Mom
xxx ooo

Covering Niagara

Cultural Studies Series

Cultural Studies is the multi- and inter-disciplinary study of culture, defined anthropologically as a "way of life," performatively as symbolic practice, and ideologically as the collective product of varied media and cultural industries. Although Cultural Studies is a relative newcomer to the humanities and social sciences, it has in less than half a century taken interdisciplinary scholarship to a new level of sophistication, reinvigorating the liberal arts curriculum with new theories, topics, and forms of intellectual partnership.

Wilfrid Laurier University Press invites submissions of manuscripts concerned with critical discussions on power relations concerning gender, class, sexual preference, ethnicity, and other macro and micro sites of political struggle.

For more information, please contact:

Lisa Quinn
Acquisitions Editor
Wilfrid Laurier University Press
75 University Avenue West
Waterloo, ON N2L 3C5
Canada
Phone: 519-884-0710 ext. 2843
Fax: 519-725-1399
Email: quinn@press.wlu.ca

Covering Niagara

Studies in Local Popular Culture

Joan Nicks and Barry Keith Grant, editors

Wilfrid Laurier University Press

WLU

This book has been published with the help of a grant from the Canadian Federation for the Humanities and Social Sciences, through the Aid to Scholarly Publications Programme, using funds provided by the Social Sciences and Humanities Research Council of Canada. We acknowledge the support of the Canada Council for the Arts for our publishing program. We acknowledge the financial support of the Government of Canada through the Book Publishing Industry Development Program for our publishing activities.

Library and Archives Canada Cataloguing in Publication

Covering Niagara : studies in local popular culture / Joan Nicks and Barry Keith Grant, editors.

(Cultural studies series)
Includes bibliographical references and index.
Issued also in electronic format.
ISBN 978-1-55458-221-1

1. Popular culture—Ontario—Niagara (Regional municipality). 2. Niagara (Ont. : Regional municipality)—History. I. Nicks, Joan, [date] II. Grant, Barry Keith, 1947– III. Series: Cultural studies series (Waterloo, Ont.)

FC3095.N5A39 2010   971.3'38   C2010-900648-8

ISBN 978-1-55458-247-1
Electronic format.

1. Popular culture—Ontario—Niagara (Regional municipality). 2. Niagara (Ont. : Regional municipality)—History. I. Nicks, Joan, [date] II. Grant, Barry Keith, 1947– III. Series: Cultural studies series (Waterloo, Ont.)

FC3095.N5A39 2010a   971.3'38   C2010-900649-6

Cover art by Niagara Region artist John Sakars: panel (48" × 48") from *Mosaic of Niagara* (2006; collage on wood triptych, 48" × 144"), photographed by Denis Cahill. Cover design by David Drummond. Text design by Catharine Bonas-Taylor.

© 2010 Wilfrid Laurier University Press
Waterloo, Ontario, Canada
www.wlupress.wlu.ca

This book is printed on FSC recycled paper and is certified Ecologo. It is made from 100% post-consumer fibre, processed chlorine free, and manufactured using biogas energy.

Printed in Canada

Every reasonable effort has been made to acquire permission for copyright material used in this text, and to acknowledge all such indebtedness accurately. Any errors and omissions called to the publisher's attention will be corrected in future printings.

For Kenji, student of "the beautiful game" —J.N.

To Zak and Gabi, who have taught me so much about popular culture —B.K.G.

CONTENTS

Quebec

St. Lawrence River

Montreal

Ottawa River

Ottawa

QUEBEC

Lake
Champlain

N

Boston

Albany

Hudson River

New York

Atlantic
Ocean

ONTARIO

Sault Ste. Marie

Georgian
Bay

Lake
Huron

Detroit

Lake Ontario

Rochester

Toronto

Hamilton

Buffalo

NIAGARA

Lake Erie

Cleveland

UNITED STATES

0   100   200

kilometres

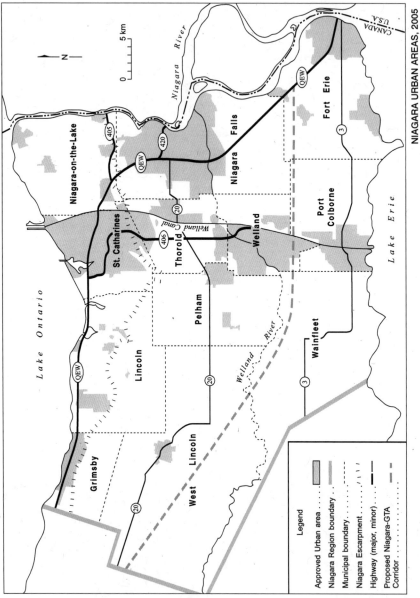

NIAGARA URBAN AREAS, 2005

Legend

Approved Urban area ....
Niagara Region boundary .....
Municipal boundary ....
Niagara Escarpment ....
Highway (major, minor) ....
Proposed Niagara-GTA
Corridor ....

Lake Ontario

Lake Erie

Grimsby

West Lincoln

Lincoln

St. Catharines

Niagara-on-the-Lake

Pelham

Thorold

Welland

Niagara Falls

Fort Erie

Port Colborne

Wainfleet

Niagara River

Welland Canal

Welland River

CANADA
U.S.A.

QEW

405

420

406

20

3

N

0   5 km

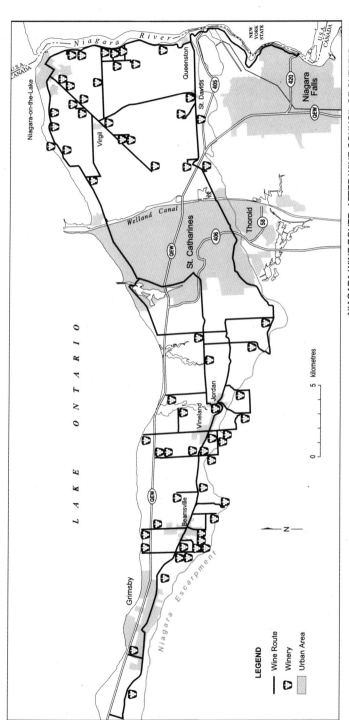

NIAGARA WINE ROUTE. AFTER WINE COUNCIL OF ONTARIO, 2009

FOREWORD | Reflections on Everyday Life in Niagara

GEOFF PEVERE

There's a paradox lodged in the very idea of writing about how a particular place shaped one's pop cultural proclivities. At least there is for me. The comforts I derived from things like movies, TV, comics, radio, and records ran in deliberate opposition to particularity. I came to love pop culture because it didn't matter where I was. What I cherished was how it erased geography.

By the time my family arrived in St. Catharines in October 1970, I was newly turned thirteen and had already moved some ten times. The why of it doesn't really matter—lest, of course, you think my parents were on the lam and they weren't—but the net result for me was a decidedly overdeveloped fondness for anything that offered both distraction and stability in an otherwise constantly changing domestic environment. With regard to root cause, my own full tilt toward pop cultural pursuits is simply explained: I chased them because they could be caught anywhere.

So, while I can't recall the particular quirk of timing that brought my family from London, Ontario, to St. Catharines on the day of my thirteenth birthday—although I'm sure the reasons weren't nearly as personal as I probably had suspected—I do remember what things concerned me the most, apart from the reasonable pubescent dread of a new school. I was worried about what shows would be available on local TV; how many movie theatres were in town; where to get regular supplies of magazines, paperback books, and records, and—most despairingly—whether there would be anyone within the city limits who shared my love of horror comics. I needed to know this place was just like every other place I'd ever lived. At least in the ways that most mattered.

Already prone to extreme affinities—by thirteen, I'd begun collections of comics, LPs, magazines, paperbacks, museum brochures, *MADs*, and *Peanuts* strips clipped from the newspaper—I found myself in an especially acute funk because I'd been compelled to arrive in the Garden City without my comics. (Really: how could anything bloom without them?) Offered a choice by my mother to keep either the comic or paperback collection, I opted for the latter in what must have seemed at the time a gesture of sorts toward maturity. Needless to say, I almost immediately regretted the decision and sunk into a pimply funk that intermittently manifested itself throughout most of my adolescence. Some of my adulthood too.

Come to think of it nearly forty years on I can still get pissed about those comics. Things came around, though, at least in the way that most mattered. School sucked, of course, but other things fell into place promisingly. The St. Catharines *Standard*, bless its soul, had the most extensive daily comics section I'd ever seen: a full page consisting of two full columns of strips, including such essentials as *B.C.*, *Pogo*, *Beetle Bailey*, and the magisterial *Peanuts*. I discovered a St. Paul Street cinema called the Palace (later sectioned off into the Towne I and II), which featured weekly discount double-bill fare like *House of Dark Shadows and Count Yorga, Vampire*. Just doors away was a used book store at which I quickly stocked up on second-hand Ian Fleming James Bond paperbacks, and just around the corner from that was Christopher's Smoke Shop, an excellent emporium in which to find such crucial reading material as *Eerie*, *Creepy*, and *Famous Monsters of Filmland*. Records of both the single and album variety were to be had at the Sam the Record Man outlet at the then still-unroofed Pen Centre shopping mall, as were the weekly CHUM-AM Top 40 music charts and required rock reading like *Rolling Stone*, *Creem*, and *Circus*.

TV and radio proved similarly reassuring. Because of its situation smack at the axis of the Golden Horseshoe, St. Catharines was a veritable repository of broadcasting bounty. TV beamed in from Buffalo, Erie, and Pittsburgh stateside, and from Toronto, Kitchener, and Hamilton. The latter was where the remarkable CHCH was based, a TV station that somehow managed to acquire broadcasting rights to movies that had played theatrically only a year or two before. At a time when movies customarily dropped out of sight for up to three or four years before resurfacing on prime time TV, CHCH was nothing short of a fall-on-your-knees-and-give-thanks godsend.

Initially, radio was welcomed for its consistency with my Top 40 listening habits elsewhere. Later, as my interests, record collection, and rock mag stash expanded, local radio took on much more substantial interest. Primarily, this was because St. Catharines was in the broadcasting purview of not one but two free-form FM radio stations: CHUM-FM, in Toronto, and WPHD, based in Buffalo. One of the most remarkable but short-lived phenomena in radio, free-form was based on the now almost inconceivably uncommercial presumption that what the DJ wanted to hear was somehow synched with what the audience wanted to hear, even if that meant an hour and a half of non-stop Frank Zappa and Mothers of Invention tracks or the collected works of Savoy Brown.

Not commercial in general terms maybe, but absolutely so in the specific case of this neophyte music snob. For me, free-form FM directly fed my music-buying habits by introducing me to things I'd otherwise never hear. After reading about interesting new music in those magazines obtained at Sam's at the Pen Centre, I'd listen for it on WPHD and CHUM-FM. If it pleased my ears, I'd be back at Sam's as promptly as my allowance would permit. As far as live concerts were concerned, the geographical situation of the city permitted relatively easy travel to both Buffalo and Toronto, both tour stops for just about every band any unreasonably fixated young suburban mall rat like myself could possibly dream of attending.

In short, within a year or so of living in Niagara, life—or at least what passed for it in my case—was officially good.

I now realize how peculiar that sounds—to define a contented life by the supply of distractions from life it provided. But that was the way of popular culture, at least for me. Not that I had an unbearable life, far from it. If anything, my growing obsession with mass-mediated experience was dependent upon a certain middle-class stability: I had the time and money to indulge my interests, not to mention the low level of daily incident that permitted those interests to take charge. Looking back at those six years I spent in St. Catharines, I find I can more easily summon memories of movies I saw and records I bought than places I went or things I did. It reads retrospectively as a kind of hazy trance, stretches of time spent floating between Friday night movies.

Later, as technology increasingly displaced the collective nature of pop cultural experience with more private forms of consumption, I came to realize how ultimately solipsistic my pleasures were. Reading had always been a particularly keen pleasure of mine, and it went hand in hand with such other solitary pursuits as organizing my comics collection and sketching superheroes and movie stars on drugstore notepads. Television was always best watched alone and free from the chatter and interruptions of others, and movies were never more fully appreciated than when viewed in a largely empty theatre during a quiet matinee. (Friends had an annoying way of finding something social in the act.) The pleasures of popular culture were always private in my case, and this probably explains how easily I adjusted to anything that enhanced this state of happy insulation: headphones, portable TV and radio initially, and later videocassette, Walkmans, personal computers, DVD players, and iPods. If it delivers pop culture directly and personally, it's doing what I always dreamed it should be doing: delivering me from everything else.

But that's the dream, a narcotic vision of perpetual trance that grows organically from my childhood attraction to popular culture as a place to go where geography didn't matter. In reality, meanwhile, my obsessions simply filled me up and spilled over into the life that seemed so much more interesting then, and by the time I graduated high school and prepared to leave St. Catharines for university, I was more or less doomed to find a way of making a life out of the very distractions I'd sought for so long. After a year spent miserably studying journalism, I found myself enrolled in a film studies program at Carleton University, almost deliriously happy with the discovery that I might actually secure some kind of legitimate academic goal while doing what I'd always felt most natural doing anyway: watching movies and writing about them, basking in the private pleasure of popular culture.

So it also is my pleasure to have the first words in this book, which with its multiple perspectives on local popular culture in Niagara not only recalls for me that time in my life but also helps illuminate it.

ACKNOWLEDGEMENTS

Appropriately, given the subject of this book, there are many people who have helped in one fashion or another, and indeed too many to mention by name. Most importantly, we wish to thank the numerous individuals from across the Niagara Region and elsewhere who agreed to be interviewed and to share their memories, stories, and memorabilia (some of which appears in these pages). In addition to the many people and sources, whether identified or not, we are particularly grateful for the individual contributions of John Burtniak, local historian and collector; Andrew Porteus, Reference Librarian, Niagara Falls Public Library, and the library staff; Wilma Morrison of the Norval Johnson Heritage Library; Sherman Zavitz, Official Historian, City of Niagara Falls; the Lundy's Lane Historical Museum staff, Niagara Falls; the Archives of Ontario; Pat Simon and Don Ede, avid collectors of local memorabilia; and the M.A. students in Popular Culture who assisted the Popular Culture Niagara Research Group.

At Brock University, the staff of the Office of Research Services, under former Vice-President, Research Michael Owen, provided excellent advice and support. Nick Baxter-Moore and Marian Bredin, former chairs of the Department of Communication, Popular Culture and Film, and current chair, Russell Johnston, have provided additional help despite limited resources. Lewis Soroka and Dave Siegel, former Deans of the Faculty of Social Sciences, both had the vision to appreciate and support the work of the Popular Culture Niagara Research Group. Anne Howe, Sharon Spiece, and Adrian Palmieri provided invaluable assistance in mounting the 2002 Colloquium, out of which much of the research for this book grew. Rob Macmorine, as always, offered dependable technical assistance with this event and the 2006 Popular Culture Niagara Conference, as did Phil Nardangeli and John Culp of Audio Visual Services. The 2002 Colloquium was partly funded by the President's Fund for the Advancement of Scholarship and by the Office of Research Services. Special Collections librarians Edie Williams and Lynne Prunskus of the James A. Gibson Library provided research assistance. Joanna Robinson, former M.A. student in Popular Culture, provided outstanding help in organizing the conference in 2006, and Dante Sicoli did an excellent job designing the promotional materials for the conference. We are particularly indebted to artist John Boyle for providing his artwork for the conference materials, and for his keynote talk on the history of the Niagara School, and to the local musicians who offered their excellent interpretations of local popular music in the concert portion of the conference hosted by Terrance Cox. Professor Gregory Waller of Indiana University, keynote speaker at the 2002 Colloquium, provided advice and encouragement as the PCN researchers were beginning their work. We are also grateful to Nick Baxter-Moore for his consultation on the Introduction, to Denis Ceci for formatting the illustrations, and cartographer Loris Gasparotto for preparing the maps.

At Wilfrid Laurier University Press, thanks to Brian Henderson, Director; Lisa Quinn, Acquisitions Editor; Rob Kohlmeier, Managing Editor; and Heather Blain-Yanke, Production Manager, as well as copy editor Wendy Thomas; we are grateful for their supportive consultations along the way. Thanks also to the text designer, Catharine Bonas-Taylor, and the marketing and publicity team at the Press: Leslie Macredie, Penelope Grows, and Clare Hitchens. We are grateful to the anonymous readers of the manuscript, who provided very helpful reviews and whose comments and suggestions are reflected in the final book. Thanks as well to local artist John Sakars for permission to use his charming depiction of Niagara's famous waterfalls, rendered from found materials, housed in Trish Friesen's Tangled Yoga Studio in the Port Dalhousie area of St. Catharines; to Denis Cahill, who photographed John's artwork for the cover; to Mike Balsom and David Sisler, Laura Secord Secondary School, for the photos of the Kenny Wheeler concert; and to Geoff Pevere for his fitting reflections in the Foreword. Finally, we thank the contributing authors represented in this collection for their original work, cooperation, and patience throughout the development of this project; and our fellow-members (Nick Baxter-Moore, Marian Bredin, Terrance Cox, Russell Johnston, Michael Ripmeester, and Jeannette Sloniowski) of the Popular Culture Niagara

Research Group for the many lively and stimulating discussions on researching local popular culture.

This research was partly funded by the Social Sciences and Humanities Research Council of Canada (Council Grant Number 410-2003-0945).

INTRODUCTION

"Popular culture is a significant and effective part of the material reality of history, effectively shaping the possibilities of our existence." (Grossberg 1992, 69)

POPULAR CULTURE AND THE LOCAL

When eight members from various disciplines at Brock University in St. Catharines, Ontario, met in 2001 to discuss the formation of the Popular Culture Niagara Research Group (PCN), it was apparent that research was independently already in progress. As these initial studies proceeded and new topics revealed themselves at a one-day colloquium in April 2002 and a conference in May 2006 at Brock, sponsored by PCN, other individuals involved in studying Niagara's popular culture were invited to become contributors to this book. The case studies presented in *Covering Niagara* are original to this collection, documenting and examining myriad forms of local popular culture in this particular part of Canada. Together, the studies represent a tapestry of expressive local activities, in geographical, historical, and social contexts, and hint at the diversity, vitality, and complexity that inform the Niagara Region's daily life. They reveal a region that is unique *and* derivative, constructed *and* consumed, and sometimes a hedge against parochial and globalized thinking, media flow, and the wireless domain.

Although there has been considerable scholarly work in popular culture and cultural studies, particularly in the United States and United Kingdom, much of it considers broad trends that subsume questions and specifics of more localized popular culture. Studies in Canadian popular culture have grown more common as traditional disciplinary boundaries have become more fluid, and we are now well past the point where studying Canadian popular culture needs justification.[1] Still, regional or local Canadian popular culture often merits discussion, both within and without Canada, only when it ascends to the national or international spotlight (Shania Twain, The Guess Who, Guy Madden, David Cronenberg, *SCTV*, Cirque du Soleil, Great Big Sea). This tendency creates historical gaps in understanding the incubation, development, lapses, shifts, and reincarnations of local practices and meanings. If we apply John Fiske's contention that popular culture is a "site of ideological struggle" (1989, 201), then we must acknowledge that any manifestation of popular culture emerges out of competing expressions. Consequently, the culture of any region, Niagara included, is not univocal, nor is it impervious to commercial, political, and globalizing interests.

Previous studies by such researchers as Elizabeth McKinsey (1985), Patrick McGreevy (1988, 1994), Patricia Jasen (1995), William Irwin (1996), and Karen Dubinsky (1999) have emphasized representations of Niagara Falls as tourist site and borderland. Niagara's history and position at the Canada–United States border are important within what is known as southern Ontario, densely populated and urbanized compared to the vast summer-cottage country and remote wilderness parks of central and northern Ontario. Viewing the Niagara Region from the Canadian side of the border, through a diverse range of local popular culture practices, reminds us of David Trend's observation that "people are too different and complex to be manipulated uniformly by monolithic institutions and discourse" (2007, 5). In the same spirit, the very methods of *Covering Niagara*'s contributors include participant interviews; archival, historical, and field research; cultural studies concepts; and textual analysis.

DEFINING NIAGARA

Niagara's small cities and towns are threaded by a major Ontario highway and local bypasses, the Welland Canal locks, and back roads leading to nature trails, wineries, produce stands, golf courses, and festivals from folk to jazz, classical to rock, and drama from Shaw to Shakespeare in the Vineyard. The regional character is picturesque, a destination, an event, and a cultivated, built environment where people enjoy all manner of popular culture as well as the enrichment and diversity that accrue from the presence and activities of a university (Brock), a community college (Niagara), a preparatory college (Ridley), and a broad multi-ethnic population. Thus, the Niagara Region represents the nexus of a number of material and symbolic landscapes—frontier, border, greenbelt, tourist site, agribusiness, among others—that together provide a special context for the unfolding of local socio-cultural practices. Niagara's significant geography and history and its immediate position at the Canada–United States border have marked this cultural landscape and its place in the busy corridor of the Golden Horseshoe, located between Toronto and Buffalo. The region's combination of historical and cross-border connections has given rise to a locality that is at once urban *and* rural, in the centre *and* on the margin, borderland *and* hinterland.

The Niagara Region lies between Lake Ontario and Lake Erie and is bounded at its eastern end by the Niagara River, which also forms the Canadian-American boundary at this point (see maps). It is across Lake Ontario from Toronto, east of Hamilton, and lies in a peninsula that borders western New York at four international crossings: one at Fort Erie, Ontario/Buffalo, New York; two at Niagara Falls, Ontario/Niagara Falls, New York; and one at Queenston, Ontario/Lewiston, New York. Waterways were as important as bridges of today, and the Niagara River crossing, which flows into Lake Ontario—separating Fort Niagara (at the corner of Western New York near Youngstown) and Fort George (in Niagara-on-the-Lake, Ontario, the historical seat of Upper Canada government)—was a passage not only for commerce and culture, but also for colonial confrontation and conflict.

Part of the traditional industrial heartland of Central Canada, and the centre of a thriving binational, borderland region, Niagara is also a peripheral area of Ontario and is sometimes perceived (not least by local inhabitants) as a cultural backwater in comparison to the cities of Buffalo, Hamilton, and, especially, Toronto. Torontonians, on the other hand, view Niagara as an escape, and on holiday weekends, traffic jams are the norm on the multi-lane Queen Elizabeth Way ("the QEW"). The local economy was based on the urban "rust-belt" industries, especially the auto industry and related manufacturing; farming and orchards in the rural areas; and a heavy dependence upon tourism, notably in Niagara Falls, Niagara-on-the-Lake, and a burgeoning grape-growing/winery sector along the Lake Ontario shoreline and below the Niagara Escarpment (a World Biosphere site). With the decline of the auto industry today, tourism, the wine, food, and hospitality industries, and small manufacturing prevail, even as the region seeks to reposition itself with digital and computing entrepreneurship. Perhaps because many jobs in tourism and related service industries are seasonal and often not unionized, average earnings in Niagara are not only well below those for Ontario, but even lag slightly behind average earnings in Canada as a whole (Statistics Canada 2006). At the same time, unemployment rates have historically been relatively higher than for other metropolitan areas in the province.

Also a politico-administrative entity, the "Niagara Region" serves as a separate sphere of government, delivering some of the services that elsewhere would be provided by constituent townships and cities. The region extends over some 1900 square kilometres (715 square miles), boasts a population of about 435,000, and consists of twelve separate municipalities, most prominently St. Catharines (132,000), Niagara Falls (83,000), and Welland (50,000), along with smaller centres such as Fort Erie, Port Colborne, Grimsby, and the historic Niagara-on-the-Lake.[2] Despite a sizable population base, Niagara is relatively small compared to its neighbouring regions, cities, and conurbations, such as Buffalo (population, including suburbs in Erie County, of close to 1.2 million), Hamilton-Burlington (700,000), and, especially, Metropolitan Toronto (the "GTA," approximately 5.5 million).

Niagara's regional government was created only in 1970. Previously, the area now administered by the regional government and its twelve constituent municipalities was divided into no less than twenty-six separate cities, towns, and rural townships. Forced amalgamation with other local units to create new municipalities often caused resentment against both the new municipal governments and the overarching region. Some people still do not accept regional government, regarding it as an unnecessarily expensive and bureaucratic additional layer of government. Even in larger communities such as Thorold (population 17,000) there is fierce local independence, politically and culturally, and strong aversion to any idea of annexation by the neighbouring city of St. Catharines, despite periodic attempts to do so. A certain parochialism persists throughout the region, reinforced, for example, by local print media: served by no fewer than three daily newspapers, Niagara also has a plethora of weekly or biweekly "community" papers.[3]

The reorganization of local government in 1970 left outside the newly constituted "Niagara Region" some communities that are part of the peninsula geographically or that serve as mini-metropoles for populations within the region. For example, the town of Dunnville, in neighbouring Haldimand County, is a service, shopping, and cultural centre for many people in Long Beach, on the shore of Lake Erie, and other parts of southwestern Niagara. Internal boundaries are not particularly clear even within the region. In numerous ways, the concept of "local" in the Niagara Region is fluid, dynamic, and contested, where multiple communities coexist and often interact, producing a recognizable local culture. Staged events by various groups have a networking function or are designed to spur public conversation on cross-border and regional matters: for example, events coordinated by the Canadian Consul General's office in Buffalo, the University at Buffalo (SUNY), Brock University, Niagara College, and regional organizers. As of this writing, the most recent of these initiatives—widely attended by representatives of the region's cultural, political, business, and institutional sectors—was "Niagarapolooza: Re-thinking Our Cities" in January 2008, with public intellectual and regionalist thinker Richard Florida as keynote speaker. The focus was on the inevitable shift from an industrial-based to a knowledge-based economy. Fittingly, as Sara Cohen defines the term, "locality" is a multi-dimensional concept, methodologically as well as practically: shifting and interweaving, neither bounded nor fixed, locality involves "networks of social relationships, practices, and processes extending across particular places" (1995, 66). This certainly is reflected in the variegated popular culture of the Niagara Region.

THE CASE STUDIES

Although we began in part with a specific set of physical-geographical and politico-administrative borders in mind, it soon became clear that cultural boundaries are in many ways far more permeable than political ones, and the authors in this collection take as a given that the local should be understood symbolically as well as literally. Each study in *Covering Niagara* considers common assumptions about the region and what popular culture is, and has been, locally. The authors have struck a balance between conceptualizing and historicizing their respective topics and analyzing artifacts, sites, and field and archival sources, to explain and make sense of specific practices in Niagara. Besides the scholarly underpinnings of each study, generally this kind of work depends on collaboration and conversation, and the researcher's curiosity and dogged pursuit of scattered historical materials: documents, newspapers, records, and random files in libraries and museums; photo albums and scrapbooks of collectors who tend to be surprised at the cultural value of memorabilia; fieldwork in the community, networking, and meeting with the people who have memories and experiences that together make up any region's vibrant popular culture. In the process, even seeming dead-end searches can result in "eureka" moments of discovery.

The three studies in "Public Showings" share the notion that the Niagara Region has been both a central and a marginal place for showcasing novelty as if for cultural betterment. First, Phillip Mackintosh demonstrates how late Victorians fled Toronto's summer heat for safe, sanitized Niagara-on-the-Lake, where they orchestrated "bourgeois gaieties." He argues that they used this space to perform their class publicly as spectacle. With bicycle parades (gymkhanas), golf and tennis tournaments, and musicales, they connected pleasure with "proper" leisure-time behaviour, modelling their sense of popular taste for public consumption by the local spectators lining the streets, hence claiming the area as their retreat and playground. Next, Russell Johnston and Michael Ripmeester examine the origins of the statue memorializing Private Alexander Watson, a "common soldier" who fell in the North-West Rebellion of the 1880s. The statue stands before St. Catharines City Hall but has faded from public interest, becoming a backdrop for an annual Christmas crèche, neither a prop to that story nor an understood historical emblem. As Johnston and Ripmeester explain, Victorian "memory entrepreneurs" and civic boosters constructed preferred meanings for Watson's funeral, turning it into a spectacle celebrating generic codes of heroic glory to meet the ideological needs of the nation-state. Concluding this section, Marian Bredin explores the implications of the Indian Village, a popular Niagara Falls tourist attraction in the 1960s, where native employees performed their "Indianness" through dances, cooking and beading demonstrations, and storytelling. Discussing the role of re-enactments and the concept of the "imaginary Indian," she argues that the Indian Village was a place of negotiated practices between the costumed employees and the many tourists who came away with positive impressions of their first contact with First Nations people, suggesting the resonance of this long-gone tourist attraction in the popular imagination.

In "Movies and Media," the three studies illuminate the ideological work of the press and media in shaping public tastes. Leading off the section, Paul Moore draws on random newspaper reports of the late 1800s to make historical sense of the occasions when early exhibitions of moving pictures and projection apparatuses came to the Niagara Region. Film footage of Niagara's famous waterfalls may have stood in for Canada elsewhere, but the region was peripheral to the Toronto-based travelling-circuit lecturers who toured Ontario's cities and towns promoting a novel technology associated with misadventure and opportunism. In their study on the local press of the 1920s and the construction of gender in promoting films and star culture, Jeannette Sloniowski and Joan Nicks show how the Niagara Falls newspaper absorbed Hollywood rhetoric but took ambivalent editorial positions on the New Woman, while encouraging boys to be groomed by civic-minded men. They argue that women and girls, especially, who were well acquainted with fanzines and "Hollywoodized" discourse, may have become discerning local and transnational readers of print, theatre ads, and celebrity stories. Then, Laura Wiebe Taylor focuses on three St. Catharines radio stations, housed in one building and owned by a radio-media corporation, to chart how the "local" in local radio mostly disappears from mass media view in its evolving commercial form. Localness has become a framing device for "talk" and "easy rock" formats and radio personalities engaged in charity events and contests. This branding of local commercial radio, she argues, plays to listener demographics and largely produces a veneer of community.

Today's growing culinary interest in Niagara is based on a significant agricultural heritage, explored in the "Food and Drink" section. Fiona Lucas and Mary F. Williamson examine the everyday life of Upper Canada in the mid-nineteenth century, when a literate farm woman, who used the moniker "A.B. of Grimsby," produced a pocket-sized manual of recipes and gardening instructions. The manual has survived to become an artifact of colonial Niagara, abundant in farm produce, game, and drink; in their reading of it, Lucas and Williamson disprove the myth that Loyalist cooking was bland—fitting today's food culture ideology of incorporating and celebrating local fare. Dan Malleck searches the lively reports of the Ontario Liquor Control Board (LCBO) inspectors to reveal the creative efforts of Niagara's public houses, and their clients, to skirt the rules. During the post-Prohibition era of the 1930s, the LCBO regulations were severely tested by social drinkers and hotel proprietors. Drinking was a common pastime and managers used clever tactics to inject music and dancing into public houses, attempting to heed, and stretch, the LCBO standards while mollifying wily patrons intent on breaking the governing conventions. In the section's final chapter, Hugh Gayler examines Niagara's wine industry for the implications of Greenbelt protection, government regulations, the Vintner's Quality Alliance (VQA), agritourism, and the entrepreneurs and "little guys" behind the wineries (over ninety to date). Though the annual Niagara Wine Festival (formerly the Grape and Wine Festival) in September draws thousands of celebrants to the region, Gayler argues that a "made in Canada" wine culture built around the beverage's purchase and consumption largely has catered to an elitist middle-class demographic interested in pursuing the "wine experience" and a cuisine built on local produce and Niagara vintages.

Whatever motives underlie the forging of community links, the three studies in "Local Connections" dig in to the personal and social character of regional culture. Terrance Cox borrows the term "kenny-ing" to identify the influential mentorship of internationally renowned jazz trumpeter Kenny Wheeler. Wheeler came of age in St. Catharines in the 1940s, left to find his place and acclaim in England and Europe, yet makes return journeys to visit family and friends and to perform. While the challenging music of the self-effacing Wheeler is not the most popular of popular culture, his seeming nostalgic attachment to place, family, and individual musicians often mystifies local devotees yet reveals the inevitable dialectic of an international artist with his local roots. In the following study, Nick Baxter-Moore takes an ethnographic approach to uncover the enduring role of the local music store, an institution that, he argues, has been overlooked in the growing scholarship on local sounds and scenes in popular music. Laying down a typology of the music store's functions—from "an advertising and communications centre" to a "day job" for local musicians—he discusses this stable haven as a "scene" in itself, serving customers, musicians, and recreational players. As purveyors of both material objects and dreams, Niagara's music stores negotiate the competing demands of commerce and community. Concluding this section, Roslyn Costanzo reads through the archives of the Niagara Artists Centre (NAC), a local parallel gallery, to compare this artist-run centre's regional-based mandate and projects of the 1970s with its recent return to original principles and programming. With a strong sense of its regional history and goals, and a permanent storefront location in downtown St. Catharines, NAC attracts both an arts and a populist audience. It operates at the "front lines"—not in culturally narrow ways, Costanzo argues, but as part of the diversity of Canadian culture and geography.

The three studies in the final section, "Borderline Matters," emphasize different modes of display, each established on iconography borrowed from elsewhere. Joan Nicks and Jeannette Sloniowski analyze the practice of "corking up" and performing the racist stereotypes, black dialect, and "coon" songs of minstrelsy far removed from its American origins. For almost half a century, these shows, often produced for charitable causes, and heavily boosted by newspaper coverage, entertained the largely white community of Niagara Falls—with no questions raised. Amateur blackface minstrel shows are an unspoken legacy in the social history of this small city, rooted in the popular professional blackface comics who toured with vaudeville circuits early in the twentieth century across a porous border of multiple uses and pleasures. In his study, Norman Ball depicts the Niagara electricity industry as a symbol of modernity and, importantly, a time saver in domestic life. In the 1920s, when "going electric" was more than a slogan, the Canadian Niagara Power Company's Cooking School in Fort Erie was a centre for educating the community on the uses of electricity. Electric stoves could be purchased "on time" and were promoted this way in newspaper ads and handbills. With demonstrations and recipes designed for "cooking electric," the school taught local women how to produce nutritious family meals and creative dishes for entertaining and became a site where their domestic lives were drastically changed and shaped. In the final chapter, Greg Gillespie situates the development of the Niagara Regional Police Pipe Band's tartan within local geography and United Empire Loyalist history. He reviews the contentious notion of "tradition invention," the myth of Highlandism, and the Scottishness and generic style associated with tartans, to demonstrate how the weaving of the landscape's colours into the "Niagara Region" tartan effects a fusion of the local and the global and serves official, material, and popular purposes.

Covering Niagara contributes to the project of searching the historical and contemporary place of local popular culture, always present or re-emerging in some form, yet evanescent. While no single volume can include every aspect of "the local," the topics herein provide a diverse "mapping" of Niagara's popular culture—undoubtedly, with more to come in future from researchers who have made Niagara their long-term study and, for others, newly discovering untapped sources. Such study has become a matter of public trust, of interest to general as well as academic readers, as records, sites, events, and aspects of everyday life are being read and interpreted, often for the first time.

NOTES

1 See, for example, *The Beaver Bites Back: American Popular Culture in Canada*, David H. Flaherty and Frank E. Manning, eds. (Montreal/Kingston: McGill-Queen's University Press, 1993); Geoff Pevere and Greig Dymond, *Mondo Canuck: A Canadian Pop Culture Odyssey* (Scarborough, ON: Prentice Hall Canada, 1996); *Pop Can: Popular Culture in Canada*, Lynne Van Luven and Priscilla L. Walton, eds. (Scarborough, ON: Prentice Hall Allyn and Bacon Canada, 1999); *Slippery Pastimes: Reading the Popular in Canadian Culture*, Joan Nicks and Jeannette Sloniowski, eds. (Waterloo, ON: Wilfrid Laurier University Press, 2002).

2 The boundaries of the Niagara Region also coincide with those of other administrative units, including the Niagara Regional Police Service and, since 1998, the Public and Roman Catholic School Boards, which deliver primary and secondary education.

3 Daily newspapers are published in St. Catharines (*The Standard*), Welland (*The Tribune*), and Niagara Falls (*The Review*). In recent years, all of these papers have been owned by the same newspaper chain (Osprey Media, now a subsidiary of Quebecor), which also owns some of the community weeklies. Once run by entrepreneurial owner-publishers who lived locally, were prominent boosters of community, and had a direct stake in running their newspapers, these dailies have lost personality under succeeding chains. Rival chains produce other community newspapers, and independents such as *Pulse Niagara* publish news and reviews on local arts and popular culture. The evolution toward consolidation of these papers is itself reflective of the challenges facing local popular culture.

WORKS CITED

Cohen, Sara. "Localizing Sound." In Will Straw et al., eds., *Popular Music: Style and Identity*. Montreal: Centre for Research on Canadian Cultural Industries and Institutions/IASPM, 1995: 61–68.

Dubinsky, Karen. *The Second Greatest Disappointment: Honeymooning and Tourism at Niagara Falls*. Toronto: Between the Lines, 1999.

Fiske, John. *Understanding Popular Culture*. Boston: Unwin Hyman, 1989.

Grossberg, Lawrence. *We Gotta Get Out of this Place: Popular Conservatism and Postmodern Culture*. New York and London: Routledge, 1992.

Irwin, William. *The New Niagara: Tourism, Technology and the Landscape of Niagara Falls, 1776–1917*. University Park: Pennsylvania State University Press, 1996.

Jasen, Patricia. *Wild Things: Nature, Culture and Tourism in Ontario, 1790–1914*. Toronto: University of Toronto Press, 1995.

McGreevy, Patrick V. "The End of America: The Beginning of Canada." *The Canadian Geographer* 32:4 (1988), 307–18.

———. *Imagining Niagara: The Meaning and Making of Niagara Falls*. Amherst: University of Massachusetts Press, 1994.

McKinsey, Elizabeth. *Niagara Falls: Icon of the American Sublime*. New York and Cambridge, UK: Cambridge University Press, 1985.

Statistics Canada. "St. Catharines-Niagara CMA Community Profile 2006." http://www12.statcan.ca/census-recensement/2006/dp-pd/prof/92-591/details/page.cfm?Lang=E&Geo1=CMA&Code1=539_&Geo2=PR&Code2=35&Data=Count&SearchText=Ontario&SearchType=Begins&SearchPR=01&B1=All&Custom=.

Trend, David. *Everyday Culture: Finding and Making Meaning in a Changing World*. Boulder, CO: Paradigm Publishers, 2007.

Part I | **PUBLIC SHOWINGS**

POLITE ATHLETICS AND BOURGEOIS GAIETIES | Toronto Society in Late Victorian Niagara-on-the-Lake

PHILLIP GORDON MACKINTOSH

Tennis week at Niagara-on-the-Lake, which begins to-morrow, promises to be as popular an attraction and as altogether enjoyable as in past seasons, and the Queen's Royal will doubtless be filled with happy guests. The attractions of golf and cycling will occupy the mornings, while something special in the way of amusement has already been arranged for the evenings. Quite a large number of people are going over from town. (Globe, July 15, 1896, 6)

INTRODUCTION

In August of 2007, an entourage of Torontonian bicyclists boarded the "Bike Train" to Niagara-on-the-Lake for an adventurous weekend of bicycling and wine tourism through the town's celebrated grape and wine district.[1] Via Rail Canada's bike service allows twenty-first century, haute bourgeois Torontonian cyclists the opportunity to repeat the leisure pursuits of their late Victorian forebears: participation in polite athleticism and bourgeois gaieties in Niagara-on-the-Lake. Curiously, the small town at the mouth of the Niagara River toward the southwest end of Lake Ontario has afforded an escape to Torontonian cyclists, and sport and leisure seekers in general, since the late nineteenth century.[2] Railway and steamer service flourished as privileged Torontonians took their desire—and often their bikes—out of the city to escape the heat and congestion. Indeed, so many comely leisure seekers took their bicycles to Niagara-on-the-Lake that Henry Winnett, a proprietor of the Queen's Royal Hotel, arguably the most famous hotel in Ontario at the time and celebrated summer home for Toronto's and the northern North

American elite in general, had to build "a bicycle stable for these silent steeds" (*Globe*, July 9, 1895, 9).

There were, of course, other reasons for bourgeois interest in Niagara-on-the-Lake, which was regarded as a suburb of Toronto (Mackintosh 2007, 130): Toronto's streets and "resorts" (parks and green spaces) were occupied by "a plague of nuisances" in summertime, from peddlers and boot blacks to noisy music makers, roving bands of rowdy boys, and drunks who made haute bourgeois pretensions and activities in public difficult.[3] Undoubtedly, some Toronto resorts, such as Munro Park in the beaches district, where an "absolute prohibition of intoxicating liquors" and "the splendid and complete manner in which the grounds were lighted and policed," maintained "excellent order" for the park-goers.[4] These places notwithstanding, suburban and exurban resorts such as Niagara-on-the-Lake became havens for haute bourgeois entertainments, as respectable Victorians sought distant locations resistant to non-bourgeois intrusions.

Late Victorian Torontonians loved Niagara-on-the-Lake. It provided seasonal recreational refuge for the beneficiaries of Toronto's burgeoning industrialism. Niagara-on-the-Lake, as an everyday extension of Toronto's urban geography, was commonly mentioned in the "General City News" column in the *Globe*. Indeed, all Toronto papers made frequent references to the town, whether in society pages, advertisements for steamer or railway excursions, social events at such "Blue Book" destinations as the Queen's Royal Hotel and the Oban Hotel, or through regular news of the military activities, reviews, and galas and hops at Fort George or the Queen's Royal.[5]

The preoccupation with Niagara-on-the-Lake as a site of polite leisure for late Victorian Torontonians was especially apparent in the summer months. The lack of refrigeration and central cooling (electric fans were becoming available only to a privileged few) compelled city people of all classes to develop heat-avoidance strategies. Polite Toronto looked elsewhere in the summer months: as the *Globe* suggested in its "Niagara-on-the-Lake" column, "It is hot in town these days and one's friends are, one and all, departing for fresh fields and new pastures ... and, in a moment, we are once more in that delightful summer-hotel the Queen's Royal" (July 20, 1895, 9). Thus, availing itself of the proliferation of steamer excursions to fashionable destinations around Lake Ontario (Niagara-on-the-Lake, Niagara Falls, Port Dalhousie, Kingston, and the Thousand Islands, among others), Toronto's Four Hundred set (haute bourgeois) also mounted extended bicycle trips into Toronto's hinterland (Mackintosh and Norcliffe 2006) and, increasingly, railway escape to exclusive resorts in the Muskoka and Haliburton lake districts of central Ontario and even points beyond.

Niagara-on-the-Lake, "The Newport of Canada" (*Globe*, July 23, 1895, 8), and described as "a garden" in Roberts's travel guide (1891, 15), was especially important to Toronto's elite social calendar in August, which revolved around the Queen's Royal Hotel, "a favorite summer resort for the aristocracy of Toronto" (Sweetser 1881, 397). During the 1890s, four discrete annual events constituted "the very bright season" for Toronto's "very gay" "summer colony" at Niagara-on-the-Lake and the Queen's Royal Hotel: the bicycle gymkhana and the international tennis tournament, and the annual golf and lawn bowling tournaments (*Globe*, Aug. 9, 1899, 8). True, these were serious athletic meets, attracting aficionados from Canada and the United States (see, for example, Kendrick 1990, 30–31). They were also something else: forums for the expression of haute bourgeois manners in public. The bicycle gymkhana, a bicycle version of the equestrian gymkhana where both dressage and riding skills were adjudicated, was of special importance; it put respectability on the ground and in public, at a time when threats to courtesy and decorum—real and imagined—were perceived to be increasing as a result of urban in-migration by foreigners and rusticated rural Canadians.

Summer mattered in the formulation of this idea of threat simply because heat generated by the summer sun in 1890s Toronto urged all Torontonians into the streets and parks—or resorts. Whether they lived in "unsanitary" clapboard hovels on Wilton Avenue, roughcast rear cottages on Elizabeth Street, tenements on King Street West, modest suburban houses on Coxwell Avenue, fancier suburban houses on Morley Avenue, or great Victorian piles on Jarvis Street, the heat of Toronto's drought-prone summer made Torontonians very public people, June to August. This put them in contact with a scrutinizing, bourgeois gaze with real effects on the public life of "Toronto the Good" (Mackintosh, "Scrutiny" 2005).

And because the bourgeoisie laid lasting claims on the public spaces of modern Toronto at this time (Goheen 2003), public space increasingly became an important receptacle for haute bourgeois propriety; "the bourgeois experience" as Peter Gay (1998) suggests, justified the moral force of the bourgeois gaze. Geographers have spent the last two decades investigating such spatial sociality under the rubric of Moral Geography, the instantiation of bourgeois moral ideologies in spaces, places, landscapes, and environments, paying particular attention to often dubious bourgeois pretenses to public space.[6] The elites' out-of-doors athletic season in 1890s Niagara-on-the-Lake was more than simple engagement in summer sports and leisure pursuits. The Torontonian desire to display the pretensions of their class in public (Mackintosh, "Scrutiny" 2005) can be read as the cultural production of a summer heat-initiated, public moral geography. So goes the reciprocity between geography and culture: heat conditions in Toronto not only contributed to the growth of Niagara-on-the-Lake as an elite, summertime tourist enclave; they also contextualize Niagara-on-the-Lake within the Great Lakes regional system of towns and cities, showing how the climatic happenings in one place influenced cultural expression in another.

In this study, I examine the haute bourgeois—upper middle and upper class—Torontonian claim on the public space of Niagara-on-the-Lake in the 1890s. I argue that the Torontonian performance of class, in the guise of polite athletics, in the streets and greenswards of Niagara-on-the-Lake transpired, in part, as a consequence of Toronto's summertime heat. City heat shifted Toronto society to Niagara-on-the-Lake (whose water frontage on two sides made it milder and breezier), where they engaged in public displays of class, which included parading on bicycles. I use Peter Goheen's work on the parading impulse as an overt pretension to public space (1992)[7] to suggest that the floral parades; the flaunting of fashion, reputation, and wealth; and the cotillions, concerts, and music that accompanied the annual international tennis tournament, the annual golf and lawn bowling tournaments, and the annual bicycle gymkhana (from 1896 to 1901) denote the presence of a bourgeois purpose grander than mere athleticism. Rather, the athletic events and their attendant "society" at Niagara-on-the-Lake came to signify all that was spatially and socially proper and refined in contradistinction to the public disorder of Toronto in summertime.

PETIT BOURGEOIS PUBLIC SPACE: HEAT AND UNRULY BEHAVIOUR IN TORONTO'S PUBLIC "RESORTS"

To understand late nineteenth-century public space is to delve into the curious interconnection between city people and industrial modernity—including tension-filled class, race, and gender relationships attending new work and living arrangements in increasingly populating cities—and the way they mediated and were mediated by the contrapuntal geography of the modern city. Beaux arts architecture on one city block challenged ramshackle buildings on another; concrete sidewalks on one side of the street, outmoded wooden on the other; asphalt pavement on this side of the intersection, misrepresented cedar blocks or macadam on that side. This urban geography was also social. The contest between the upscale, haute bourgeois virtues and manners, and the less formal and less tutored behaviour of the petit- and nonbourgeois gave Toronto its moral edge and was responsible for its moniker "Toronto the Good"—so-called because C.S. Clark (1898) demonstrated chapter and verse that it was not "good," though its gatekeepers tried very hard to make it so. Add to these, at least in cities around Lake Ontario, the environmental difficulties of extremes of climate, ranging from winter deep freezes to summer heat waves. The result was public space with a wide range of both uses and expectations.

The attempt to ameliorate geographically this variety of "Bourgeois Nightmares" (Fogelson 2005)—Toronto's social, cultural, and climatic conditions— meant that those who saw themselves as the guardians of the city, haute bourgeois professional and lay reformers, secular and clerical (but also those who simply believed their status in "high society" lent merit to their opinions), worked to stamp their values on Toronto's public space. With varying degrees of success, leagues of social hygiene and school art, nosy church and citizens groups, and local councils of women and their various city and street committees attempted to imprint the streets with their views.[8] Yet, in spite of bourgeois moralizing about the proper uses and disposal of the public, Peter Goheen argues that public spaces in 1890s Toronto "remained remarkably available to all its residents for a wide repertoire of activities. They were the preferred locale for public purposes ranging from the most dignified to the most disreputable, and from the highly organized to the spontaneous" (1994; 2003, 74). And nothing facilitated the Toronto public's rehearsal of its "wide repertoire of activities" better than its summer-heat conditions.

Everyday life in Toronto was understandably hot in the summers during the 1890s; the Toronto weather station shows a gradual average rise of more than 4°C (7°F) in July and August temperatures from the beginning of the decade to the end—74.3°F/23.5°C in 1891 to 81.41°F /27.45°C in 1900.[9] Such an average temperature for July and August meant summer in the city could get uncomfortably warm. The *Evening Star* even asserted "This Heat Does Kill," noting a death by heat prostration (July 29, 1898, 1). Indeed, Richard Anderson has shown a measurable urban heat-island developed from the building boom of the 1870s that resulted in the erection of many hectares of public buildings and housing fabricated with heat-retaining materials.

Torontonians justifiably complained of the city's "Hot Weather Housing," designed by builders who seemed to devise their housing schemes in the dead of the Canadian winter, forgetting that Toronto often saw summer temperatures that significantly breached 90°F/32.22°C. Toronto's heat experience demanded "bigger balconies, bigger windows, more light and air," and importantly, "less [heat-retaining] brick wall" (*Toronto Daily Star* July 16, 1901, 4). During the hot, humid summers for which Toronto is well known, the streets were often "burning hot," exhaling "the heat stored up in brick and stone and asphalt" (July 6, 1901, 12).

Little wonder the fortunate and the privileged fled the city at the first sign of excessive warmth—and had their subscriptions to the *Toronto Daily Star* forwarded to the summer destinations (July 7, 1900, 4). Numerous steamers sailed the Great Lakes and St. Lawrence River, offering tickets to destinations everywhere between Lake Superior and the Maritimes.[10] The Niagara River Line shipped Torontonians clamouring for cooling breezes across Lake Ontario to Niagara, sailing up and down the Niagara River, and of course stopping in Niagara-on-the-Lake. "The Steamer Lakeside" ran from Toronto to St. Catharines (a little west of Niagara-on-the-Lake on Lake Ontario), its "popular" Wednesday and Saturday trips allowing for "two hours in the Garden city," sailing "through the locks and up the canal," a journey "unsurpassed for beauty and pleasure" (*Globe*, Aug. 7, 1891, 2). The Muskoka Lakes District, now famous as Ontario's cottage country and the summer playground of Toronto's haute bourgeois, acquired its reputation as a cool and salubrious antidote to summer in the city. Muskoka became one of the standards for cool, breezy health in late Victorian Toronto, providing elite city people of all ages access to pure air and water in an era that ached for both.[11] The Toronto Star Fresh Air Fund arose in part as a response to summer heat, raising money to send underprivileged children and mothers in Toronto's worst and hottest neighbourhoods on steamer and railway excursions to the cooler, airier climes of Toronto's hinterland, including Lake Ontario (Mackintosh and Anderson 2009).[12]

While abandoning the city for extended periods was available to the wealthy, for most people escape was temporary; a bourgeois population was bound by work, housing, family maintenance, and other responsibilities. They provided the "funny" fodder for the *Evening Star*'s "Hot Time Snap Shots," descriptions of the "circus" of "cool breeze seekers" during the heat wave of July 18–29, 1898 (July 21, 1898, 2). For them, and for the many slum dwellers trapped in Toronto, the city provided public bathing areas, bath houses, and parks and playgrounds, "resorts" to which literally thousands of hot Torontonians flocked: 18,000 people used the baths and beaches at Woodbine, Don River, Fisherman's Island, Western Sandbar, and Sunnyside during a heat wave in July of 1901.[13] Yet, even in the cooler weather of August, the *Globe* reported 13,711 bathers at the same locations that same summer (Aug. 9, 1901, 6). In August 1896, none of the beach houses at Balmy Beach were "vacant ... which [spoke] well for this resort" (Aug. 7, 1896, 8). Enough people used the campgrounds at Kew Beach and Balmy Beach—the latter "growing rapidly into a large sized town" by the early 1900s (*Globe*, July 13, 1904, 12)—in the east end of the city to elicit comment by the *Toronto Star* when they began to abandon them en masse at the end of the summer (Aug. 26, 1896, 1). Summering in Toronto was a perennial hunt for "a cool spot [like] Munro Park" (*Toronto Daily Star*, June 28, 1901, 9).

It is easy to imagine that all such urban summer resorts, with their huge numbers of people and a heterogeneous mix of class and ethnicity, attracted the judgmental, scrutinizing bourgeois gaze (Mackintosh, "Scrutiny" 2005). In an era when conspicuous consumption demanded not only appropriate individual demonstrations of "tasteful" manipulation of disposable income, but also the ability to comport oneself as a respectable bourgeois,[14] social behaviour at public gatherings were indications of the acquiescence to or rejection of the polite norm. When public drinking created "conditions which promoted disorder" at one east end Toronto beach, its respectability as a "quiet family resort" free "from the rough element and disorderly conduct" began to wane, urging the cry to "Keep the Park Orderly" (*Evening Star*, June 20, 1895, 4).

The *Evening Star* stated the problem of resorts plainly in an editorial on Long Branch, a resort to the west of the city (in what is now the southwestern corner of Etobicoke). Lauding the "beaut[iful] grounds and buildings [with] perhaps no equal in Ontario," the writer entertained "no wonder that the young people delight to hold their picnics at this resort, protected and free from the rough element that sometimes visit other resorts" (June 29, 1895, 4). This "rough element," too, sought escape from the heat, but did so improperly, as one observer of Victoria Park noted. An important summer resort in the city, Victoria Park attracted the ire of a *Globe* letter writer who complained of "wives sitting all around with their drunken husbands lying in the grass," rendering the park unsuitable and unsafe for "women, children and respectable men" (May 7, 1895, 7). Tally this with other such threats in resorts and public spaces in general and we get a rather powerful intimation of indifference toward bourgeois deportment in the resorts of 1890s Toronto: "disorderly boys" in Bellevue Park; a "catapult nuisance" in Queen's Park (created by too many "city boys" taking slingshots into the parks to shoot songbirds); overly enthusiastic evangelists in High Park, Reservoir Park, and Queen's Park, "the resort of thousands of reputable citizens"; too many bicyclists disturbing the peace in High Park, "two to three thousand young men and women there at one time"; rowdies "howling" through the summertime band concerts in the city parks; the hurdy-gurdy and tambourine players and other "street music nuisances" made by Italian buskers, creating "a groan of anguish" in the "average resident"; "distant cheers resembling the yells of victorious armies" coming from "rooters" at the city parks' baseball diamonds; women wearing improper—"frightful"—bathing costumes at Toronto beaches; and finally "indecent bathers" "insulting" boating parties on the Humber River with their "improper exposure."[15] Such a varied repertoire of public behaviour, especially in summertime, meant that elite Torontonians would look to Niagara-on-the-Lake for more genteel, public enjoyments.

CONSTRUCTING HAUTE BOURGEOIS PUBLIC SPACE: POLITE ATHLETICS IN SUMMERTIME NIAGARA-ON-THE-LAKE

Heat conditions in Toronto at the end of the nineteenth century help explain the summertime preoccupation with upscale resorts frequented by the city's haute bourgeois in the summer excursion season.[16] Toronto newspapers report weekly of the life at "The Summer Resorts" and, in the case of Niagara-on-the-Lake, the "Merry Doings of ... Summer Visitors at the Hotels and Cottages of the Pretty Village at the Mouth of the Turbulent River" (*Toronto Daily Star*, July 7, 1900, 9). The Queen's Royal Hotel advertised a "Temperature of 65 Degrees [F or 18.3°C]" and, importantly, "reduced prices for those staying two weeks or longer," to lure Toronto's social crowd to its "delightful" bathing beaches and park-like grounds (*Globe*, July 7, 1894, 5; July 14 1894, 20). Indeed, *Cutter's Guide to Niagara Falls* described Niagara-on-the-Lake as an aristocratic wonderland of sorts:

> In the broad bay formed by the sweep of the river, the fleets of both American and Canadian yachts are gathered annually for regattas and pleasure excursions, and the waters are, during the summer season, continually dotted with white sails and pleasure boats. Back, beyond the shady streets of the little town, are many of Canada's best summer homes, and still further back, on the shores of the lake are the buildings of the new Chautauqua. (1900, 33)

The Queen's Royal Hotel, described fawningly in the same guide, suitably matched its exclusive environs:

> Amid this scene of repose and beauty is situated a charming summer hotel, "The Queen's Royal." The broad veranda . . . faces the green waters of the Lake, and the clear waters of the River where they meet, and on the other three sides are beautiful groves, flower gardens, shady walks, golfing links, tennis courts, and every provision which may add to the comfort of the guest in search of rest and pleasure. (1900, 34)

Little wonder those of means in Toronto and other Canadian and American places sought out Niagara-on-the-Lake and the Queen's Royal as a summer home.

The cost of seasonal summer accommodation in such a place probably excluded all but the haute bourgeois and the aristocracy. Apparently, "$200 for the season [would] rent a commodious and well-furnished house" (*Globe*, July 5, 1900, 3) in the town proper. Such a price most certainly prohibited labourers and clerical workers, whose average annual income in 1905 was $384.53 (Lowe 2006 , 184). Not that this could keep them from visiting Niagara-on-the-Lake, for "the railroad companies and steamboat lines" offered "crowds" of Torontonians "cheap holiday fares" for day trips (*Globe*, July 1, 1896, 10). Thousands of heat-avoiders regularly boarded the Niagara River Line steamers, *Chicora*, *Chippewa*, *Cibola* (which burned in July of 1895), and later *Corona*, from the Yonge Street wharfs for Niagara, Queenston, and Lewiston at seventy-five cents a trip (*Evening Star*, July 17, 2; *Globe*, July 8, 1898, 5). However, it was Toronto's haute bourgeois who benefited most from the town's summertime attractions and could afford the rates at the Queen's Royal Hotel and the Oban Hotel. The *Canadian Guide-Book* notes the rates at the Queen's Royal were $3.50 a day in the 1890s which, even adjusting for inflation—between $90 and $100 CDN today—would not exceed the resources of the average salaried employee, at least for a brief respite from the heat (Roberts 1899, 334). The Queen's Royal had "Hops every Saturday" and advertised a $5 package, "good for steamboat fare and board at hotel from Saturday to Monday" (*Globe*, Aug. 4, 1891, 8); the Dominion Day holiday (July 1) rate for the same package was $5.50 (*Globe*, July 1, 1993, 15). Seasonal stays at the Queen's Royal and "all the delights of summer life" (*Globe*, July 19, 1894, 8) remained, however, the prerogative of the privileged.

Especially noteworthy at the Queen's Royal were sporting events that occurred in August. Throughout the 1890s, Niagara-on-the-Lake was the site of the annual bicycle gymkhana, an international tennis tournament, and the annual local golf and lawn bowling tournaments—high society attractions that marked the summer social "season" for many elite Torontonians and Buffalonians. Participants came from as far afield as Cincinnati, Chicago, St. Louis, New York City, and Washington, D.C., though they, like the Torontonians, were probably already summering in Niagara-on-the-Lake. Their enthusiasm for conspicuous consumption and proper comportment found articulation in the town's streets and greenswards and the Queen's Royal Hotel, which served as the centre of the activities (*Globe*, July 30, 1897, 24).

Summer sports at Niagara-on-the-Lake largely constituted the August social season in the resort town that drew hot leisure seekers from many of the major cities on or near the great lakes. A "Chit Chat" column in the *Globe* in the summer of 1899 noted that "the very gay week [of August 1] which culminated in a fancy dress ball on Friday, the floral parade and bicycle gymkhana on Saturday" was followed (Tuesday August 8) by a "night of delightful entertainment ... in the Queen's Royal ballroom." The next week

FIGURE 1.1 View of Queen's Royal Hotel, c. 1900, from Lake Ontario. Niagara Historical Society and Museum.

(of August 14) offered the bowling championship, the week after (beginning August 22) the International tennis championships. Lastly, on August 31, the golf tournament rounded off "a very bright season."

These annual summer sports, such as the international tennis tournament, attracted talented athletes and "noted players" from Canada and the United States, but the events and their geographies were equally celebrated for their "artistic standpoint" (*Globe*, Aug. 20, 1898, 15). The Queen's Royal tennis courts during the international tennis tournament

> were remarkably pretty ... especially when witnessed from the end of the courts nearest the hotel, for the beautiful trees cast their deep shade in sharp contrast to the brilliant sunlight on the lawn, and the terraces are filled with ladies in gay summer gowns, together with men, who for the most part, have donned white flannels and duck suits; and as one turns one's face slightly there are the deep blue waters of Lake Ontario for a background, crowned with great white caps that dance and leap right merrily before the breeze. (July 10, 1895, 3)

It may well have been newsworthy that the players competed so fiercely that "great excitement prevailed among the spectators"; however, equally important were the certain society "ladies and gentlemen ... noticed on the terraces." The evening gatherings were also requisite: newspaper notices regularly announced that the tournaments included concerts, dances, plays, cotillions, and tournament balls. I suggest that such attention by the newspaper to the social detail of these sporting events elevates them beyond the commonplace of athletic competition.

FIGURE 1.2 Participants, 1898 International Tennis Tournament, Niagara-on-the-Lake. Niagara Historical Society and Museum

The international tennis tournament organizers seemed especially committed to "the social point of view" and to making the "social side of the tournament ... a charming feature of the Niagara season" (*Globe*, Aug. 24, 1895, 20). Indeed, this was an annual week of "gaieties" (Aug. 22, 1896, 24), where "Toronto society [would] undoubtedly gather in large numbers" (*Globe*, Aug. 17, 1899, 5). Festivities promising to make the week of tennis the climax "of the gayest season Niagara has known in many years" always followed the daily matches (Aug. 24, 1897, 5). With events as varied as costume concerts, evenings of musical selections, and calico cotillions ("in which the ladies wear calico gowns of varied hues and the gentlemen wear waistcoats and ties of the same material," the joke being that calico was a material used by the poor), amateur theatrics, tableaux, and vaudeville, and even a cake walk, the week of international tennis sponsored by the Canadian Lawn Tennis Association was not only about sports but also about manufacturing a sense of the "delightful" in the vacationers at the Queen's Royal.[17] This included the use of D'Alesandro's Mandolin Orchestra performing for the benefit of the tony spectators (and perhaps the annoyance of the competitors) (July 11, 1895, 4). The noted Canadian oil painter E. Wyly Grier, who offered art classes at the Queen's Royal during the summer, also sketched

FIGURE 1.3 Close of Niagara-on-the-Lake Golf Tournament, 1902. Niagara Historical Society and Museum

the players and apparently contributed his baritone singing voice to evening musicales.[18]

The annual golf tournament emphasized fashion and gaiety, sometimes at the expense of the sport. As central to the reportage on the tournament's "representative golfers from the United States and Canada" was the idea that "the presence of a number of smart people from New York and Chicago [would add] to the éclat of the affair" (*Globe*, Sept. 4, 1895, 10). So, too, would the "eminent tenor" Signor Tesseman, "who fairly electrified" the audiences with his singing of ballads and who was booked to give a "grand concert" at the Queen's Royal during the 1895 tournament (Aug. 30, 1895, 8). Indeed, the respectability of the event, garnered through the attendance of society folk, was so important that the 1895 tournament was postponed from Friday to Saturday "to suit the convenience of the Toronto ladies" expected both to play and cavort (Sept. 4, 1895, 10).

The Niagara lawn bowling championship, sponsored by the Ontario Lawn Bowling Association and considered the "premier bowling event of the year" (*Toronto Daily Star*, July 11, 1900, 6), in contrast to the mannered conduct of the golf and tennis tournaments and, as we will see, the bicycle gymkhana, was not the same type of society affair. In the newspaper coverage of the competition for "the Queen's Royal Challenge trophy," the bowling mattered, especially to "the large gathering of enthusiastic spectators" (*Globe*, Aug. 3, 1895, 18; Aug. 23, 6); McGaw and Winnett even provided the gold medals for the trophy winners of the August 14, 1900, match (*Toronto Daily Star*, July 11, 1900, 6) which, despite the bad weather and conditions of the lawn, saw aggressive competition full of "surprises" (*Globe*, Aug. 15, 1900, 6). However, along with the faithful reporting of the winners and losers of the round-robin competition for the challenge trophy in what appears to have been a five-day event, there were hints of the importance of respectable, social geography.[19] The Queen's Royal provided "the pleasantest of surroundings" for the bowlers and spectators (Aug. 21, 1896, 8). And if the description was accurate, "no prettier scene [could] be imagined than the crowd of 100 or more gentlemen with white or vari-colored blazers, who covered the smooth green lawns of the Queen's Royal Hotel in August of 1893" (Aug. 24, 1893, 6). What a remarkable difference in tone and style from the "disgrace" and "rowdyism" associated with a sport such as lacrosse, which was well supported in neighbouring St. Catharines, an immigrant entrepôt in southern Ontario.[20]

The Queen's Royal lawn bowling tournament provided once more a venue of lawns, terraces, and "fine shade trees" for "fair spectators," "well-dressed ladies and their escorts," to see and be seen (The Oban, too, held lawn bowling tournaments, such as "The Canadas" [*Globe*, Aug. 1, 1898, 1]). And because the sport was fairly new to Canadians in the early 1890s, many of the society women were unfamiliar with the rules; their ignorance elicited the occasional "'hush, dear and don't mention it'" (*Globe*, Aug. 24, 1893, 6). Yet whether or not the many elite spectators understood what they were witnessing was, I contend, less important than their haute bourgeois presence on the greens of southern Ontario's premier summer resort.

"BATTLE OF FLOWERS": THE BICYCLE GYMKHANA

The annual bicycle gymkhana at Niagara-on-the-Lake, hosted by the Queen's Royal Hotel, illustrates the easy affinities between polite athletics and bourgeois decorum in public space. An amalgamation of flower arranging and dressage for bicycles, it catered to invited elite bicyclists who performed feats of bicycling prowess while maintaining their elevated social status (Mackintosh 2007, 145–50). A two-day event, the first day involved parading through the streets on bicycles artfully decorated with flowers, plants, and bunting (flags, ribbons, silks, lace, etc). The second day consisted of bicycle games testing the riding skills of both child and adult bicyclists. Combined, the parading and gaming produced a haute bourgeois spectacle that appeared to counter the unseemly anti-bourgeois behaviour·in and at Toronto's summer resorts.

FIGURE 1.4 Floral parade arriving at or leaving the Queen's Royal Hotel, c. 1899, when cart and carriage entrants were permitted in the bicycle gymkhana's floral parade. Niagara Historical Society and Museum

The floral parade in 1899 flaunted "gaily colored wheels ... [touring] the town, going around the main square and finally [drawing] up in front of the Queen's Royal grounds for judging." As the 1897 gymkhana parade concluded, spectators, performing a type of bourgeois benediction, pelted the procession of bicyclists with flowers when it returned to the Queen's Royal, a projectile-launching behaviour quite different in kind and intent from the "catapult nuisance" in Toronto's Queen's Park (*Globe*, Aug. 7, 1899, 2).

If indeed the floral parade "doubtless surpassed the expectations of the many admirers, who literally thronged the principal square of the town, by which route the cyclists proceeded," it had much to do with the veneration accorded class and art at this time in Canada (Lochnan et al. 1993, Hill 1995). Art and aesthetics had become a haven for bourgeois aspirations at the turn of the twentieth century, and horticulture had become the latest art form in cities that referred to parks and public gardens as "municipal art."[21] As *The Times* (of Niagara) commented, the 1896 bicycle parade of artfully arranged flowers, bicycles, and handsome and decorous bicyclists was "exceptionally artistic and pleasing."[22]

Accordingly, parade entrants and their wheels were bedecked in floral art. Despite the *Globe*'s comment regarding the same floral parade—"it would be difficult to give any description of the decorations of the wheels [bicycles] that would at all do justice to their prettiness"—the description of haute bourgeois propriety on the streets and greenswards of Niagara-on-the-Lake and the Queen's Royal Hotel was exactly the point. It was necessary to convey to readers of the *Globe* that users of the Niagara-on-the-Lake resort not only were well behaved but also fashionably accounted. In a description of the 1897 floral parade, we learn that "Miss Fowler's wheel" (the entrant and bicycle won "best decorated wheel") was "decked … with quantities of pink ribbons and roses, smilax and white Japanese lilies, in the front under the handle bars. Miss Fowler wore a white duck gown, with pink muslin blouse and flower-trimmed hat." The bicycle ridden by Miss Eliza Winnett, a native of the town, "was covered with asparagus [fern], and had big bunches of golden brown flowers on the handle bars and down the posts [forks]." The wheel of "little Miss Hoyt … was a mass of white and pink ribbons and flowers. In her dainty little frock of white organdie muslin, with pink satin sash and bows, bare arms and legs, with short socks she looked a dainty picture" (*Globe*, Aug. 7, 1897, 20).

Men, too, participated in the gymkhana's "Battle of Flowers" (*Globe*, Aug. 4, 1899, 10). In the 1896 gymkhana, for example, all twenty-two members of the Niagara Fire Brigade, led by "Chief Reid," entered their bicycles festooned with red flags. The firefighters themselves wore red shirts and white caps. Riding with one hand, they "carried Japanese parasols" in the other. Gymkhana organizer and honorary secretary, E. Scott Griffin of Toronto, entered the same floral parade on a bicycle "decorated with red carnations and geraniums, interspersed with smilax."[23] The following year, one notable male was "Mr. Oscar McGraw [who] carried Upper Canada College colors on his wheel, which looked extremely well. The spokes were entwined with deep blue and white paper while the same colors were entwined on the frame, which was decorated with asparagus fern and white asters." Not to be outdone, "Mr. Boughton of Buffalo chose scarlet and green as his colors, and carried out the design with a scarlet ribbon and smilax, and also a huge bunch of geraniums on his handle bars, from which sprang here tall peacock feathers" (Aug. 7, 1897, 20). In a bourgeois world that continuously berated men for masculine indiscretions,[24] we can imagine such artful, masculine, and public behaviour credited the men riders.

If the first day of the bicycle gymkhana was, as the *Globe* noted, "exceptionally elegant and enjoyable," the second day (of the 1896 gymkhana, for example) was a "fashionable gathering [numbering] in all about 1,100"

FIGURE 1.5 Bicycle gymkhana "games" on the green of the Queen's Royal Hotel, c. 1901. Niagara Historical Society and Museum

(Aug. 17, 6). These were "ladies and gentlemen" come to see the events "on the beautiful terraces and lawn" of the Queen's Royal Hotel. "A marked increase of visitors from Toronto and other Canadian points and [an] exceptionally large attendance of ladies" witnessed a variety of bicycle games, all "keenly contested":

> *Maiden's scurry*. For girls sixteen years of age and under, with turn and obstacle [sic] eighteen inches high over which the wheel must be lifted.... *Obstacle race*. Start, ride ten yards, dismount, lift wheel over obstacle, ride 30 yards, pick up handkerchief with hands without dismounting, ride twenty yards further over bicycle hurdle and then to finish between upright posts.... *Tortoise race*. Fifty yards; person finishing last without falling or stopping to win.... *Needle and necktie race*. Gentlemen must thread needle while lady who is waiting at turning point ties necktie. Points given for the neatest bow. Hurdle at finish.... *Parasol race (for ladies)*. Rider must wheel fifty yards, dismount and pick up parasol, mount and open parasol and arrive at finish holding up parasol....
>
> *Tent-pegging*. Rider with lance must pick up peg; best three trials out of five.... *Tankard race (for men only)*; competitors must ride to a point where pewters stand in a row, dismount, and take pewter in hand, mounting again and must drink contents without spilling them and return to finish holding pewter.

D'Alesandro's Mandolin Orchestra again accompanied the contestants as they vied for recognition as the most stylish and capable rider.[25]

CONCLUSION: BOURGEOIS CONGRUITY AND THE SUMMERTIME PUBLIC

I have suggested elsewhere that these two days of polite sport and parading at the Niagara-on-the-Lake gymkhana, melding the stylishness of the contestants with the propriety of the activity, "perhaps evinces the social meaning" of an exhortation by bicycling etiquette writer Maria E. Ward: "'look well at all times when bicycling' so as not to appear 'incongruous'" (Mackintosh 2007, 148). "Incongruous," of course, can mean inharmoniousness with surroundings (OED), and the potential for incongruity in the public of the late Victorian city is significant to students of public space. We already know that Victorians and Edwardians embraced moral environmentalism and osmotic beauty, believing that "proximity to beautified environments infused citizens with a desire to behave in a morally acceptable manner."[26] Such values blended with their propensity to associate spatial order and disorder with orderly or disorderly social behaviour, a reflection of their devotion to environmental determinism. If "incongruity in public" denotes the improper behaviour of petit- and non-bourgeois Torontonians in the city's urban and exurban resorts, then "congruity in public" describes the polite athletics and bourgeois gaieties performed in the streets and greenswards. The town's summer crowd of polite athletes and gaiety seekers not only displayed a congruity suited to their haute bourgeois status. They also affirmed their role as spectacle producers, a responsibility they increasingly shouldered as promulgators of conspicuous leisure and consumption (Mackintosh 2007).

This study shows something else, equally important in our contemporary world where environmental concerns and environmental history obtain increasing relevance: there is an intimate connection between the culture of the southern Ontario historical public and its climate, specifically Toronto's summertime heat conditions and Niagara-on-the-Lake's ability to accommodate Toronto's anxious heat-avoiders. While many Torontonians of all classes took day trips to the town, haute bourgeois Torontonians used their privilege to circumvent the perceived disorderly public consequences of summertime heat: a hurly-burly of anti-bourgeois behaviours and "nuisances" made public by the hot conditions in residences and the openness of Toronto's public resorts to all Torontonians. Toronto, as public as it was, seemed to encourage those with privilege to vacate the city for a more a congruous geography suited to the polite pastimes of summer.

NOTES

1 Saturday Special, the Niagara Falls *Weekend Review*, Aug. 4, 2007, 1; "Babes and Bikes in Niagara's Vineyards," *Globe and Mail*, Aug. 18, 2007, accessed at http://www.theglobeandmail.com/servlet/story/LAC.20070818.BIKE18/TPStory/specialTravel.

2 Driving mileage today between Toronto and Niagara-on-the-Lake is 132 kilometres (82 miles), although the steamer trip took approximately two hours and most people went to Niagara by steamer or train.

3 "Plague of Nuisances," *Toronto Evening Star*, Apr. 30, 1898, 7.

4 "In Munro Park," *Toronto Daily Star*, July 3, 1901, 6.

5 Winnett and Dick McGaw also owned Toronto's Queen's Hotel—now the Fairmont Royal York Hotel. See *The International Railway and Steam Navigation Guide*, 1875, 41, 42.

6 See Driver 1988; Entrikin 1994; Matless 1994, 1997; Sibley 1995; Cresswell 1996; Sack 1999; Domosh 2001; Howell 2001; Smith 2000; Goheen 2003; Mitchell 2003; Mackintosh 2005 "Scrutiny" and 2005 "Development," 2007; Baldwin 2009.

7 See also Davis 1988, Scobey 1992, Newman 1997, Ryan 1989.

8 See Valverde 1991, Goheen 2003, Strange 1995, Walden 1997, Mackintosh 2005 "Development," Mackintosh 2005 "Scrutiny."

9 The following are average temperatures for July and August, 1890 to 1900: 1890, 75.11°F/23.95°C; 1891, 74.3°F/23.5°C; 1892, 77.63°F/25.35°C; 1893, 77.9°F/25.5°C; 1894, 74.3°F/25.3°C; 1895, 75.92°F/24.4°C; 1896, 78.53°F/25.85°C; 1897, 78.35°F/25.75°C; 1898, 81.05°F/27.25°C; 1899, 80.69°F/27.05°C; 1900, 81.41°F/27.45C. "Daily Data Reports for July and August, 1890–1900—Toronto Ontario," *Environment Canada—Climate Data Online: National Climate Data and Information Archive*, accessed at http://climate. weatheroffice.ec.gc.ca/climateData/daily data_e.html.

10 A *Globe* article, "Passenger Steamers: Toronto a Great Centre of Traffic," explains just how expansive navigation activity was on the Great Lakes at the time (Aug. 16, 1890, 1). By 1898, the Niagara River Line offered "5 Trips Daily—on and after ... June 20th" to Niagara-on-the-Lake (*Globe*, Aug. 23, 1898, 5).

11 See Valverde 1991, Rosen 1995, Stradling 1999, Melosi 2005.

12 The Toronto Daily Star Fresh Air Fund recommended sending children sick with "summer complaints ... to Muskoka or the highlands north of the city" because "it resulted in improved health for the little sufferers. Children who cannot sleep at all here [in hot Toronto] will sleep well in Muskoka, where the air is fresh" (Aug. 3, 1901), 11.

Steamer excursions for needy children were first reported in the *Globe* (June 12, 1888, 1) in the 1880s and assumed a permanent role with the Toronto Daily Star Fresh Air Fund by the early 1900s (see, for example, July 23, 1901, 1).

13 "At the Free Baths," *Toronto Daily Star*, July 15, 1901, 4.

14 See Veblen 1953; Leach 1984; Blumin 1985; Horowitz 1985; Abelson 1989; Mackintosh 2005, 2007; and Mackintosh and Norcliffe 2006.

15 *Globe*, Aug. 30, 1890, 16; *Globe*, Apr. 22, 1896, 10; *Saturday Night*, June 12, 1897, 1; *Globe*, July 27, 1891, 5; *Saturday Night*, July 20, 1896, 1; *Globe*, May 2, 1896, 6; *Toronto Evening Star*, July 21, 1898, 4; *Toronto Evening Star*, July 25, 1898,

1, 2; *Globe*, July 2, 1896, 4; *Toronto Evening Star*, July 28, 1894, 8; *Toronto Evening Star*, June 27, 1895, 5. One notable cartoon shows a woman in a bathing suit that looked more like a bulky petticoat than the typical Victorian bathing costume, with the caption, "I made it myself out of a postage stamp" (*Toronto Daily Star*, June 23, 1900, 11).

16 Ironically, the weather station closest to Niagara-on-the-Lake—in Welland—reported higher average July temperatures in the 1890s than the Toronto station, peaking at 83.66°F/28.7°C in 1898. "Daily Data Reports for July, 1891–1900—Welland Ontario," *Environment Canada—Climate Data Online: National Climate Data and Information Archive*, available at http://climate.weatheroffice .ec.gc.ca/climateData/dailydata_e.html.

17 *Globe*, Aug. 22, 1896, 24; Aug. 12, 1899, 20; May 2, 1896, 6; Aug. 17, 1899, 5.

18 *Globe*, July 22, 1897, 7; July 11, 1895, 4; Aug. 19, 1897, 7; Aug. 24, 1897, 5.

19 See, for example, the implication that this is so, in "The Winners at Niagara," *Globe*, Aug. 22, 1896, 20.

20 *Toronto Evening Star*, July 2, 1898, 5. By the 1920s, as one bourgeois Torontonian recalls, whenever he took the ferry to Port Dalhousie, his mother would admonish him "not to go to St. Catharines," because of its working class, immigrant reputation (William Clements, RCA [Royal Canadian Academy of the Arts], personal communication).

21 See Lears 1981, Blanchard 1995, Boisseau 2000, Mackintosh 2005 "Development," 692.

22 "Bicycle Tourney," *The Times* (of Niagara), Vol. III, No. 1, Aug. 20, 1896.

23 "Bicycle Tourney," *The Times* (of Niagara).

24 See Carnes and Griffen 1990; Chauncey 1994; Bederman 1995; Kimmel 1997; and Mackintosh 2007.

25 "Bicycle Tourney," *The Times* [of Niagara]. The spelling for "D'Alesandro" varies: I've seen "D'Alessandro" and "D'Alsandro."

26 See Mackintosh 2005 "Development," 713; Baldwin 2009.

WORKS CITED

Abelson, Elaine. *When Ladies Go A-Thieving: Middle Class Shoplifters in the Victorian Department Store*. New York and Oxford: Oxford University Press, 1989.

Anderson, Richard. "Sweltering Under a Broiling Sun: Towards an Historical Geography of Toronto's Heat Island," a paper presented at the Annual General Meeting of the Canadian Association of Geographers, University of Saskatchewan, Saskatoon, Saskatchewan, May 29–June 2, 2007.

Baldwin, Andrew. "The White Geography of Lawren Stewart Harris: Whiteness and the Performative Coupling of Wilderness and Multiculturalism in Canada." *Environment and Planning A* 41 (2009), 529–544.

Bederman, Gail. *Manliness and Civilization: A Cultural History of Gender and Race in the United States, 1880–1917*. Chicago: University of Chicago Press, 1995.

Blanchard, Mary. "Boundaries and the Victorian Body: Aesthetic Fashion in Gilded Age America." *American Historical Review* 100 (1995), 21–50.

Blumin, Stuart. *The Emergence of the Middle Class: Social Experience in the American City, 1760–1900*. Cambridge and New York: Cambridge University Press, 1989.

Boisseau, Tracy. "White Queens at the Chicago World's Fair, 1893: New Womanhood in the Service of Class, Race, and Nation." *Gender & History* 12.1 (2000), 3–81.

Carnes, Mark, and Clyde Griffen, eds. *Meanings for Manhood: Constructions of Masculinity in Victorian America*. Chicago: University of Chicago Press, 1990.

Chauncey, George. *Gay New York: Gender, Urban Culture, and the Making of the Gay Male World, 1890–1940*. New York: Basic Books, 1994.

Clark, C.S. *Of Toronto the Good. A Social Study. The Queen City of Canada as It Is*. Montreal: The Toronto Publishing Company, 1898.

Cresswell, Tim. *In Place/Out of Place: Geography, Ideology and Transgression*. Minneapolis: University of Minnesota Press, 1996.

Cutter, Charles. *Cutter's Guide to Niagara Falls, and Adjacent Points of Interest*. Fourth Edition. Published by Charles Cutter, 1900.

Davis, Susan. *Parades and Power: Street Theatre in Nineteenth-Century Philadelphia*. Berkeley: University of California Press, 1988.

Domosh, Mona. "The 'Women of New York': A Fashionable Moral Geography." *Environment and Planning D: Society and Space* 19 (2001), 573–92.

Driver, Felix. "Moral Geographies: Social Science and the Urban Environment in Mid-nineteenth Century England." *Transactions of the Institute of British Geographers* 3:3 (1988), 275–87.

Entrikin, J. Nicholas. "Moral Geographies: The Planner in Place." *Geography Research Forum* 14 (1994), 113–19.

Fogelson, Robert. *Bourgeois Nightmares: Suburbia, 1870–1930*. New Haven and London: Yale University Press, 2005.

Gay, Peter. *Pleasure Wars, The Bourgeois Experience: Victoria to Freud*. New York and London: Norton, 1998.

Goheen, Peter. "Parading: A Lively Tradition in Early Victorian Toronto." In Alan Baker and Gideon Biger, eds., *Ideology and Landscape in Historical Perspective: Essays on the Meanings of Places in the Past*. Cambridge, New York: Cambridge University Press, 1992: 330–51.

———. "Negotiating Access to Public Space in Mid-Nineteenth Century Toronto." *Journal of Historical Geography* 20:4 (1994), 430–49.

———. "The Assertion of Middle-class Claims to Public Space in Late Victorian Toronto." *Journal of Historical Geography* 29 (2003), 73–92.

Hill, Charles. *The Group of Seven: Art for a Nation*. Toronto: McClelland and Stewart, 1995.

Horowitz, Daniel. "Frugality or Comfort: Middle-class Styles of Life in the Early Twentieth-Century." *American Quarterly* 37 (1985), 239–59.

Howell, Philip. "Sex and the City of Bachelors: Sporting Guidebooks and Urban Knowledge in Nineteenth-century Britain." *Ecumene* 8:1 (2001), 20–49.

The International Railway and Steam Navigation Guide. Montreal: C. R. Chisholm and Bros., 1875.

Kendrick, Martyn. *Advantage Canada: A Tennis Centenary.* Toronto: McGraw-Hill, 1990.

Kimmel, Michael. *Manhood in America: A Cultural History.* New York: Free Press, 1997.

Leach, William. "Transformations in a Culture of Consumption: Women and Department Stores, 1890–1925." *Journal of American History* 71 (1984), 319–42.

Lears, T. Jackson. *No Place of Grace: Antimodernism and the Transformation of American Culture, 1880–1920.* Chicago: University of Chicago Press, 1994.

Lochnan, Kathryn et al. *The Earthly Paradise: Arts and Crafts By William Morris and His Circle from Canadian Collections.* Toronto: Key Porter Books, 1993.

Lowe, Graham. "Class, Job, and Gender in the Canadian Office." In Laurel Sefton MacDowell and Ian Radforth, eds., *Canadian Working-class History: Selected Readings.* Toronto: Canadian Scholars' Press, 2006: 178–98.

Mackintosh, Phillip Gordon. "Scrutiny in the Modern City: The Domestic Public and the Toronto Local Council of Women at the Turn of the Twentieth-Century." *Gender, Place, and Culture* 12:1 (2005), 29–48.

———. "'The Development of Higher Urban Life' and the Geographic Imagination: Beauty, Art and Moral Environmentalism in Toronto, 1900–1920." *Journal of Historical Geography* 31:4 (2005), 688–722.

———. "A Bourgeois Geography of Domestic Cycling: The Responsible Use of Public Space in Toronto and Niagara-on-the-Lake, 1890–1900." *Journal of Historical Sociology* 20 1/2 (2007), 128–57.

——— and Glen Norcliffe. "Flâneurie on Bicycles: Acquiescence to Women in Public in the 1890s." *The Canadian Geographer* 50:1 (2006), 17–37.

——— and Richard Anderson. "The Toronto Star Fresh Air Fund: Transcendental Rescue in a Modern City." *Geographical Review* 99:4 (2009), 539–62.

Matless, David. "Moral Geography in Broadland." *Ecumene* 1 (1994), 127–55.

———. "Moral Geographies of Landscape." *Landscape Research* 22 (1997), 141–55.

Melosi, Martin. *Garbage in the Cities: Refuse, Reform and the Environment* (revised edition). Pittsburgh: University of Pittsburgh Press, 2005.

Mitchell, Don. *The Right to the City: Social Justice and the Fight for Public Space.* New York: Guilford Press, 2003.

Newman, Simon Peter. *Parades and the Politics of the Street: Festive Culture in the Early American Republic.* Philadelphia: University of Pennsylvania Press, 1997.

Roberts, Charles G. D. *The Canadian Guide-Book: The Tourist and Sportman's Guide to Eastern Canada and Newfoundland.* New York: D. Appleton and Company, 1891.

———. *The Canadian Guide-Book: The Tourist and Sportman's Guide to Eastern Canada and Newfoundland.* New York: D. Appleton and Company, 1899.

Rosen, Christine Meisner. "Businessmen against Pollution in Late Nineteenth Century Chicago." *The Business History Review* 69:3 (1995), 351–97.

Ryan, Mary. "The American Parade: Representations of the Nineteenth Century Social Order." In Lynn Hunt, ed., *The New Cultural History*. Berkeley: University of California Press, 1989: 131–53.

Sack, Robert. "A Sketch of a Geographic Theory of Morality." *Annals of the Association of American Geographers* 89:1 (1999), 26–44.

Scobey, David. "Anatomy of the Promenade: The Politics of Bourgeois Sociability in Nineteenth-Century New York." *Social History* 17 (1992), 203–27.

Sibley, David. *Geographies of Exclusion*. London: Routledge, 1995.

Smith, David. *Moral Geographies: Ethics in a World of Difference*. Edinburgh: Edinburgh University Press, 2000.

Stradling, David. *Smokestacks and Progressives: Environmentalists, Engineers, and Air Quality in America, 1881–1951*. Baltimore: Johns Hopkins University Press, 1999.

Strange, Carolyn. *Toronto's Girl Problem: The Perils and Pleasures of the City, 1880–1930*. Toronto: University of Toronto Press, 1995.

Sweetser, Moses Foster. *New England: A Handbook for Travelers*. Seventh Edition. Boston: James R. Osgood and Co., 1881.

Valverde, Mariana. *The Age of Light, Soap, and Water: Moral Reform in English Canada, 1885–1925*. Toronto: McClelland and Stewart, 1991.

Veblen, Thorstein. *The Theory of the Leisure Class*. New York: Mentor, 1953[1899].

Walden, Keith. *Becoming Modern in Toronto: The Industrial Exhibition and the Shaping of a Late Victorian Culture*. Toronto: University of Toronto Press, 1997.

A PROMISE SET IN STONE
St. Catharines Honours a Common Soldier

RUSSELL JOHNSTON
MICHAEL RIPMEESTER

INTRODUCTION

"Step by deliberate step, pallbearers in brilliant red tunics" brought the soldier "home." Veterans of past conflicts saluted as the coffin passed through
the streets of St. Catharines. With them stood civilian onlookers and schoolchildren, many holding flags, lining the streets as the entourage passed.
Police officers paid their respects, and an honour guard of firefighters attended
silently at the cemetery. Then, at the graveside, "a deafening silence fell" following the traditional riflemen's salute, only to be filled with the Last Post
and a piper's lament. These scenes brought a distant conflict very close to
home.[1]

This was December 2006. Corporal Albert Storm, a native of Fort Erie,
was killed on active duty in Afghanistan. Storm was a member of the Royal
Canadian Regiment based in Petawawa, but the Lincoln and Welland Regiment stationed in Niagara opened its St. Catharines armoury and mounted
a full military funeral for their fellow soldier. Known as "Stormy" to his
friends, he left behind his wife and two children, his parents, and siblings.
They were embraced by the troops on hand and the community. The armoury
was filled to capacity. Some mourners had to be turned away.[2]

This was also June 1885. Three blocks away from the armoury, a worn
grey monument reminds passersby of another soldier whose life and death
were honoured by the people of Niagara. Private Alexander Watson, a native
of St. Catharines, fell at the Battle of Batoche during the North-West Rebellion of 1885. Like Storm, Watson served with a regiment based in another

city: Winnipeg's 90th Battalion, now the Royal Canadian Rifles. Nonetheless, the Lincoln and Welland regiments, then operating as two separate units, put all of their manpower behind an impressive military funeral. Then, too, the local community stood behind Watson's parents and siblings as they grieved the loss of their only son and brother.

Times do not change when honouring the death of a local soldier. Communities rally to comfort the family and articulate their own collective sense of grief; according to Snezhana Demitrova, they also celebrate the "citizen who possesses the power and spirit that allows absolute self-denial in the name of sacred duty," hoping to preserve the memory of the dead (2005, 184).[3] However, the initial fervour of remembrance and celebration does not seem to last. Watson was hailed as a hero in the months following his death. He was accorded two funerals, and a third ceremony—the unveiling of the monument—served as a fitting memorial service. If the service for Albert Storm reveals a depth of popular support for local soldiers today, Watson's memorialization reveals that popular support for local soldiers was no less strong in the Victorian era. Today, however, Watson is unknown to most residents of St. Catharines (Johnston and Ripmeester 2007). How do we account for the break between the immediate, spontaneous recognition of specific soldiers and the gradual loss of their names and stories? Despite the persistence of memorials, perhaps the effort to remember a particular soldier sits most heavily upon the generation that lost a son, a lover, a father, and a friend.

This observation points to the ambivalent relationship between the intentions of "memory entrepreneurs" and the sensibilities of their audiences. Elizabeth Jelin uses the term "memory entrepreneur" to identify individuals and groups "who seek social recognition and political legitimacy of one (their own) interpretation or narrative of the past" (2003, 33–34). The literature on popular memory suggests that the maintenance of specific narratives is a politically charged process. Looking at the creation of memory infrastructures (such as archives, museums, school curricula, and historic sites) most often reveals the desires of specific groups with access to the necessary resources to perpetuate their own preferred readings of the past. Subsequently, learning about the past becomes structured by mnemonic socialization; we are rewarded for appropriate understandings (for example, graded as a good student while in school) or reprimanded for inappropriate or uninformed understandings (for example, chastised as a poor citizen by newspaper editorialists). Within these infrastructures, a preferred understanding of the past can become naturalized as the *only* understanding of the past. In this regard, Niagara is little different from elsewhere in its commemoration of local history.[4]

That said, most citizens betray a genuine ambivalence regarding these kinds of memory infrastructures. There is no reason why any audience must internalize the mnemonic prompts they convey. Thus, any interpretation, no matter its source, requires an audience not only willing to hear it but willing to perpetuate it. As well, audiences may attach their own, alternative meanings to particular people, places, and events. As John Bodnar argues, commemoration relies upon a process of compromise between official and "vernacular" perspectives. Without some popular participation or at least acquiescence in the process of commemoration, the work of memory entrepreneurs may bear few results (1992, 13–20). Similarly, Roy Rosenzweig and David Thelen contend that mnemonic prompts remain effective through time only when they remain significant in the popular imagination. As the local contexts of remembering shift with trends in society, the economy, or politics, so too can the significance of particular historical narratives (1998, 115–46).[5]

This draws us back to the parallel between the funerary rituals dedicated to Alexander Watson and Albert Storm. Examining the commemoration of Watson's death reveals the fervour and politics that surrounded the North-West Rebellion and how Niagarans marked events of national significance. Over time, the specific details of Watson's story have been lost to popular memory, subsumed by other conflicts and changing perspectives. Nonetheless, the generic intent of his monument endures in the commemorations for contemporary soldiers like Storm.

THE NORTH-WEST REBELLION

The story of the North-West Rebellion has been told many times, how in 1885 the Métis and their Native allies fought Ottawa over land claims in the Prairie west. It was the second of two uprisings prompted by the same issue: the federal government under Sir John A. Macdonald wanted farm communities to flourish west of Lake Superior, farm communities built by newly arrived European immigrants. Planning began in 1869 with a land survey of the Red River Valley in what is now southern Manitoba. Unfortunately, there was no guarantee the lands held by Natives and existing white settlers would be recognized. To protect themselves, they established a provisional government under Louis Riel, a Métis schoolteacher who emerged as a powerful spokesman for the community. Riel's government successfully negotiated the community's entrance into Confederation as the province of Manitoba. At the same time, it was not afraid to use force to defend its jurisdiction. In one instance, it jailed, tried, and executed a man who rejected its authority.

Certain quarters of Ontario were outraged by this act and viewed the entire situation as treasonous; they lobbied heavily to have Riel brought to justice. Macdonald subsequently deployed the militia to the Red River, and the provisional government collapsed. Riel fled. He was later pardoned while in exile (Stanley 1960, Pannekoek 1991).

In 1885, the struggle was renewed when a railway company co-operating with the federal government began linking British Columbia with Ontario. Again, Macdonald's government neglected to settle land claims before development began. Again, the Métis under Riel formed a provisional government to protect their interests. This time it was located at the village of Batoche, roughly eighty-five kilometres north of Saskatoon. Riel hoped a combination of political posturing and sabre-rattling would force Macdonald to negotiate with them as equals. To many outsiders it appeared that Riel's forces controlled the district and could easily extend their power. Macdonald responded quickly, but not with negotiations. The Canadian militia mustered some 8,000 men from Manitoba, Ontario, Quebec, and New Brunswick to form a "Northwest Field Force" and face the rebels. This time the provisional government did not back down and Riel remained to lead it. Canada was at war (Morton 1972, Beal and Macleod 1984).

Alexander Watson was a volunteer with the 90th Battalion in Winnipeg. In 1881, aged twenty-four, he had headed west alone while his family remained in St. Catharines. Like many young Canadians, he likely sought his fortune by following the railway. In four years he achieved a modest success. He was a carpenter, and the building trades were in high demand in booming Winnipeg. Socially, he joined a Presbyterian church where he was a popular Sunday school teacher. Local papers also report that he was engaged to a young woman from a prominent Winnipeg family (Mulvaney 1885, 242). He also found companionship in the militia. The rebellion began when the provisional government came into being on March 18, 1885; the 90th was called immediately, and Watson's company boarded trains for the journey west just twelve days later. He first saw action on April 24 and managed to avoid sniper fire that ambushed the Field Force at the Battle of Fish Creek—the Métis' strategic defence point on the land route from Saskatoon to Batoche. On May 12, at the Battle of Batoche, he was not so fortunate. Watson was mortally wounded during the final charge that took the Métis capital. He died three days later. He was one of only eight soldiers in the Field Force to be killed.[6] Batoche was decisive. Several Métis leaders surrendered or were captured in the ensuing days while their riflemen dispersed. Riel himself surrendered, was tried for treason, and was found guilty. He was hanged six months later.

FIGURE 2.1 Alexander Watson, 1885.
C.P. Mulvaney, *Canada's North-West Rebellion* (Toronto: Hovey, 1885)

The rebellion and its aftermath prompted conflicting responses from Canadians. There were many who believed that the Natives' land claims were legitimate. Indeed, the Liberal opposition blamed Macdonald's government for the outbreak of violence because it had obstinately refused to address these claims even as it pushed forward with the railway and settlement (Flanagan 1983, Mailhot and Sprague 1985). In Niagara, the Welland *Tribune* argued that "the Ottawa Government is largely responsible for neglecting the grievances and warnings of trouble wafted from the Northwest for months before the outbreak actually occurred" (May 22, 1885, 5). Nonetheless, the rebels' decision to use force was roundly condemned. Even to partisan eyes, this was a fatal mistake. Again in Niagara, the Thorold *Post* captured this spirit in an editorial discussing the number of deaths on both sides: "Their crimes can never be atoned for, even were all their worthless lives sacrificed."[7] The Field Force volunteers were both Protestant and Catholic, both anglophone and francophone. Among the Natives, several Prairie bands rejected Riel's leadership. The government's response to the rebellion seemed to be widely accepted (Morton 1972, Beal and Macleod 1984).

While most Canadians agreed with the militia's deployment, they did not agree on a suitable punishment for Riel. Much of English-speaking Canada viewed Riel as a traitor who had led an armed revolt; the justice of his cause was irrelevant. The *Post* referred to Riel as "an inciter of treason, and, if not a red-handed assassin himself ... directly responsible for the deeds of the irresponsible hordes who were inspired by him." A court found him guilty, the sentence was death, and justice was served. The *Tribune* concluded, "Riel well deserves hanging" (May 22, 1885, 5). By contrast, French-speaking Quebec saw things quite differently. The rebellions were not condoned but were pardonable because the Native cause was thought to be fundamentally just. Seen in this light, Riel's execution appeared to be unnecessarily harsh. His jury had recommended mercy, but the anti-Catholic Orange Lodge had lobbied relentlessly for his death. Worse, the Lodge's vitriol and violent language suggested that French-speaking Catholics were not welcome on the Prairies. These suspicions were confirmed five years later when Manitoba abolished its Catholic school system (Owram 1982, Trofimenkoff 1982, Silver 1988).

The events of 1885, then, did not recount a simple heroic plot in which good triumphed over evil. From the outset, the government's handling of the affair deepened tensions between Natives and whites, francophones and anglophones, and Catholics and Protestants. At the same time, it was an enormously popular campaign among those who supported it. The celebrations began with the 90th Battalion itself, whose members wrote a music hall farce—"a musical and dramatic burlesque"—en route back to Winnipeg. *The 90th on Active Service* was a hit on the Winnipeg stage and the libretto was published for sale. The dead were barely five weeks in the ground and already there was little mention of them in the show. At best, the score contained this brief verse from the newly penned regimental march: "We fought the rebels at Fish Creek and drove them out of sight/While many of our good men and true fell battling for the right" (Tascona and Wells 1983).[8] These two lines emphasize the gallantry of the unit rather than the death of individuals. It was a theme repeated by the campaign's proponents in the stories, books, and memorials that later marked the campaign.[9]

A SOLDIER'S FUNERALS, 1885

Dead Field Force soldiers were honoured almost from the moment battles ended. News dispatches from the front reached Winnipeg and Niagara within forty-eight hours. Unfortunately, they were not always clear or accurate. The first list of casualties from Batoche reported that "Watson of the 90th" had fallen. This prompted a rather sad episode in Winnipeg since an officer in the same battalion, Sgt.-Maj. John Watson, was wounded the same day. Anxiety gripped the city. Both the Winnipeg *Free Press* and the *Times* were beset by family and friends of the two young men. Over the next forty-eight hours the papers frantically awaited further dispatches to discover the soldier's true identity. The *Free Press* noted that the sergeant-major "has a wife and six children in this city, and should the report of his death be confirmed it will be a sad bereavement.... [He] was universally liked and was a great favorite [sic]."[10] The private may have had fewer friends, but the papers made up for this unintended slight. Once his death was confirmed, he and his dead comrades were lionized with biographical notes illustrated with their portraits.[11] These pieces were later reprinted in the leading Montreal and Toronto papers.[12]

Under British military custom, dead soldiers were buried in the field of battle. During the American Civil War the Union army altered this practice. It sought to recognize the effort of every citizen-soldier in defence of the nation, and to do so it created national war cemeteries to honour its dead. Apparently the Canadian government understood the powerful propaganda effect of these efforts and adopted similarly political procedures. After temporary interment at the battleground, the Department of Militia paid to have the remains returned to their families. This decision made camp life disquieting as soldiers sought closure with respect to their dead comrades. One veteran later wrote of the dead, "As a rule the men shun them until they are carried out. They seemed to be forgotten in the excitement of the moment" (Rusden 1983, 293). On the home front, however, this decision had startling results. The home community of every dead soldier took possession of his name and transformed not just officers but rank-and-file soldiers into national war heroes (Tascona and Wells 1983, 39).[13] Rather than offer sombre eulogies over the tragedy of war, each community trumpeted its own contribution to the military victory achieved in the Northwest.

In this enthusiastic atmosphere, Watson had two funerals. The first funeral took place in Winnipeg. The city took great pride in the 90th Battalion's role at Batoche and gave the men a massive public reception when they returned in July. Their parade route was marked with a victory arch, and local newspapers competed to sing their praises. Weeks before this, however, the bodies of Watson and five fellow soldiers arrived on May 22. Their reception, though sombre, was no less grand. The town of Moose Jaw, Saskatchewan, provided an early indication of how certain Canadians felt about the campaign and their men in uniform. The train carrying the coffins stopped there en route and was met by "a large number of citizens and the home guard" who wished to pay their respects.[14] In Winnipeg, city council arranged a public, military funeral with the co-operation of Grace Presbyterian Church and the Montreal Garrison Artillery (who were then awaiting orders in the city). The bodies laid in state overnight in city council chambers until a service was held at the church the following day. A military procession led by the

Garrison Artillery band then took three coffins to St. John's Cemetery. One military chaplain estimated that some 15,000 people lined the route, "besides those who looked from windows."[15] The remaining three coffins, including Watson's, returned to the rail yard to continue their journey to Ontario. The Winnipeg *Free Press* reported that Watson had been widely known as "a noble Christian and a gallant soldier."[16] He had been in Winnipeg only four years, but there was an obvious desire among the locals to honour the fallen volunteer and claim him as their own.

The occupation of public space became a common feature of events marking the campaign. The modest scenes first observed in Moose Jaw and repeated more grandly in Winnipeg had their echoes throughout Ontario. The return of one battalion to Toronto was delayed in every town it had passed through as cheering crowds met the troops.[17] Two points warrant emphasis. First, the organizers of these events tended to be individuals in positions of authority, either in municipal government, church life, or militia units. These were groups with access to the required resources to claim public space and imprint their values through parades, public gatherings, and temporary structures such as arches. Nothing suggests that these events were purely spontaneous expressions of public enthusiasm. At the same time, it must be remembered that the public did attend them and demonstrated an impassioned enthusiasm, as reported by the newspapers of the day and suggested in contemporary images. And, as enthusiastic as the public's responses might have been, it is also clear that there were rituals associated with similar public events: the end of a war, the return of the troops, and the commemoration of the dead. As many scholars have shown, such rituals can open space for alternative behaviours and give voice to alternative opinions (Davis 1986; Ryan 1989; Goheen 1992, 1994; Heron and Penfold 2005). For the most part, participants in the end-of-war celebrations across English-speaking Canada did not break from their expected roles. If anything, their over-enthusiasm became a point of comment. The same access to public space, the same rituals, and the same enthusiasm were evident in St. Catharines to honour the memory of Private Watson.

Watson's second funeral took place in St. Catharines one week after the first in Winnipeg. Here, again, the city, local churches, and local militia units co-operated to stage a public, military funeral. According to the Hamilton *Spectator*, his family consented to a public event only at the "urgent request of a large number of citizens."[18] The body sat in his parents' home in St. Catharines until the day of the burial, Friday May 29. It was then moved to the courthouse for public viewing. The coffin was decorated with his uniform, the red ensign flag, and several floral tributes. St. Andrew's Presbyterian Church in Winnipeg sent two arrangements, a floral pillow and a floral crown; the city of St. Catharines ordered a floral anchor. The courthouse was filled to capacity. For two hours, every seat was taken and a steady stream of visitors paid their respects. The Welland *Telegraph* expected a big turnout, not because Watson had been well liked or came from a prominent family, but because his death itself was significant, "as this is the first victim of the Northwest insurrection to be buried in this district."[19] The service was solemn, consisting of prayer, scripture, and hymns. The pastor of the Watson family's church, Rev. John H. Ratcliffe of First Presbyterian, led the proceedings, assisted by Rev. O.J. Booth, rector of St. Thomas Anglican.

A military procession took the coffin to Victoria Lawn Cemetery, St. Catharines' most prominent graveyard. The order of those participating was carefully orchestrated: the local police came first, followed by a firing party, the men of 19th Regiment (St. Catharines), their band, and the band of the 44th Regiment (Welland). Next came the coffin itself, carried on a gun carriage pulled by four horses, with an escort of six pallbearers representing the infantry, artillery, and cavalry. Behind it were the family and the clergy in carriages. Then came a parade of representatives from local organizations: the officers of the 19th and 44th Regiments, the men of the 44th, the men of the 3rd Regiment of Cavalry, a veteran of the War of 1812 (driven in a carriage), the Fire Department, the local lacrosse club, employees of two local firms, elected city officials, judges and county officials and prominent citizens (the last three groups all in carriages). Along the three-kilometre route, shops were closed, several businesses were draped in black, and flags flew at half-staff. Onlookers lined the streets. The dedication at the cemetery was relatively simple, with Rev. James G. Foote of Welland Avenue Methodist Church performing the last rites. A firing party split the air with three volleys. The day concluded with a rendition of "God Save the Queen."[20]

The funeral received detailed coverage in the St. Catharines *Journal*, and it was front-page news in nearby cities such as Welland and Hamilton and in distant Winnipeg. The *Journal* reporter described everything surrounding the day in heroic fashion: "The funeral of this gallant young soldier," an "active and zealous member" of the church, was the "largest and most imposing affair of the kind" the city had seen; his remains were enclosed "in a massive polished chestnut casket," and flowers were "a profusion of magnificent … offerings of rich and rare colors [sic]." As it lay in state, the coffin sat on "a raised catafalque draped in deep black, from the sides of which sprung festoons of heavy crape from whose apex was suspended a sculptured snow white dove." The elaborate funeral procession was described in detail. The report concluded, "The echo of the falling earth upon the coffin lid told all that was mortal of a brave Canadian soldier, who died in the path of duty, was forever enshrouded in the bosom of mother earth."[21] The reporter's use of superlatives and high diction bids readers to view this common soldier in an uncommon way. It characterizes Watson's actions in terms of bravery, honour, and sacrifice—all heroic qualities to be emulated by those who survived him.

Watson was not the only Northwest casualty to receive such tributes. The events of Winnipeg and St. Catharines were repeated in Toronto for the funerals of Lieutenant W.C. Fitch and Private Thomas Moor[22]; in Perth, Ontario, for the funeral of Lieutenant A.W. Kippen;[23] and, in Port Hope, Ontario, for the funeral of Colonel A.T.H. Williams.[24] Everything about Watson's funeral—lying in state, the floral tributes from multiple organizations, the elaborate military procession to the graveyard, the participation of local militia units and civilians, and the patronage of townsfolk—was replicated in these other services. Even the newspaper accounts echoed one another, employing the popular tropes of the day. The articles on Moor's and Williams's funerals were almost word-for-word copies of the write-up for Watson's funeral in the *Journal*. Historian Desmond Morton notes that this was the first campaign the Canadian military had completed without the support of British regulars (Morton 1999, 99–106). Many Canadians saw the campaign as the Dominion's first trial by fire that provided suitable material for nation-building and hero-worshipping.

A SOLDIER'S MEMORIAL, 1886–1898

Within days of Watson's second funeral, residents of St. Catharines formed a memorial committee to ensure that his name and actions would not be forgotten. None of the committee's records survives but the gist of their work can be pieced together from newspaper accounts. Two members are known: the chair, Dr. Edwin Goodman, a city alderman, and the treasurer, Major George C. Carlisle of the 19th Battalion. The committee wanted a statue, but not a likeness of the dead man, and decided on a generic "Canadian Volunteer" representation to honour all of Watson's comrades-in-arms. A competition was held for the design and the winner was James Munro, owner of a local granite and marble works best known for its gravestones. The statue was his masterwork. Thirty years later, an etching of the statue still illustrated his advertisements. By August 1885, $780 had been raised to pay for it. The "Watson Memorial Concert," held at the Grand Opera House in downtown St. Catharines, generated $200 of this amount, city council donated

FIGURE 2.2 Postcard view of City Hall and Monument, c. 1890. St. Catharines Public Library, Special Collections Room

$50, and the employees of Riordan Paper Mills donated another $50. No other donors were named in reports.[25]

The monument was originally intended for Watson's grave, but a month before its unveiling city council agreed to place it at city hall. The decision suggests a desire to place it in the public eye. City hall sat downtown at the corner of James Street and Church Street and shared a block with the farmers' market, police station, and courthouse. By contrast, the cemetery was three kilometres outside the core and surrounded by farmland. St. Catharines had no public park at the time, and the local militia did not have a permanent armoury. City hall, then, was the most prominent and visible public location for a memorial.[26] Beyond such practical concerns, perhaps the memorial committee also believed that city hall carried a significant symbolic weight. City hall represented an official and secular landscape in contrast to the spiritual and sacred landscape of the cemetery. If Watson's sacrifice had been viewed in religious terms, then it is worth noting that every prominent faith had a grand church downtown and one of them might have provided a suitably sacred location. Knox Presbyterian Church faced the city hall lawn while St. George's Anglican, the garrison church for the local militia, was one block removed. The monument's placement suggests that Watson's death as a patriotic citizen-soldier trumped his life as a good Christian.

The monument stands roughly seven metres tall, carved from Queenston limestone drawn from the Niagara escarpment. It does not bear Watson's likeness. As requested by the committee, the statue portrays a common

FIGURE 2.3 Watson Monument, 1886. St. Catharines *Standard*, "The Garden City of Canada," *Anno Domini*, 1907 (St. Catharines: Standard Printing, 1907)

soldier in period uniform standing at ease. That did not deter the Winnipeg *Free Press* from commenting that the visage was a fair portrait of the dead man.[27] Looking at its uniform, one might note that Watson wore a rifleman's distinctive green tunic and black busby. Yet the soldier portrayed in grey limestone is easily imagined wearing a red tunic and white helmet. Hence, this uniform is not a rifleman's as the 90th Battalion (Winnipeg) wore but an infantryman's, just as the 19th Battalion (Lincoln) wore. One wonders how much influence Major Carlisle had over the winning entry. Everyone on the monument committee knew Watson's correct dress because his uniform was displayed at the funeral. Apparently, recasting the local hero in the garb of the local militia was a popularization of reflected glory, embodied in the statue's artful representation.

Watson's name appears in relief at the base of the monument and represents the most prominent text. On the front, the original inscription read:

> Erected To the memory of
> Alexander Watson,
> 90th (Winnipeg) Battalion Rifles,
> Canadian Volunteers,
> And his companions in arms who fell in
> Battle during the Rebellion in the
> Northwest territories, A.D., 1885.

At the rear were the names of the campaign's four major battles: Duck Lake, Fish Creek, Cut Knife, and Batoche. Relief carvings, unfortunately lost to erosion, appeared on all four sides of the pedestal's cap. One featured crossed rifles and a busby, another an artillery piece. The statue faced James Street in front of city hall and stood on a square bed of grass approximately 30 centimetres higher than the surrounding lawn. Notably, the city already possessed two cannons, which were placed on either side of the building's front steps. Council planned to have them placed on either side of the monument, but they were never moved. Instead, flowerpots decorated each corner of the raised bed.[28]

Once the location and design were set, the committee held an unveiling ceremony on Tuesday, September 14, 1886. It was the first monument raised in Ontario for the Northwest campaign, but the city did not publicize this fact. It found another way to enhance the pageantry of the day and draw the country's attention: General Frederick Middleton, the officer who led the Northwest Field Force during the campaign, agreed to preside. The unusual mid-week date was set to coincide with a biennial militia training camp in Niagara-on-the-Lake and all the volunteers were invited to "make a great day of it."[29] They did. The ceremony involved speeches by prominent men, the transfer of the monument's deed to the city, and the unveiling itself. It was a grand event for the small city. One reporter claimed that it was the largest crowd ever assembled in St. Catharines, "fences, trees and every spot that could hold a sight-seer being occupied."[30] Indeed, a photograph shows people sitting on the roof of city hall. Nonetheless, reporters felt that it was not well planned. The speakers' platform stood only 30 centimetres high and, despite the efforts of police, onlookers took "complete possession of the ground right up to the monument."[31] As a result, it was difficult to hear the speakers from any distance. A dismayed reporter noted that "not a single cheer was heard from beginning to end" since the audience missed its cues.[32] Still, the day was not lost: It ended with a particularly bloody lacrosse match between the St. Catharines Saints and a Toronto team, with the former winning. By all accounts the Torontonians were not eager to return given the beating they endured. The unveiling was front-page news in Winnipeg, but only made the sports page in Toronto.[33]

FIGURE 2.4 Unveiling the Watson monument, 1886. John Burtniak Collection, St. Catharines

CONCLUSION

The Watson monument was as much a celebration of St. Catharines as it was a memorial to Alexander Watson, the rebellion, or even the defence of constituted authority. Historically, the rebellion was the first action undertaken by the Canadian militia without the support of British regulars. The militia's apparent success and efficiency was celebrated in the home community of every unit that went west—this, despite the fact that its deployment was also considered a tragedy in other quarters. The military funerals in Winnipeg and St. Catharines, both arranged by civic officials, heralded each city's contribution to the national cause and the streets themselves were converted into sites of commemoration. The death of an individual soldier became the pageantry and celebration of duty, courage, and gallantry ascribed to an entire community. The location and timing of the Watson monument's unveiling suggest the same conclusion. St. Catharines city hall hosted an event timed to include the country's top soldier, with his troops in tow, and thereby ensured a measure of publicity in the national public sphere.

Watson's significance in the self-image of St. Catharines has long since faded. His monument barely survived demolition in the early 1970s. Perhaps this reflects current popular opinion of the rebellion, one that views the Métis sympathetically and the government's motives with disdain, but other conflicts have taken precedence in local popular memory. For tourists, Niagara's military legacy is promoted with reference to Sir Isaac Brock, Laura Secord, and the defence of Upper Canada during the War of 1812. For local people, public recollection of the region's military heritage is situated at the many cenotaphs that dot the region and return to mind each November (Johnston and Ripmeester 2007, 2009).[34] One may guess that the same politics of remembrance, the same erosion of memory, may also subsume the name of Albert Storm. The town of Fort Erie hopes to preserve his name with a very practical memorial, something that will invite daily interaction rather than annual observance: a children's playground.

The funerary honours bestowed upon Watson and Storm can reveal the confluence of memory entrepreneurs and popular memory. We might conclude that the Watson monument was only an expression of late nineteenth-century civic boosterism. We might also conclude that Storm's public funeral promoted Canada's continued involvement in "the war on terror." At the same time, we cannot discount the popular sentiment that these deaths evoked. In Watson's case, city councils and local militia units may have orchestrated the events, but it was the public that lined the streets, formed the crowds, attended the concerts, made donations, and paid their respects to the dead soldier. Whether or not the public believed in the justice of the cause, the bodily sacrifice of family, friends, and fellow citizens, or the broader structures that provoke wars, they bestowed honour upon those who went into battle. This has not changed. Like the mourners of 1885, the mourners of 2006 marked the passing of someone they believed represented the best qualities of their community. Niagara may not remember the name of Albert Storm a century from now, but it may still honour the idea of his service and sacrifice.

NOTES

1 Grant Lafleche, "Final Farewell," St. Catharines *Standard*, Dec. 9, 2006, A1, A2.

2 Lafleche, "Final Farewell Hundreds Expected," *Standard*, Dec. 7, 2006, A4; "Students to View," *Standard*, Dec. 8, 2006, A4.

3 See also Thomas Laqueur, "Names, Bodies and the Anxieties of Erasure," in T.R. Schatzki and W. Natter, eds., *Social and Political Body* (New York: Guildford, 1996), 123–41.

4 On Canada generally, see Ian McKay, "Among the Fisherfolk: J.F.B. Livesay and the Invention of Peggy's Cove," *Journal of Canadian Studies* 23:1 (1988), 23–45; Jill Delaney, "Ritual Space in the Canadian Museum of Civilization: Consuming Canadian Identity," in Rob Shields, ed., *Lifestyle Shopping: The Subject of Consumption* (New York: Routledge 1992), 136–48; Claude Rocan, "Images of Riel in Contemporary School Textbooks," in Ramon Hathorn and Patrick Holland, eds., *Images of Louis Riel in Canadian Culture* (Lewiston, NY: Edwin Mellen Press, 1992), 93–126; Alan Gordon, *Making Public Pasts: The Contested Terrain of Montreal's Public Memories, 1891–1930* (Montreal: McGill-Queen's University Press, 2001). On Niagara, see Thomas Ritchie, "Memorial on a Hero: Brock's Monument on Queenston Heights," *Canadian Geographical Journal* 78:5 (1969), 164–69; C. James Taylor, *Negotiating the Past: The Making of Canada's National Historic Parks and Sites* (Montreal: McGill-Queen's University Press, 1990); Norman Knowles, *Inventing the Loyalists: The Ontario Loyalist Tradition and the Creation of Usable Pasts* (Toronto: University of Toronto Press, 1997); Paul Litt, "The Apotheosis of the Apothecary: Retailing and Consuming the Meaning of a Historic Site," *Journal of the Canadian Historical Association* 10 (1999), 297–321; Colin M. Coates and Cecilia Morgan, *Heroines and History: Representations of Madeleine de Verchères and Laura Secord* (Toronto: University of Toronto Press, 2002).

5 See also Charlene Mires, *Independence Hall in American Memory* (Philadelphia: University of Pennsylvania Press, 2002); S. Purcell, "Commemoration, Public Art, and the Changing Meaning of the Bunker Hill Monument," *The Public Historian* 25:2 (2003), 55–71.

6 "The Killed," Winnipeg *Free Press*, May 14, 1885, 1; "The Official List," Welland *Telegraph*, May 15, 1885, 8; "Private Watson," Hamilton *Spectator*, May 19, 1885, 1; editorial, Thorold *Post*, May 15, 1885, 2; A.N. Mowatt, "Decoration Date," St. Catharines *Standard*, May 11, 1946, 12. Also see Mulvaney 1885, Morton 1972, Beal and Macleod 1984.

7 "What Will Be Done with Riel?" Thorold *Post*, May 22, 1885, 2; Welland *Tribune*, May 22, 1885, 5.

8 Lyrics by Lawrence Buchan quoted in George Broughall, *The 90th on Active Service* (Winnipeg: George Bishop, 1885).

9 For example, see Horace G. Dunlevie, *Our Volunteers in the North West: A Ready Reference Handbook* (Ottawa: Daily Free Press, 1885); Charles P. Mulvaney, *Canada's North-West Rebellion* (Toronto: Hovey, 1885); Ernest J. Chambers, *The 90th Regiment: A Regimental History of the 90th Regiment*, Winnipeg Rifles (Ottawa: the author, 1906); 90th Regiment, General Anniversary Committee, *The Winnipeg Rifles, 8th Battalion, CEF Fiftieth Anniversary, 1883–1933* (Winnipeg: 90th Regimental Headquarters, 1933); Roy S. Stubbs, *Men in Khaki: Four Regiments of Manitoba* (Toronto: Ryerson, 1941); Royal Winnipeg Rifles, *Royal Winnipeg Rifles,*

1883–1958: Seventy-fifth Anniversary (Winnipeg: RWR Regimental Headquarters, 1958).

10 "City Notes," Winnipeg *Free Press*, May 19, 1885, 1.

11 "The Rebellion," Winnipeg *Free Press*, May 18, 1885, 4; "Casualties at Batoche," Winnipeg *Sun*, July 3, 1885, 19.

12 "The Casualties," Toronto *Globe*, May 15, 1885, 2; "North West Rebellion," Montreal *Star*, May 18, 1885, 1; "Our Fallen Heroes," Toronto *Mail*, Sept. 15, 1886, 8.

13 "The Soldiers' Graves," Toronto *Mail*, May 16, 1885, 4; "To Be Buried at Home," Hamilton *Spectator*, May 23, 1885, 1. For the American practice, see D.G. Faust, "'The Dread Void of Uncertainty': Naming the Dead in the American Civil War," *Southern Cultures*, 11 (2005), 7–32.

14 "Bodies of the Dead" and "From Winnipeg," Hamilton *Times*, May 22, 1885, 1.

15 "Arrival of the Dead," Winnipeg *Free Press*, May 23, 1885, 1.

16 "Letter from Rev. Mr. Gordon," Winnipeg *Free Press*, May 23, 1885, 1.

17 "Reception at Toronto," Kingston *Daily British Whig*, July 21, 1885, reprinted in N. Mika and H. Mika, eds., *The Riel Rebellion 1885* (Belleville: Mika, 1972).

18 "From St. Catharines," Hamilton *Spectator*, May 29, 1885, 1.

19 "Military Funeral," Welland *Telegraph*, May 29, 1885, 1.

20 "From St. Catharines," Hamilton *Spectator*, May 30, 1885, 1; "St. Catharines," Thorold *Post*, June 5, 1885, 3; "Private Watson," Welland *Tribune*, June 5, 1885, 1.

21 "Private Watson," Welland *Tribune*, June 5, 1885, 1; see also "Private Watson," Welland *Telegraph*, June 5, 1885, 1; "From St. Catharines," Hamilton *Spectator*, May 30, 1885, 1; "A Tribute to the Dead," Winnipeg *Free Press*, May 30, 1885, 1.

22 "From Toronto" and "The Funeral of Lieut. Fitch," Hamilton *Spectator*, May 28, 1885, 1; "The Burial of Private Moore [sic]," Hamilton *Spectator*, May 30, 1885, 1; "At Rest," Toronto *Globe*, June 2, 1885, 6.

23 "Lieu. Kippen's Funeral," Toronto *Mail*, May 29, 1885, 1.

24 Montreal *Gazette*, July 21, 1885, and Kingston *Weekly British Whig*, July 23, 1885, both reprinted in N. Mika and H. Mika, eds. *The Riel Rebellion 1885*.

25 St. Catharines, City Council minutes, June 8, 1885, mflm 171–315; "Neighbourhood News: St. Catharines," Hamilton *Spectator*, June 2, 1885, 2; June 24, 1885, 2; and July 11, 1885, 2; "St. Catharines," Toronto *Globe*, Aug. 4, 1885, 2; "St. Catharines," Thorold *Post*, Sept. 17, 1886, 2.

26 St. Catharines, City Council minutes, Aug. 6, 1886, mflm 171-315; "St. Catharines," Thorold *Post*, Nov. 20, 1885, 2; and Aug. 13, 1886, 2.

27 "St. Catharines," Winnipeg *Free Press*, Sept. 14, 1886, 1.

28 St. Catharines, City Council minutes, May 23, 1887, mflm 171-316; "St. Catharines," Hamilton *Spectator*, Sept. 15, 1886, 1.

29 "St. Catharines," Thorold *Post*, Sept. 3, 1886, 2; and Sept. 10, 1886, 3.

30 "St. Catharines," Thorold *Post*, Sept. 17, 1886, 2.

31 "St. Catharines," Welland *Tribune*, Sept. 17, 1886, 8.

32 "St. Catharines," Thorold *Post*, Sept. 17, 1886, 2.

33 "St. Catharines," Winnipeg *Free Press*, Sept. 15, 1886, 1; "Our Fallen Heroes," Toronto *Mail*, Sept. 15, 1886, 8.

34 "Watson's Watch," St. Catharines *Standard*, Apr. 6, 1971, 9; "Third Restoration Firm," St. Catharines *Standard*, Apr. 29, 1971; A. Dreschel, "Has Time Tainted Hero's Renown?," St. Catharines *Standard*, May 22, 1982, 9.

WORKS CITED

Beal, Bob, and Rod Macleod. *Prairie Fire: The North-West Rebellion of 1885*. Edmonton: Hurtig, 1984.

Bodner, John. *Remaking America: Public Memory, Commemoration, and Patriotism in the Twentieth Century*. Princeton, NJ: Princeton University Press, 1992.

Davis, Susan G. *Parades and Power: Street Theatre in Nineteenth-Century Philadelphia*. Berkeley: University of California Press, 1986.

Demitrova, Snezhana. "'Taming the Death': The Culture of Death (1915–18) and Its Remembering and Commemorating through First World War Soldier Monuments in Bulgaria (1917–44)." *Social History* 30:2 (2005), 175–94.

Flanagan, Thomas. *Riel and the Rebellion: 1885 Reconsidered*. Saskatoon: Western Producer Prairie, 1983.

Goheen, Peter G. "Parading: A Lively Tradition in Early Victorian Toronto." In Alan H. Baker and Gideon Biger, eds., *Ideology and Landscape in Historical Perspective*. Cambridge: Cambridge University Press, 1992: 330–51.

———. "Negotiating Access to Public Space in Mid-Nineteenth Century Toronto." *Journal of Historical Geography* 20:4 (1994), 430–49.

Heron, Craig, and Steve Penfold. *The Workers' Festival: A History of Labour Day in Canada*. Toronto: University of Toronto Press, 2005.

Jelin, Elizabeth. *State Repression in the Labours of Memory*, trans. Judy Rein and Marcial Godoy-Anativia. Minneapolis: University of Minnesota Press, 2003.

Johnston, Russell, and Michael Ripmeester. "A Monument's Work Is Never Done: The Watson Monument, Memory and Forgetting in a Small Canadian City." *International Journal of Heritage Studies* 13:2 (2007), 117–35.

———. "Awake Anon the Tales of Valor: The Career of a War Memorial in St. Catharines, Ontario." *The Canadian Geographer* 53:4 (2009), 404–26.

Mailhot, P.R., and D.N. Sprague. "Persistent Settlers: The Dispersal and Resettlement of the Red River Métis, 1870–1885." *Canadian Journal of Ethnic Studies* 17 (1985), 1–30.

Morton, Desmond. *The Last War Drum: The North West Campaign of 1885*. Toronto: Hakkert, 1972.

———. *A Military History of Canada*, 4th ed. Toronto: McClelland and Stewart, 1999.

Mulvaney, Charles Pelham. *Canada's North-West Rebellion*. Toronto: Hovey, 1885.

Owram, Douglas. "The Myth of Louis Riel." *Canadian Historical Review* 63:3 (1982), 315–36.

Pannekoek, Frits. *A Snug Little Flock: The Social Origins of the Red River Resistance of 1869–70*. Winnipeg: Watson and Dyer, 1991.

Rosenzweig, Roy, and David Thelen. *The Presence of the Past: Popular Uses of History in American Life*. New York: Columbia University Press, 1998.

Rusden, Harold Penryn. "Notes on the Suppression of the North West Insurrection." In R.C. Macleod, ed., *Reminiscences of a Bungle ... and Two Other North-West Rebellion Diaries*. Edmonton: University of Alberta Press, 1983: 241–312.

Ryan, Mary. "The American Parade: Representations of the Nineteenth-Century Social Order." In Lynn Hunt, ed., *The New Cultural History*. Berkeley: University of California Press, 1989: 131–53.

Silver, A.I. "Ontario's Alleged Fanaticism in the Riel Affair." *Canadian Historical Review* 69 (1988), 21–50.

Stanley, George F.G., *The Birth of Western Canada: A History of the Riel Rebellion*. Toronto: University of Toronto Press, 1960.

Tascona, Bruce, and Eric Wells. *Little Black Devils: A History of the Royal Winnipeg Rifles*. Winnipeg: Royal Winnipeg Rifles/Frye Publishing, 1983.

Trofimenkoff, Susan Mann. *The Dream of Nation: A Social and Intellectual History of Quebec*. Toronto: Macmillan, 1982.

NIAGARA FALLS INDIAN VILLAGE
Popular Productions of Cultural Difference

MARIAN BREDIN

INTRODUCTION

A current visitor to the Canadian city of Niagara Falls, Ontario, probably would notice the residual presence of First Nations peoples in the sights and scenery of the area. These traces include the name Niagara itself, often described in the tourist literature as a derivation of the indigenous peoples' word for the waterfalls (commonly called "the Falls"); the lingering myth of the Maid of the Mist as generic Indian Princess and sacrificial victim in some unnamed tribal ritual; and the Native tourist souvenirs available in many gift shops, ranging from "authentically" outfitted brown-tinted plastic dolls to up-market carvings and prints created by First Nations artists. While these signs of "Nativeness" are everywhere, the more observant traveller might note the remarkable absence of actual First Nations people in the public spaces and tourist venues of Niagara Falls. This was not always the case, however. Throughout the nineteenth and much of the twentieth centuries, Native people were actively present at Niagara Falls, creating and selling baskets, carvings, and other souvenir crafts along the main thoroughfares, and performing and dancing at local tourist sites. As the active involvement of First Nations peoples in the Niagara Falls tourist economy has declined, their significance to this location in the North American imagination has been only marginally maintained with the dominance of other types of tourist experiences and commodities.

This study traces the shifting forms of popular representation of First Nations peoples in the Niagara Region, with a primary focus on a once-thriving local tourist destination, the Niagara Falls Indian Village. The Indian

Village is one example, among many others throughout the history of Niagara Falls as a tourist destination, of how the popular meaning of the natural experience of the Falls was produced in conjunction with the consumption of Aboriginal cultures, narratives, and souvenirs. As this case study demonstrates, the performance of Native identity that took place at the Village was constrained by its commercialized tourist setting and worked to construct Aboriginal people as part of the natural history of the Falls. Yet within these constraints, First Nations people had a place within local popular memory, actively participating in and negotiating their own representation, a place that is now almost entirely erased.

In this analysis, Niagara Falls is viewed as the nexus of material and symbolic landscapes—frontier, border, tourist site, "natural," historic—that together provide a unique context for the unfolding of socio-cultural practices. The reconstructed Indian village and the collaborative construction of First Nations culture by employees and visitors can be linked to a broader understanding of Niagara as the site of a liminal encounter between nature and culture, Aboriginal and European. The Indian Village was a product of the history of representations of Native heritage at Niagara Falls and an expression of popular modes of making meaning in the 1960s, both processes negotiated and influenced by Native participants. Today, the "living exhibit" of Aboriginal people is not part of the tourist experience at the Falls, and its demise can be linked to the growing disjuncture between the "performing Indian" and North American Native people's emerging political presence in the 1970s and '80s. Though the staging of Native cultures occurred in the context of racist attitudes and neo-colonial practices in post–World War II Canada, and First Nations communities had no direct economic or administrative control of tourist venues like the Indian Village, neither of these factors entirely explains Aboriginal people's participation in the production of cultural difference at this site. The interactions between Natives and non-Natives were negotiated, and meanings of First Nations culture were produced and reproduced at this popular Niagara Falls tourist destination.

The Niagara Falls Indian Village operated between 1960 and 1968 as an "authentic Iroquois village" with the goal of luring tourists (mainly Americans) beyond the Falls to spend their money on local attractions. In this period, the Niagara Falls tourist economy was being consolidated on a more comprehensive scale to attract regional, national, and international visitors. The village was a unique configuration of representations of the Falls, the Niagara Region, and Canadian and North American First Nations' cultural history. Thus, several related questions have guided this study: what were the explicit and implicit commercial, cultural, and educational goals of the operators and employees at the village? How did Aboriginal and non-Aboriginal participants in the operation of the village articulate and act upon these objectives? Why was the village appealing to visitors and what led to its ultimate decline? What part did the Indian Village play in generating awareness of First Nations' history and culture in local citizens? Finally, how was this awareness shaped by larger political shifts in relations between First Nations people and other Canadians in this period? The synthesis of local accounts of the village and its place in the tourist economy demonstrates how local identity is produced by complex and often contradictory discourses of cultural difference. Relying on a survey of archival material and local tourist publications of the period, this study documents the operation of the village as a tourist site and describes the daily performances and re-enactments of Native activities there. Interviews with local residents and Aboriginal people who were employed at the site at its height of popularity illuminate the mutual production and reproduction of popular memory and the construction of cultural difference at the Indian Village.

POPULAR CULTURE, TOURISM, AND REPRESENTATIONS OF NATIVE HERITAGE

The heritage sites of the Niagara Region must be understood as aspects of popular culture but are unlike cinema and music or other media texts analyzed by popular culture scholars. Heritage sites do not circulate as cultural artifacts or commodities but are geographically fixed, and people must circulate among them. This is the most significant difference between "heritage sites" and "media texts" when we compare them at the level of production and reception. Mass-mediated texts like popular cinema, recorded music, television programs, and mass market books and magazines are produced in those relatively few centres of the twenty-first century global (or Euro-American) entertainment industry: London, New York, Los Angeles. But the site of media reception is primarily local: the neighbourhood cinema, local radio station or dance club, bookstore, library, our own living rooms. Hollywood films screened, say, in Niagara Falls were also likely screened in Saskatoon, rural England, and the Southern United States. The response of the local audience to mass media varies according to those specific contexts.

In contrast, heritage sites, as fixed expressions of historical significance and commemoration, are by and large produced locally, created by local heritage and tourism stakeholders such as local history associations, tourist operators, municipal governments or parks, and provincial heritage agencies.

	Media Texts	Heritage Sites
Production	Global	Local
Reception	Local	Local
Reader/Spectator	Local	Global

FIGURE 3.1 Media texts and heritage sites

Local heritage, by definition, cannot be mass-produced but, like the mass media text, the site of reception is local; the use or "consumption" of heritage sites requires a visit, in this case to Niagara. The reader or spectator at the heritage site is not, however, predominantly local. The audience for the heritage text is a global audience, made up of widely dispersed individuals, who bring their own particular socio-cultural contexts to bear in the interpretation of popular memory.

Global tourists encounter local heritage informed by their prior expectations and pre-existing media information and intertextual "knowledge" of the place and its significance. For many Americans and foreign visitors touring the United States, the cross-border city of Niagara Falls and its immediate environs are the only part of Canada they will visit. Thus, local heritage in Niagara can be seen as a key site for working out stories of national as well as local cultural identities, stories that get played out before a global audience.

The Indian Village in the 1960s fits into this paradigm of local heritage produced locally but consumed primarily by global tourists. Tourists came to Niagara with predetermined expectations about the grandeur of the Falls and its link to the exotic indigenous peoples and their colourful traditions. Shaped by the history of the Falls and its place on international tourist maps dating back to the eighteenth century, the post–World War II tourist economy in Canada depended on the production of Aboriginal cultures and performances for its success. If we write the history of the past in terms of the present, then we make sense of heritage sites in terms of the stories we have selectively told about the past.[1] As this analysis of the Indian Village shows, the production and reception or recognition of First Nations heritage has changed over time, evolving from the type of popular entertainment and generic Indian "performance" characterized by the Indian Village to a more critically informed and historically accurate representation of indigenous cultures in Canadian museums and local heritage tourism sites, now more often operated or managed by Native people. Examples of this evolution include the archaeological exhibits at Head-Smashed-In Buffalo Jump in Southern Alberta, and the visual arts and interpretive displays at the

Woodland Cultural Centre in Brantford, Ontario. In both these instances, the reception and interpretation of heritage sites are influenced by changing attitudes toward the groups and events being remembered, especially attitudes toward Aboriginal people. The closure of the Indian Village in the late 1960s is related paradoxically to the rising awareness of contemporary Aboriginal people and politics in Canadian society.

The description and analysis of Niagara's Indian Village must also be located within existing analyses of heritage tourism, popular memory, "Indian" images, artifacts, and performances as expressions of popular culture. The literature on popular tourist representations of Native people in specific locales and historical periods considers how indigenous peoples and cultures have been appropriated and commodified for the mainly white European and North American "tourist gaze." This research helps establish a conceptual framework for understanding the construction of the "tourist Indian" in Niagara during the 1960s and locate the Indian Village within past and present popular memory of Aboriginal heritage in the region. A site like the Niagara Falls Indian Village can be traced back to early displays of indigenous peoples as "living exhibits," designed and scripted by anthropologists for the national and international fairs of the late nineteenth and early twentieth centuries. The first tourist site of this kind may have been the immense outdoor village of Native people collected from communities all over the United States at the 1904 Louisiana Purchase Exposition in St. Louis. According to Nancy Parezo and John Troutman, this early Indian village was "arranged to create a sense of uniqueness, 'strangeness,' and inherent inferiority as prototypic representatives of races considered less technologically, intellectually, and artistically evolved than enlightened civilization represented in its high form by Euro-Americans" (2001, 3). The ethnographic display at the turn-of-the-century Indian village played an educational role in demonstrating pre-contact material cultures and forms of social organization, but at the same time it also played a fundamental ideological role in establishing the "primitiveness" of indigenous peoples. By locating Native cultures firmly and irrevocably in the past, especially in the context of an exhibition celebrating Western progress and civilization in the New World, these reconstructed villages obscured the colonial practices and military actions of American and Canadian governments. Placed in the context of an exhibition, Native societies were implicitly cast as less advanced and therefore inevitably doomed to disappear. The same colonial agents that organized these living displays were actively involved in the destruction of actual First Nations communities and the incarceration or assimilation of indigenous peoples.

At the opposite end in the continuum of representations of Native heritage were exhibits designed as pure entertainment, without educational or ethnographic value, as Daniel Francis describes the "Wild West Shows" of the late nineteenth century: the "performing Indian" had a certain lowbrow popular appeal based on a "manipulation of nostalgia [that] ... allowed non-natives to admire aspects of aboriginal culture safely located in the past without confronting the problems of contemporary Native people" (1995, 96). In Canada, the performing "wild Indian" was key to the popularity of events such as the Calgary Stampede and the Banff Indian Days in the first half of the twentieth century. These and other Indian parades and performances were a significant tourist attraction in the western provinces at the time. In her analysis of the western Canadian Indian shows and parades, Marilyn Burgess points to the fundamental contradiction of these events: "Indian people at Banff Indian Days were portrayed as without history and without culture, belonging to the pre-colonized, pre-industrial past; nomadic wanderers in a mysteriously vanished space-time" (1993, 358). To properly occupy their position as the Euro-Canadian cultural Other, Indians could not be accepted as part of contemporary society or participate in the wage economy. Burgess argues that Indian cowboys, like champion rodeo competitor Tom Three Persons, threatened this myth of the timeless savage. No longer content to play the exotic Indian on display by the 1960s and 1970s, the Stoney and other Alberta Indians demanded to be part of the present. Burgess suggests that the White elite lost interest in the Indian as tourist object when differences between Native and non-Native could no longer easily be contained in the Indian Days performances. Their position in the tourist gaze prevented Indians from being part of the political present, and this became increasingly important in Canada after 1969. This year marked Native peoples' rejection of the federal White Paper on Indian Affairs and represented a watershed in relations between Aboriginal peoples and the government and the emergence of a new national awareness of Native rights in Canada.

As Patricia Jasen notes, all tourists are engaged in an exchange of meaning between the places and sites consumed, and the values and experiences assigned to the tourist product (1993, 13). First Nations heritage sites are no exception, and images of the Indian become saleable commodities in the tourist industry. The analysis of these representations of Native heritage must be located at the intersection of the imaginary and the material, the cultural and the economic; or, as Valda Blundell states, between the tourist site and its meaning, the product and its value (2002, 48). In the case of Aboriginal heritage at Niagara Falls, the intersection between the imaginary and the material connects Native people to the natural history of Niagara such that, in the tourist's perception, they become a kind of extension of the natural land-scape (Dubinsky 1999, 59). Philip Deloria extends this argument to suggest that Indianness in the North American context has become inextricably linked to representations of the natural world, and that it became closely connected with the very experience of North American newcomers' identity: "For those who came here from other countries, the ultimate truths of America's phys-ical nature—rocks, water, sky—were intimately linked to a metaphysical American nature that would always be bound up with mythic national iden-tities. The secrets of both natures lay in 'Indianness'" (1999, 183). At Niagara Falls, the overwhelming "physical nature" of the Falls seemed to appeal even more strongly to the mythic aspects of Canadian and American national iden-tities as reflected in Indian performance, reconstruction, and souvenirs.

As Karen Dubinsky argues, the fantasy consumption of Aboriginal expe-rience alongside the encounter with the power and mystique of Niagara Falls was made concrete by watching a staged performance of Native dances and legends at sites like the Indian Village or in the actual purchase of Aborigi-nal souvenirs: "Both of these collaborative, if not on equal terms, encounters—imagining native people and buying from them—reveal the two-sided nature of relationships in the contact zone: exchange and appropriation" (1999, 65). Niagara becomes a central site for imagining the cultural Other, but also for interaction and negotiation. While the relationship between tourists and Aboriginal people was clearly imbalanced, it was not entirely one-sided.

In their analysis of a similar contemporary tourist site called Tillicum Vil-lage in Seattle, Katie N. Johnson and Tamra Underiner suggest that focus-ing only on the experience of appropriation denies the conscious involvement and intervention of the Native performers, their enthusiasm for the dance, and the authorization of the performance by the elders (2001, 56). Tillicum's dinner theatre productions, though managed and produced by non-Native owners, require the willing creative involvement of the local Pacific North-west tribes: "the Native American participants of Tillicum Village have always exercised a degree of control over what is presented of and by them and are compensated both for their participation and for the handicrafts they sell in the tourist market there. However, if the Native Americans control the dances, they cannot fully control the subtle messages inherent in the way they are promoted and presented" (54).

Thus it seems that the experience of exhibition, performance, and display at the Indian Village must be a contradictory and variously determined one. If, as Dubinsky, Deloria, and Johnson and Underiner, and others have sug-gested, cultural interaction occurs at sites like the Indian Village, then the pro-duction of cultural difference must be recognized as a kind of collaborative "constructive negotiation" in which Native performers are active participants (Johnson and Underiner 2001, 56). Jasen points out that most of the history of tourism is produced from accounts of white tourists and tourist operators, official and government agents: "these efforts do not take us inside the Native communities affected by tourism or give us access to the experiences of those who acted as guides, souvenir sellers or simply as objects of the tourist gaze" (1993, 6). Thus, the accounts of First Nations employees are necessary to help develop an understanding of the Indian Village as more than just a commercial object for tourist consumption.

Valda Blundell divides First Nations cultural tourism into two categories: those where Native people have little or no control over their representation, as in public museums and historical sites, as well as those commercial tourist attractions representing Native heritage but owned and operated by non-Natives; and those sites where Native people do control the representation of their past and present culture, such as the Woodland Cultural Centre at Six Nations or Head-Smashed-In Buffalo Jump in Alberta, which use a "representational strategy that juxtaposes knowledge derived from Western science and knowledge encoded in local aboriginal oral traditions without privileging one form of understanding over the other" (2002, 53). Where First Nations people are authorizing their own cultural identification, exhibits place archival documents and historical accounts alongside indigenous legends, art, and material culture, as a means of bringing subjugated and marginalized knowledge to the active expression of living heritage. This is clearly a future objective for the representation of Aboriginal heritage at Niagara Falls and elsewhere, though it remains largely unrealized. The Indian Village as it was operated in the 1960s does not fit so comfortably into either of Blundell's categories. While most of the financial investment came from a non-Native family in Niagara Falls, there was substantial First Nations participation in the design and coordination of activities at the Indian Village site. For the period in which it operated, traditional knowledge and commercial objectives, the dual imperatives of education and entertainment, were in a kind of shifting balance at this local heritage site.

NIAGARA FALLS INDIAN VILLAGE IN CONTEXT OF LOCAL HERITAGE

At Niagara, the story of First Nations heritage has been marginal to the narratives of white conquest of nature in the New World and colonization of the "wilderness." Though there is evidence of nearly 4,000 years of continuous occupation of the Niagara Region by Iroquoian peoples and their ancestors, there is little or no representation of either the long pre-contact Native occupation of the region or of the strategic role the Iroquois played in the European, and later North American, powers' struggle for control of the Great Lakes and the Niagara River. Local museums at St. Catharines and Fort Erie, as well as the Lundy's Lane Historical Museum in Niagara Falls, make only passing reference to First Nations history in the region. However, in September 2006 a new exhibition, "Mewinzha," was created as a permanent exhibit in the lobby of the Peace Bridge Administration building in Fort Erie to commemorate the Iroquoian heritage of the area. Featuring tools and weapons dating back 11,000 years alongside contemporary Native artwork, this display recognizes the indigenous peoples who lived on the shores of the Niagara Peninsula. Some of the archaeological artifacts were excavated during the construction of the building, which was specially designed and built so as to minimally disturb the ancient indigenous peoples' gravesites and human remains that lie beneath it. This exhibition space is unique in the Niagara Region because it was produced in a partnership of the Buffalo–Fort Erie Public Bridge Authority, the Town of Fort Erie, Fort Erie Museum Services, and the Fort Erie Native Friendship Centre (Fort Erie Museum, 2006).

The other current manifestation of First Nations heritage in Niagara is the annual Border Crossing Parade dating back to 1928. This commemorative event was first organized by the Tuscarora chief Clinton Rickard of the Six Nations to mark the restoration of Indians' right to travel and trade freely across the border as originally guaranteed by the 1794 Jay Treaty. The march is still held every third weekend in July and is organized by the Indian Defense League of America. Taking place at the Whirlpool Rapids Bridge (one of two international bridges connecting the cities of Niagara Falls, Ontario, and Niagara Falls, New York), the starting point of the border crossing alternates from year to year between the United States and Canada (IDLOA, 1996). While the museum exhibits represent an objectified and distant past, the annual parade is a symbolic re-enactment of First Nations sovereign status in relation to the national governments of Canada and the United States. Its political origins as an expression of the Aboriginal right to cross international borders freely is not widely understood by local residents of Niagara. While visitors to the region might tour the museums and gift shops, they are less likely to witness the parade or to have any awareness of its historical significance. The goal of the border-crossing re-enactment is to draw attention to the political significance of Aboriginal people in a trilateral relationship among nations, but the small-scale annual parade has little impact on local popular memory. While the displacement of Aboriginal people from the land and the violent history of colonialism are often marginalized in Niagara's public history, the largely commercialized representation of Native heritage creates a romantic image of the noble savage, a placeless and timeless construction of the non-Native imagination.

The Niagara Falls Indian Village, while it purported to be an "authentic Iroquois village," partially, though not entirely, played into this construction of the imaginary Indian. At the village, as elsewhere in Niagara, Native heritage was represented through commercial tourist activities, performance at staged events and souvenir sales. At its large naturalized setting on Portage Road in Niagara Falls, Ontario, the Indian Village combined a reconstructed settlement with Native inhabitants, featuring regular stage shows based on dances from the Iroquoian tradition, as well as other Native social dances, and souvenir and craft sales.

It was built and operated by a commercial tourist venture, Phildrake Enterprises, whose three partners were non-Natives: Mr. and Mrs. Murray Ruta of Niagara Falls, and Raymond Logan, a status Indian living in Thorold.[2] The Rutas had won the Irish Sweepstakes and used some of the money for their initial investment in the village. Ruta had visited the reconstructed Huron mission village at Ste. Marie and was convinced that a similar attraction could be appealing and profitable in Niagara Falls. Ste. Marie Among the Hurons was located in Ontario on the site of an eighteenth-century Jesuit mission, but the Niagara Falls Indian Village did not have any direct links to archaeological precursors or specific historical First Nations settlements. Its location on Portage Road linked it loosely to the "original Indian trail" around the Falls. In planning the village, Murray Ruta made trips to the Six Nations reserve where he attended dance competitions. His partner, Raymond Logan, did not live on the reserve, but through his wife, Frankie, had family connections to Six Nations. Her brother-in-law Leeman Johns helped to hire several of the Native employees who were drawn from among friends and relatives on the reserve. Ray Logan's involvement in the Indian Village encouraged participation by artisans, dancers, and performers from the Native community.

The original site was on four acres of unused wooded land well above the "Horseshoe" (Canadian) Falls, including a three-acre lot for free parking. The land was originally owned by the Oakes family, prominent investors in Niagara Falls,[3] and was first occupied by the Ohio Brass Company in the 1930s. In the 1940s, it was the site of the Chippawa Barracks,[4] and in 1960 Murray Ruta leased the land for the Indian Village from the Oakes family. The original investment in the site ($40,000) went to construct a large log palisade enclosing several structures, including a Plains-style tipi and two longhouses, one built from poles and bark and the other built from logs, and housing Indian "relics" and wood carvings. As well, the owners acquired an eighteenth-century log house from Johnsville on the Six Nations reserve nearly

FIGURE 3.2 Indian Village brochure. Niagara Falls Public Library

100 kilometres away and had it moved to the palisade for reconstruction there. The cabin was identified as belonging to an elder named Una Buck.

The compound included several small shelters, a "wigwam," a sweat lodge, a central stage for dance performances, and, of course, a souvenir shop. While Ruta consulted with members of Six Nations about the design of the village and construction of the longhouse, he contracted a local builder, Adam White, to do most of the construction of the palisades and structures. Josephine and Angus Beaucage, a Native couple who were not from Six Nations, were employed early in the first year (1960) to help with the construction. The builder recalls collecting sheets of bark from a local sawmill, while Beaucage went into the woods on site to find the appropriate fibres from ironwood trees to hold the structures together. The construction process was relatively authentic to pre-contact Iroquoian methods. No nails or concrete were used, and White researched the various types of indigenous building methods used in the region.

The performers at Niagara Falls Indian Village were what the *Niagara Falls Review* referred to as "Reservation Indians" (Mar. 28, 1960), meaning that many of the female craftspeople and male singers and dancers were from Six Nations, though some employees were from other Iroquois communities in Ontario such as Deseronto and Tyendinaga, while still others were members of Native bands in northern Ontario. In the first few years at least, most employees were from Six Nations, and on a daily basis there was only one non-Native employee at the site, the woman who ran the gift shop. In a 1960 photograph of the First Nations performers, it is apparent that a range of ages and both men and women were represented at the site. The men were the dancers and singers who engaged in tanning hides, lacrosse demonstrations, and other such activities between shows, while the women did beading, baking, and leather working. One of the employees acted as the "Chief" and was responsible for greeting visitors and giving them an introductory description of the village as it would have existed in the traditional territory of the Iroquois. The introduction was tied into the mythic aspects of the Falls and made reference to traditional stories about the cultural and spiritual significance of the Niagara River and cataract.

The village was open from 10 a.m. until dusk every day during July and August, and for weekends from May to September at the beginning and end of the season. The Indians were expected to "live" on site during operating hours. Ruta contracted both the younger dancers, many of whom were still in high school, and the older people for the summer. Their transportation to, and lodging in, Niagara Falls was arranged through the federal Department of Indian Affairs. At that time, it was difficult for First Nations people to find

FIGURE 3.3 Indian Village performers, 1960. Niagara Falls Public Library

employment off the reserve and the rate of pay and working conditions at the Indian Village presented an excellent opportunity, especially for the young people. Every hour during the day there were performances of dances, including the Rain Dance, Hunters Dance, Spear Dance, Snake Dance, and the Pow Wow of Elders. In the later years of its operation, non-Native high school students were hired as village guides, responsible for explaining the activities and performances of the Indians and leading the visitors through the site.

The Niagara Falls Indian Village seems to have been a relative commercial success in competing for tourist dollars at Niagara Falls. It provided a steady source of employment for Native and non-Native people and by the mid-sixties was highlighted on most tourist maps of the area. It occupied the Portage Road location by itself until 1965 when another tourist attraction, Marine Wonderland and Game Farm, opened an aquarium and game farm. By the late 1960s this attraction's name was shortened to Marineland and its activities expanded rapidly from a small-scale aquarium and petting zoo to a full-fledged amusement park. At the same time, the Niagara Falls Indian Village suffered declining attendance. Part of the structure was destroyed by a windstorm in 1964, and it proved costly to maintain and staff. Finally it closed down after the 1968 season and the land was transferred to Marineland, which still operates a highly successful, though not uncontroversial, marine mammal show and theme park on the site.

FIGURE 3.4 Indian Village damaged by a windstorm in 1964. Courtesy of Don Ede

PRODUCTION OF FIRST NATIONS HERITAGE AT THE VILLAGE

Both Native and non-Native employees interviewed have been quite clear that the goals of the Indian Village were primarily commercial—and in this respect were certainly achieved—but it also had other value. For its initial years of operation, the village was a new and appealing tourist attraction, quite unlike anything that existed elsewhere in Niagara Falls or in southern Ontario. Attendance was high, the craft and souvenir sales were profitable, and the Native performers were paid a reasonable salary and also made tips from visitors for posing for photographs. For the most part, relations between the owners and the Six Nations employees were good. Though Ruta did enforce the working hours from the beginning of the season to the end, one Native performer commented, "He was excellent. He came to the site, he participated and saw the shows that we were doing."

The First Nations employees had considerable creative control over the type of activities and dances performed. Primarily, Fred Williams from Six Nations, who in his youth had been an actor and performer in Wild West shows, organized the dancers. Although many of the dances were based on traditional Six Nations Longhouse ritual dances, they were never exactly like those performed in the sacred context of the longhouse ceremonies. The dancers were aware of the need to entertain and so dances were adapted to audience tastes. The "Snake Dance," for example, was not Iroquoian at all. Modelled on a Southwestern Native American dance, it featured all the dramatic elements of drumming, whooping, a wigged and costumed dancer, and a very realistic rubber snake. At the height of the performance, the snake was once accidentally tossed into an audience of elderly women on a bus tour and, as may be imagined, havoc and hysteria ensued. Although the goals of the village were primarily commercial, it had a less explicit educational function. Both owners and employees wanted visitors to be more aware of the history and culture of First Nations people, and considerable effort was made to be as accurate as possible in recreating the material culture and practices of the pre-contact period.

How did Aboriginal and non-Aboriginal participants in the operation of the village variously articulate and act upon its commercial and educational objectives? There was a conscious effort on the part of Murray Ruta, Ray Logan, and the Native staff to create and maintain the sense of the Indian Village as a "living site." At the local level of production, the Indian Village was seen as more than just a commercial tourist attraction. As one employee recalled, "You don't really realize it until you're really into it. Because everything else was very authentic, but its premise was begun as a sheer money-making venture by Ruta ... but, when we arrived in there, we would perform, or replicate, it would become a living site." The Native performers were aware of other heritage sites such as Upper Canada Village at Morristown, and thought, "'Well, why can't we do that, as well?' And so that was one of the things, why the women did their beading, or making cornbread, or sometimes the boys played lacrosse. And we would talk about that. And so when we did do that education work, we thought we were doing very good things, though it certainly had that umbrella of being a very commercial venture." This conscious recognition that heritage could be reconstructed and historical experiences could be re-enacted by Euro-Canadians at other local heritage sites, such as Fort George in Niagara-on-the-Lake, led to the logical conclusion by Indian Village participants that First Nations heritage should be accorded the same degree of public awareness and popular appeal.

Both Native and non-Native people interviewed commented on the intergenerational dynamics of the Indian Village for the First Nations employees. There was a general consensus that the village was a good place to work, with a strong sense of camaraderie. One employee recalled games of hide-and-seek throughout the village later in the evening when few tourists remained— once resulting in severe damage to a beaded outfit as the wearer tried to get "home" without being caught. Apart from impromptu games, the younger dancers and performers also were exposed to rituals, traditional knowledge, music, and dances unfamiliar to them, which they otherwise might not have learned. The structured environment of the village meant that they had the opportunity to work together while learning more about their own cultural heritage:

> It was a good time, for myself ... working with all of the people there ... [who] were all traditionalists. So that many of the rituals and songs that I know even now today, I learnt in that Village, because I was there from nine 'til ten each day, hearing these songs over and over. And when I was hearing them, certain songs of the ritual would never have been performed, but there would be adaptations that would be performed, but if you knew the Long-house tradition, you would say, well, I don't know if they should be doing that, it's kind of close to the real song. But they were making such adaptations so that they could get away with it. I would hear that and know that. So all of the things that I know in terms of music ... and social dance music, comes from my experience there, from those people that worked there.

This atmosphere made the village appealing to visitors, with its sense of participation in daily life, both through the romanticized image of a pre-contact Native community and the vibrant interactions among the contemporary Native people who worked there. But non-Native visitors in the 1960s also seemed to have had at least a superficial interest in the factual and culturally accurate representation of First Nations tradition and history. In this respect, the Indian Village did play a role in generating awareness of First Nations culture locally and nationally. Most people interviewed thought representations of First Nations people at the Indian Village were positive and generally had an impact. One person elaborated, "I would say very positive, although I think it was positive because we were who we were. And we were very much aware of our situation. We weren't trying to act like a seventeenth-century Iroquoian warrior at Niagara Falls, for instance. We were doing other things, and bringing things up that were very *au courant* to the site." The Native employees were quite aware of contemporary relationships between Indians and non-Indians in North America and of their own role in the tourist exchange. In this context, the "authenticity" of the Indian Village had less to do with the accuracy of the reproductions and performances and more to do with the shared recognition of First Nations heritage and identity. The dances were a hybrid of the ceremonial and the social, the authentically Iroquoian and the pan-Indian. The costumes were a pastiche of Plains, Woodland, and Iroquois, while the design and structure of the village combined both pre-contact and post-contact dwellings. The "living site" was not completely controlled by the dictates of historical accuracy, nor was it given over to a purely romantic Imaginary Indian. There seems to have been a negotiated appeal to both fact and fantasy within the confines of the palisade, but the "real Indians" featured in the village brochures were indeed really Indians. It was their presence that established the credibility of the site as a form of both education and entertainment. In this respect, the Indian Village departed from other representations of First Nations peoples in the Niagara Region and from past perceptions of indigenous people in North America.

CHANGE IN POLITICAL AND SOCIAL CONTEXTS

In the post–World War II period it was widely believed that "real Indians" had been either exterminated or assimilated, and most of their cultures "lost." In Canada the long years of residential school education, and the forced enfranchisement and dispossession of Native women and men under the Indian Act—including elements that prevented Native people from moving freely and organizing politically—resulted in extensive cultural harm and social upheaval in First Nations communities. These negative effects of federal Indian policy were compounded by the overt racism of Canadian society, resulting in the suppression of Native languages and cultures across the country. But the late 1960s represented a watershed for First Nations relations with other Canadians and the beginning of a revitalization of Native societies throughout North America. Native rights movements of the era did not emerge out of nowhere, but were shaped by a long history of resistance to the forces of the state, the church, and capitalism. Strategic resistance that attracted media attention beginning in the 1960s appeared to be "new" only because dominant discourses had until then effectively silenced dissenting voices. The 1960s marked a shift from coercion to negotiation in relations between the state and Aboriginal groups.

In the post-war decades two major federal policy directions reflected these political and discursive shifts. The first was articulated in the 1966 *Hawthorn Report*, an internal study that recommended that the federal Department of Indian Affairs act as a more forceful advocate of Indian interests. Hawthorn's *Survey of Contemporary Indians of Canada* was part of a wider political recognition of the colonial and racist principles underlying the administration of Indian affairs. The second, somewhat contradictory, direction was expressed in the *White Paper on Indian Policy*, tabled in Parliament in 1969. It called for the termination of special status for Indians and transfer to the provinces of responsibility for Aboriginal people. The *White Paper* was a second attempt to radically transform the administration of Indian affairs in Canada by proposing in effect that Native rights be terminated. The policy was rationalized in terms of "helping" Indians to participate in Canadian society, while suggesting that they had little choice in their encounter with the modern industrial world. These two policy statements engaged core elements of a liberal discourse of equal rights. They emerged in a political context of expanding social programs for Native people and public pressure on governments to address the extremes of poverty and racism in Canada. The federal government's general program to modernize the administration of Indian affairs included increased educational access and extension of welfare and social assistance programs to reserves. In 1960, status Indians and Inuit were permitted to vote in federal elections for the first time.

These two documents were widely publicly debated and triggered strong political opposition within the Native community. At the same time, on the cultural front, Expo 67 in Montreal created a new sense of self-awareness for the Canadian public. For Canada's indigenous peoples, the Indians of Canada Pavilion at Expo represented the first time that Native cultures and heritage were presented separately and on their own terms in such an international venue. The pavilion, which was produced in consultation with Native curators and designers, included contemporary documentary photographs of the living conditions on Canadian reserves and featured both ethnographic displays and the work of emerging Native artists (Library and Archives Canada, 2007).

The combination of an emerging Native rights movement along with a cultural renaissance in many First Nations communities in the 1960s made the popular mixture of fact and fantasy at the Indian Village more difficult to negotiate. The tourist economy of Niagara Falls was also beginning to shift again in the second half of the decade as the first large hotels and the "panoramic" glass and concrete Seagram, Skylon, and Oneida Towers were built to overlook the Falls. More sophisticated American visitors may have found the low-tech homemade aspects of the Indian Village less appealing. Canadian tourists, more aware of the political and social issues facing Aboriginal people, were less comfortable with the "performing Indian." In the last years of the 1960s, new social programs and increased educational and economic opportunities for local Native people likely contributed to staff shortages at the village. These combined factors all played some part in the closure of the Niagara Falls Indian Village after 1969.

CONCLUSION

The Indian Village was both a product of the history of representations of Native heritage at Niagara Falls and of ethnographic and popular modes of making meaning. As a commercial undertaking, it constructed First Nations people as an object for the tourist gaze, but that construction was both negotiated and influenced by Native performers at the village who gave it some authority. The demise of tourist exhibits and re-enactments of Aboriginal heritage at Niagara Falls can be linked to the growing contradiction between the consumption of the tourist Indian and Native people's emerging political presence in 1970s Canada. This rising political awareness, fostered by documents like the *Hawthorn Report* and the *White Paper*, made many Canadians more sensitive to colonial realities. Liberal discourses of the era made the commodification of Native culture and heritage more contentious.

Today, the exchange of meaning between the natural experience of the Falls and the tourist consumption of Native cultures, narratives, and souvenirs continues largely in the absence of active First Nations participation and control. Though it is not possible to imagine a site like the Indian Village operating at Niagara Falls today, there were aspects of the performances and participation of the Native employees at the village that cannot be dismissed merely as forms of commercial entertainment. The presence of Aboriginal people in the local tourist economy inscribed them as part of the natural history of Niagara Falls, but it also prevented their complete erasure from local expressions of national identity. Local popular memory had a place for First Nations peoples and cultures, however misrepresented and now lost.

Since the demise of the Indian village, the global tourist likely leaves Niagara with fewer meaningful encounters with Native heritage. However, one remarkable anecdote perfectly illustrates the means by which global spectators (in this case tourists) carry away their own interpretation of local heritage and Aboriginal identities from Niagara Falls. A Native employee who played the role of "Chief" at the village told this story about a chance meeting long after the Indian Village had disappeared:

> I can remember that much later, that about ten or twelve years later, I went off to New York City, and I can remember at a club … this guy came up to me and he said "I know you" and I said "No you don't, I haven't ever been to New York." And he said "Yes I do, I've got your picture in my wallet" and he pulled a picture from his wallet, one of these photos from the Village. He was from Brooklyn…. He said, "You made such an impression" and I said "That's weird, carrying my picture around." It was [me and] him, and his two boys, and I thought that was so weird, but he said "Oh, I've always loved that picture, I liked you because of what you said, and I've always imagined…" He had a romantic impression of an Indian and he said "It was one of my favourite pictures so I carry it around in my wallet."

In the post-colonial era, the former object of the tourist gaze himself becomes a global tourist, suggesting that the production of cultural difference at the Indian Village occurred at this intersection of the local and the global. The exchange of meaning between the site of the Indian Village in the landscape of Niagara and the values assigned to the tourist experience was not only a commercial exchange, but also a moment in the mutual production of personal and cultural identities.

Thanks to the many individuals who assisted me in the research for this study, especially several current and former residents of Niagara Falls and employees of the Indian Village who kindly consented to be interviewed. Thanks to Don Ede for generously sharing information and copies of historical photographs, to Andrew Porteus and Cathy Simpson at the Niagara Falls Public Library for locating material from the James Collection, to Edie Williams and Lynn Prunskus in Special Collections, James A. Gibson Library, Brock University, and to John Burtniak, for their invaluable advice and research assistance.

NOTES

1 See Michel Foucault, "Nietzsche, Genealogy, History," in *The Foucault Reader*, Paul Rabinow, ed. (New York: Pantheon Books, 1984), 76–100. In his discussion of the method of "genealogy" Foucault argues that traditional devices for constructing a continuous historical narrative of the past must be dismantled. The purpose of history, as shaped by genealogy, is "not to discover the roots of our identity, but to commit itself to its dissipation" (95). In this manner, Foucault presents a critique of traditional history as always imbued with the perspectives and interpretations of the present and as situated within networks of domination, while genealogy, as the analysis of heritage, descent, and emergence, "permits the dissociation of the self, its recognition and displacement as an empty synthesis, in liberating a profusion of lost events" (81).

2 In Canada, a status Indian is recognized under the federal Indian Act. Indigenous people with status under the Act include individuals who are members of "bands" that originally signed treaties with colonial or Canadian governments. Indian status entitles individuals to certain rights and benefits, but status could be "lost" by forms of voluntary or involuntary enfranchisement before Native people were granted the federal vote in 1961, or by women, through marriage to a non-status Indian or non-Indian before 1985. Although interpretations and applications of the Indian Act have changed over the last century, it still serves as one of the key juridical determinants of indigenous identity in Canada.

3 "Harry (later Sir Harry) Oakes, who struck gold in northern Ontario in 1912, was one of the most prominent men in Canada during the time he lived in Niagara Falls (from 1924 to 1934). He donated the land on which Oakes Garden Theatre was built as well as the property for Oakes Park." Taken from the caption for a photo of Oakes, in Sherman Zavitz, et al., *Images of a Century: The City of Niagara Falls, Canada, 1904–2004* (Niagara Falls: Centennial Committee/Maracle Press, 2004), 102.

4 See Paul Ozorak, *Abandoned Military Installations of Canada*, Vol. 1, Ontario. (Canada: self-published, 1991). Ozorak explains the war-time uses of the site: "Given that canals and power stations make attractive targets for sabotage during war-time, the Canadian Army was instructed to post guards at ... 'Vulnerable Points'.... The regiment guarding power stations at Queenston and Niagara Falls, the Welland River and the upper part of the Chippawa Power Canal was headquartered at Chippawa Barracks and at a sub-depot at Victoria Park.... In addition to guarding the above key points, whatever regiment that happened to be on duty was also required to provide escorts to visiting dignitaries [for example, Prime Minister Winston Churchill's "secret visit to the Falls in August 1943"], [140].... Chippawa Barracks were established in the Canadian Ohio Brass Company factory on Portage Street [Road]. After guard duty ceased in the peninsula, they were used as the No. 91 Military Detention Barracks, this from October 1945 to 1946" (141).

WORKS CITED

Blundell, Valda. "Aboriginal Cultural Tourism in Canada." In Joan Nicks and Jeannette Sloniowski, eds., *Slippery Pastimes: Reading the Popular in Canadian Culture*. Waterloo: Wilfrid Laurier University Press, 2002: 37–60.

Burgess, Marilyn. "Canadian 'Range Wars': Struggles over Indian Cowboys." *Canadian Journal of Communication* 18:3 (1993), 351–64.

Deloria, Philip. J. *Playing Indian*. New Haven and London: Yale University Press, 1999.

Dubinsky, Karen. *The Second Greatest Disappointment: Honeymooning and Tourism at Niagara Falls*. Toronto: Between the Lines, 1999.

Fort Erie Museum. "Mewinzha—A Journey Back in Time," 2006. Available at http://www.museum.forterie.ca/WebSite/museumweb.nsf/0/7389C35BE0EB 5EE4852571D10069AD23?OpenDocument, accessed June 26, 2007.

Francis, Daniel. *The Imaginary Indian: The Image of the Indian in Canadian Culture*. Vancouver: Arsenal Pulp Press, 1995.

Indian Defense League of America. "Border Crossing Celebration," 1996. Available at http://www.idloa.org/pages/borcross.html, accessed June 26, 2007.

Jasen, Patricia. "Native People and the Tourist Industry in Nineteenth Century Ontario." *Journal of Canadian Studies*, 28:4 (1993), 5–27.

Johnson, Katie. N., and Tamra Underiner. "Command Performance: Staging Native Americans at Tillicum Village." In Carter Jonas Meyer and Diana Royer, eds., *Selling the Indian: Commercializing and Appropriating American Indian Cultures*. Tucson: University of Arizona Press, 2001: 44–61.

Library and Archives Canada. "Expo 67 Man and His World—A Virtual Experience, Indians of Canada Pavilion," 2007. Available at http://www.collections canada.ca/expo/0533020206_e.html, accessed June 26, 2007.

Parezo, Nancy. J., and John W. Troutman. "The 'Shy' Cocopa Go to the Fair." In Carter Jonas Meyer and Diana Royer, eds., *Selling the Indian*. Tucson: University of Arizona Press, 2001: 3–43.

Part II | **MOVIES AND MEDIA**

EARLY MOVIE-GOING IN NIAGARA
From Itinerant Shows to Local Institutions, 1896–1910

PAUL S. MOORE

INTRODUCTION

In August 1910, a moving picture named *Scenes in Ontario* was advertised playing at the Princess Theatre in Niagara Falls, Ontario. The film was part of a Canadian-themed bill, one of three different programs to appear at the Princess that week. At the time, just as movie-going was becoming an every-day routine and a local institution in Niagara Falls and across North America, each short film was presented almost interchangeably. Individual pictures were not yet advertised as having special interest, let alone presented as having local interest for particular audiences in Niagara or anywhere else. Not yet nicknamed "movies," films came and went in constant variety. In just this week at the Princess, twelve pictures were shown, interspersed with a variety of illustrated songs, musical selections, and short plays on stage. The films included comedies, melodramas, westerns, and scenic or newsworthy pictures from around the world.[1] The picture of Ontario scenes was nothing special. Compared to more popular genres and more exotic locations, the movie-going public of Niagara Falls was probably disappointed to see the selection. After the first show, however, the Niagara Falls *Record* excitedly reported that this particular film had "created quite a little comment last night," because it was "a local picture which shows scenes along the Niagara, St. Catharines and Toronto Railway from Port Dalhousie to Falls View."[2] Indeed, the Princess changed its advertising to elaborate: "*Scenes in Ontario*, including N., St. C. & T. Ry, Falls View to Lake Ontario." Even more remarkably, this film stayed for an extra two days "by special request," even when the other films on the program changed.

While the definitive debut and origins of cinema are debatable, the novelty became publicly exhibited worldwide in 1896, and in every present-day Canadian province and most Canadian towns by the end of 1897. From the very first months of commercial cinema, people in towns and cities around the world marvelled at images of Niagara Falls from afar. Yet the earliest exhibitions of moving pictures in the Niagara Region itself in 1896 and 1897 notably failed to include those scenes of Niagara's famous waterfalls. If cinema specialized in showing the world, beyond local experience, its global, mass culture was nonetheless built upon gatherings of local audiences. By 1910, moving picture theatres had become anchored local institutions, each connecting people to modernity through the world on screen. In that context, with a film of a tram ride through St. Catharines and Thorold to the city of Niagara Falls, and only then to the site of the Falls themselves, the people of Niagara clamoured to appreciate their own region on screen as part of the modern world, knowing audiences elsewhere were seeing the same film.

Moving pictures of Niagara's waterfalls were the first images of Canada filmed and are central to any history of early Canadian cinema. The same cannot be said of movie-going in Niagara. Film distribution and exhibition in the Niagara Region (Welland and Lincoln counties) was organized commercially as a marginal part of a Toronto-based mass market, itself a marginal affiliate of a global industry soon dominated by the United States. Niagara's theatres and audiences are absent from the record of Canada's film history, but hardly more than any other region because local sites are altogether sidelined as a result of the global reach of film production, distribution, and exhibition. Niagara's local relation with mass culture can thus be taken as paradigmatic for Canada as a whole—an international flow of popular culture easily crossed the Canada–United States border at Niagara; the region received magazines and newspapers, touring shows and circuses, and later radio and television broadcasts directly from south of the border. The people of Niagara could also casually cross the border in person, and in many ways their metropolis was Buffalo, not Toronto. My argument is that, if images of the natural wonder of the Falls themselves stand in for the entirety of early Canadian cinema, then the cultural experience of modernity that grew from the Falls can be understood as a condensed version of the Canadian experience of American popular culture. On the one hand, this historical case study of the beginnings of movie-going in Niagara is valuable as an example of the more general, even globalized, emergence of mass culture. On the other hand, this history recovers the origins of the region's movie theatres as important local institutions, as part of Niagara's regional culture and public practice. Movie theatres became gathering places, fondly remembered and significant in everyday life, alongside schools, libraries, or churches (and likely attended more often, with excitement, for fun). The exceptional moment when local culture appeared on screen, such as at the Niagara Falls Princess Theatre in 1910, sheds a light on the routine of constantly varied imported mass media, embedded in local experience, but always in view of wider cultural contexts.

The earliest film exhibitions—in Niagara as elsewhere—presented the modern world in motion, bringing glimpses of foreign lands and marvels from across the oceans: New York and Paris streets, royalty and presidents, colonial peoples, exotic animals and scenery, and always a careening express train headed straight toward the seated audience. Did any actual viewer of the first moving pictures really duck and run away from the oncoming locomotive? The "train effect" is known as one of the primal scenes of cinema's modern grammar (Bottomore 1999), but Niagara Falls is another constant scene in early cinema shows around the world. At the very first display of moving pictures in Ontario in July 1896, the Falls were ballyhooed as an attraction on the program.[3] Although more distant scenes from Europe and America predominated in the promotional rhetoric across Canada in the first year of cinema, in smaller towns across Ontario the Falls were a constant draw (albeit always second-rate compared to trains and racing fire brigades or royal parades). First to capture the Falls on film was an unknown camera operator working for the Thomas Edison Vitascope Company early in 1896. With Edison's celebrity behind it, the Vitascope claimed the title of "invention" as the first projected, paying, public showing of moving pictures in North America, making its debut in New York City in April 1896, dismissing earlier efforts as experiments.[4] In France, the Lumière brothers had even earlier introduced their Cinématographe to Paris in December 1895, arriving in North America in Montreal to become the first exhibition of moving pictures in Canada on June 27, 1896 (Lacasse 1984).[5]

Because the Lumière films of Niagara's Falls did not enter their catalogue until 1897, the first public showing of films of the Falls in Canada happened with the official debut of Edison's Vitascope at an Ottawa amusement park on July 21, 1896.[6] The Vitascope opened next in Toronto on August 31, 1896, at a Yonge Street vaudeville theatre and dime museum called Robinson's Musée (later the first Toronto branch of Shea's Vaudeville). Those Vitascope views of Niagara appeared in Toronto, too, promoted for just one week in September 1896. Peter Morris, in the first academic history of Canadian cinema, notes how Niagara Falls was "the mecca of all early motion picture cameramen" and how two more picture operators stopped to capture the

Falls in September and October 1896: Felix Mesguich for Lumière, and W.K.L. Dickson for the American Mutoscope and Biograph Company.[7] Scenes included the American and "Horseshoe" (Canadian) Falls, the Whirlpool Rapids of the Niagara River, and the *Maid of the Mist* bringing boatloads of tourists into the spray at the foot of the Falls. One of these films—it is difficult to know which in these first months—was part of a program of the Motograph in Toronto early in February 1897. Another was noted as an important part of a show of the Anamatagraph in Aurora, north of Toronto, in January 1897, and again mentioned when that show toured in Ontario to Berlin (now Kitchener) and Hamilton in February. Yet another projector called the Canadagraph was made in Toronto and, in an opening exhibition in Richmond Hill in April 1897, featured moving pictures of the Falls—later touring through Muskoka and up to Sudbury, Sault Ste. Marie, and the twin cities of Port Arthur and Fort William (now Thunder Bay).[8]

Whether in northern small towns or metropolitan cities, the history of the beginnings of movie-going in Canada is archived primarily in local newspapers, for most communities the *only* record of early cinema. Every small town and village newspaper had a local gossip column, "Town Topics" or some such heading, an informal compilation of indiscriminate social and commercial happenings of the past week. These columns often recorded the first appearances of cinema in not-quite-rural places across North America. Altogether they paint a surprisingly detailed picture of the regional dispersion and institutionalization of the novelty in the years before it was a mass practice. The crux of my previous study of early movie-going in Toronto emphasized urban routines and city governance as the foundation for making a mass culture out of metropolitan movie-going.[9] Now that I have also carefully studied early picture shows in regional small towns, such as in this discussion of the Niagara Region, I must modify my argument to emphasize how the emergence of mainstream cinema was metropolitan—not simply urban—insofar as it almost simultaneously included entire regions in a mass market for entertainment. Newspapers are an important empirical record of early cinema-going because they were a similarly modernizing means of connecting readers anywhere to the modern, mass market everywhere.

For the city of St. Catharines in the 1890s, the daily *Standard* consistently included advertising for entertainments and usually printed small articles about business developments—cinema events in the city are easily found. Unfortunately, both the Niagara Falls newspapers *The Daily Record* and the weekly *Review* were lost before December 1908. I have relied instead on local notes from Niagara Falls published in the Welland weekly papers. The paper in St. Catharines also included daily notes of town gossip and happenings in Niagara Falls, Thorold, Welland, and Niagara-on-the-Lake. The everyday life of culture and consumption was rarely reported as news but instead shows up as passing comments in these "town topics" columns like needles-in-haystacks. The three Welland papers in this period, in particular, included columns of news from everywhere in Niagara *except* St. Catharines, and they luckily make up for the gaps in the early newspaper records of Niagara Falls and other towns—albeit with the need for patience and a magnifying glass because the news was written as notes without headlines.[10]

TOURING THE ATTRACTION OF CINEMATIC TECHNOLOGY

In these first months of cinema, the entertainment was usually named after the brand-name apparatus; the content of the show was at first secondary to the technology itself. Let me clarify something implicit in the preceding tracing of films of the Falls as they travel around Ontario: in this first year of commercial cinema, 1896, the projector, showman-operator, often a pianist, and a lecturer all travelled with the canisters of films as an itinerant, mobile evening of entertainment, criss-crossing the territory (Pryluck 2008). To provide further context before discussing film shows in Niagara itself, it is important to understand the very beginnings of cinema in relation to travelling dramas, vaudeville, circuses, and fairground attractions. In my tracking the routes of the first year of cinema across Canada, I found several types or classes of moving picture shows. First were the prominent, licensed exhibitions of particular picture programs, which did *not* cross the Canada–United States border but toured interprovincially to small cities, but not small towns. In the Niagara Region, these shows stopped only in St. Catharines. Second were the cinema machines, which were a supporting "act" on a large-scale vaudeville bill of a syndicated American touring show; these *did* cross the border but stopped only in major cities. In 1896–97, there were no theatres in Niagara on these routes, but these shows did stop in Buffalo, Hamilton, and Toronto. And third were the small-scale exhibitions extensively touring a territory, usually run by a regional showman; these did *not* cross the border. In Niagara, these shows toured through the smaller cities, and this last type was especially typical in small towns in southern Ontario, the only part of Canada that was densely populated with extensive rail networks.

Except for when cinema was attached to American vaudeville acts, the impermeability of the border arises from film being a licensed industrial product rather than a performance, making moving pictures distinct from prior commercial amusements. In the 1890s, even small-time touring dramas and minor circuses travelled throughout North America, treating the U.S. border as all but irrelevant. Film was different because local entrepreneurs purchased its amusement as an industrial product, competing against others with identical content. Ironically, the technological reproducibility of cinema imposed territorial borders on exhibition circuits, even as costs lowered to make it more viable to include small towns as well as villages within those entertainment routes. The effect for the Niagara Region (a borderland) was to sever it from Buffalo and render it marginal to Toronto, part of a Toronto-centric network in a rail-based mass market. Another effect is to squarely privilege St. Catharines as the biggest city in the region.

Moving pictures debuted in Niagara on November 30, 1896, with an engagement of the Lumière Cinématographe, "Here for Three Days Only" at the Victoria Chambers in St. Catharines—"If you miss it now, you will be sorry when it's gone! Greatest Wonder of the Age!"[11] The Ontario licensee for the Lumière machine was H.J. Hill, manager of the annual Toronto Industrial Exhibition, where the show opened on September 1, 1896, then stayed in Toronto for another month at a Yonge Street storefront site.[12] In October, the Cinématographe toured west through Hamilton, London, and six other Ontario cities, ending its tour in St. Catharines before returning to the Yonge Street location for another two months. Playing at the town hall auditorium instead of the Grand Opera House in St. Catharines was typical, as Hill's booking agents needed specific dates (and surely lower costs) to plan their routes with the machine in tow. Only here in St. Catharines was the full program of films printed in the advertising, a total of twenty-two scenes, all from England, France, and Spain except for a "Negro Bathing Scene" noted as off the coast of South Africa. Typical of a Cinématographe program, the moving pictures were accompanied by a lecturer, William Ramsay, and turned into a formal, almost educational event as much as an entertainment (Steven 2003). Despite the variety of distinct scenes, there was a logical progression: the program started with the landing of a steamship, scenes from London, then Brighton Beach on the coast. Then came a segment of visual and comic scenes before arriving in Spain with scenes of its armies, and onto France with domestic scenes reflecting the French origins of the Lumière invention. Last, of course, an approaching train completed the show with dramatic effect. The cost was fully twenty-five cents, a dime for children, and the show ran from 2 to 6 p.m. and again from 7:30 to 10 p.m.—probably four shows a day in all. Representatives of the St. Catharines *Standard* attended the first show, reporting the next day that "everyone should see the Cinématographe. That's the unbiased advice the *Standard* has to offer ... every movement is depicted very realistically, in fact, absolutely true to life," singling out the military, seaside bathing, and railway scenes.[13]

Here for Three Days Only

If You Miss It Now You Will be Sorry When It's Gone !

GREATEST WONDER OF THE AGE!

The Great French Electrician and Photographer, M Lumiere's Marvelous Invention, the

CINEMATOGRAPHE

IN VICTORIA CHAMBERS

MONDAY, TUESDAY, WEDNESDAY

NOV. 30 and DEJ. 1 and 2.

PROGRAMME :

1. Landing from the Steamer.
2. Regent St., London.
3. Rotten Row, Hyde Park, London.
4. Visiting Friends in London.
5. Sea Shore on the South Coast of England, Brighton Beach.
6. Garden Hose Scene.
7. Pulling down an Old Building.
8. The Village Blacksmith.
9. Many Faces under One Hat, by M. Drewee.
10. Bark Leaving Port.
11. Sardine Fishing on Coast of France.
12. Spanish Artillery at Gun Practice.
13. Review of Imperial Troops in Spain.
14. Spanish Soldiers Dancing.
15. Children and their Toys.
16. Negro Bathing Scene.
17. Burning Weeds in Garden of M. Lumiere.
18. A Game of Cards.
19. The Gulf of Lyons.
20. Coming out of Cologne Cathedral.
21. M. Lumiere, Wife and Child at Breakfast.
22. Arrival of Train.

Open from 2:00 p.m. until 6:00 p.m. and from 7:80 to 10.00 p.m.

Admission, 25c ; Children, 10c.

FIGURE 4.1 Ad for Cinématographe, St. Catharines *Standard*, Nov. 1896

Newspapers across Canada reported the arrival of cinema as a novelty entertainment rather than a newsworthy invention. In London, Ontario, a review in the *Advertiser* is perhaps the most evocative: "The performance is so marvelous that one is appalled by the genius of the human mind that could produce such wonders.... To a person of imaginative mind, the exhibition is peculiarly attractive. He is transported in quick succession to France, Spain, England and Africa—to scenes and places that no writing, however graphic, can make so real to him as this little miracle, the Cinématographe. It has almost the power of the magic cap in the Arabian Nights."[14] This ecstatic impression certainly contrasts with the reception on the next tour of the Cinematographe around Ontario in February and March 1897, when newspapers merely reprint Hill's own press releases; we can assume the reading public was now familiar with the conventions of cinematic entertainment.

Within months, the marvel and novelty of the technology itself had worn off, and moving pictures of prominent special events were featured on a variety bill of assorted other unnamed scenes. The Magniscope pictures of Queen Victoria's Diamond Jubilee Procession arrived in St. Catharines in September 1897 for two days. This time, the shows were booked into the Grand Opera House.[15] All across Canada, even in Quebec, local events in June 1897 had celebrated the British Monarch's Jubilee, mirroring the Queen's own procession and celebrations in London, England. Newspapers and magazines rushed to print special issues with photographs of the event, but moving pictures nonetheless drew audiences months later. The filming of such newsworthy events was proving the commercial viability of cinema, which was still strongly connected to its verisimilitude and ability to photograph events in movement. Strictly speaking, moving pictures were operating as newsreels, as a "cinema of attractions" (Gunning 1990) rather than merely providing "harmless entertainment"(Grieveson 2004). This was all the more evident with another moving picture show of an equally newsworthy event. Veriscope pictures of the Jim Corbett–Bob Fitzsimmons heavyweight boxing prizefight arrived in St. Catharines for one night in October 1897 at the Grand Opera House.[16] The fight had taken place in March in Carson City, Nevada, where it was legal—but prize fights were illegal in Ontario and most other parts of North America, and this film led to the first debates over film censorship in the Canadian Parliament, in the Toronto city council chambers, and in dozens of meeting rooms around the continent. In fact, such controversy had erupted on a smaller scale when a "fake" fight film toured Ontario earlier, in summer 1897. Calling itself the Feriscope and claiming to depict the Corbett–Fitzsimmons fight, it was actually a poor-quality film from 1894 of Corbett staging a boxing match with Peter Courtney for the Edison cameras making a Kinetoscope picture (a peepshow predecessor of projected cinema). This film, too, came to the St. Catharines Grand Opera House for a night in June 1897.[17] In other Ontario cities, for example in Chatham, the show was stopped and the showman arrested and fined, but the tour moved on without incident in Niagara.

TOURING NIAGARA'S SMALLER TOWNS

By the time moving pictures came to the smaller communities of the Niagara Region in February and March 1897, over a dozen different machines had shown exhibitions in six provinces already and had visited at least forty different towns and cities elsewhere in southern Ontario. The first show to tour Niagara was for a machine called the Ametomagnoscope, owned by T.H. Duncombe, manager of the Duncombe Opera House in St. Thomas, Ontario. The apparatus was advertised as "an invention which produces colored animated bodies upon a screen, as in life." There was a staff of five working on this cinema side-business from November 1896 until April 1897, when Duncombe sold the outfit.[18] Travelling with the machine was a lecturer, electrician, and operator, plus a secretary to collect receipts and a publicity agent to book shows and handle advance advertising. Duncombe purchased the Ametomagnoscope from Thomas Amet's Illinois factory and originally planned to debut it on Thanksgiving Thursday, November 26, 1896, in his own St. Thomas theatre, but the machine arrived late and, instead, had its first show in nearby Aylmer the next week.

The device had to be set up in each new hall, and technical problems with electric current and projection were typical; in Aylmer for its first performance, the newspaper reported, "the results were not good.... Some improvement in the motion and in the clearness of the pictures is still possible."[19] Indeed, local reception of the showmanship behind the new moving picture machine was essential at first, and in Aylmer, Duncombe offered free admission to all who had paid for the first failed performance, "thus doing all in his power to go square with the public, as he always does." Subsequent exhibitions in St. Thomas, Petrolia, and Chatham were well received, at least according to the local press. The show's films were evidently American and derived from early titles from Edison's Vitascope: *Ocean Storm*, *Children's Parade*, *Camels*, and *The Kiss*, the last an already famous close-up of a moment between May Irwin and John C. Rice from a Broadway play called *The Widow Jones*.[20] Two films on the program, *Eating Watermelons* and *Pickaninnies*, attest to how early cinema inherited racial themes and stereotypical preoccupations from minstrelsy and the popular culture that preceded it.[21]

After extensive exploitation of the densely populous area between Sarnia and Woodstock, the Ametomagnoscope toured Niagara, opening in Welland on Monday, February 22, 1897, for four days. By then, the lecturer accompanying the moving pictures had been supplemented with an Edison Graphophone playing recorded music and famous speeches. The Welland *Tribune* reprinted a review from Brantford that placed as much emphasis on the music as the moving pictures: "It sings, talks and laughs and gives selections from Sousa's, Gilmour's and other bands."[22] The publicity in the Welland *Telegraph* was more extensive, striking a defensive tone to differentiate this entertainment from others: "The Ametomagnoscope Co. do not cater to the class that always go anyway, but to those that class all shows the same. Now stop a minute and think. You see a picture on the wall and then each individual person, streetcar, bicycle, whatever it may be begins to move, as in life. You hold your breath in surprise."[23] Admission was 20 cents for adults and 10 cents for children; seats could be reserved without extra charge at Garner's bookstore. In Welland, the show was far from a success, as the *Tribune* remarked afterwards, almost mocking the townsfolk for being stuck in conventional expectations about amusements: "Perhaps few comprehend what these moving pictures are—and then there was no brass band, you know."[24]

Judging from notes in the Welland papers, audiences in Niagara Falls were more appreciative when the moving pictures were exhibited there for two days in the Clifton Town Hall: "The Ametomagnoscope exhibitions in the town on Saturday and Monday evening last was a great success, considering the bad weather.... The reproductions from life are so perfect that one is disposed to believe life is actually in the pictures, while no less interesting were the productions by the Graphophone." Separate notes from Niagara Falls South report, "A large number from here went to Clifton ... to see the wonderful Ametomagnoscope in the town hall there and were highly delighted."[25] A return date was set for March although it is not clear whether it actually happened. It is certain, however, that Duncombe's moving pictures continued on for three days at the Bridgeburg Oddfellows Hall, two days in Matthews Hall in Port Colborne, and finally two days in St. Catharines at the Victoria Chambers where the Cinématographe had played three months earlier.[26]

As the Ametomagnoscope finished its Niagara tour, another small-scale picture show toured the region, with a gimmick marketed especially to women. Purchased by a Hamilton firm—apparently the manufacturers or retailers of a local baking powder—a machine called the Cinagraphoscope exhibited pictures for two weeks in St. Andrew's Hall in Hamilton: "A program of wonderful animated pictures. Admission 15c. children 10c. Note— to every lady will be given a free sample half-lb. tin of the famous Jersey Cream Baking Powder. Cosy Hall—good music. Come!"[27] In the newspaper ads for its second week, when it had to compete against another picture show, the baking powder almost received top billing: "While giving this strictly first-class entertainment to advertise our celebrated Jersey Cream Baking Powder, we are trying to give as good value for money as we give in our powder. We trust every lady in Hamilton will attend. Two hours' solid enjoyment. Lumsden Bros. Wholesale Grocers."[28]

This special show, perhaps the first use of moving pictures for product placement targeting women as shoppers, came to the Welland Opera House for three days beginning March 10, 1897. The Welland *Telegraph* reported that the Cinagraphoscope's strange use for advertising baking powder led to its leaving town with a deficit of $35 rather than a profit.[29] The show had better luck in the town of Niagara Falls (known before as Clifton). The local notes column in the *Telegraph* reported that the show "met with great success. The wonderful moving pictures shown by this machine excels all others ever shown here. In addition to the pictures, Mr. Allan Douglass, the popular Scotch baritone, who is possessed of exceptionally rich talent, delighted the large audiences with some beautiful selections in the dialect in which he is particularly gifted." Again, there was special clamour among those who had travelled from Niagara Falls South: "The wonderful Cinagraphoscope, which has given such great amusement in the town hall, Clifton, has by special request of a number of prominent citizens been induced to give an entertainment in the town hall here."[30] Early cinema shows were apparently not uniformly well received, and a show might hold over or return to an enthusiastic community. This particular machine played five days in Niagara Falls (Clifton), reportedly to packed houses, but was a failure in its three days in Welland and stopped in St. Catharines for only a single day.[31]

PICTURE SHOWS BECOME THEATRES: A PLACE TO SPEND YOUR NICKELS

Cinema continued to depend on touring showmen for another decade, stopping for a few days in the local opera house or town hall just like any itinerant show or travelling vaudeville program. The situation changed entirely in 1907 when some showmen and local entrepreneurs turned downtown storefront spaces into small-time picture shows. Although at the time it seemed these might be a passing fad, they are considered in hindsight to be the first movie theatres. Converting storefronts to small theatres seating around 200 people had happened as early as 1896, but the Vitascope Hall in Buffalo or the Cinematographe set up on Yonge Street in Toronto were temporary sites. Where there was Keith's Vaudeville—as at the major Shea's Theatres in Buffalo and Toronto—moving pictures were first available on an everyday basis as the last act "chaser" on their variety bills from 1899 onward. The storefront theatre as a permanent, small-scale picture show took hold as a fad throughout the midwest United States in 1905 where it became known as a "nickelodeon"(Bowser 1990). The first "scope" opened in Montreal early in 1906, and the first "theatorium" in Toronto in spring 1906. The first Ontario nickel show to open outside those metropolitan cities was the Theatorium in Brantford, in November 1906.[32] By the end of 1907 more than thirty Ontario towns and cities had picture shows running daily, including St. Catharines and Welland, with plans to open shortly in Niagara Falls.

Many years later in a special issue of the St. Catharines *Standard*, Henry P. Nicholson wrote a nostalgic article, "Remember Those Early Movies?"[33] He recalled the first picture theatre in St. Catharines was called the Bijou and located on Queen Street across from the *Standard* offices, where, as a boy, he would pick up papers daily for delivery. He recalls vividly his first trip to the pictures came with a fellow newsboy when the newspaper was delayed one afternoon: "When we got inside, the place was dark and the show had started…. When the picture was over, an announcement came on the screen saying, 'Those who came in late can remain for the start of the next show.' The exit doors opened and about 75 percent of the people went out, including two dumb little boys who did not understand the meaning of the announcement. I still remember and still laugh." Nicholson also recalls how early picture shows included two acts of small-time vaudeville, performing popular songs on stage. In its first several years, the program presented at most nickel shows was indeed a combination of short films, usually shown silent, interspersed with illustrated songs—popular music sung by a paid performer accompanied by projected slide images, with a chorus slide for everyone to join in singing together (Altman 2004). It took several years for picture shows to set up two projectors and a piano accompanist to allow for a continuous multiple-reel feature lasting one hour or more.

There is no trace of the Bijou except Nicholson's memories, but there are large ads leading up to the opening of the Hippodrome on downtown St. Paul Street in June 1907. Owned and managed by a Mrs. Hastings, who operated a show of the same name in Buffalo, the Hippodrome offered "the latest and most up-to-date moving pictures," gave away souvenir fans to the first 150 ladies for its opening, and featured Charles O'Donnell with illustrated songs—all for five cents from 2 to 6 p.m. and 7 to 10:30 p.m.[34] O'Donnell was described as "St. Catharines Favorite Singer," and he had frequently sung in travelling Vitagraph shows in the previous year at the Grand Opera House. Within the first week, song and film titles were advertised daily, and the first Friday afternoon was free to children. Summer heat was immediately a problem; although it was years before air conditioning was standard, the Hippodrome promised ventilation with special electric fans. In November, a third nickel show called the Gaiety, owned by two men (James and Watson), opened in St. Catharines on Ontario Street at St. Paul Street.[35] Against its new competition, the Hippodrome arranged to exhibit a blockbuster feature film, *The Passion Play of the Life of Christ*, "two miles of beautiful, interesting, hand-colored film that touches every heart-string." This picture was the five-cent show's first blockbuster, playing for fourteen weeks in Detroit starting in August 1907 and prompting Toronto theatoriums to advertise in newspapers for the first time in October.[36] At the Hippodrome in St. Catharines, admission was a dime instead of a nickel.

Religious films like *The Passion Play* were important to the entrepreneurs of picture shows because these new, permanent daily places to see moving pictures were already drawing the criticism of religious ministers, parents, and police. Their primary audience was children and young women, and the immaturity and feminine character of the pastime cast aspersions on exactly the cheap freedom of entertainment it offered (Uricchio and Pearson 1993). They offered a space of fun and amusement without supervision, at a cheap price almost anyone could afford. In Chicago in April 1907, protests came from moral reformers supported by investigations of danger and vice, reported by the *Chicago Tribune* (Grieveson 1999). At exactly the same time in Toronto, calls came for film censorship but the Staff Inspector of the Police morality squad announced he had already been confiscating objectionable moving pictures and inspecting the theatoriums. An undercover reporter for the *Mail and Empire* visited several downtown Toronto picture shows and had to report, "Five Cent Theatre Harmless Here."[37] The controversy happened on a smaller scale in Welland.

The first picture show in Welland, the Grand Theatorium, was owned by William Dawdy and opened in November 1907 on East Main Street. A small news article reported in the *People's Press* that the theatre was "fresh evidence of Welland's new order of things ... modeled after the style of the five-cent shows on the main streets of the metropolis, which have been all the craze, and the price will be the same."[38] Dawdy's advertising the following week made a case for the merit of amusement: "The one great craving in human nature is to be entertained. We hope to satisfy that longing," no doubt to the consternation of churches trying to satisfy what they thought to be people's one great need. The ad continued, "Moving pictures make recreation more delightful, as a result work is made easier and sleep more restful…. Come and enjoy yourself."[39] The new, secular order of things was all the more clear when a second picture show opened in Welland in January 1908 on West Main Street in an old church. The Star Nicklette was owned by Charles DeGraff of Buffalo and run by a man named Mr. Sider from nearby Ridgeway. The Welland *Tribune* noted wryly, "Just think of it girls! Another place to spend your nickels and your dimes."[40] As before in St. Catharines, the Grand booked *The Passion Play* to ward off the new competition. By March, the *People's Press* commented on the state of affairs of commercial versus sacred amusement on Saturday night in town: "Both five cent theatres were crowded—standing room only—whilst a contingent of Free Methodists conducted service at the end of the canal bridge and the Salvation Army held the fort in front of the bunch of hotels on East Main Street."[41] If the moral consequences of nickel shows were debatable, one harmful side effect would soon lead to regulation: the material base of film itself was highly flammable.

SOCIALLY COMBUSTIBLE: REBUILDING FOR SAFETY AFTER TRAGEDY

In January 1908, a fourteen-year-old projectionist died of burns after the film he was showing caught fire at the Hippodrome in St. Catharines. The news was reported widely across Ontario even before his injuries turned fatal: "A spark from the electric light fell upon the combustible film and an explosion followed…. Panic followed and several were trampled under foot…. The machine was being operated by Lorne McDermott, a boy under 15 years of age. The lad was severely and seriously burned about the hands and all over the face."[42] The *Standard* interviewed eyewitnesses: Annie Markle, the ticket seller who was working immediately below the projection room, said, "The people came crowding out in a bunch, some of them completely losing all control of themselves…. I grabbed the money and pushed my way out."[43] Another woman was working in her store across the street: "My first impressions were that the crowd coming out had enjoyed a good show and were laughing over it. On second thought, however, I could see that something unusual had happened. The pen where the operator sits was a mass of fire." A young lady who had been in the audience said, "All seemed to rise at once, and jumping over chairs and anything which might be in their way, made a dash for the door." John Sawyer was managing the theatre: "I had just concluded singing an illustrated song which was given after the pictures…. I endeavored to keep the crowd quiet and tell them to take their time, but it

The Daily Standard.

ST. CATHARINES, WEDNESDAY, JANUARY 15, 1908

CLAIMING THE BODIES

Sad Scenes Attend the Opening of the Four Temporary Morgues at Boyertown, Pa. To-day.

Full Investigation Into the Fatality Will be Made---Many of the Bodies Burned Beyond Recognition.

(Associated Press. Special to Standard.)
Boyertown, Pa., Jan. 15.—With the opening today of the four improvised morgues, in which lay the victims of Monday night's theatre holocaust, the inhabitants of this little borough began to realize the awful extent of the tragedy. The hand of death has touched probably every family in the town, and in neighboring villages, where families were not directly affected by the terrible panic and fire, through the loss of relatives, everywhere is mourning for lost friends or acquaintances.

from the burning building, died this morning.
Coroner Ctrasser is making an investigation preliminary to the official inquest. "It was the saddest picture I ever looked upon," he said. "No living soul can depict the scenes. It was simply indescribable. I made a thorough investigation leading up to what I consider the most terrible fatality that ever occurred in Eastern Pennsylvania."
The coroner's attention was called to the fact that oil lamps were used for foot lights in the opera house in place of a stationary illumination. He said he would make a thorough inquiry.
But two members of the cast so far as can be learned were killed. This was due to the precaution taken by Mrs. Della Mayer. She had a premonition that something would happen. At a luncheon given to the members of the cast in the hall several days ago she said she feared some thing. There ought to be a means of escape, she said. The rear entrance was spoken of and at her suggestion the doors were taken off the hinges so that in case of accident egress could easily be accomplished.
Henry W. Fischer of Carlisle, Pa., the operator of the calcium light which was the original cause of the terrible disaster, was severely burned. He said: "The accident to the calcium light was caused by a cap on one of the tanks blowing off. This caused a sharp report and flash which startled the people in the audience. I stuck to my ap-

EXTRA

HIPPODROME WAS GUTTED BY FIRE

Panic Follows Explosion of Film But Fortunately No One Was Seriously Injured

Lorne McDermott the Youthful Operator Was Badly Burned and is Now in the Hospital.

Flames, which broke out shortly after 3 o'clock this afternoon, caused three o'clock this afternoon, caused by the setting fire to the celluloid film, used in the moving picture machine at the Hippodrome, totally gutting that building, and doing damage of a large amount to the adjacent buildings.

FIGURE 4.2 Tragic celluloid film fires make the news. St. Catharines *Daily Standard*

was useless." Finally came the thoughts of the proprietress, Mrs. Hastings of Buffalo. The Hippodrome was in the same building as the McDermott family store, and her loss of $2,000 seemed nothing compared to their tragedy, although she said he was hired "against her desires and out of deference to the wishes of himself and his family."

McDermott's death followed on the heels of a theatre disaster in Boyertown, Pennsylvania, where 170 people died in a panicked rush to flee a fire reportedly resulting from the explosion of a moving picture projector. Although moving pictures were ultimately cleared of culpability in Boyertown, the tragedy remains associated with the dangers of early movie-going (Smither 2002, 433).[44] Horrific details from Pennsylvania shared the front page of the *Standard* with news of the fire, panic, and injury at the local theatorium. The death in St. Catharines showed how the still-novel technology seemed to escape the bounds of even the most stringent requirements in the construction of theatres, although the city introduced a much stricter building code for public buildings as a result. Within months of the fire and death came the first provincial law from Queen's Park specifically addressing the cinematograph and its flammable film material. Film was identified as a hazardous substance needing careful bureaucratic inspection and licensing. These fire safety laws were soon extended into elaborate film bureaucracies encompassing inspection, censorship, taxation, and restricted admissions (barring unaccompanied children from attending films, for example). The first Ontario law addressing the cinematograph in 1908 amended the existing regulation of safety exits in public buildings, which had previously meant churches and theatres, but now applied to "all places of amusement" as well. The amendment went further than its nominal interest in exits, however, and there were provisions for a provincial licence of all moving picture machines and their projectionists, both instituted a year later in 1909.[45] But the law *immediately* required the inspection and approval by municipal police of every "cinematograph or similar apparatus" and all locations handling or storing "combustible film more than ten inches in length." From this time forward all over Ontario, moving picture machines would be strictly regulated as part of community policing.

After the Hippodrome fire, safety was paramount in the promotional rhetoric of new picture shows. Another nickel show opened in St. Catharines soon after the fire, Mr. Harris' Lyric, next to the trolley station, "The Prettiest Theatre in Canada." When the Lyric opened in April, it featured Charles O'Donnell in illustrated songs, just as the Hippodrome had nearly a year earlier. But this time, a fire drill was performed in addition to the entertainment: "The theatre was emptied of its largest audience in exactly 55 seconds."[46] When the Hippodrome itself was rebuilt and reopened in May, fire safety was promoted as much as its decoration or entertainment. "No expense or labor has been spared in making the theatre thoroughly fire proof, so that even the most critical patron, who besides desiring to see a good show, thinks more of his or her safety, will feel perfectly at ease."[47] Again, the opening of Griffin's Family Theatre in November presented its fire exits as its "most consoling feature.... It can, almost in an instant, be cleared of an overcrowded house, the exits being so arranged that it is next to impossible to be dangerous." This new theatre had even hung a framed painting in its lobby of the city fire chief alongside pictures of St. Catharines' first mayor, and Sir Wilfrid Laurier and Sir John A. Macdonald. The Family theatre was a class higher than the earlier nickel shows. Purpose-built, part of a theatre chain, with a stage curtain, box seats, and a balcony, "It is just like Shea's," the *Standard* reported as the "general exclamation" of those who attended

FIGURE 4.3 Proscenium of Griffin's Family theatre. *Billboard* 1908

opening night.[48] John Griffin was the pioneer theatorium owner in Toronto, opening the city's first four nickel shows between March and August 1906, adding several more in the next two years, and expanding to other cities— first here in St. Catharines, as reported in the American amusement trade paper, *Billboard*: "There is no finer structure devoted to refined vaudeville and motion pictures on the continent and Mr. Griffin is to be congratulated for his laudable ambition."[49]

With the opening of the Family theatre at the end of November 1908, the city of St. Catharines now had four picture shows operating (perhaps five if the Bijou was still open). But the business had been booming all over Niagara, from the shore of Lake Ontario to the shore of Lake Erie: a picture show called the Idle Hour had opened in Port Dalhousie back in May, as did a "nickelodium" at an expanded Crystal Beach Amusement Park. In November, a Prof. Scott had opened the Nicklette in the Osbourne House block in Thorold.[50] Niagara Falls now had two nickel shows. At the end of January, the *People's Press* noted that the Reeb Brothers, Port Colborne merchants, were converting part of the Gay Brothers block on Queen Street in Niagara Falls to a moving picture theatre. Just after the Hippodrome fire, the newspaper also noted that the site had "good means of exit" and that the picture apparatus would be "entirely fire-proof." The Amuseyou opened in March to a packed house, offering a change of program three times a week.[51] News

Coming here

Every Wednesday

Starting

WEDNESDAY, NOV. 4, 1908

Oddfellows' Hall, Thorold,

— THE —

Vanetograph Company

2—HOURS AMUSEMENT—2

OF

High-class Moving Pictures
And Illustrated Songs

This Company plays in the following places
each week, with full change of Pictures each
week—

Grimsby—Mondays
Beamsville—Tuesdays
Thorold—Wednesdays
Port Colborne—Fridays
Welland—Saturdays

Doors open 7:45

Children 5c, Ladies 10c, Gents 15c

FIGURE 4.4 Vanetograph Company
in Thorold's Odd Fellows Hall.
Thorold *Post*, Nov. 1908

of plans for another show in Niagara Falls first appeared in September.
Located in the Woodruff block on Bridge Street, Mr. Taylor's Princess Theatre
was the city's mainstay for entertainment until 1914, after a larger theatre had
opened. The Niagara Falls notes in the *Standard* reported of its opening in
November 1908, "No expense has been spared in fitting up the building, both
inside and out. The entrance is wonderfully pretty, numerous electric lights
being artistically arranged."[52] A few days later came another newsworthy
event: "On Saturday night his establishment was packed and there were so

many people waiting outside that the services of the police were requisitioned to keep the sidewalk clear for passersby. The high-class entertainment provided was thoroughly enjoyed, especially the singing and dancing of little Miss Olga Durham."[53] The Princess was off to a good start.

Another development bridged the early years of the itinerant travelling showman and the nickel show as a local institution. In November 1908, Fred VanDyke started a weekly moving picture circuit across Niagara, routinely scheduling shows for the first time in Grimsby, Beamsville, and Port Colborne, and also competing against the daily nickel shows in Welland and Thorold. VanDyke and other members of his family had been operating the Twentieth Century Roller Rink in Welland, as well as rinks elsewhere in Ontario. His Vanetograph Company offered a two-hour show in established venues like the Oddfellows Hall in Thorold, travelling along the street railway line from Grimsby to Port Colborne and ending on Saturdays in his own roller rink in Welland. He charged five cents for children, ten cents for ladies, and a hefty fifteen cents for gents.[54] It is difficult to judge his success; like many of the early nickel shows, VanDyke's Vanetograph circuit is noted only when it first opened. How long did these small shows last? It is easier to answer how bigger theatres soon replaced them, long-lasting "picture palaces" still remembered in contrast to these forgotten first picture shows.

CONCLUSION

By 1910, moving pictures were a constant, daily part of life in Niagara. By then, moving pictures were playing regularly in the Town Hall in Niagara-on-the-Lake; Port Colborne had its own show, the Dreamland; Moore's Picture Palace had opened in Grimsby Park; the Grand in Welland and the Princess in Niagara Falls had expanded from around 200 seats to 600 or more, as newer, purpose-built theatres were planned to compete against them.[55] When the nickel shows first opened, most of the films were made in France by the Pathé Company, although they were imported to Toronto via New York. By 1910, as film historian Richard Abel has detailed, almost all of the pictures themselves were produced in the United States, although the film industry there was not yet centred in Los Angeles and not yet called "Hollywood"(Abel 1999, 2006; Olsson 2008). A major step in becoming a big business was the creation in 1910 of the General Film Company, a chain of distributors across North America, including Canada, directly owned by film production companies.[56] In the next decade, movie studios also purchased control of local theatre chains. In Canada, for example, Paramount helped create Famous Players Theatres in 1920, and the chain dominated the country's first-run theatres for the rest of the twentieth century. In light of this emerging corporate consolidation, let me return in conclusion to the film of the local tram ride that played in 1910 in Niagara Falls.

In August 1910, the Princess Family Theatre advertised daily in the *Record*. Musical director Joseph Hopkins changed the vaudeville program twice weekly, on Mondays and Thursdays, but the motion pictures changed every two days, on Mondays, Wednesdays, and Fridays. The local management would have had almost no choice in the films that came to town; the General Film Company in Toronto, a branch of the American company controlled by film producers, would have simply sent around a constant change of almost interchangeable titles. On Wednesday, August 10, the pictures changed like any other, with a two-day show consisting of five pictures from American film companies, but with a Canadian theme: 1. *Trappers and Redskins*; 2. *That's What They All Say*; 3. *Scenes in Ontario*; 4. *Canadian Northern Railway Construction*; 5. *General Farming in Canadian North-West*. As I noted in my introduction, Thursday's *Record* excitedly reported that the scenes in Ontario had actually included a film of local interest, "a local picture which shows scenes along the Niagara, St. Catharines, and Toronto Railway from Port Dalhousie to Falls View."[57] Exploiting the unusual interest in this otherwise routine program, the Princess changed its advertising to make the local content explicit. Unlike other films at the time, this picture stayed for an additional two days, even when the rest of the program changed on Friday. For over a decade already, moving pictures of scenes from around the world had entertained audiences in the Niagara Region. For several years already, picture theatres had provided a daily variety of constantly changing amusement and distraction. All forms of sensation and spectacle had become routine. Yet, here this once, the local theatre provided a special experience never seen before as the screen flickered with images of home.

NOTES

1 Advertising for the Princess Theatre, Niagara Falls *Record*, Aug. 8–13, 1910.
2 "Princess Theatre," Niagara Falls *Record*, Aug. 11, 1910.
3 The Falls of Niagara is promised as a feature of "Edison's Vitascope at West End Park," *Ottawa Journal*, July 20, 1896. On the Vitascope, see "Edison Manufacturing," in Richard Abel, ed., *Encyclopedia of Early Cinema* (New York: Routledge, 2005), 200–203.
4 For the filming of Niagara Falls, see Peter Morris, *Embattled Shadows: A History of Canadian Cinema, 1895–1939* (Montreal and Kingston: McGill-Queen's University Press, 1978 [2nd ed. 1992]), 29, 276 n16, 280 n2.

5 "Le Cinématographe," Montreal *La Presse*, June 29, 1896. On the Cinématographe, see "Lumière, Auguste and Louis," in Abel, *Encyclopedia of Early Cinema*, 398–99.

6 An apparently unlicensed Edison Vitascope actually opened in Winnipeg on Portage Avenue before the official Ottawa debut. See "The Vitascope," Winnipeg *Tribune*, July 20, 1896.

7 Morris, *Embattled Shadows*, 29.

8 The Whirlpool Rapids are noted as part of the New Motograph show in the ad for the Bijou Theatre, Toronto *World*, Feb. 6, 1897. Niagara Falls showing the *Maid of the Mist* is noted for the Anamatagraph show in "Town Topics," Aurora *Banner*, Jan. 15, 1897. A scene of Niagara Falls is noted as part of the Canadagraph show in "Vaudeville Entertainment," Richmond Hill *Liberal*, Apr. 8, 1897.

9 Focusing on Toronto, Paul S. Moore, *Now Playing: Early Moviegoing and the Regulation of Fun* (Albany: State University of New York Press, 2008), traces the emergence of theatoriums and their transformation to a mass culture of movies.

10 This methodology is developed further in a forthcoming publication by Paul Moore, "The Social Biograph: Newspapers as Archives of the Regional Mass Market for Movies."

11 Ad for the Cinématographe, St. Catharines *Standard*, Nov. 30, 1896.

12 Morris, *Embattled Shadows*, 7–9. Also see Walden.

13 "City and Vicinity News," St. Catharines *Standard*, Dec. 1, 1896.

14 "A Delightful Exhibition," London *Advertiser*, Oct. 27, 1896.

15 Ad for the Queen's Diamond Jubilee Magniscope at the Grand Opera House, St. Catharines *Standard*, Sept. 16, 1897.

16 Ad for the Corbett-Fitzsimmons Veriscope at the Grand Opera House, St. Catharines *Standard*, Oct. 7, 1897.

17 Ad for the Corbett-Fitzsimmons Feriscope at the Grand Opera House, St. Catharines *Standard*, Jun. 7, 1897. The arrest in Chatham was the last show; coincidentally word had got round that the films were falsely advertised. "Verescope Showmen Arrested," Chatham *Daily Planet*, June 14, 1897. On fight films and fake fight films, see Dan Streible, *Fight Pictures: A History of Boxing and Early Cinema* (Berkeley: University of California Press, 2008); entry on "Boxing Films," in Abel, *Encyclopedia of Early Cinema*, 80–81.

18 "It Did Not Come," St. Thomas *Times*, Nov. 27, 1896. "Town and Vicinity," Aylmer *Sun*, Dec. 3, 1896.

19 "Town Topics," Aylmer *Express*, Dec. 3, 1896.

20 "The Ametomagnoscope," Strathroy *Dispatch*, Dec. 9, 1896.

21 For more on blackface and minstrel shows in the Niagara Region, see Joan Nicks and Jeannette Sloniowski, "Entertaining Niagara Falls: Minstrel Shows, Theatres, and Popular Pleasures," in this volume. For an analysis of the experience of early black audiences in the United States, see Jacqueline Stewart, *Migrating to the Movies: Cinema and Black Urban Modernity* (Chicago: University of Chicago Press, 2005).

22 "Town and Vicinity," Welland *Tribune*, Feb. 19, 1897.

23 "News Around Town," Welland *Telegraph*, Feb. 19, 1897.

24 "Town and Vicinity," Welland *Tribune*, Feb. 26, 1897.

25 "Niagara Falls" and "Niagara Falls South," Welland *Telegraph*, Mar. 5, 1897. Upon amalgamation in 1856, the town name became Clifton and remained as such

until 1904, when, with further amalgamation, it became the city of Niagara Falls. See Sherman Zavitz, et al., *Images of a Century: The City of Niagara Falls, Canada, 1904–2004* (Niagara Falls: Centennial Committee/Maracle Press, 2004).

26 "Port Colborne" and "Bridgeburg," Welland *Tribune*, Mar. 5, 1897; "News of City and Vicinity," St. Catharines *Standard*, Mar. 8, 1897.

27 Ad for the Cinagraphoscope, Hamilton *Spectator*, week of Feb. 15, 1897. See Jeannette Sloniowski and Joan Nicks, "Hollywoodization," in this volume, for details about the marketing of movies to women in Niagara Falls in later decades. See also Jane Gaines, "From Elephants to Lux Soap: The Programming and Flow of Early Movie Exploitation, " *Velvet Light Trap* 25 (1990), 29–43.

28 Ad for the Cinagraphoscope, Hamilton *Spectator*, week of Feb. 22, 1897.

29 "News Around Town," Welland *Telegraph*, Mar. 19, 1897.

30 "Niagara Falls" and "Niagara Falls South," Welland *Telegraph*, Mar. 19, 1897.

31 "News of City and Vicinity," St. Catharines *Standard*, Mar. 16, 1897.

32 Ad for Theatorium, Brantford *Courier*, Nov. 10, 1906.

33 Henry P. Nicholson, "Remember Those Early Movies?" St. Catharines *Standard*, Feb. 14, 1976.

34 The Hippodrome opened June 22, 1907. See ads in the St. Catharines *Standard* leading up to the opening. Also see note on owner Mrs. Hastings of Buffalo in "Fire in Moving Picture Theatre," Welland *Telegraph*, Jan. 21, 1908.

35 The Gaiety opened Nov. 21, 1907. See "The Gaiety," St. Catharines *Standard*, Nov. 22, 1907.

36 Ad for *Passion Play* at Hippodrome, St. Catharines *Standard*, Nov. 18, 1907. For the Toronto exhibition of the film, see Moore, *Now Playing*, 69.

37 "Five Cent Theatre Harmless Here," Toronto *Mail and Empire*, Apr. 13, 1907. See also Moore, *Now Playing*, 24–25.

38 The Grand opened Nov. 16, 1907. See "Moving Picture Theatre," Welland *People's Press*, Nov. 12, 1907.

39 Ad for The Grand, Welland *People's Press*, Nov. 19, 1907.

40 The Star Nicklette opened Jan. 29, 1908. See "All for a Nickel," Welland *Tribune*, Jan. 17, 1908, and "Star Theatre Opening," Welland *Tribune*, Jan. 31, 1908.

41 "Town and Country," Welland *People's Press*, Mar. 24, 1908.

42 "Hippodrome Was Gutted by Fire," St. Catharines *Standard*, Jan. 15, 1908; "Was Nearly Disaster," Brockville *Times*, Jan. 16, 1908; "Was Nearly a Disaster," Belleville *Intelligencer*, Jan. 16, 1908.

43 "Some Late Particulars of the Hippodrome Fire," St. Catharines *Standard*, Jan. 16, 1908; "Lorne McDermott Dies After Brave Struggle," St. Catharines *Standard*, Jan. 17, 1908.

44 See also Moore, *Now Playing*, 53–61.

45 See the chart of moving picture legislation in Toronto in Moore, *Now Playing*, 138–39.

46 The Lyric opened Apr. 11, 1908. See "Successful Opening of the Lyric Theatre," St. Catharines *Standard*, Apr. 13, 1908.

47 A rebuilt Hippodrome opened May 29, 1908. See "The Opening of the Hippodrome," St. Catharines *Standard*, May 28, 1908.

48 Griffin's Family opened on Nov. 30, 1908. See "Pretty New Theatre Opened," St. Catharines *Standard*, Dec. 1, 1908.

49 *Billboard*, Dec. 12, 1908, 8. For more on Griffin's chain of theatres, see Moore, *Now Playing*, 84–92.
50 The Idle Hour in Port Dalhousie advertised its opening in the St. Catharines *Standard*, May 29, 1908. A new nickelodium is noted as one of the "Crystal Beach Wonderful Improvements," Welland *People's Press*, May 19, 1908. The Nicklette opening on Nov. 19, 1908, is reported in Thorold notes, St. Catharines *Standard*, Nov. 20, 1908.
51 The Amuseyou opened Mar. 12, 1908. See "Niagara Falls," Welland *People's Press*, Jan. 28, 1908; "Niagara Falls," St. Catharines *Standard*, Mar. 13, 1908.
52 The Princess opened Nov. 19, 1908. See "Niagara Falls," St. Catharines *Standard*, Nov. 20, 1908; "Niagara Falls," Welland *People's Press*, Sept. 15, 1908.
53 "Niagara Falls," St. Catharines *Standard*, Nov. 23, 1908.
54 Vanetograph ad, Thorold *Post*, Nov. 3, 1908, and following weeks; "Local News," Beamsville *Express*, Nov. 12, 1908; "Moving Pictures at Rink," Welland *People's Press*, Nov. 17, 1908.
55 Moving Pictures begin daily in Niagara-on-the-Lake on June 14, 1909. See "Camp Entertainment," *Niagara Times*, June 11, 1909. The Dreamland opened in Port Colborne on July 30, 1910. See "Amusement House," Port Colborne *Times*, Aug. 4, 1910. Moore's moving pictures begin on May 24, 1910, in a rebuilt commercial Grimsby Beach. See ad, Beamsville *Express*, May 5, 1910. "The Grand Theatre," Welland *Tribune*, Apr. 28, 1910. "Princess Theatre," Niagara Falls *Record*, Feb. 1, 1910, and July 18, 1910.
56 On the General Film Company in Canada, see Moore, *Now Playing*, 98–99.
57 "Princess Theatre," Niagara Falls *Record*, Aug. 11, 1910, and advertising, Aug. 10–13, 1910.

WORKS CITED

Abel, Richard. *Americanizing the Movies and Movie-Mad Audiences, 1910–1914*. Berkeley: University of California Press, 2006.
———.*The Red Rooster Scare: Making Cinema American, 1900–1910*. Berkeley: University of California Press, 1999.
Altman, Rick. *Silent Film Sound*. New York: Columbia University Press, 2004.
Bottomore, Steve. "The Panicking Audience?: Early Cinema and the 'Train Effect.'" *Historical Journal of Film, Radio, and Television* 19:2 (1999), 177–216.
Bowser, Eileen. *The Transformation of Cinema, 1907–1915*. Berkeley: University of California Press, 1990.
Grieveson, Lee. *Policing Cinema: Movies and Censorship in Early Twentieth Century America*. Berkeley: University of California Press, 2004.
———. "Why the Audience Mattered in Chicago in 1907." In Melvyn Stokes and Richard Maltby, eds., *American Movie Audiences from the Turn of the Century to the Early Sound Era*. London: British Film Institute, 1999: 79–91.
Gunning, Tom. "Cinema of Attractions." In Thomas Elsaesser, ed., *Early Cinema: Space, Frame, Narrative*. London: British Film Institute, 1990: 56–62.
Lacasse, Germaine. "Cultural Amnesia and the Birth of Film in Canada." *Cinema Canada* 108 (June 1984), 6–7.

Olsson, Jan. *Los Angeles Before Hollywood: Journalism and American Film Culture, 1905 to* 1915. Stockholm: National Library of Sweden, 2008.

Pryluck, Calvin. "The Itinerant Movie Show and the Development of the Film Industry." In Kathryn Fuller-Seeley, ed., *Hollywood in the Neighbourhood: Historical Case Studies of Local Moviegoing*. Berkeley: University of California Press, 2008: 37–52.

Smither, R.B.N. *This Film Is Dangerous: A Celebration of Nitrate Film*. Brussels: FIAF, 2002.

Steven, Peter. "Pleasing the Canadians: A National Flavour for Early Cinema, 1892–1914." *Canadian Journal of Film Studies* 12:2 (2003), 5–21.

Uricchio, William, and Roberta Pearson. *Reframing Culture: The Case of the Vitagraph Quality Films*. Princeton, NJ: Princeton University Press, 1993.

Walden, Keith. *Becoming Modern in Toronto: The Industrial Exhibition and the Shaping of a Late Victorian Culture*. Toronto: University of Toronto Press, 1997.

"HOLLYWOODIZATION," GENDER, AND THE LOCAL PRESS IN THE 1920s
The Case of Niagara Falls, Ontario

JEANNETTE SLONIOWSKI
JOAN NICKS

INTRODUCTION

By the 1920s, movies and movie-going were an established form of popular culture produced by an aggressively capitalistic American studio machine. The studios' talent for advertising penetrated local newspapers and widely circulated American fanzines and women's magazines. In his comprehensive study of popular culture in early Lexington, Kentucky, Gregory Waller refers to "Hollywood" as a "broadly understood ... site and subject of discourse during the 1920s":

> "Hollywood" was *constructed* [emphasis ours] on a national scale, through shorts and features and newsreels, and all manner of publicity and promotional material.... Fanzines, trade journals, and general interest magazines all played crucial roles in this discourse.... Publication of advertising, editorials, and syndicated or wire service materials ... [were] ... disseminated (and contextualized) in local papers. (1995, 239)

"Hollywoodization" did not stop at the American border. Local newspapers—*The Daily Record*, followed by the long-standing *Niagara Falls Evening Review* (1918–present)—delivered Hollywood tastes and values to conscript readers to embrace movie-going and support hometown theatres.[1] As Paul Moore argues in his study of early movie-going in Toronto, "journalism and promotion did not merely reflect and comment on the place of film in society. Newspapers fundamentally were agents themselves in reshaping the meaning and practice of going to the movies" (2008, 14).

In Niagara Falls, Ontario, the business of running a local newspaper thrived on revenue from local entrepreneurs who built and ran theatres and advertised movies. Ad copy and movie columns were largely studio generated and fed a newspaper discourse that enveloped product endorsements by stars and wire stories on Hollywood scandals and production practices. The local newspaper printed the stories, interpreted them, and offered editorials about movie culture, tailored to community concerns and locally rooted moral values. Thus "Hollywood" became a social issue and public topic, as did changing gender roles influenced by screen style. Debates about the New Woman, her fashion and desires, preoccupied newspapers and magazines, as well as American writers such as F. Scott Fitzgerald; bobbed hair, the style of screen vamps, was a hot topic of the day that fostered press commentary, magazine and literary stories, and contests in local theatres.

In this study of "Hollywoodization," we examine the conventions of local newspaper discourse and how contradictions within this discourse shaped a rhetorical debate about popular culture in the 1920s, with cautionary messages for all members of the community, and the promotion of Hollywood culture for those eager for its exciting new fashions, mores, and stars—far from Hollywood but locally accessible at the movies, in the newspaper, and in fanzines.[2] The burgeoning commercialization of movies and stardom, and the interest in and obsession with "Hollywood," marked the beginnings of modern celebrity culture and the spread of celebrity-related consumerism. An undercurrent of our argument is that induction into the propaganda and pleasure of all things "Hollywood" through the local newspaper—the *Review* cost two cents in 1929 and was available for delivery six days a week—may have produced early media literacy, not only fandom and consumerism, at least for discerning readers of the day. As Kathryn Helgesen Fuller argues, for small-town movie-goers, "the proliferation of movie fan magazines, the evolution of male and female movie fans, the cults of movie star worship, the spread of movie references to other parts of popular culture, even the linkage of movie stars to consumer culture through product endorsements—all worked to compensate small-town movie fans for any perceived deficiencies in their local experience" (Fuller 2002, 47–48). Samantha Barbas describes a significant shift for the young women who did not make it to Hollywood: "Most of these fans had come to terms with the fact that they would never see their names in lights.... But that did not preclude other ways of exerting influence over Hollywood. Many fans actually learned to draw on their power as purchasers to leave their mark on the studio system" (2001, 82). Some readers wrote letters to *Photoplay* magazine in the 1920s saying they "were inspired by movies to improve their lives: to find a job, to go back to school" (63).[3]

Consumers of entertainment and fashion could be discriminating read-ers. In an essay on audience surveys of the 1920s and 1930s, Melvyn Stokes emphasizes the place of newspapers in movie-going decisions: "Girls, boys, usually selected which movie to see themselves, independently of the par-ents, and were most influenced in their choice by reports in the daily news-papers" (1999, 47). Many newly enfranchised women and girls of the Jazz Age were eager to reject rigid Victorian moral codes and to adopt the newer, more revealing fashions and behaviour displayed in Hollywood films; mod-ern hair styles, on and off screen, became a flashpoint in the press and popular magazines. On the other hand, the Niagara Falls Rotary Club's "big brother" campaign groomed local boys for their traditional public roles through a special school program and theatre event, heavily boosted by the *Review* (May 20, 1922, 8) (discussed below). These gender contradic-tions bring into relief a social climate that informs our study and illuminates the local newspaper's skilful integration of Hollywood promotion, widely distributed by wire services, to engage readers' popular interests and develop a sense of decorum deemed appropriate to the citizens of this unique border city.

NIAGARA FALLS MOVIE HOUSES: CANADIAN PLAYERS OR HOLLYWOOD SERVANTS?

Besides vaudeville and staged presentations, Niagara Falls movie theatres in the 1920s thrived on Hollywood fare, with an occasional Canadian film, and more often a British film, advertised as a drama of *excellence* from the mother country. For a short period, Albert Huttlemeyer, an entrepreneur from Niagara Falls, New York, who built the Queen Theatre in 1913, the first stand-alone theatre in Niagara Falls, Ontario, ran a drama season with tour-ing and resident stage companies. This attempt to inject "culture" into a vaudeville/movie house was only marginally successful, and feature films supplemented the effort. Although Huttlemeyer presented the stage musi-cal *Mademoiselle From Armentières* with the original all-Canadian cast of soldiers (*Review*, Jan. 16, 1922, 6), the touring *Winnipeg Kiddies* (Oct. 24, 1921, 4), and the *Broadway Vanities of 1921*, promoted as the "Biggest Attraction Ever Brought to Niagara Falls At Pre-War Prices" (Oct. 8, 1921, 3), he, like the city's other theatre owners, was hamstrung by what Waller calls "sabbatarian demands" (Waller, 219). The Ontario Lord's Day Act did not permit movie screenings on Sunday, and on many such afternoons the Queen Theatre was the venue for free fire-and-brimstone lectures by stern representatives of the International Bible Association. The large newspaper

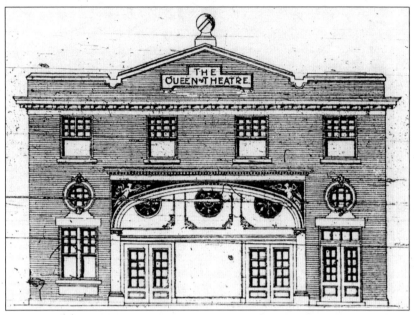

FIGURE 5.1 Blueprint, Queen Theatre, Niagara Falls, Ontario. *The Daily Record*, 1912

ads promoting these lectures fit the Christian values of the *Review*'s publisher, Frank H. Leslie. The ads also served Huttlemeyer as owner-operator of a theatre that needed to maintain its social standing in a downtown with three nearby churches: St. Patrick's Catholic, St. Andrew's Presbyterian, and Christ Anglican.

By the time Famous Players Canadian Corporation bought the Queen Theatre in 1926, renovated and converted it to sound technology, and renamed it the Capitol, the corporation dominated film distribution and exhibition in Canada.[4] Huttlemeyer's former Queen Theatre had become "Hollywoodized" into a corporate asset suitable for bigger movies and theatre events, and an extensive supplement in the *Review* makes a celebrity of the Capitol's newly minted identity as a Famous Players Canadian theatre. Fitted with state-of-the-art sound technology, the Capitol opened with the musical *Show Boat* (Universal Pictures, d. Pollard, 1929). The lavish two-page newspaper spread was a piece of Hollywood promotion extolling the breakthrough musical spectacle. Though the film's narrative was stilted and the sound elements meagre, Niagara Falls, Ontario, had been earmarked by Famous Players as a location ripe for the expansion of its Canadian holdings, and the community responded enthusiastically to this exciting new era of movies.[5]

FIGURE 5.2 Centre section, panoramic photo of 75 Famous Players Canadian Corporation managers, posed with the American waterfall as central backdrop, 1929. Capitol Theatre manager, Jack Ward, second row, third from left. Courtesy of Gary and Pat Ward

In 1929, seventy-five theatre managers of the Famous Players Canadian Corporation convened in Niagara Falls, deemed to be "an ideal spot by the gathering" (*Review*, July 6, 11). The "talkies" and sound were the main items on the agenda, only weeks before the Queen-to-Capitol name change, decorous upgrade, and conversion to sound technology were announced in the newspaper. In a panoramic photo taken by a Pathé photographer, the Canadian managers are a handsome lot in smart suits, posed on the site that later became the formal Oakes Garden Theatre in Queen Victoria Park (figure 5.2). The American waterfall—as it is known, to distinguish it from the Canadian "Horseshoe" waterfall at the far right of the photo—is clearly visible as the central backdrop. How natural and attractive "Hollywoodization" looked from the Canadian side of the border, yet how groomed and staged it was!

THE LEARNING CURVE: TEACHING AN EARLY FASCINATION FOR MOVIES

As early as 1910, readers of the *Daily Record* could learn about marvellous apparatuses like the *camera obscura* (Oct. 6). In 1912, the newspaper published a piece headed "SHOOT AT PICTURES—Charging Infantry Thrown on Screen a Most Realistic Target." The story explains in detail the technical use of "the cinematograph" by the French army, where recruits in training fire at "phantom soldiers" as they advance on screen (Sept. 17). Ambitious mothers may have been amused by a naïve, short, gendered piece headed "The Child Actress," which feminizes the claim that children simply are born to act: "From the time she learns to walk she dances, pirouettes and minces her way along" (Sept. 2, 1920). The perceived social impact of movie reception is unmistakable in a reprinted article from a *Times* (London) educational supplement that glowingly discusses the classroom use of moving pictures and advances the moral value of children drawing parents away "from the public houses to performances" (Sept. 17, 1912). Stories about notable men like Thomas Edison emphasize their genius, taking the great-men-do-great-things approach. A story on the Pathé Frères (Paris) Company agents, who filmed a dummy *Maid of the Mist* sent plummeting over Niagara's famous falls in a canoe, played up the staging and shooting of the scene as a public *event* of great local interest (Sept. 15, 1910).

These newspaper conventions are rooted in turn-of-the-century promotion of theatres run by competitive managers who booked popular stage dramas, playlets, vaudeville acts, blackface comics, and short-reel films—and also ran amateur nights. In Niagara Falls, Ontario, such regular programming at the Bridge Street Princess Theatre (1908–14) was supported by weekly, sometimes daily, ads and write-ups in the *Record* and the Niagara Falls, New York, *Gazette*. By the 1920s, the movie/theatre ads in the *Review* were well illustrated, and the Hollywood stories and promotion often included studio photos. Theatres in Niagara Falls, New York, competed for nearby Canadian audiences with regular, sometimes larger and more elaborately illustrated ads in the Niagara Falls, Ontario, newspapers. Only one of the great advantages of living in a border community is this easy access to another culture. Niagara Falls, New York, more than twice the size of Niagara Falls, Ontario, in this period, had more and larger movie houses, as well as elaborate vaudeville programs until well into the 1930s. Border crossing was cheap and easy, and even Canadian drugstores advertised and sold tickets for theatres on the American side of the border.

The *Review* ran a regular Music and Drama column in the 1920s that described the plots and stars of Hollywood films playing locally. Write-ups like this one could only have been studio material: "BLACKFEET TRIBE STAGE FIGHT FOR MOTION PICTURES—Chief Who Posed for the Buffalo Nickel Head, Portrays Role of Sitting Bull" (May 17, 1922, 6). A column entitled "Filmland" conveys insider knowledge about production and movie people. One extols movies as science rather than art (May 29, 1922, 9). In the late 1920s, the Hollywood Film Shop column (byline Duane Hennessy) was full of insider news and gossip about Hollywood productions and, in one instance, instructs readers on the wholesomeness of the western: "Parents will like them for the morals they teach" (July 12, 1929, 13). An Associated Press piece from Hollywood stretches reader interest to include European influences on Hollywood production, namely the painstaking detail of F.W. Murnau's direction of his first American film, *Sunrise* (1927) (Jan. 25, 1927, 9).

Not only was "Hollywoodization" aimed at newspaper readers, by 1931 the *Review* itself had been schooled in all things "Hollywood" and, in a long editorial (reprinted from the Woodstock, Ontario, *Sentinel Review*) argued that newspapers should protect themselves from the Hollywood studios' threat to put advertising on screen, "presented in the guise of entertainment." The editorial concludes with a self-serving rejoinder, "to advertise extensively in the newspapers" (May 28, 1931, 14). A decade of playing Hollywood's game had become instructive for small-town newspapers, not only their movie-going readers, and publishers protected their own interests.

THE *REVIEW*'S GUIDING VOICE

Frank H. Leslie, publisher of the *Review*, was highly regarded in Niagara Falls and among Ontario publishers.[6] His commitment to the city reads like a mission statement: "Published every afternoon except on legal holidays and Sundays by F.H. Leslie Limited (Member of Canadian Press Ass'n) at the corner of Clifton Avenue and Park Street ... devoted to the interests of Niagara Falls, Canada" (Aug. 31, 1922, 2). Leslie valued what small communities stood for, apparent in the editorial "The Small Town" (reprinted from another small Ontario newspaper), which liberally references a "scheme for a chain of small cities from 30,000 to 50,000 population," found in the "epoch-making book" *Garden Cities of Tomorrow*.[7] The editorial draws on political rhetoric to make its case, quoting from a lecture by Ontario Premier Ernest Charles Drury in praise of "small town communal cohesion"—"there the cultural influences that belong as essentially to the country as to the town can best be maintained" (Mar. 24, 1922, 2).

In the small city of Niagara Falls—population 15,936 in 1922 and 16,412 in 1923 (Sept. 6, 1923)—the *Review* took on the multiple roles of community voice, consumer guide, world-news source, social register, and booster of local development, business, and education. Only rarely were there bylines to inform readers of a reporter's identity or locale. It was the newspaper itself that spoke with journalistic and moral authority to, and for, the community, albeit often with striking contradictions between editorials, movie/theatre ads, Hollywood studio copy and columns, and large product-endorsement ads featuring studio stars. Hollywood and its ideology was part of the education. Like the earlier *Daily Record*, the *Review* was a major purveyor of popular culture and, at the same time, suspicious of its influences, particularly Hollywood's excesses. Yet, the *Review* borrowed Hollywood's visual codes in fashion ads it produced for local businesses (discussed below). Contradictions between a publisher's principles and business practices, and playing to the already well-developed popular interests of readers, were as common to newspapers of the 1920s as they are to print and broadcast media today.

In this period, the public was developing a hearty appetite for what Waller calls "cheap amusements" (1995, xiv), and local newspapers subscribed to Hollywood's self-promotion and propagandizing work. The newspaper was an instrument in what Fuller terms "the creation of movie fan culture" (2002, 47). Newspapers were quick to report on the establishment, activities, and potential of new theatres in the community in the early 1910s and 1920s. Where grand picture palaces were big-city showcases, in small cities and towns the building or renovation of *any* theatre, however modest, was important business and social news—more so when, in Niagara Falls, controversies erupted at city hall and in pulpits over the perceived detriment to the orderly development of the downtown/Queen Street business corridor. This was the case well before the American Albert Huttlémeyer built the Queen Theatre in 1913 (*Record*, Sept. 17, 1912).[8]

Under owner-publisher F.H. Leslie, the *Review* was a substantial newspaper and publishing operation with an average daily circulation of 3,725 in 1921 (Oct. 26).[9] A photograph in the city's one-hundredth anniversary commemorative book, *Images of a Century*, shows Leslie front and centre in 1929, surrounded by thirty-three staff members, seven of them women (Zavitz et al. 2004, 11). The working woman was a factor in Leslie's newspaper operation, and perhaps in pushing the appeal of "Hollywood" for women readers. Another photograph from 1925 includes more than sixty newspaper carriers (all boys, it appears), an indication that many households subscribed to the *Review*. These period photos reveal the vitality of the local newspaper and its employees, though the *Review*'s journalistic style was light on investigative reporting, sometimes having to recant hard news stories within a day of misspeaking facts. Editorial apology was not yet thought necessary. Gossipy speculation on a suicide's possible motives were part of the paper's voyeuristic interest as were sometimes grotesque descriptions of death and catastrophic injuries—including grim industrial accidents and suicides and the all too common drownings in the Niagara River—for the paper served as the city's trusted voice in an era when the publisher was well known to the community, and not a media-generated abstraction as in corporate newspaper ownership today. This is key to understanding how Leslie, as local publisher-owner of a newspaper mandated by him to serve Niagara Falls, Ontario, could adopt and distil Hollywood discourse and develop the character of the *Review* with a keen sense of commerce, public good, and journalistic licence.

Typically, early theatre ads in the *Daily Record* and the *Review* were clustered on "amusements" pages, promoting local entertainments such as dancing, skating, band concerts, road shows, fairs, and rodeos. Short promotional inserts for the theatres on the front page were positioned as if news, reinforcing the movie ads on the amusements pages. The common rhetoric of theatre ads in 1910 and 1912 assured readers of the "refined pictures" and "high class" vaudeville acts, and catered to families. The Princess Theatre on Bridge Street (1908–14) promoted itself as the "Princess *Family* Theatre," charging ten cents admission for adults and five cents for children for Saturday matinees (*Record*, Dec. 7, 1910).[10] Readers were promised that American and British election results would be "flashed on the canvas" (Nov. 8, Dec. 16, 1910), and World Series pictures shown, with "no advance in price" (Nov. 15, 1910). Physical upgrades and investments in new technology, such as the latest Edison moving picture machine at the Princess, were made prominent in press stories and theatre ads (Feb. 10, 1910). By the 1920s many wire stories on the social dangers of movies and indulgent Hollywood stars were reprinted in the *Review* as editorials—the voice of the newspaper for local consumption—pitched to appeal to the moral standards of God-fearing citizens while also managing to titillate readers. In Hollywood, as Stokes argues, this was a "crucial period" of change, namely through "the growth of the studio system, the further development of movie 'stardom,' the innovation of sound, and the beginnings of more formal self-regulation of the industry" (1999, 42). Young star-struck fans read anything "Hollywood" found in fanzines, in the amusements and women's pages of newspapers, and in mother's *Ladies' Home Journal*—and were in tune with the times.

Deep concerns prevailed about the possible effects of Hollywood and its movies before the Motion Picture Producers and Distributors of America (MPPDA) instituted the regulatory Hays Code in 1922 (Cook 1981, 216). The *Review*'s readers would have been well tutored by an uncredited article on the U.S. Postmaster General Will Hays, the man from Washington hired by the studios to clean up Jazz Age Hollywood's reputation, sullied by two major scandals. The front pages updated readers daily on the lurid details of comedian Roscoe "Fatty" Arbuckle's arrest and murder trial, and the (then) unprintable charges in young Lila Gray's divorce suit against Charlie Chaplin, described in a *Los Angeles Times* wire story as "a cruel and faithless husband" (Jan. 11, 1927, 1). These silent-film clowns were characterized in the press as figures of debasement, part of the Hollywood "dream factory" gone wrong. From the *Review*'s front page, to the editorials, to the theatre pages with their eye-catching illustrated movie ads and studio promotion pieces, Niagara Falls readers got a taste of a Hollywood full of appealing contradictions: stories of immorality, photos of glamorous stars, and movies that titillated and thrilled and also, importantly, dramatized social ills and brought images of change into public view.

The Arbuckle case is informative on all counts, especially as sensational news turned moral lesson in the *Review*.[11] The newspaper took its cue as moral guardian by printing the well-orchestrated Hollywood response reported in big-city American papers. The wire stories played into Hollywood's public damage control. Within three days of Arbuckle's arrest, the *Review* began publishing front-page reports from San Francisco and New York on the Arbuckle murder charge and possible perjury by witnesses—"no effort spared to bring the guilty ones to their just deserts" (Sept. 12–13, 1921, 1). Wire pieces from Providence and Chicago were strung onto the main story like a righteous litany designed to script public thinking, concluding with the warning that Arbuckle films "would be laid on the shelf for the present." A day later the *Review* inserted a two-line announcement in the City News section: "The local theatres have cancelled the bookings of Arbuckle films. The Queen Theatre had several bookings but wired Monday canceling them" (Sept. 14, 1921, 4).[12] Eight months later, Arbuckle's acquittal was relegated to a brief insert: "ARBUCKLE FREE—Judge takes five minutes to decide verdict in prisoner's favor" (Apr. 13, 1922, 8). A *Review* editorial the following week seized the opportunity to lambaste "the deviltry of a few motion picture people," liberally quoting Hollywood's police chief (unnamed) to prove the lesson to be learned: "In the motion picture industry as in other lives, the man or woman who gets big returns for little work is apt to go downhill" (Apr. 22, 1922, 2). With this strategy, the local newspaper absorbed "Hollywood" to sermonize on its immoral conduct and, at the same time, to attract attention and promote films.

While indulgent Hollywood life was sensational news in the 1920s, so were the dramatic newspaper and screen pleas for social action on poverty in a city with an adjacent ghetto known as Tintown (*Review*, Jan. 25, 1922, 1). A month before the Arbuckle scandal broke, the *Review* ran a bold front-page plea under the headline, "GIVE A MAN OR WOMAN A JOB" (Feb. 13, 1922). The story pokes at the conscience of the city to act like a "brotherhood ... babies are going hungry ... the dole system is vicious ... city relief comes out of the people's pockets." The following week an ad for the Queen

Theatre promoted "the sensational" success of the film *Over the Hills to the Poor House* (d. Millard 1920), featuring a stark illustration of a broken man at his wife's knees (Feb. 17, 1922, 7). The plot of this remake of a 1908 film involves a mother who is threatened with the poor house but is rescued by one of her abandoned children. The ad reinforces the film's dire domestic theme, and in timely fashion the *Review*'s hard headline story prompting citizens to act charitably found "proof" in the power of the screen melodrama.

BOBBED HAIR—A FLASHPOINT

Though the *Daily Record* and the *Review* were instruments in the "Hollywoodization" of local readers, the newspapers had ambivalent feelings about many of the values that Hollywood was seen to endorse. A prime example is the great hair debate, which surfaced with some regularity in the newspapers until the early 1930s. Study of women's hairstyles may seem a trivial concern, the stuff of fanzines and celebrity gossip; however, feminists have argued since at least the end of World War I that the choice of whether "to bob" or not "to bob" has some disturbing social implications. The Britney Spears shaved-hair affair of our own era is hardly something new in the world of women's efforts to speak through radical-seeming hairstyles and gestures, even though conservative American mainstream media in 2007 viewed Spears not as a woman making a statement but merely as a candidate for rehab. Rose Weitz has argued, using Michel Foucault's figure of the "docile body" (2001, 668), that far from a trivial concern, hairstyle can be an important marker of women's resistance to, or accommodation of, mainstream gender roles—resistance and accommodation being two sides of the same coin (670). For Weitz, rebellious hairstyles allow women "to distance themselves from the system that would subordinate them, to express their dissatisfaction, to identify like-minded others and to challenge others to think about their own actions and beliefs. These everyday, apparently trivial, individual acts of resistance offer the potential to spark social change and, in the long run, to shift the balance of power between social groups" (670). Hair, then, is hardly a trivial affair.

The years after World War I were particularly fraught with respect to gender relations and the decision "to bob" or not "to bob" took on considerable importance in Canada, the United States, and Europe. The battle between the image of the traditional Victorian woman and the Jazz Age flapper was conflicted for both men and women, and the act of cutting the hair became symbolic of women's subordination or liberation.[13] Both women and men

FIGURE 5.3 Victorian up-swept hair. *Daily Record*, 1910; Jazz Age star Gloria Swanson with bobbed hair. *Niagara Falls Evening Review*, 1923

had ambivalent feelings about the New Woman, and so did Hollywood, the Niagara Falls newspapers, and, as described below, at least one movie theatre manager, Jack Ward.

This ambivalence toward a liberated and aggressive woman is nowhere better demonstrated in that era than by F. Scott Fitzgerald's lovely but disturbing short story, "Bernice Bobs Her Hair" (1922). Bernice, a young woman from Eau Clair, is on a month's visit with her cousin Marjorie. An attractive but traditional young woman, unlike Marjorie, she is not a success with the local swells. Frustrated with her old-fashioned, respectable manners and dress, Marjorie shoves Bernice into the Jazz Age with a change of wardrobe and some seemingly *progressive* values. In her new, more aggressive persona, Bernice brazenly announces to Marjorie and her friends that she is going to bob her hair to become "a society vampire." Although she considers the hair cut "unmoral" (129), the telling and planning of the deed excites her as she watches her friends' shocked faces. She has no plans to go through with this "radical" act but continues to tease her friends with the very thought of such social impropriety. Eventually backed into a corner by Marjorie, Bernice is forced to go through with the cut or lose face in front of her various beaux. In an agonizing car ride to the barbershop, which she likens to Marie Antoinette going to the guillotine, she sees the cut as a test of her "sportsmanship" in a man's domain (135). Fitzgerald, in a wonderful rendering of Bernice's fear and excitement, notes her courage and a "narrowing of her eyes," which marks her secret pleasure in the outrageous act (136). Ironically, the bob makes Bernice far less attractive and is doubly ironic in that she must attend, that very night, a lecture called "The Foibles of the Younger Generation" held by the matrons at the Thursday Club with a special discussion of the abomination of bobbed hair. Bernice has thoroughly shocked her friends and family, and at least one of the beaux believes that she "shouldn't have been allowed to go to the movies so much" (138), as though the movies are the source of such "radical" ideas.

The story ends on an unsettling and humorous note as Bernice now realizes that Marjorie in her jealousy goaded her into this anti-social act. As retribution, Bernice sneaks into the sleeping Marjorie's room and amputates her luxurious blond pigtails, and on her way by foot to the train station to return home, she flings the severed pigtails with joyous abandon onto the porch of Marjorie's boyfriend, as though unloading all the social baggage of her gender. Not only has Bernice recognized that her own haircut has "carried consequences" (139), but she is oddly exuberant and "no longer restraining herself" despite the unattractiveness of her new do (140). This remarkable short story embodies both the fears and desires of Jazz Age women caught between an older and more sober respectability and the desire to be done with Victorian restrictions on their freedom. With a discerning eye, Fitzgerald captures the excitement and consequences of breaking the rules even in such a small gesture as cutting the hair.

Movie stars and other entertainers entered the debate about hair length. Irene Castle, a famous dancer of the time who is credited as the first well-known woman to adopt the bob, appeared at the Cataract Theatre in Niagara Falls, New York, as star of the revue *Dances and Fashions of 1923* (*Review*, Apr. 2, 5). In an article in the *Ladies' Home Journal*, Castle glories in the convenience of her bob, which gives her "joy and comfort," but worries that popularizing the style caused her to be blamed for "the homes wrecked and engagements broken because of clipped tresses" (1921, 124). Mary Garden, a well-known singer, also spoke out about her bob. More liberated, or perhaps less diplomatic than Castle, she argues, "I consider getting rid of our long hair one of the many little shackles that women have cast aside in their passage to freedom. Whatever helps their emancipation, however small it may seem, is well worth while" (1927, 8).

Canadian-born Mary Pickford, one of the most popular movie stars of the period, was less enamoured of the bob and did not cut her hair. Her reasons are practical and careerist: she claims that fans write her constantly, urging her not to cut her famous hair. She also reasons that her spouse and mother would be upset if she fell for the short hair "epidemic" and the unattractive "shaved neck" that accompanied it (1927, 9). Her power resides in her feminine curls, and although she sometimes envies those with the easy-to-manage short cuts, she perceives that the new hairstyles express a "radical" position; as a conservative woman, she is unable to follow the new trends even though being "old-fashioned" was not a good thing in Pickford's time. Here, too, there is ambivalence about the New Woman, although in the end Pickford rejected what Mary Garden saw as progressive.

Hollywood films of the period attempted to have it both ways as well. Some of the great female stars of the time, including Pickford and the Gish sisters, gloried in their long curly hair and reticent Victorian personas. Others like Louise Brooks, Clara Bow, and Barbara Stanwyck epitomized the flapper with their sleek, boyish figures and bobbed hair. Like much mass culture that has as its primary goal making enormous amounts of money, having it both ways, with both Vamps and Virgins, is a clever marketing strategy: Hollywood could cater to the youthful, progressive women and their more traditional sisters at the same time. However, movie ads in the *Review* do show the bob and the flapper to be the great attractions of the time, despite the ambivalence of many articles and editorials written about them. A marvellous ad for Lux Soap epitomizes the attractions of the New Woman (May 12, 1931, 7). The ad, for a soap said by actor Lew Ayres to inhibit aging, is almost a full page long and lavishly illustrated with movie star images, forty famous women in all, in an era when photographs were still relatively few in the *Review*. Only two of the famous women do not have bobbed hair! The preferred Hollywood image is youthful, beautiful, and short-haired.[14]

The *Review* eagerly announced that the days of the hair bob were numbered—and happily so, despite the fact that women were flocking to see "flappers" in Hollywood films. Nevertheless, the paper frequently published ads for local clothing stores featuring short-haired, boyish women. The other common, if unexamined, ploy of 1927 was to publish articles written or endorsed by hairdressers announcing that the day of the bob and the flapper are over and that women want to become more "feminine again." In "Beauty Experts Rap Bobbed Hair," one expert comments that the bob "should be abolished forthwith and forevermore" (*Review*, Jan. 4, 11). Mrs. Ruth J. Maurer, head of the National School of Cosmeticians, claims that the bob is "the worst crime committed in the name of beauty"—a bob-haired woman looks like "a Fiji Islander or a cedar mop." In "Short Hair Issue Bobs Up Again," a group of cosmeticians and barbers, meeting in New York City "in solemn convocation," announce the end of the bob (Jan. 25, 1927, 11). Noting that the hair issue had "rent" the country, they announce, "It is high time that hair and hips come back." As late as 1931 this issue was still making news, in a report on a fashion show that featured the return of more "feminine" fashion and false curls to cover shaven necks, and "the strongly feminine garment [the petticoat] … to aid and abet the 'womanly woman' in her seasonable metamorphosis from the athletic flapper type" (Apr. 17, 1931, 18). All of the "professionals" mentioned in these articles share the view that the flapper body and style had become something to cover over, for a more appropriate look. All made large profits from seasonal changes of female fashions and hairstyles, but stress the perceived "unfeminine" nature of the modern woman and disguise the mercenary aspect of their expertise.

Not to be left out of the gender debate, Jack Ward, a much respected and long-time manager of the Capitol Theatre (and later the Seneca, built in 1939 by the Famous Players Canadian Corporation), promoted exhibitor stunts that appealed to young women.[15] The most notable was the great "Screen Opportunity Contest" (Review, June 18, 1927, 3).[16] Ward personally ran various events such as Funny Face contests, dish giveaway promotions, and an "Unbobbed Hair Contest," clearly placing himself on the conservative side of the great hair debate. First prize in the contest was a five-dollar gold piece. In "Ladies Have You Bobbed Your Hair Yet?" readers are told that the women in the contest will be arranged on stage so that the audience cannot see their faces, only their long, lovely hair (Jan. 12, 1927, 7). The publicity goes on to speculate that "inside a year there will be more ladies allowing their hair to grow instead of attending the barber shop" (according to unnamed reports from the "larger cities in Canada and the United States"). One ad for the unbobbed hair contest is part of the larger movie theatre advertisement for the feature, Stranded in Paris (d. Rosson 1926). A picture of the film's star, Bebe Daniels, starring in her "latest gloom chaser," accompanies the movie ad.[17] Ironically, Ms. Daniels sports a bobbed hair style in the ad.[18]

EDITORIALS, MORALS, AND GENDER

The Review's preoccupation with cautionary messages in the 1920s reveals publisher F.H. Leslie's moral thinking and standing as a respected publisher and business leader with great influence in shaping the community. In 1923, an editorial appeared on the folly of diluting church services with "Jazz in the Pulpit," said to be disgusting to "the regular church-goer" (Aug. 31, 2). The newspaper regularly ran large ads in this period for "The Review's Bible Offer," obtainable by mail order (Nov. 13, 1923, 9). In a 1925 editorial, Leslie fiercely supports movie censorship in Ontario and calls for strict control of "so-called literature, which pours across the border."[19] Leslie's pointed remarks on the subject exhibit his Christian values and role as community guardian: "Every observant man and woman knows that there is a veritable flood of smutty publications being imported to Canada ... which pander to the lowest passions of humanity.... To mature persons such publications have little or no appeal; but, to young and immature people, there is a deadly suggestion about such things, dangerous for peace of mind. One scanned the other day, for such publication ... seemed to have been written with gutter mud instead of honest ink."

Editorial essays in the *Review* often praise progress for women that allows them greater freedom ("Athletics for Women," Oct. 26, 1927, 2). One encourages women to enter the work force, in appropriate secretarial roles ("Women Are Becoming Jills of All Trades")—although the editorial does not hesitate to look forward to women taking on more physical jobs like welding or steeple-jacking: "The trend is patently toward greater freedom, broader opportunity for women and—more interesting women. Even those who cry out that the home is being deserted cannot deny that women are more alert and show more intelligent purpose than in the past" (Feb. 15, 1929, 2).

Other editorials and articles are leery about rapid changes in what were previously stable gender roles. The famous (infamous?) Ruth Elder, the "Lady Lindy," the first woman to fly across the Atlantic, is scolded in the *Review*'s editorial "Ruth Elder's Husband"; it is one thing to become a secretary, but another to usurp a man's role! Although Elder is praised for her achievements, the editorial ponders what it must be like to be her husband, the unfortunate Lyle Womack—a man whose wife will not even take his "less euphonious" name. Mr. Womack, quite rightly the editorial points out, refuses to attend the reception held to celebrate his wife's achievements because the "average" man cannot stand such a diminished role (Nov. 23, 1927, 2). An ambitious woman was a troublesome woman.

Women's vulnerability to Hollywood's lure was the subject of much negative public debate, as Stokes argues: "During the 1920s, many parts of the American population disapproved of anything linked to 'flapperolatry,' which they associated with women who wore short skirts, used too much make-up, smoked, and liked modern dances" (1999, 52). The antithesis of the Jazz Age city woman was the homemaker, and early in the decade, the editorial "Home-Making" urges "all girls who do not intend to become teachers" to enroll in a new homemaking course at the city's technical school (*Review*, Aug. 29, 1921, 2). Another editorial waxes glowingly about "What Farm Women Think" (May 31, 1922, 2). However, the consuming woman is given the edge in a full-page promotion of Niagara Falls businesses catering to June brides.

Included in the spread is an ad for the Queen Theatre (6). The iconic, modern-looking bride-to-be, sketched with bobbed hair, is happily engaged in shopping in every cameo ad, as if posing for a series of movie stills anticipating her life's narrative as a wife. In the Queen Theatre cameo she gazes into a vanity mirror that reflects back her star qualities. The film advertised for her patronage is *Bought and Paid For* (d. de Mille, 1922), a melodrama about a woman beset by the question "Is a woman ever justified marrying for money?" (5). As a movie selection for the June bride, this was either coincidental or deliberate programming—or a jest at the consumer-wife.

Such contradictions may have prompted readers to resist editorial biases by actually increasing their movie-going and indulgence in pastimes questioned by the newspaper. Going "over the river"—as local people called border-crossing—to a Niagara Falls, New York, theatre made it possible to see seemingly racy films that might not play on the Canadian side. This mobility stimulated the processes of "Hollywoodization," the notion of what "local" meant to the Niagara Falls, Ontario, community in the 1920s, and what women's desires looked like. Canadians, for example, could see Pola Negri in *Mad Love* (d. Buchowetzki, 1921), depicted in a Bellevue Theatre ad as a vamp with kohl-lined eyes and loosened hair, posed on a bed beside a man wearing a tuxedo (*Review*, Apr. 19, 1923, 6). In their appeal to keep moviegoers on the Canadian side, the Niagara Falls, Ontario, theatres booked movies of similar appeal. The Queen ran films with titillating titles and copy, including *White and Unmarried* (d. Forman, 1921): "Falling heir to a fortune, she graduated from burglary into society" (Jan. 14, 1922, 3). The Web Theatre on Main Street announced a new policy of changing programs "three times a week, Monday, Wednesday, and Friday" (Nov. 16, 1923). Double bills were common. But it was hard to compete with the large ad the *Review* ran in a Saturday edition for *Flaming Youth* (d. Dillon, 1923), starring Colleen Moore, playing at the Strand theatre in Niagara Falls, New York—with the added attraction of four vaudeville acts and "no advance in price." In the flashy newspaper ad, Moore is depicted with loose bobbed hair, dancing so wildly she is propelled high above the jazz club scene below (Nov. 15, 1923, 8). The ad copy is a litany of gender codes associated with the out-of-control Jazz Age city woman.

Columns such as "Good Form" and "Milady's Mirror" for "women folk" appeared in the *Daily Record* as early as 1910 (July 6, July 16), regularizing the newspaper's section for women readers; these were an improvement over the 1909 front-page report of an "Old Maids" Convention in Niagara Falls (Jan. 23). By 1921 the *Review* published *front-page* reports on sewing circles (Aug. 26). Women's domestic roles *were* their social roles. Preoccupation with women's ornamental value undoubtedly interested readers; however, we wonder if women of the day complained when reports of their community service were subsumed under the belittling header "Feminine Gossip" (May 27, 1922, 5).

F.H. Leslie's *Review* of the 1920s either did not comprehend, or chose to ignore, the dilemmas of passionate movie-mad girls, and it was disingenuous to craft a front-page headline, as if hard news, based on a clergyman's advice at a Girl Guide convention: "Girl Guides an Antidote for Affectation, Eye-Brow Pencil, Lipstick, Powder Puff and the Rouge Pot" (May 29, 1922). These were the very beauty tools of the jazz era's liberated screen vamps, commonly pictured in movie ads on the *Review*'s amusement pages and scanned by movie-savvy girls and women.

There were no editorials or forewarnings about the star-struck girls Barbas discusses in *Movie Crazy* (2001). As Barbas tells it, *Photoplay* magazine and other fanzines were part of a "campaign … beginning in 1923 [that] warned women of the 'sex-crazed, hard-boiled' city"—Hollywood. It "had become a 'port of missing girls'" (76). The studios and fanzines tried to undo the overwrought fandom they had encouraged and consumerized, to deter young women from taking off for Hollywood. No such concern was expressed in the *Review*. However, the paper and the city are implicated in a letter sent to Mayor Newman by organizers of a Miss Canada contest, claiming, "Large moving picture studios have been invited to send their representatives to the contest for the purpose of choosing suitable girls for training for movie stars" (1923, Oct. 25). "Training" is the operative word—"Hollywoodization" by another name. As invitation and trial balloon, the published letter conflates civics, Hollywood, and local star quality—omitting the ugly side—to appeal to local young women eager for the spoils and fame of celebrity.

Boys, on the other hand, were targets of a "big brother" campaign run by the city's Rotarians in 1922. The *Review* boosted this public lesson on civics, duty, and morals, said to develop "the boy into a clean, healthy, loyal, God-fearing man … commencing on Sunday … which day will be known as 'Father and Son Day' or 'Every Boy in Church'" (May 18, 1922). "No boy need fear to ask a Rotarian for advice on the question of making the right choice of his life work … to lay the foundation of good citizenship on the corner-stone of the growing boy" (May 20, 1922, 6). Rotary Club members visited every school in the city specifically to speak to boys. Large ads in the *Review* promoted their special theatre night, with Rotarians as companions, to see the wholesome comedy *School Days* (d. Nigh, 1921), said to be "As Clean and Sweet as a Summer Breeze Blowing Through The Meadows" (8).[20] Another screening was reserved for the city's "employed boys," and

FIGURE 5.4 Strand theatre ad for *Flaming Youth*, starring Jazz Age actress Colleen Moore. *Niagara Falls Evening Review*, 1923

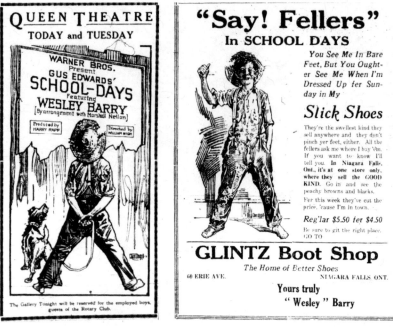

Figure 5.5 Ad for *School Days*, Queen Theatre; tie-in ad for Glintz Boot Shop. *Niagara Falls Evening Review*, 1922

the tie-in ad for a local shoe store featuring the movie's character/actor encouraged all boys to shop in Niagara Falls, Ontario, for quality and style. Gender values, fun, material goods, and local loyalty were turned into a complete package, including country bumpkin copy that literate city boys might mimic.

CONCLUSION

In this racially white, church-observant, small border city—with immigrants, blacks, ethnic groups, and the poor at the margins—F.H. Leslie's *Review* boosted community development and promoted social action campaigns to spur the city's direction. The booster campaigns that produced Niagara Falls' first arena on Victoria Avenue, and the city's supervised playgrounds, were civic projects involving service clubs, city hall, churches, entrepreneurs, prominent citizens, and, crucially, the newspaper.[21] Wholesome and civic-minded populist events often were tied to local movie-going and theatres; the theatres were venues for reporting election results and hosting bible-thumping lectures, beauty pageants, and memorials for British monarchs attended by the city's schoolchildren.

In his study of early movie-going, Moore emphasizes Toronto's metropolitanism—a claim that could not be made about Niagara Falls. However, his argument about the role of the press is generally applicable and certainly pertains to the Niagara Falls *Review* under publisher Leslie: "If the press is an alternative way to map everyday life, it is as partial and inscribed with ideology as any statistical table or map" (2008, 160). Lesley's ideology as a publisher was given to social and moral virtue, as he saw it, in the best interests of a cross-border city he hoped would retain small-town values. At the same time, his newspaper nourished the public's appetite for Americanized popular culture, particularly movies and star culture in a period when the studios' work of selling Hollywood penetrated newspapers across North America.

With the "Hollywoodization" of the public, as well as the newspaper, local movie-goers became more worldly, and, at the same time, the community more subtly Americanized than it already was as a border city. Through the 1920s, local newspaper discourse became preoccupied with movie culture and gender roles, in editorials, theatre promotions, and film production and celebrity news. Women and girls especially were avid movie-goers, and Hollywood materials in print in newspapers and fanzines catered to their interests, as did the theatre managers who ran exhibitor contests and stunts aimed at them. In a city that listened to its newspaper and knew and respected its owner-publisher, the paper cleverly interpreted Hollywood stories for a local audience by editorializing on movieland culture. The rhetoric likely prompted at least some readers to be wary of the newspaper's over-determined concerns about the New Woman and the sins of Hollywood, and thus become media-literate about the movies and what they read.

In the 1920s, theatres in Niagara Falls, Ontario, were still being built (the Web), and envisioned (the Niagara Grand)[22]—with the atmospheric Seneca Theatre still to come a decade later. Throughout, managers were creative, appealed to their home audiences, and skilfully marketed their theatres. Ushers and projectionists were loyal, and movie-goers of all ages felt safe and often satisfyingly delinquent from school or work on a weekday afternoon watching movies. When pranksters broke the rules of theatre conduct (loosely monitored, though regulated by legislation and bylaws), there were few repercussions and a teenager might sneak in through a fire door, often with the aid of a known usher.

By the late 1920s, Leslie's *Review* welcomed the corporate investment of a major theatre chain in downtown theatres, speaking for the city and the movie-going public. Nevertheless, even after the takeover of Huttlemeyer's Queen Theatre by the Famous Players Canadian Corporation there remained a unique *localness* in the practice of shopping and movie-going on both sides of the border, until the Great Depression, when the focus changed radically with newspaper ads urging the citizens of Niagara Falls, Ontario, to shop at home and with the Capitol Theatre hosting events like the Salvation Army's "Great Mass Meeting," presided over by Mayor Swayze, city council, clergy, and "leading citizens" in aid of community relief (*Review*, Apr. 11, 1931, 7). In later decades, when the impersonal multiplex became the norm for movie exhibition, all the original theatres eventually went out of business or were demolished—in retrospect, a pointed signal of the downtown's eventual slow decline and the de-centring of the community.

Niagara Falls' theatres had served as the city's social centres—at once *constructing* community and *reproducing* "Hollywood," in line with the value-laden work of the newspaper and the agendas of the studios and the times. The city's movie-going public would be confronted with novelties other than Hollywood movies in the 1940s when sex-ed and marital-relations films were exhibited at the Capitol Theatre; the public came in droves but panicked at this clumsy, gender-segregated attempt to educate and contain them. The local public had a voice, albeit the voice of mayhem.[23]

Thanks to the many Niagara Falls residents who so willingly agreed to be interviewed, to the ever helpful and resourceful Andrew Porteus and staff at the Niagara Falls Public library where we spent many months searching newspaper archives, to Pat and Gary Ward for the Pathé photograph of Famous Players Canadian Corporation theatre managers (including Gary's father, the late Jack Ward, long-time manager of the Capitol and Seneca theatres), and to Scott Leslie for informal conversations about his great-grandfather Frank H. Leslie.

NOTES

1 In 1918, The *Daily Record* evolved into the *Niagara Falls Evening Review* under a new publisher. Generally we refer to *The Review* (its current name), shortened with the switch to morning delivery. Page numbers are included where possible.

2 The first fanzine, *Motion Picture Story Magazine*, was established in 1911 by the head of Vitagraph studio; in 1912 its "Answer Man" column apparently received some 2,500 letters from readers (Barbas 2001, 24–25). Although *Photoplay*, the rival fanzine (also established in 1912), generally confirmed fans' hopes that stars' lives resembled their screen roles, sarcastic truth-telling was also part of the rhetoric: one letter writer was told by a columnist "to forget the 'reel' [movie star] Alice Hollister" (26). To many, this would have been sobering news; to others, instructive reading.

3 In a conservative city like Niagara Falls, women fans would have been embarrassed to send such letters to the local newspaper, and we doubt that the paper would have published them; the writers of the few letters-to-the-editor we found were all men.

4   See Paul Moore (2008), 109–11. By the late 1920s, the "vertical nexus of producer-distributor-exhibitor created a model on which the international success of Hollywood was based. In Canada, Famous Players Canadian Corporation ... controlled first-run theatres in all major cities. This may not have been, in itself, a problem but, directly or through subsidiaries, the company also controlled the supply of films to theatres.... The stifling control ... in Canada was to lead, in 1930, to an investigation under the Combines Investigation Act." Peter Morris, *Embattled Shadows: A History of Canadian Cinema 1895–1939* (Montreal and Kingston: McGill-Queen's University Press, 1978), 176.

5   An uncredited review of *Showboat* in *Time* magazine (Mon., Apr. 29, 1929) reads, "Having bought the cinema rights to Miss Ferber's book ... [producer Carl Laemmle] bought also the rights to the musical comedy that Florenz Ziegfeld had made out of it. Somehow the stretched narrative had to be delayed long enough to make it vocal. The best singing is done in a prologue, related to the text only by its tunes, in which Helen Morgan, whose voice is later apparently heard issuing from the lips of Laura La Plante, sings 'My Bill' and 'I Can't Help Lovin' That Man.'... Director Harry Pollard has made a picturesque, old-fashioned, tedious melodrama, full of conventional photography and exaggerated acting."

6   Scott Leslie describes his great-grandfather, F.H. Leslie, as "a very religious man and big on temperance, nature, literature and history ... interested in parks, churches and historical sites."

7   Written by Sir Elenezer Howard and published in 1898 in England, then revised and reissued in 1902 as *Garden Cities of Tomorrow*.

8   Huttlemeyer's Queen Theatre became an important hub of business, entertainment, and community events in the developing downtown corridor but was roundly disavowed before it was even built. The *Daily Record* covered the city council meetings in 1912 over the licensing of the theatre, conditional on the addition of a second storey to comply with city regulations. Huttlemeyer agreed and got the go-ahead to begin construction, despite the delegation of property owners and the minister of St. Andrew's Presbyterian, who feared the immorality of movies and "registered a hearty kick against the proposition," concerned that "the location of the theatre ... would depreciate" property values (Sept. 17, 1912, 1).

9   The *Review* was a family-run newspaper with F.H. Leslie at the helm for over sixty years (1918 to 1973). In 1973 the paper was sold to the Thomson group, then in the mid-1990s to the Hollinger Corporation, then to CanWest News Service, then in 2003 to Osprey Media (under Sun Media, a Quebecor Media Company) (*Review*, June 13, 2006).

10   See Richard Abel, "The Movies in a 'Not So Visible Place,'" in Kathryn H. Fuller-Seeley, ed., *Hollywood in the Neighborhood: Historical Case Studies of Local Moviegoing* (Berkeley: University of California Press, 2008), 107–29. Abel discusses local film distribution and exhibition in Des Moines, Iowa (1911 to 1914), with particular focus on the "unique perspective" of newspaper discourse there, contributing to the rise of star and fan culture, with special appeal to, and for, local women readers.

11   Waller writes, Arbuckle was "charged with manslaughter in the death of actress Virginia Rappe at a party in 1921. From this date until early 1923, through the comedian's three trials and Hays' deliberations concerning Arbuckle's future in

the industry, this situation remained prime copy for newspapers in Lexington and across the country.... The sheer quantity of front page coverage ... attests to the drawing power, if not the symbolic import, of this story of decline and fall" (1995), 236.

12   Arbuckle was popular with fans; however, when the scandal broke in newspapers many wrote to fanzines urging "studios to ban the actor from films" (Barbas, 28). They had followed the newspaper coverage of the case and could not be naïve about Hollywood's human failings.

13   See http://www.gotothebible.com/HTML/RiceJohn.html for a very regressive take on gender relations and women's hair.

14   The Eton Crop was an extreme cut, exceedingly short and Brylcreemed flat to the skull. Performer Josephine Baker was notorious for her Eton crop.

15   See Richard Koszarinski, *An Evening's Entertainment: The Age of the Silent Feature Picture 1915–1928* (Berkeley: University of California Press, 1994). Stunts (contests, amateur shows, giveaways) were common in this era, geared to getting people into movie theatres and also engaging in cultural debate.

16   First prize was an all-expenses-paid trip to Hollywood for the "lucky young lady and her chaperone" for a screen test—a contest deemed irresistible to star-struck young girls. The prize included a new car (an Overland-Whippet Six). Local merchants donated money and prizes, and thirty Ontario theatres were involved in the contest, an exhibitor stunt that originated in the Famous Players Canadian Corporation. Ward participated avidly in this contest as he did in other ventures promoting Hollywood and its movies.

17   In a *New York Times* movie review (Dec. 13, 1926), Mordaunt Hall writes, "Miss Daniels, as Julie, goes through this picture in a rollicking fashion. She is a poor girl, who is the fortunate winner of a ticket to Paris ... dropped by an airplane in an exploitation scheme to advertise a brand of perfume. As the tale skims along Julie is beheld in the French capital, the victim of an ignominious apache with boundless nerve. Later Julie is mistaken for the Countess Pasada, who apparently has a habit of traveling incognito. The mere fact that Julie is offered a magnificent suite in a hotel does not dismay her any more than does the arrival of a half dozen trunks filled with dazzling gowns."

18   The *Review* sometimes dropped its cautionary rhetoric, publishing such wire stories as "Bobbed Brains Worse Than Bobbed Hair" (Oct. 26, 1921, 1), which quotes an American college president who admires smart women, but not without assuming how they think: "The average girl of the day is far better equipped mentally than the girl of a generation ago.... [She] wants to be useful as well as ornamental."

19   The Ontario Censor Board was appointed by government in 1911 and has had a colourful history of cases, opponents, and supporters. It was renamed the Ontario Film *Review* Board in the 1980s. See Waller (1995) for a discussion of how two local dailies in Lexington, Kentucky, took opposing editorial views in a period of wide lobbying for movie censorship and gender-appropriate films: *The Leader* was the "vigilant watchdog for decency" (235) while *The Herald* took the position that "the good sense of the American public and of [movie] industry leaders" would progress (236). Also see Moore (2008), Chapter 4, "Senseless Censors and Startling Deeds: From Police Beat to Bureaucracy," 113–52.

20 "School Days," co-written in 1907 by vaudevillian, publisher, and producer Gus Edwards, with Will Cobb, was a hit song that "inspired a craze for school acts." See Frank Cullen and Florence Hackman, *Vaudeville, Old and New: Encyclopedia of Variety Performers in America* (New York: Routledge, 2006), 350. The "school days" title-theme was reproduced in several films in the 1920s, including animation shorts and a documentary. In Nigh's 1921 feature, schoolboy pranks provide the fun, and in the narrative's turnabout, a fourteen-year-old orphan (Wesley Barry) learns the values of education and family.

21 We are indebted to Joan and Ron Brown for a charming snapshot showing British actor Michael Redgrave—circa 1940s, by which time the Odeon (Rank) chain owned the Capitol Theatre. Redgrave is surrounded by a group of smiling children at a Hermes Club-sponsored playground, probably the one that was located at Erie Avenue and Huron Street behind the old farm-market site.

22 Following months of publicity and large ads calling for share-holders, Mayor Stephens turned the sod for the planned "amusement house and business block" at the corner of Queen Street and Buckley Avenue (*Review*, Aug. 2, 1921, 1). The theatre was never built, and the excavation remains a hidden hollow behind the block of shops.

23 The sexes were separated for the sex-ed and marital-relations films, which included talks. As a teenage usher in the Capitol theatre in the 1940s, Ron Brown witnessed the reactions to the "pseudo sex movie" *Mom and Dad* and a compilation U.S. Navy training film "depicting the ravages of venereal disease." In retrospect he wrote, "Chaos resulted—patrons fainted and fights broke out. Police and first aid personnel were at every performance. This continued for a solid week with the lineups extending from Queen Street to Park Street" (*Weekly Chronicle*, July 31, 1998, 5).

WORKS CITED

Barbas, Samantha. *Movie Crazy: Fans, Stars, and the Cult of Personality*. New York: Palgrave, 2001.

Castle, Irene. "I Bobbed My Hair and Then...." *Ladies' Home Journal* (Oct. 1921).

Cook, David A. *A History of Narrative Film*, 3rd. ed. New York and London: Norton, 1996.

Fitzgerald, F. Scott. "Bernice Bobs Her Hair." In *Flappers and Philosophers*. New York: Charles Scribner's Sons, 1922: 116–40.

Fuller, Kathryn Helgesen. "At the Picture Show." In Ina Rae Hark, ed., *Exhibition: The Film Reader*. London and New York: Routledge, 2002: 41–49.

Garden, Mary. "Why I Bobbed My Hair." *Pictorial Review* (Apr. 1927).

Moore, Paul S. *Now Playing: Early Moviegoing and the Regulation of Fun*. Albany: State University of New York Press, 2008.

Pickford, Mary. "Why I Have Not Bobbed Mine." *Pictorial Review* (Apr. 1927).

Stokes, Melvyn. "Female Audiences of the 1920s and Early 1930s." In Melvyn Stokes and Richard Maltby, eds., *Identifying Hollywood's Audiences: Culture, Identity and the Movies*. London: British Film Institute, 1999: 42–50.

Waller, Gregory A. *Main Street Amusements: Movies and Commercial Entertainment in A Southern City, 1896–1930*. Washington: Smithsonian Institution Press, 1995.

Weitz, Rose. "Women and Their Hair: Seeking Power through Resistance and Accommodation." *Gender and Society*, 15:5 (Oct. 2001), 667–86.

Zavitz, Sherman, et al. *Images of a Century: The City of Niagara Falls, Canada, 1904–2004*. Niagara Falls: Centennial Committee/Maracle Press, 2004.

WHERE IS THE LOCAL IN LOCAL RADIO? | The Changing Shape of Radio Programming in St. Catharines

LAURA WIEBE TAYLOR

INTRODUCTION

Turn on a radio in St. Catharines, Ontario, and you will hear strong broadcast signals coming in across the dial, spanning the spectrum of FM and AM wavelengths and music and talk formats. Five of those signals—four of them from commercial radio stations—originate within the city itself, constituting and constructing the St. Catharines community from inside its geographical and municipal borders, while competitors from several nearby cities both smaller (Welland and Niagara Falls) and larger (Hamilton and Toronto in Canada, Buffalo in the United States) strive to enfold St. Catharines in their own expansive definitions of the local. Three of the five St. Catharines radio stations broadcast from under the same roof, a historic downtown landmark known officially as the William Hamilton Merritt Broadcasting House, more familiarly as "The Whitehouse of Talk" and "The Whitehouse of Rock."[1] The recent ownership of these stations has less local currency than their physical home; in legal and financial terms, 610 CKTB, 105.7 EZ Rock, and 97.7 HTZ-FM belong to Astral Media, "the largest radio broadcaster in Canada."[2]

Despite corporate ownership of radio stations—the norm rather than the anomaly—radio's "localness" is one of its key attractions for many listeners. In 2005, Canadian survey respondents consistently ranked local radio among their top three sources for access to local information, including news, weather, events, and activities.[3] Broadcasters are highly conscious of radio's local appeal, and terms like "local" and "community" are deeply imbedded

FIGURE 6.1 William Hamilton Merritt Broadcasting House, home of CKTB, EZ-Rock, and HTZ-FM

in radio discourse, forming a part of broadcasting rhetoric, if not always its practice. But traffic and weather reports, advertisements for local businesses, and station identifications or promotional spots that refer to the station's hometown may be the only truly local elements of a contemporary-format radio broadcast (Berland 1998, 139; 2003, 234, 237). Although radio has the potential to contribute to and "nourish" local communities, it often falls short, and programming generally offers little substantial engagement with the community it purportedly serves (2003, 235).

At the same time, the "localization" of a station's broadcast provides one of the few ways in which radio can differentiate itself in the contemporary mass media environment. By striving to create a sense of community ownership and project a distinct identity, radio stations seek to assert their continuing relevance despite playlists and scheduling grids that closely mirror those of countless other stations throughout North America. Constructing a sense of local identity out of the particular demands and demographics of the local market—a recognizable (if not recognizably) local face—has long been one of radio's competitive strategies, particularly in its struggle to retain listeners and advertisers that might otherwise turn to television (Berland 2003, 237). The need for distinct local expression is becoming even more pronounced in the industrialized North American entertainment/infotainment market, with so many outlets drawing from the same news sources and music lists, and competing with the decentralized multimedia immediacy of the Internet and satellite feeds. Localization is a pressing need for the stations themselves, competing for their share of the public's attention, but also for the many communities that are disappearing from mass media view.

This case study focuses on the efforts of the three Astral radio stations in St. Catharines to construct and maintain their local identities even in the face of corporate ownership. The oldest of these stations, CKTB, has made efforts to develop and maintain this identity since 1933—through changes in fortune, ownership, and broadcast trends, the addition of sister stations and competitors in the local market, and the rise of new technologies and flashier media attractions to claim listeners' attention. I explore the means by which these stations—CKTB, EZ Rock, and HTZ-FM—foster the perception of their local identities, namely by advertising their local orientation, encouraging local audiences to interact with the stations or their representatives; programming local or locally produced content, and engaging (or failing to engage) with local artists and community events.

As part of the Astral Media radio group, AM station Newstalk 610 CKTB, and FM stations 105.7 EZ Rock and 97.7 HTZ-FM share house nationally with many other radio outlets following the "Newstalk," "Best Rock," and "EZ Rock" formats.[4] CKTB'S efforts to produce a sense of its local identity are ongoing and multi-faceted. While CKTB, HTZ-FM, and EZ Rock adhere fairly closely to the standardized models the commercial radio industry favours (where "local" is inserted into a formatted matrix of non-localizing programming), locality has been and remains an important emphasis for these stations and a crucial construction in their relationships with the audiences they aim to serve. CKTB and its affiliates have relied on their ability to maintain some sense of local relevance and community ownership within St. Catharines, even when "the local" in local radio holds little more substance than the airwaves.

Besides occupying a significant place in broadcasting rhetoric and strategies, the issue of "the local" in radio has been taken up in studies from differing perspectives and a range of disciplines, from popular music to cultural and communication studies. Eric Rothenbuhler and Tom McCourt, for example, have situated "the local" of local radio within the shift from network programming to format radio (2002); for Matthew Killmeier it is part of the move from mass appeal broadcasting to narrowcasting (2001). Jody Berland finds "the local" only in advertisements and deejay conventions that insert local markers into what is otherwise an abstract and imaginary space (1998, 2003). Some scholars see "the local" as a casualty of industry consolidation and corporate mergers (Huntemann 1999), or of rationalized programming strategies (Rothenbuhler 1987). Others see "the local" as a significant influence on programming decisions despite corporate ownership and industry trends (Ahlkvist 2001). In St. Catharines, localness serves as a framing device more than a substantive component of commercial radio programming. Interpreting, defining, and enacting localness varies between radio formats, with the city's "newstalk" station, CKTB, demonstrating a closer relationship to the local than the music stations. As St. Catharines' oldest radio station, CKTB is the one most invested in the local community.

The picture emerging from the critical discourse on radio broadcasting tends to depict commercial radio's relationship with local communities as tenuous, a useful construction that has more to do with the station's mailing address and the business of selling listeners to advertisers than it does with local culture. Radio, according to Antoine Hennion and Cecile Meadel, is more mediator than media, constructing the audience it claims to serve and seeks to sell through a network of transformations and negotiations in which that audience has no independent existence or voice (1986, 294, 297–300). Contemporary-music format radio, Jody Berland observes, both addresses and represents its target community (2003, 236), each station constructing a distinct "musical identity" attuned to a specific demographic whose tastes are already predefined by market research: "the community which speaks and is spoken through [radio] is also constituted by it" (232). By such means, contemporary commercial radio maintains that it is "the local medium," even as the medium becomes increasingly delocalized (231). For commercial music radio, local information comes more as a series of regular interruptions rather than serving as a focal point. Music radio does not simply divorce audiences from a sense of the local; it displaces them, situating listeners in an "abstract" or "imaginary" space, which is, Berland notes, either "semantically elsewhere or without any perceptible signification of place," unless that place is the mythical California invoked by numerous pop songs (1998, 134).

Eric Rothenbuhler argues that format radio programmers' reliance on broadcasting and music industry information sources in the decision-making process means that local audience interests have little effect on radio playlists (1987, 89–92). Additionally, changes to broadcasting policy in North America and the media mergers that followed have intensified many critics' concerns about radio stations' local focus and the decline in local broadcasting content and autonomy (Huntemann 1999, 390–92). Yet corporate ownership and industry consolidation have not caused most commercial radio stations to de-emphasize their local affiliations, and the constructed "localization" that radio continues to effect invites further study. Individual stations may draw upon similar conventions and practices to negotiate the balance of the local and non-local in their programming and self-promotion, but an examination of the ways in which particular commercial radio stations work to produce the communities they target offers a more detailed picture in the context of a rapidly changing and globalized multimedia environment.

RADIO IN ST. CATHARINES

The first sustained commercial radio enterprise in St. Catharines emerged with the founding of CKTB in 1930 by local brewery owner Edward T. Sandell.[5] The station initially aired small segments of programming through a radio station broadcasting from Hamilton, Ontario, but began broadcasting on its own wavelength on November 7, 1933.[6] The "TB" of the station's call letters came from the name of Sandell's brewery, Taylor and Bate, and local translations of the radio station's call letters included "Cool Keg of Taylor and Bate" or "Canadians Know Their Beer." CKTB's business name was the Silver Spire Broadcasting Station Limited, after its "silver spire" transmitter tower, the first self-supporting vertical radio antenna used in Canada,[7] and Taylor and Bate began to produce Silver Spire lager and ale in its honour.[8] Sandell owned the station until his death in 1943, when its ownership passed to the Burgoyne family, publishers of the St. Catharines daily newspaper, *The Standard*, and the Silver Spire Broadcasting Station became the Niagara District Broadcasting Company Limited.[9] The Burgoyne family owned CKTB until 1981, when they sold their radio interests to Standard Broadcasting.[10]

CKTB's first sister station, originally called CKTB-FM, went on air in 1949,[11] initially sharing the AM channel's programming and operating simply as a mirror of the other's signal.[12] By 1975 CKTB-FM was broadcasting with increased power and sound quality, and in 1979 the FM station established its own distinct identity by switching to a country format and new call letters: CJQR.[13] The station adhered to the country music format until 1986 when it again took on a new name—CHTZ, or HTZ-FM—and changed to a mix of classic and contemporary rock.[14] Local light rock station CHRE 105.7 FM was a late addition to the "family," joining CKTB and HTZ-FM after a series of ownership changes in the late 1990s and early 2000s. Standard Broadcasting sold CKTB in 1996 and HTZ-FM in 1998 to the Niagara-based Affinity Radio Group, which took control of CHRE as well, in 1999, and CHRE moved into the Merritt House at 12 Yates Street in 2000 when the larger Telemedia Radio Group purchased all three stations from Affinity.[15] Light Rock became EZ Rock a year later before CKTB, HTZ-FM, and EZ Rock changed hands again as part of a large exchange between Standard Radio and Telemedia in 2002 (CCF 2005). All three stations became the property of Astral Media when the corporation purchased Standard Radio in 2007.[16] By the late 1990s CKTB, like many AM stations, had adopted the news and talk-radio format, but both CHRE and HTZ-FM maintained their music formats—soft rock and hard rock, respectively.

RADIO'S COMMUNITY RHETORIC

Under Standard Radio, CKTB, EZ Rock, and HTZ-FM all emphasized their community commitment, declared in promotional material the stations provided on their websites. CKTB called itself "a vital community partner." EZ Rock presented its local dedication as part of the station's business philosophy: "Being involved in the local community is vital to ... success." HTZ-FM, in the spirit of its more aggressive format, expressed its commitment to the local community in active rather than philosophical terms: "HTZ-FM takes every opportunity to make a difference in the community." In all three cases, like Standard Radio itself, the stations primarily equate a commitment to the local community with promotional support and fundraising for charities, although the individual stations stress their work with local organizations: the Niagara Peninsula Children's Centre (CKTB and HTZ-FM), local children's charities (EZ Rock and HTZ-FM), and local women's shelters and hospitals (EZ Rock). Astral Media, on its website, indicates a more national and less charity-oriented focus but the company also stresses that its recently acquired radio stations are to remain rooted in their local communities.

Station employees, past and present, like CKTB employee Mike Saunders, echo the website's reference to local charity work. Saunders expands on the station's local focus and engagement: "knowing what's going on in the community" and being "in the community" are both significant aims for CKTB.[17] One implication of this attitude is the need for local programming content as well. The station "must know the market and what matters. It can't be all syndicated," Saunders explains. He sees sister stations EZ Rock and HTZ-FM as less community-oriented, although he admits that even at CKTB the commitment to the community was "not always as strong as it could have been" and "drifted in and out" between the early 1980s and 2000 when the station passed through several sets of (mostly corporate and non-local) hands. Former CKTB employee Bob Johnston also remembers a loss of local focus in the 1980s after Standard Broadcasting took over at CKTB,[18] but several letters to the editor and articles published in the *Standard* in the early and late 1990s indicate later low points, suggesting that station reorganization and imported programming had produced a decline in service, particularly local news and events coverage. Saunders asserts that Standard Radio became very committed to the station's local involvement, so that by 2006 CKTB was "very much a part of the fabric of life in the community."

FIGURE 6.2 "Walk a Mile in Her Shoes" benefit for Gillian's Place, Oct. 2007. Jack Peets (EZ-Rock), Iron Mike Bensson (HTZ-FM), and Tim Denis (CKTB), Market Square, St. Catharines

Astral, it seems, has yet to embark on any dramatic changes to the station's programming approach.

CKTB's relationship with the local community has long been part of its rhetoric, elaborated in a 1941 article in the *Standard* by Lou Cahill, former member of the Niagara News Bureau.[19] The article quotes Edward Sandell describing his station as "local," and reports on CKTB's dedication to the St. Catharines community, notably "the station's reputation as an outlet for sports broadcasts," its "musical, civic development, and programs for shut-ins," and in a foreshadowing of radio rhetoric to come, its fundraising work for charity. The article ends with the assertion that, despite its commercial interests, CKTB "has never neglected any effort to promote the city or its people." More than sixty years later, Lou Cahill still remembered CKTB and Sandell as "community-minded" (interview, Sept. 6, 2005).

Positive portrayals of CKTB's role within the St. Catharines community began even before the station was officially on the air. Introducing CKTB to local audiences three days in advance of the station's first sign-on, the November 4, 1933, edition of the *Standard* described Sandell, already known for "public-spirited activities," and his intention to make room for local Rotary Club fundraising during his station's first day of programming. An article in the same edition of the newspaper reported that CKTB would provide St. Catharines with "the best talent available," meaning local talent, whenever it did not compromise program quality, even though CKTB would be part of a small but "ambitious" three-station Ontario network. The article also characterized CKTB as a "milestone in the progress of St. Catharines," akin to major local developments such as the city's securing "a dock of its own on the great Ship Canal," its "location on the main permanent highway," and its airplane "facilities" (1933, 4). Eight years later in 1941, Cahill depicted CKTB as not merely a marker of accomplishment but as an active force contributing to St. Catharines' "steady progress."

Like Cahill, Bob Johnston used the words "community" and "local" when he reminisced about CKTB, characterizing the station's local focus as "deliberate" and arguing that addressing the local, and covering their own area, is what private radio stations do best: "If you weren't local, what was the sense of being a radio station?" In the decades following the publication of Cahill's article, references to the community continued to play a significant role in the station's rhetoric and self-promotions; more recent newspaper advertisements and features on CKTB tend to echo Johnston's sentiment. The station underlined its community involvement in a fiftieth-anniversary feature printed in the *Standard*, quoting both founder Sandell and Bob Reinhart (then general manager) on CKTB's dedication to community service: Reinhart declared that CKTB "must live in the community, not live off of it."[20] A similar message appears in an address delivered on January 14, 1981, to the St. Catharines Chamber of Commerce by Standard Broadcasting president Don Hartford after the Toronto-based Standard Broadcasting took over CKTB and CJQR: Hartford assured his listeners that the stations "must cater always to the local needs of St. Catharines and its neighbours."

Hartford's local references highlight the sometimes arbitrary and subjective way in which community boundaries are defined, yet concepts of the local are frequently constructed along such geographical and political lines. Although Hartford invokes municipal borders, in Canada "local" can take on a national sense, where regional differences within the country are less significant than distinguishing Canadian culture from that of the United States. The conflation of the local and the national informs Canadian documents such as the 1957 government report on broadcasting, which refers to radio's capacity for "increasing knowledge and understanding of regional problems throughout the whole country" while discussing American broadcasting as a threat to Canadian national identity.[21] Yet for St. Catharines radio stations, so near the Canada–United States border, preserving any particular "Canadian-ness" seems to be less important than constructing a local identity that encompasses the communities within their reach and within which they are physically located. Buffalo is no farther from St. Catharines than Hamilton, Toronto is farther by half, and Niagara Falls, New York, is closer than all three. However, while the St. Catharines radio stations' definitions of local are primarily Canadian, they are not exclusively so, tied more to the Niagara Region than to Canada.

Sandell identified CKTB's audience as comprising residents of Ontario and "neighboring American states" (Cahill 1941). Over many years of broadcasting, CKTB's definitions of the local have ranged from the city in which it resides (St. Catharines), to the broader region (Niagara) or, as in Hartford's address, the city and the surrounding communities. Only in its sportscasting did CKTB position itself as a Canadian station.[22] CKTB defines its local community as Niagara both on air and on its website: Station slogans have described CKTB as "the voice of Niagara" or "Niagara's News, Talk and Sports," and show titles include *Niagara at Noon* or *Rewind Niagara*. Such references are common examples of format-radio conventions, and when used on air they serve to emphasize a station's "localness, immediacy and accessibility"—as Berland describes the "live and local context" (2003, 237). With similar taglines EZ Rock has offered a definition of the local community that resembles CKTB's, identifying itself both on-air and on-line as "Niagara's Best Variety of Yesterday and Today," or simply "Niagara's EZ Rock." HTZ-FM originally pursued a similar sense of the local, depicting itself as "Niagara's Rock" in early print advertising (June 20, 1986), but the station now casts the net of locality a little wider, promoting itself as "Southern Ontario's Best Rock." However, HTZ-FM also announces events across the border in Buffalo and Niagara Falls, New York, and on its website identifies its audience as listeners from Niagara, southern Ontario and Western New York—"Buffalo to Toronto, and all points in between."

While promotional material and event announcements by CKTB, EZ Rock, and HTZ-FM reveal their respective takes on defining "the local," sponsors and advertisers represent another way in which commercial radio sets boundaries to target communities and remind listeners of the stations' local affiliations. Saunders mentions local businesses along with local charities when elaborating on the station's community involvement. Berland notes that local advertisers provide private broadcasters with the majority of their revenue—and "the only tangible proof" of their "local allegiance" (2003, 234). So it is not surprising if local businesses figure high in a station's concept of local engagement. Early radio relied heavily on network advertising (Rothenbuhler and McCourt 2002, 378), using tie-ins to local dealers of nationally advertised products to inject local references into network programs.[23] After World War II, when network advertising shifted to television and the number of radio stations dramatically increased, local advertisers became significantly more important to the survival of individual stations (Rothenbuhler and McCourt 2002, 378). Early advertising on CKTB revealed a mix of local and national sponsorship, or national advertisements with local tie-ins. For example, Canadian oil company McColl-Frontenac sponsored a program featuring James Melton (American singer and radio performer), promoting a tie-in to the local dealer of the company's Red Indian motor oils.[24] Sandell's own brewery sponsored a local musical group called the Taylor and Bate Barnstormers,[25] but other local advertisers, such as Macdonald's Battery [and] Tire Service, sponsored specific broadcasts or programs as well.[26] Footwear supplier Dillon and Moore presented a fifteen-minute Wednesday-evening program to help listeners "regain the joy of youthful feet,"[27] and the *Standard* sponsored daily performances by the Allan Roth Orchestra at 5 p.m.[28] Other programs broadcast by CKTB came complete with national sponsorship, including the Catelli-backed Friday-night children's quiz show, *Young Canada on Parade.*[29]

CKTB still broadcasts a mix of national and local advertisements, and local and national commercials air on EZ Rock and HTZ-FM as well. Although the national ads tend to avoid specific spatial or geographical references, instead promoting businesses one might find in any city or directing listeners to 1-800 phone numbers and websites, commercials for local businesses generally reflect each station's own designation of its community's geographical boundaries. An advertisement for the restaurant East Side Mario's, for example, is the same commercial broadcast on radio signals in other Ontario and Canadian cities, including Kitchener-Waterloo and Edmonton. On the other hand, advertisements for St. Catharines businesses such as the Pen Centre Mall (on EZ Rock) or Kala's Home Hardware (on CKTB) are unlikely to air outside the Niagara area and thus anchor the stations to the city from which they broadcast. Other commercials demonstrate the stations' efforts to expand their local definition beyond the city. A promotional spot for the duty-free shop at the Peace Bridge linking Fort Erie, Ontario, and Buffalo, New York, stretches all three stations' communities to the lower corner of the Niagara Peninsula, while a commercial for a strip club (Whiskey A GoGo) in the

FIGURE 6.3 "Have a Heart" Radiothon, Pen Centre Mall, St. Catharines. Mark Monroe, Laurie Walsh, Jack Peets (EZ-Rock), Kevin Jack, Tim Denis (CKTB), and Iron Mike Bensson (HTZ-FM)

Greater Toronto Area demonstrates HTZ-FM's more diffuse conception of locality and attempts to appeal to an audience distinct from that of its sister stations. HTZ-FM targets adults—"men and women alike"—but particularly young men, while EZ Rock identifies its audience as "female adult listeners 25 to 49 and established families" (website), and CKTB targets a wide and mixed demographic (Saunders).

LOCAL RADIO AND ITS LISTENERS

The three stations' self-identification with specific geographical areas is closely linked to their efforts to encourage a sense of community ownership. Fostering the notion that they belong to, and speak for, the local community is tied to a broader discourse, the rhetoric surrounding the role of radio broadcasting in Canada. The country's Broadcast Act of 1991 declares that "the Canadian broadcasting system shall be effectively owned and controlled by Canadians" but also states that the actual radio frequencies are "public property." Thus, slogans like "Southern Ontario's Best Rock" (HTZ-FM) or "Niagara's Best Variety" (EZ Rock) anchor the stations within particular regions or municipalities but also imply that they belong to the regions they target. The promotional spots and advertising campaigns describing Newstalk 610 as the "voice of Niagara" express CKTB's claim to speak for the community whose boundary it simultaneously defines, suggesting to local listeners that the station expresses listeners' opinions and beliefs (rather than informing and forming them). CKTB has used this tactic for a long time, for example, in newspaper ads for the station that identified CKTB to readers as "Your Station" (*Standard*, Sept. 30, 1944, 3), "Your Niagara District Station" (Feb. 12, 1949, 19), and the "Voice of the City" (June 27, 1967). Johnston's recollections from his time at CKTB suggest that listeners responded at times to this idea of the audience holding a stake in the station's programming: "In the early days, every time we tried to make changes we'd get calls from listeners saying, 'What are you trying to do to *our* radio station?'" (2005, emphasis Johnston's).

Radio stations also encourage a sense of community ownership by suggesting that they are receptive to feedback, and that listeners have a say in programming through solicited responses and participation. Although audience engagement has changed over the years, particularly technologically, a few common means for audiences to interact with stations and their representatives have been in place for decades, such as submitting comments or requests, entering contests, and participating in surveys and discussion groups. The stations use airtime to remind listeners of these opportunities, but also promote them in newspaper advertisements and, more recently, on station websites.

For CKTB, the primary method of engaging with local audiences—and maintaining a "community focus" in daytime programs (Saunders)—is through the open-line talk show. During the late morning and afternoon "drive" shows, listeners may call to share their opinions on issues discussed by the program's host. Although this does not give CKTB's audience much influence over the station's programming, Saunders stresses that listeners have an impact on the topics under discussion: "If we don't talk about what they want, they won't call." Interviews and issues must be "local or something local people are interested in" to keep them tuned in and calling. The open-line talk show has a long history on AM radio generally, and on CKTB specifically. Johnston recalls that, like other AM stations, CKTB "got into" talk radio (a precursor to the station's later adoption of the "newstalk" format) in the 1970s, mixing talk shows with music programming. Saunders identifies the program hosted by Laura Sabia, a St. Catharines and Toronto-based feminist politician and activist, as a "pioneer of open-line" at CKTB.[30] Although Sabia's tenure with CKTB was interrupted mid-decade and came to an end in 1977,[31] CKTB later returned to the open-line format with other controversial hosts such as John Michael, a local broadcaster who joined the station in 1989.[32] More recently, in-house hosts such as Larry Fedoruk (weekday afternoons) open the phone lines to CKTB listeners to voice their own opinions, responses, and questions over the air.

While EZ Rock and HTZ-FM do not have open-line shows, both stations give audience members the chance to voice their opinions over the airwaves now and then. EZ-Rock maintains Facebook and Twitter pages as well. On HTZ-FM, listeners are likely to hear occasional impromptu conversations with callers. Like most commercial music stations, both EZ Rock and HTZ-FM take listener requests by telephone, e-mail, or on-line forms, making it easier for people to voice their opinions (Saunders). HTZ-FM, like several of Astral's other stations, also depends on listener input for its new music countdown program broadcast in the evenings; its *Top 9 @ 9* charts have tended to differ only slightly from similar charts at affiliated rock stations. On May 10, 2006, for example, under Standard Radio ownership HTZ-FM's *Top 9 @ 9* shared five charting songs with Standard's other rock stations. However, the rest of its list favoured "hard" or "heavy" rock (bands like Korn and Godsmack) rather than the "lighter" contemporary and classic-sounding rock popular on the other stations (artists such as Sam Roberts, Pilate, and Mobile charted on other lists but not on HTZ-FM's).

Stations EZ Rock and HTZ-FM have gauged local taste by recruiting listeners as "Assistants" or "Online Music Directors," giving participants the opportunity to rate selections from the stations' playlists through an on-line survey. The surveys tend to focus on newer songs, although occasionally older music is put to the test, asking participants to rate short song clips according to criteria such as familiarity, likeability, and whether they have been over-played. Additional survey questions relate to musical taste or lifestyle—another way for stations to learn about their audience—and occasionally offer prizes to participants. HTZ-FM, true to its harder rock format, has been more aggressive with these surveys than EZ Rock, which ceased issuing such "invitations" in 2008; invitations from HTZ-FM to participate continue to arrive more regularly, and the window for taking the survey is shorter. Less frequently, participants receive invitations to take part in a listener advisory panel, a means for the stations to obtain more specific and personal comments on their programming and listener demographics. Panel invitations may specify a precise target group—women 35 to 44 in one EZ Rock session (April 24, 2006) and males 18 to 35 in a similar HTZ-FM panel (March 10, 2006)—but this practice does not necessarily indicate the overall target demographic of the station.

Volunteering to be an assistant or on-line music director may not give listeners any direct control over playlists, but it does imply that local audiences can have an impact on station programming, particularly through the

FIGURE 6.4 Iron Mike Bensson (HTZ-FM), Friday the 13th bikers' gathering, July 2008, Port Dover

rhetorical use of the title "music director." As Saunders points out, while CKTB has "always listened to people," listening does not necessarily translate into action. Suggesting that audiences can influence programming benefits the stations, and CKTB has long encouraged this impression, for example, in a *Standard* ad ("We've Been Listening, St. Catharines") announcing the arrival of "Your New B610" (Dec. 31, 1986). Historically, CKTB solicited listener feedback on its programming early on and, through direct communication, measured audience interest and response. The station solicited feedback through its weekly radio column in the *Standard* beginning in 1945[33] and invited listeners to participate in surveys and discussion groups on radio as early as the mid-1950s.[34] CKTB received letters from listeners even before it was officially on the air,[35] and when Sandell owned the station his dinner companions could request changes in programming, which he would relay to the studio by telephone then and there (Cahill 2005). CKTB bands such as The Barnstormers would learn new songs upon listeners' requests and hear back if they got it wrong (LePage 1976). Johnston recalls *The San Show*, an early request-driven program that targeted "shut-ins" living in a local sanatorium.

Contests offer another way for the stations and their audiences to interact. By phoning, or e-mailing, listeners of CKTB, EZ Rock, or HTZ-FM can enter contests for a wide variety of prizes promoted on-air and on the dedicated contest sections of websites. One of EZ Rock's ongoing contests offered tickets to Paramount Canada's Wonderland and the chance for listeners' kids "to be a star on the radio." Special-event contests offer passes to station-presented musical performances by artists such as David Usher (March 2007, EZ Rock), 54-40, and the Foo Fighters (June 2005, HTZ-FM). Other contest prizes range from DVDs to vacations in locations such as Myrtle Beach, Virginia (March 2007, CKTB). In the 1930s, CKTB awarded children "Eskimo [ice cream] Pies" for singing the song "An Earful of Music" (Stevens 1980, 7A); later programming included the "You Win" contest, which offered a prize of $114 for identifying a mystery singer.[36]

RADIO CONTENT AND THE LOCAL

Despite the efforts of private stations to convey their "localness," their programming content rarely reflects the same level of community investment. If news is a primary marker of commercial radio's local content, then CKTB, with its newstalk format, is at an advantage, airing frequent news reports and often incorporating local news and issues into its daytime programs, or with the dedicated news shows *Niagara at Noon* and *The Six O'Clock News Hour*. Saunders cites the immediacy of radio news and the frequency of news reports as important selling features for the three Merritt House stations, as well as the in-house news team, which in early 2006 was its largest in the past twenty-five years, allowing them to air information with a local focus rather than relying primarily on national and international news services. In the 1960s, CKTB facilitated its news programming with a news studio at the *Standard*, enjoying access to wire services and the newspaper's own newsgathering team (Johnston 2005, Stevens 1980). Johnston describes CKTB as being "big on news" and particularly proud of its news department from the 1960s into the 1980s.

HTZ-FM and EZ Rock air news with less frequency, but the stations' programming content (popular music) otherwise maintains a tenuous link with the local area, broadcasting mostly songs and artists with little or no relationship to St. Catharines or Niagara, thus distancing not only local issues but also the relationship between broadcasting and the local production of music and programming. Corporate broadcasters can save money by using satellite networks and syndicated programming, inserting local advertisements and station identification spots at pre-arranged points (Huntemann 1999, 400). CKTB and EZ Rock rely on syndicated programming to complete their broadcast days, and HTZ-FM incorporates deejay-free blocs into its program schedule, where prerecorded station identifications, promotional spots, and commercials punctuate a steady stream of music without the "personal touch" of live on-air hosts.

At EZ Rock, in-house deejays host much of the programming, but the station shifts to syndication for most evenings and overnight, mostly American syndicated radio programs—*The John Tesh Radio Show* and *Delilah*—which maintain the station's soft-rock music format and occupy the majority of its broadcast week. The John Tesh approach to radio even infused the rest of EZ Rock's schedule to the point where local deejays adapted Tesh's "Intelligence for Your Life" informational segments to "Intelligence for the Workday," providing general interest information and lifestyle tips throughout the day. EZ Rock hosts its own Friday-night "disco" show live from Casino Niagara in Niagara Falls, but Astral's other EZ Rock stations air a similar type of show; other shared programming has included the *Classic Café*, an all-request show featuring hits of the past (a similar format aired on EZ Rock London), as well as the syndicated programs *Hollywood Confidential with Leeza Gibbons* and *Heart to Heart with Joanne Wilson*. Of the three stations broadcasting from the Merritt House, EZ Rock's programming most closely resembles its EZ Rock counterparts, including website design and colour scheme, although Astral has now standardized most of its radio stations' websites. HTZ-FM has produced its own programming, if not its playlists, but like all commercial music format stations, its music is mostly from non-local sources—with a certain percentage required to be Canadian, though not necessarily local.[37] Although HTZ-FM still does not share its programming with Astral Media's other broadcast rock stations, its music playlists are not substantially different either, except perhaps in the ratio of new-to-classic rock or in minor accommodations to local taste, as determined through surveys and other local audience research.

Although CKTB's morning and news programming is primarily produced in-house, like EZ Rock, CKTB relies on syndication—perhaps even more so since the Astral takeover—with its largest blocs of programming devoted to *Coast to Coast*, a popular American show dealing with strange or unexplained phenomena, airing seven nights a week. CKTB's weekend daytime schedule also intersperses locally produced and syndicated programming, including the local show *Uncorked* (formerly the pub, wine, and beer program *A Taste of Niagara*), the Canadian show *Renovations Cross Canada*, and the American program *The Kim Komando Show*. Saunders attributes CKTB's reliance on syndicated programs to a commitment to quality programming, concentrating during the day on what it does best—maintaining the local element "front and centre"—and leaving non-local programming to the "experts." Despite the hours of CKTB's broadcast week devoted to syndicated programming, CKTB remains distinct from Astral's other newstalk stations. There are now only three other Astral stations adhering to the strictly newstalk format: in Toronto, Montreal, and London, while Kelowna offers news, talk, and sports. Although the stations structure their daily broadcasts along similar lines, the actual content is largely different; individual stations share only segments of their programming schedules, overlapping on, for example, *Coast to Coast* or *Ann Shatilla's Hollywood Trend Report*. Saunders suggests that CKTB's smaller market size (compared to Toronto's) may give the station more freedom to stretch the structure of its format but notes that there is "no such thing as unformatted radio anymore."

CKTB's blend of network programming and local variations on broadcasting trends reaches back to the station's founding, before the advent of format radio. In the early days of commercial radio broadcasting, network programming offered benefits to individual stations and to networks: higher quality programming than small stations could produce on their own and "low distribution costs and uniform scheduling" for broadcast networks (Rothenbuhler and McCourt, 369). Canada's first radio network, CNR Radio, founded in 1923, sponsored local programs, often music-oriented, which "encouraged the development of musicians and singers as radio artists."[38] On its opening, CKTB was part of the central Canada service, a small network that included Toronto's CKCL and Brantford's CKPC.[39] Much of the early network programming available in St. Catharines came from non-local competition, the closest competition during this period coming from Hamilton, while more distant stations broadcast *Amos 'n' Andy*, *Rudy Vallee*, *Bing Crosby* (on CRCT in Toronto and WBEN in Buffalo), and *The Yodelling Cowboy* (on CFRB in Toronto and WGR in Buffalo) (Mar. 12, 1936, 14). Presumably, early St. Catharines listeners could tune in to any of the many broadcasts listed in the *Standard*,[40] and the lure of network programs originating in the United States must have been strong. Lou Cahill remembers having to schedule evening meetings of the St. Catharines Auto Club around broadcasts of *Amos 'n' Andy*. CKTB's access to syndicated programming throughout most of the 1930s and 1940s relied on the station's affiliation with the CBC radio network and programs "supplied through the Canadian Broadcasting Corporation Chain" (Cahill 1941). Advertisements in the St. Catharines *Standard* from the period indicate that network programming provided CKTB listeners with access to the music program *Borden's "Canadian Cavalcade"* (Sept. 28, 1944, 11), speeches by Canadian federal and Ontario politicians (Dec. 3, 1936, 17; Sept. 28, 1944, 11), and the popular American detective series *The Thin Man* (Sept. 29, 1941, 15).

Over the years, network feeds shared CKTB's airtime with locally oriented programs that maintained the station's explicit links to the St. Catharines community. The early interview show *Around Your Town*[41] provided a much-needed local element in a schedule that, by the mid-1950s, offered popular recorded music most of the day, mixed with drama, quizzes, and mysteries, as well as news and sports over the dinner hour.[42] CKTB's sports coverage was a particularly strong local element with sportscasting celebrity Rex Stimers and his assistant and eventual replacement, Tommy Garriock (Stevens 1980, 6A and 8A). Stimers directed his "phantom" sportscasts—reports he created in the studio from wire copy and descriptions received over the phone (Stevens 1980, 6A)—at an explicitly local audience, which got him into trouble at times: Cahill recalls an incident in which people from Brockville (over 400 kilometres from St. Catharines) complained after hearing Stimers attribute a St. Catharines sports team with leads it never held during a game on the road. Stimers died in 1966 (Stevens 1980, 7A), but Garriock's unstructured late-night sportscasts continued to attract high numbers of listeners to CKTB, even after television began to eat away at the station's evening audience.[43]

Originally, live music made up a substantial portion of CKTB's locally produced content; in the 1930s and early 1940s CKTB relied largely on local bands and piano players performing live in its studios (Stevens 1980, 6A). The station's original home, in the Welland House hotel at the corner of Ontario and King streets, included a studio to accommodate "choirs and large orchestras" and a smaller room for "soloists" and small groups,[44] and both this and its later home in the Merritt House contained viewing rooms where audience members could watch the performances.[45] Local musicians appearing on CKTB included pianist Clarence Colton, who was with the station at its founding,[46] as well as Bob McMullen, who started at CKTB performing with his family and in groups such as The Tennessee Hillbillies, which included his brother Tom and local fiddler Abbie Andrews.[47] Such bands were more local in fact than in name. Others included The Cabineers, The Sod Busters, and The Mountaineers (LePage, 1976), their music (often "old time fiddling music") evoking nothing inherently local in sound. CKTB also broadcast the music of local women, including organist/pianist/vocalist Eva Griffin, who performed live on the station's inaugural program and had her own weekly show.[48] After World War II, CKTB, like radio in general, featured more musical recordings than live performances (Stevens 1980, 6A), but live music did not immediately vanish from CKTB's schedule. Colton continued to play five days a week until he was elderly (Johnston 2005), and after serving in the army in World War II, Andrews returned to CKTB with his Canadian Ranch Boys.[49] With CKTB's programming moving toward recorded music, network broadcasts disappeared as announcers in the late 1950s began playing records throughout the evening (Johnston 2005).

Today EZ Rock and HTZ-FM broadcast music from the Merritt House, and although most popular music conveys little indication of any local identity or affiliation, EZ Rock and HTZ-FM do air the occasional St. Catharines, Niagara or, more often, Ontario-bred musician. HTZ-FM is somewhat more likely to identify an artist as local, particularly if the performers are previous winners of the station's annual Rock Search contest, which solicits demo recordings from unsigned rock bands and provides the top entrants with limited airplay followed by a live showcase; the winning act receives equipment, studio time, and professional support. Two of the most successful past finalists, Finger Eleven (originally The Rainbow Butt Monkeys) and The Trews, were based within HTZ-FM's definition of local (Burlington and Niagara Falls) and still receive substantial airplay. Other winners have vanished from playlists, suggesting that HTZ limits its sustained on-air support to local artists who gain more widespread commercial success. EZ Rock broadcasts the music of Canadian artists after they have achieved recognition elsewhere and rarely mention the artists' origins, even when playing St. Catharines' exports like acclaimed singer-songwriter Ron Sexsmith.

In the absence of local programming content, particularly in the case of EZ Rock and HTZ-FM, the stations use public appearances and community fundraising campaigns to foster their local identities. Saunders suggests that part of a radio personality's job is "representing the station," and deejays from all three stations serve as recognizable members of the community, not "disembodied voices"—covering, hosting, and promoting concerts, live-to-air club nights, and local festivals. Public appearances and community-based activities have stretched into the region to include an annual "radiothon" involving deejays from CKTB, HTZ-FM, and EZ Rock—a three-day fundraiser for the Niagara Peninsula Children's Centre in St. Catharines—as well as golf games with radio contest winners at the Royal Niagara Golf Club in Niagara-on-the-Lake, and live broadcasts from Casino Niagara in Niagara Falls. Long gone are the live broadcasts from the Grand Ballroom of the Brock Hotel in Niagara Falls (Stevens 1980, Cahill 2005) and the reports, which continued into the 1970s, on city parades and lost dogs and cats (through which many a lost pet was found) (Johnston 2005). However, the live broadcasts of midnight mass from a local church continue today, as before, every Christmas Eve.[50]

The broadcasting industry underwent dramatic changes in the mid-twentieth century, influenced by the increased competition from numerous new stations (Rothenbuhler and McCourt 2002, 371), the "mobility" of listening brought about by car radios and transistor technology (378), a newly designed Top 40 programming format, and the emergence of television, teenagers,

FIGURE 6.5 Christmas 2007, 75th consecutive broadcast of Midnight Mass, Cathedral of St. Catherine of Alexandria, St. Catharines. Mike Saunders, Rector Bishop Wingle, Msgr. Wayne Kirkpatrick

and rock and roll (Barnes 1988, 10–12). However, the industry was slow to change and this resistance bears on the stations' community focus. While many broadcasters were attempting to create a "total station sound" (Rothenbuhler and McCourt 2002, 381), CKTB was still trying to please its established "maturing" audience with a mix of programs and content (Johnston 2005). When Johnston arrived at CKTB in 1955, he was surprised to find the station still programming blocs of time in the style of early radio (Barnes 1988, 10; Rothenbuhler and McCourt 2002, 370). For many years the station avoided the "new" rock and roll music, maintaining a middle-of-the-road (MOR) philosophy rather than following industry trends (Johnston 2005). With no Niagara Region competition before 1947 and no in-town competition until 1967 (CCF 2005), CKTB did not feel pressured to follow the path of other stations until well into the 1970s (Moffatt 2005). As Cahill remembers, the Burgoyne family ran CKTB on a traditional model, much like it had been operated by Sandell, and he recalls a banquet speech from the Burgoyne period in which both the station's studios and management style were described as "historic." Murray Moffatt cites the longevity of many CKTB staff members' careers at the station as further indication of its "historic" quality; it was one of the last stations in southern Ontario to retain a music librarian on staff and many early (and a few later) employees spent twenty-five to thirty years at CKTB, while living within the boundaries of the community the station defined.

CONCLUSION

CKTB's audience-focused approach to programming in its first few decades of operation resembles a style Jarl Ahlkvist describes as the "surrogate consumer philosophy" (2001, 347). Ahlkvist argues that programming philosophies depend on several concerns: musical aesthetics, market research, responsibilities to the music industry, and obligations to local audiences. The surrogate consumer programmer makes local obligations a priority: "For these programmers, 'radio is not rocket science or brain surgery,' all that is required is a willingness to 'give the people what they want' and the only people that matter are the potential listeners in the local market. This locality orientation leads programmers to take direct listener input, such as call-in requests or informal contact, quite seriously" (348). Ahlkvist argues that the surrogate consumer philosophy tends to produce "more familiar" or "less risky" music programming, because "it is customized for the local audience" (352). Local customization was certainly the case at CKTB, which continued its proven, local-audience-pleasing formula long after most other stations had abandoned the "make-everyone-happy" approach for new industry formats. As Johnston remembers, direct contact with station listeners was CKTB's primary method of learning about its audience, and the station did not turn to professional research consultants until after the Burgoyne family sold the station in 1981.[51]

Listening to employees like Mike Saunders, one gets the impression that the listener-focused philosophy may still hold some validity for CKTB; however, in EZ Rock and HTZ-FM's programming the surrogate consumer approach seems overshadowed by what Ahlkvist calls the "programming professional" philosophy, which relies on "objective" research into "the target [demographic's] response to the station's programming" (348). The listener surveys and audience music-director roles of HTZ-FM and EZ Rock combine the rhetoric of the surrogate consumer philosophy—"letting the listeners program your station"—with the practice of the professional programmer.

My reading of CKTB, HTZ-FM, and 105.7 EZ Rock lines up with Ahlkvist's argument that several factors influence radio programming, some of them local and some of them generic to commercial radio. Although it does not represent a comprehensive analysis of commercial radio in St. Catharines, or the Niagara Region, it does shed light on how the "local" fares in the programming and promotions of these three corporate-owned stations. Definitions of the local in St. Catharines radio are not fixed or tightly bounded, and vary according to station format, with rock radio demonstrating the loosest conception of locality. The amount of locally produced programming differs, with the newstalk format exhibiting a stronger connection to local issues and audiences. Although local commitment varies as station ownership changes, historically local owners who had other stakes in the community, such as Sandell or the Burgoyne family, likely favoured local audiences over industry trends and demands.

In Berland's ideal view, radio has the capacity to make a dynamic contribution to local identity, culture, and history, connecting the local with "other spaces and cultures" (2003, 235). In other words, radio could respond to the complexity and fluidity of locality, mediating and negotiating between a station's immediate community and the rest of the world. Yet the aim of commercial radio stations seems less a matter of negotiating the relationship between local culture and the national, the continental or the global, and more about bringing non-local production into the community while at the same time constructing enough local identity to keep listeners from turning to nearby stations playing much the same thing. In a market where national and global radio is now accessible through satellite and Internet access, where news and music are available at the click of a computer mouse, a broadcast radio station's local identity is even more valuable: an essential tool and a matter of survival. Change, of course, is a difficult process, and broadcasters (and their accountants or the shareholders they report to) may prefer to let computers and network feeds take over in the studio than to risk re-infusing commercial radio with local culture. However, even as media mergers and consolidation may threaten the autonomy of local stations, commercial radio's sense of local identity and connection within the community would be intensified if stations were forced to concentrate on what sets them apart: that is, a locally grounded broadcasting strategy, which is already the practice of underfunded campus and community radio stations.

Thanks to Lou Cahill (in memoriam), Bob Johnston, Murray Moffatt, and Mike Saunders for sharing their memories of CKTB and its sister stations; and to Mike and to Astral Radio Media Niagara for permission to use the pictures.

NOTES

1 CKTB has broadcast from its current location on Yates Street in St. Catharines since 1938. In 1981, radio station management officially renamed the white building known as Oak Hill Mansion in honour of Merritt, a nineteenth-century local statesman and the mansion's original owner (CKTB Brochure, St. Catharines

Museum Archives; Johnston, "CKTB, St. Catharines/Niagara—A Brief History";
St. Catharines *Standard*, Nov. 28, 1981). The building's more popular names are
self-designations, promotional taglines used within station identification
announcements.

2 Before becoming part of Astral Media in 2007—a public corporation dealing in
national television, radio, Internet media, and outdoor advertising— CKTB, EZ-
Rock, and HTZ-FM belonged to Standard Radio, which had been the "largest privately owned broadcasting company" in Canada. See 105.7 EZ Rock, "Niagara's
Best Variety of Yesterday and Today," Standard Radio, Inc. http://www.1057ezrock,
accessed June 7, 2005; Apr. 19, 2006; Feb. 26, 2007; Astral Media. http://www
.astralmedia.com, accessed Aug. 10, 2008.

3 Decima Research Inc., *Local Content and Its Sources—A Decima teleVox Study*, prepared for the Department of Canadian Heritage (Feb. 2005, 8), http://www.pch
.gc.ca/progs/ac-ca/progs/ri-bpi/index_e.cfm, accessed Apr. 28, 2006.

4 "Branding" in radio broadcasting is common, the result of "music selection" and
"narrowcasting" (Rothenbuhler and McCourt 2002, 368). Under Standard Radio
Inc., EZ Rock was identified as one of "the most recognized and listened-to brands
in the industry." See Standard Radio, "History," http://www.standardradio.com,
accessed May 16, 2005; Apr. 30, 2006; Mar. 3, 2007; "Get to Know London News-
Talk 1290," Standard Radio Inc., http://www.cjbk.com, accessed Apr. 30, 2006,
and Mar. 3, 2007; "610 CKTB," Standard Radio, Inc. http://610cktb.com, and
HTZ-FM. "Southern Ontario's Best Rock," Standard Radio Inc., http://www
.htzfm.com, accessed May 16 and June 7, 2005; Apr. 18, 2006; Feb. 26, 2007.

5 J.N. Jackson and S.M. Wilson, *St. Catharines: Canada's Canal City*, St. Catharines:
St. Catharines Standard Ltd. (1992), 259.

6 "CKTB-AM," Canadian Communications Foundation (CCF), *The History of Canadian Broadcasting*, http://www.broadcasting-history.ca, accessed May 12 and 16,
2005.

7 Jackson and Wilson, 259.

8 Tom Torrance, "Taylor and Bate Brewery 1834–1935," *Let's Talk Business* (Winter, 1985), 54–55.

9 CCF 2005, "CKTB-AM"; Jackson and Wilson, 289.

10 Linda Bramble, "The End of an Era," *Alive and Well* (Nov. 1981), 44–45; CCF,
"CKTB-AM," St. Catharines *Standard* ad, Sept. 16, 1981.

11 Bob Johnston, "CKTB."

12 "CHTZ," CCF, 2005.

13 CCF 2005; Johnston, "A Brief History."

14 Doug Herod, "New Hard Rock Station Going on Air June 27," St. Catharines *Standard*, Apr. 23, 1986, 11; Karen Martin, "A New Sound Hits the Airwaves: HTZ-FM
in St. Catharines Is Niagara's Newest Radio Station," *Let's Talk Business* (Summer, 1986), 50–51.

15 CCF 2005; Angela Murphy, "Local Radio Stations Reunited by Affinity,"
St. Catharines *Standard*, Jan. 29, 1998, A11; Linda Shutt, "Former CJRN Owner
Buying CKTB," St. Catharines *Standard*, Local section, Aug. 10, 1996.

16 Astral Media, 2008.

17 At the time of my interview (Jan. 18, 2006) with Mike Saunders, he had been
with CKTB for nearly twenty-five years, since May 1981, and was working in

production and promotions. Although his name was later removed from the CKTB website (noted Feb. 26, 2007), he was still employed by the station as morning show producer.

18 Bob Johnston began working at CKTB in 1955, became station manager of CJQR in 1979, and returned to CKTB briefly in 1986 before he left to teach broadcasting at Niagara College (interview, Sept. 8, 2005).

19 Lou Cahill, "Radio Serves the Modern Community: St. Catharines Is Proud of the Record of Station CKTB," St. Catharines *Standard*, Apr. 21, 1941.

20 Gene Stevens, "610/CKTB: Still the One, 50th Anniversary Supplement," St. Catharines *Standard*, Oct. 2, 1980.

21 Royal Commission on Broadcasting, *Report* (Ottawa: Queen's Printer and Controller of Stationery, Mar. 15, 1957).

22 CKTB's coverage of the Royal Canadian Henley Regatta (a North American rowing event held in the Port Dalhousie area of St. Catharines) was broadcast around the world. Such international exposure may have motivated the slogan "Canada's Sports Station," used in an advertisement printed in the 1943–44 season program for the St. Catharines Garden City Arena. Cahill 1941; also Stevens, "610/CKTB," 6A.

23 Timothy Taylor, "Music and Advertising in Early Radio," *Echo: A Music-Centered Journal* 5:2 (2003), http://www.echo.ucla.edu, accessed Aug. 8, 2005.

24 St. Catharines *Standard*, Sept. 30, 1944, 13.

25 Lorraine LePage, "Played on Radio: The Barnstormers Were a Popular Orchestra," St. Catharines *Standard*, Feb. 14, 1976, 24A.

26 St. Catharines *Standard*, Nov. 7, 1933, 2.

27 Ibid., Nov. 7, 1933, 6.

28 Ibid., Feb. 5, 1949, 14.

29 Ibid., Mar. 27, 1941, 21.

30 Joe O'Donnell, "Go Ahead Please, You're on the Air," St. Catharines *Standard*, Apr. 26, 1973, 8; Stevens 1980, 7A.

31 O'Donnell, 1975. Rosalie Simpson, "Laura Says Program Off Because of Her Canadian Unity Views," St. Catharines *Standard*, June 24, 1977.

32 John Michael got himself and the station into trouble in the mid-1990s in the form of a rebuke from the Canadian Broadcast Standards Council and a libel suit from an ex-government minister. His controversial shock-radio style had led to similar problems in the past, jeopardizing the broadcast licence of a previous employer, Niagara Falls radio station CJRN. See Dean Beeby, "John Michael's Remarks Put CJRN License in Jeopardy," St. Catharines *Standard*, Apr. 15, 1988, 8; Shawn Berry, "CKTB Confirms Michael Deal," St. Catharines *Standard*, Aug. 2, 1989; Carol Alaimo, "Colourful Match-up in $2-million Libel Suit," St. Catharines *Standard*, Mar. 31, 1994, A1; also Carol Alaimo, "CKTB Pays Ex-Minister $50,000 in Libel Suit," St. Catharines *Standard*, Apr. 1, 1995, B1.

33 Charlie Walls, "At Radio Ringside," St. Catharines *Standard*, May 5, 1945, 14.

34 Elda Flintoff, "Elda's Radio Ringside," St. Catharines *Standard*, Apr. 16, 1955, 33.

35 *Standard*, Nov. 7, 1933, 4.

36 Flintoff, *Standard*, June 8, 1957, 5.

37 Canadian Radio-television and Telecommunications Commission (CRTC) policy requires all radio stations to "ensure that 35% of their popular musical selections

are Canadian each week" (2004). Commercial radio stations have an additional obligation to maintain 35% Canadian content during primetime hours, which for radio run from 6:00 a.m. to 6:00 p.m., Monday through Friday. See Broadcasting Act, "Broadcasting Policy for Canada," Canadian Radio-television and Telecommunications Commission, 1991, http://www.crtc.gc.ca/eng/LEGAL/BROAD.htm, accessed Oct. 13, 2005; CRTC, fact sheet, Canadian Content for Radio and Television. Canadian Radio-television and Telecommunications Commission, 2004, http://www.crtc.gc.ca/eng/INFO_SHT/G11.htm, accessed Apr. 28, 2006.

38 Greg Gormick and J. Lyman Potts, "Canada's First Network: CNR Radio," *The History of Canadian Broadcasting* (Canadian Communications Foundation, 1998), http://www.broadcasting-history.ca, accessed Oct. 5, 2005.

39 St. Catharines *Standard*, Nov. 4, 1933, 1.

40 On the day that CKTB first broadcast on its own radio signal, the St. Catharines *Standard* listed the wavelengths and programming schedules of thirty-nine other radio stations as close as Hamilton, Ontario, and as far away as St. Louis, Illinois, Nov. 7, 1933, 11.

41 Linda Bramble, "Man Alive Survives—And Thrives," *What's Up Niagara*, Apr., 1983, 6–10; St. Catharines *Standard*, May 9, 1857, 35.

42 Flintoff, *Standard*, Apr. 16, 1955, 33.

43 Sept. 6, 2005, interview with Murray Moffatt, a newscaster at CKTB from 1976 to 1989.

44 St. Catharines *Standard*, Nov. 4, 1933, 1.

45 CCF 2005; Stevens 1980, 6A.

46 St. Catharines *Standard*, May 9, 1957, 35.

47 Bob McMullen, interviewed by Terrance Cox, May 3, 2000.

48 Lily M. Bell and Kathleen E. Bray, "Women of Action 1876–1976," typescript. St. Catharines Museum Archives.

49 Lorraine LePage, "They'll Honor Fiddler Abbie Andrews," St. Catharines *Standard*, Oct. 14, 1982; John Morrison, "Abbie Andrews Still Involved with Music and His Fans Still Remember," St. Catharines *Standard*, July 6, 1978.

50 Bill Currie, "Peace Will Be Message at Midnight Mass: CKTB Will Broadcast Service for 70th Year," St. Catharines *Standard*, Dec. 24, 2003, A5.

51 CKTB, cue sheet, Niagara District Broadcasting Co. Ltd. (Jan. 1981).

WORKS CITED

Ahlkvist, Jarl. A. "Programming Philosophies and the Rationalization of Music Radio." *Media, Culture and Society* 23 (2001), 339–58.

Barnes, Ken. "A Fragment of the Imagination: Top 40 Radio." In Simon Frith, ed., *Facing the Music: Essays on Pop, Rock, and Culture*. New York: Pantheon Books, 1988: 8–50.

Berland, Jody. "Locating Listening: Technological Space, Popular Music, and Canadian Mediations." In Andrew Leyshon, David Matless, and George Revill, eds., *The Place of Music*. New York: Guilford Press, 1998: 129–50.

———. "Radio Space and Industrial Time: The Case of Music Formats." In Justin Lewis and Toby Miller, eds., *Critical Cultural Policy Studies: A Reader*. Malden, MA: Blackwell, 2003: 230–39.

Hennion, Antoine, and Cecile Meadel. "Programming Music: Radio as Mediator." Trans. Nicholas Garnham. *Media, Culture and Society* 8 (1986), 281–303.

Huntemann, Nina. "Corporate Interference: The Commercialization and Concentration of Radio Post-the 1996 Telecommunications Act." *Journal of Communication Inquiry* 23:4 (1999), 390–407.

Killmeier, Matthew A. "Voices between the Tracks: Disk Jockeys, Radio, and Popular Music, 1955–60." *Journal of Communication Inquiry* 25:4 (2001), 353–74.

Rothenbuhler, Eric W. "Commercial Radio and Popular Music: Processes of Selection and Factors of Influence." In James Lull, ed., *Popular Music and Communication*. Newbury Park, CA: Sage, 1987: 78–95.

Rothenbuhler, Eric, and Tom McCourt. "Radio Redefines Itself, 1947–1962." In Michele Hilmes and Jason Loviglio, eds., *Radio Reader: Essays in the Cultural History of Radio*. New York: Routledge, 2002: 367–87.

Part III | **FOOD AND DRINK**

FROLICS WITH FOOD | *The Frugal Housewife's Manual* by "A.B. of Grimsby"

FIONA LUCAS
MARY F. WILLIAMSON

INTRODUCTION

The Frugal Housewife's Manual (1840) is the first original cookbook to be published in Canada that was not a reprint of a foreign cookbook.[1] Written by a Canadian gentlewoman known only as "A.B. of Grimsby," it opens an unexpected window onto the popular culinary culture of the fertile Niagara area of the late 1830s. In our early twenty-first century minds, its title may conjure images of the unpleasant necessity of parsimonious meals in times of economic hardship, but nothing could be farther from the truth. We read of fruit cakes redolent with spices and wine, cookies rich in butter and caraway, pears delicately simmered with lemon and brandy, homemade tomato catsup improving the sauce for baked meats, sliced eggplant accompanying fried ham, and poultry roasted to perfection in front of the open hearth. Mouths water while one reads the recipes. The author has created an evocative image of the elegant dessert Floating Island, in which beaten egg whites are piled high over custard and sometimes fruit and jam. She describes it as "a very ornamental dish by candle light, together with a dish of snowballs"— another elegant dessert of balls of sweet rice in a wine sauce—"on the opposite part of the table." Indeed, A.B. was as keen on presentation as high-end restaurant chefs are today.

Not all of the recipes in the *Manual* speak to a diet that is rich in calories, although the active lives led by most men and women depended on the consumption of energy-producing foods. For her cookbook, A.B. focused on instructions for preparing baked goods, puddings, and preserves whose success

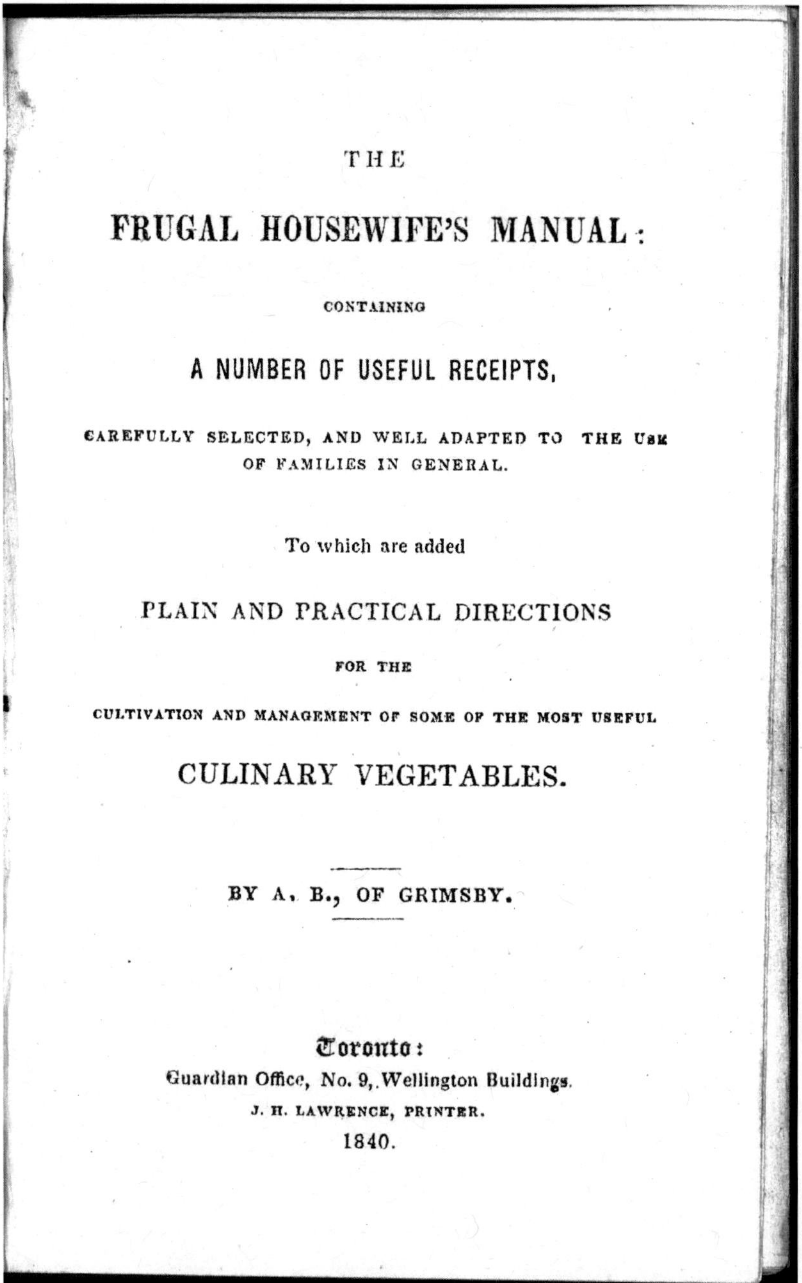

THE

FRUGAL HOUSEWIFE'S MANUAL:

CONTAINING

A NUMBER OF USEFUL RECEIPTS,

CAREFULLY SELECTED, AND WELL ADAPTED TO THE USE
OF FAMILIES IN GENERAL.

To which are added

PLAIN AND PRACTICAL DIRECTIONS

FOR THE

CULTIVATION AND MANAGEMENT OF SOME OF THE MOST USEFUL

CULINARY VEGETABLES.

BY A. B., OF GRIMSBY.

Toronto:
Guardian Office, No. 9, Wellington Buildings.
J. H. LAWRENCE, PRINTER.
1840.

FIGURE 7.1 Title page, *The Frugal Housewife's Manual* by "A.B., of Grimsby." Private Collection

requires close attention to detail. In her preface she instructs readers to be "careful to attend to every particular of the directions given, or they may condemn the work unjustly. It may be thought unnecessary to observe trifles; a little experience will convince any one of their importance." Despite A.B.'s appeal to frugal housewifery, which simply meant applying restraint, even a casual reading of the *Manual* evokes the vivid flavours and aromas of foods enjoyed in mid-nineteenth-century Ontario. These were served at public celebratory gatherings and were enjoyed on a daily basis by the lucky ones who had graduated from the subsistence fare of the early settlers.

THE MYSTERIES AROUND A.B.'S COOKBOOK

In advertisements, beginning April 8, 1840, the *Manual* is attributed to a "Canadian Lady" who, like many women authors of the time, preferred anonymity.[2] She simply called herself "A.B. of Grimsby," presumably after the Niagara area village she called home, situated on the south shore of Lake Ontario midway between the larger centres of Hamilton and St. Catharines. By 1840, the cookbook's year of publication, Grimsby was well settled by agricultural United Empire Loyalists and their descendants. A.B. was probably an educated and prosperous farm woman who was accustomed to preparing large communal meals for her extended family, farmhands, and other servants, and maybe boarders. Her tiny manual of seventy-two food recipes and instructions for planting and cooking twenty-eight vegetables reflects popular culinary practice and kitchen gardening knowledge in her community. It was probably directed at rural women like herself, used to thriftiness but still interested in preparing delicious meals from their home-grown produce: vegetables and orchard fruits; maize; chickens and ducks; eggs; lard; suet and maple molasses; and homemade pickles, catsups, jams, and fruit cordials. By 1840, the wives and daughters of the small farmers and self-employed artisans who predominated in this relatively established district would have been literate. Here was a potential market for the cookbook. Tiny and unpretentious, it could be tucked into an apron pocket for quick referral in both the kitchen and the vegetable garden. We don't know how many copies were printed, but only three copies are known to survive today, two of them in libraries and one in a private collection.[3] That all three copies were useful to their original owners is tellingly revealed by the evidence of spattering in the cake sections.

A.B. is credited on the title page with authorship of *The Frugal Housewife's Manual*, but technically she mostly compiled it from other books and interjected her own editorial comments. She had two main sources. Colin

FIGURE 7.2 (above left) "Floating Island." *Cassell's Dictionary of Cookery*, v.1, c. mid-1870s.
FIGURE 7.3 (above right) St. Catharines in 1828, after a drawing by Capt. Basil Hall. Logo for *The Farmers' Journal*. Library and Archives Canada.

Mackenzie's encyclopaedic *Five Thousand Receipts* was published in England in 1823 and from 1829 until 1860 in several expanded American editions.[4] The other source was Lydia Maria Child's very popular *American Frugal Housewife*, first issued in 1829 and advertised through the late 1840s by booksellers in villages all over southern Ontario.[5] It was, without a doubt, the best-known American recipe book in Upper Canada in the 1830s and '40s. A.B. took a single recipe, Mince Pies, from Amelia Simmons's *American Cookery* (1796), the first American cookbook.[6] A.B.'s other recipes were taken either from sources not yet identified or were her own versions of recipes that were widely known and found in family manuscript recipe collections. Parts of the meat and fish section seem to be original.

Lydia Child's *The American Frugal Housewife* was offered for sale by the Methodist Book Depot, the *Christian Guardian* newspaper's bookshop outlet in Toronto. Indeed, A.B.'s cookbook was printed by Joseph Lawrence and published by the *Guardian* office on King Street. The *Guardian* advertised A.B.'s cookbook weeks before, and after, and on the same day (Sept. 9, 1840) as the twentieth edition of Mrs. Child's cookbook was declared to be "a work containing many particulars which every female should know who has a house of her own."[7] Considering the respect given to Mrs. Child's book and the similarity of titles, the publication of A.B.'s cookbook poses a mystery. The answer may lie in the financial difficulty being experienced at that moment by the Methodist Church's Book Committee, which just months earlier had decided to expand into non-religious books. It is likely that *The Frugal Housewife's Manual* was what we might call today a vanity publication with the author/compiler financing the publication, expecting few sales, and wishing only for the satisfaction of giving copies to extended family members and friends. Possibly the printer, Joseph Lawrence, along with his wife, Sarah, had a hand in the enterprise. Unlike Mrs. Child's book, A.B.'s cookbook was not listed in the Methodist Book Depot's catalogue, and apart from a string of advertisements in the *Christian Guardian*, few other than Methodist subscribers would have heard about it. Furthermore, since arriving in the province, Upper Canadians had been exposed to a number of American and British cookbooks that were best-sellers in their own countries. For example, St. Catharines and Niagara booksellers were advertising, and presumably selling, Ude's *The French Cook*, *The Housekeeper's Book*, Kitchiner's *The Cook's Oracle*, and Mrs. Lee's *The Cook's Own Book*.[8]

Why did A.B. choose the prescriptive adjective "frugal" in her title when it had already been used for other well-known cookbooks? Likely because in the nineteenth century frugality was prized as a virtue by all classes of society and had not acquired the pejorative connotations routinely assigned to it today in a more affluent culture. Providing the cakes, puddings, and meats that made up three large meals each day for a hungry crowd required speed, efficiency, and self-discipline; because her vegetables were home-grown and her fruits were gathered from her own orchards and berry patches, they were fresh, seasonal, and flavourful. These were all aspects of familial thriving within frugality. Above all, a frugal housewife was not wasteful, the ultimate failing in the thinking of other housewives.

THE NIAGARA COMMUNITY

We are assuming that A.B.—"a Canadian Lady"—really did live in the Township of Grimsby, and if we look at this agricultural community of around 1,700 residents, we catch a glimpse of the food-related activities that permeated every aspect of daily life in 1840. The township was still only partially developed, but boasting a relatively mild climate and good soil, it held great promise. In 1831 the surveyor Joseph Bouchette had observed the area's "excellent fertile locality," and "the numerous settlements which are emerging from the rudeness of primitive cultivation, and exhibit some appearance of agricultural success and rural comfort" (98). Back in 1820 a Scottish traveller, John Howison, had been greatly impressed by what he saw: "The soil and climate here seem to be admirably adapted for the production and growth of fruit. Numerous apple and peach orchards ornament the sides of the road, and are, every season, loaded with a profusion of delightful fruit" (1821, 66).

The village of Grimsby was directly on the mail route that passed through St. Catharines on its way from Hamilton to Niagara. In 1835, Adam Hope, a recent immigrant from Scotland to Hamilton, made a journey on horseback between the two towns, sharing his observations with his father in a letter:

"Grimsby," he wrote, "is a pretty thriving village…. It possesses Churches with *Steeples*, Flour & Grist Mills & some good stores. A good deal of Flour is manufactured here" (Crerar 2007, 132). But the political turmoil of 1836–38 had put agricultural development and economic opportunities on hold. Lingering grievances over land policy and oligarchic governance in the colony underlay abortive attempts at rebellion around Toronto, and Brantford to the west. While the majority of the population remained "neutral" during the rebellion outbreaks, frustration over the status quo was more widespread. For example, work begun in 1835 on a macadamized road from Niagara to the western limit of Grimsby Township was far from complete. The same year a proper harbour with breakwater had been approved, but by 1840 nothing had been accomplished. Clearing fields for cultivation was a priority. In the following decades the township's earlier promise was realized through the efforts of generations of growers. Today, Grimsby occupies a proud place on the Niagara wine route, its first winery having been established in 1858 when W.W. Kitchen began to produce wines from grapes and rhubarb on his farm (Turcotte 2007, 107).[9]

According to the 1851 census, slightly over half of the farmers and farm labourers, millers, distillers, church ministers and teachers, and their families and servants living in Grimsby, had been born in the province. Of the remainder, the majority were settlers from the United States with various European backgrounds, followed by Irish and English immigrants.[10] On a visit to St. Catharines in 1820, Howison had observed "large wagons carrying loads of amphibious Dutch"—that is, "Deutsch," or Germans—who were making their way to church (1821, 134). A majority of domestic servants were young Catholic Irish girls, commonly illiterate, who had to be taught by their mistresses how to cook and perform other duties around the house.[11]

Fundraisers, popular entertainments, celebrations, sporting events, and "bees" were organized around the community and its churches, with food and drink the lure that encouraged participation, much as they do today. The Loyalists had brought the idea of a "bee," meaning a work-oriented gathering where families happily joined in to help each other, from the United States. There were numerous excuses, such as house-raisings, barn-raisings, apple-drying, and maple sugaring, and a variety of foods were inevitably involved. A logging "bee" attended by Susanna Moodie in the backwoods north of Lake Ontario sported a "rude board" of "pea-soup, legs of pork, venison, eel, and raspberry pies, garnished with plenty of potatoes, and whiskey to wash them down, besides a large iron kettle of tea" (1852, 74). The family's womenfolk, with assistance from neighbours, prepared the meals consumed at such local "bees."

On important public occasions, however, meals were often organized by professional caterers, with the diners' eclectic tastes and sense of status in mind. In the spring of 1840, a district fanatic blew up the wooden Brock Monument on Queenston Heights. Forty-seven military officers who had been stationed in the Grimsby area during the Upper Canada Rebellion, together with farmers and residents of the village, subscribed to the fund to reconstruct the monument, which was about twenty-one miles east on the border with the United States. In honour of General Brock, all public and private business in the province was suspended, and a public holiday that included "all classes" was declared for July 30. A temporary pavilion was constructed for a meeting and dinner on the Heights "near to where the hero fell." Close to 1,000 "loyal" citizens arrived—many of them borne from Toronto on four steamers festooned in evergreen garlands—and after the speeches they tucked into dinner. Each diner paid 7 shillings and 6 pence for a knife, fork, and wine glass, and several kinds of meat, bread, and cheese, and decanters of wine, all supplied by Toronto caterer Thomas Craig. Other foods would have been brought in locally. One journalist was impressed by "the sharp pop of champagne corks" that accompanied the "airs and melodies" played by the band of the 34th Regiment and amply sustained a series of toasts to the good health of a long list of dignitaries.[12]

The bright young people of Niagara enjoyed themselves during the winter of 1845 with "several gay parties," according to one newspaper. Among the gayest of them was the Ball and Supper of the Sergeants of the Royal Canadian Rifle Regiment at Butler's Barracks in Niagara—now Niagara-on-the-Lake—about twenty-six miles east of Grimsby. Following dancing, "the supper room was furnished in a style alike satisfactory to the eye and to the appetite."[13] For some, these were the years of elegant dining in Upper Canada, when the food was plentiful and the drink flowed freely, and everybody danced to a live band.

In 1838, the English writer Anna Jameson, travelling with friends by sleigh from Toronto to Niagara, took a tumble in a snowbank near Beamsville, just east of Grimsby. She is full of admiration for the landlady of a nearby inn who produced dinner at very short notice: "The supper table was spread, a pile of logs higher than myself blazing away in the chimney; venison steaks, and fried fish, coffee, hot cakes, cheese, and whiskey punch (the traveller's fare in Canada) were soon smoking on the table; our landlady presided, and the evening passed merrily away." The next morning when Mrs. Jameson woke up she felt ill and had no interest in breakfast, but her landlady insisted on offering her "her best tea, kept for her own drinking (which tasted for all the world, like must hay) and buttered toast, i.e. fried bread steeped in

FIGURE 7.4 "Lunch in the Woods," sketches of Ontario Methodist camp ground, Grimsby. *Illustrated Historical Atlas of the Counties of Lincoln and Welland, Ontario, 1876*

melted butter, and fruit preserved in molasses—to all which I shall get used in time—I must try, at least" (1838, 75–76). The foodways of the Canadians still required some adaptation on the part of new arrivals from Great Britain.

As for the descendants of slaves who had been brought to Canada from the United States by the United Empire Loyalists, they were spread out in the Niagara Region and over the decades had merged with the general population as soldiers, farm labourers, and cooks. On August 1, 1840, the "coloured population" of St. Catharines assembled for their annual celebration of the anniversary of emancipation, which had been declared officially by the British government in 1833. A reporter for the *St. Catharines Journal* made special note of a parade headed by members of the 3rd Battalion of militia brought from Niagara for the occasion, and of speeches by dignitaries complimenting the assembly on their "orderly proceedings." Following the singing of hymns and three cheers for the Queen, to the tune of "Rule Britannia" about two hundred celebrants, including children, proceeded to a "substantial dinner" in a temporary shed where they ate "a variety of dishes and most abundantly supplied."[14]

Let us imagine A.B. helping to prepare for a picnic, a favourite amusement in summer but also during the winter lull when there was little work to do on the farm. Snow and strong winds seldom deterred the settlers from the prospect of a picnic. Bundled into sleighs lined with furs, they would head across fields and into the woods where a fire had been kindled and cauldrons installed for hot soup and chowder. Portable tables set under the trees would be laden with hams, venison, pork, and chicken for which A.B. supplied the necessary cooking directions. Currant Jelly, Pickled Onions, and Pickled Cucumbers may have been brought along as suitable accompaniments to the meats. Then on to the dessert course: an Apple Pie, Ginger Bread, Albany Cake, and a rich Baked Custard. As the favourite homemade wine of Upper Canadians, Red Currant Wine was likely enjoyed by the picnickers, plus a warmed-up alcoholic cider from local cider-maker John Moore, or whiskey from licensed distiller William Harris.

A.B.'S COOKBOOK AND KITCHEN

Compiling an inventory of kitchen equipment and vocabulary based solely on what is stipulated or implied in her recipes and garden instructions does not provide a full picture of A.B.'s kitchen. She likely had other cookbooks, but in conjunction with other resources such as an 1844 advertisement by L.D. Winchester for tin and copper wares, the few surviving images, together with old kitchens that still exist in the Grimsby area and recreated kitchens at historic houses, we can visualize A.B.'s kitchen and how it reflected both her milieu and her community. Despite the intriguing, unanswered questions about her motivation, identity, and relationship to the *Christian Guardian*'s printer, A.B. of Grimsby reveals her personality and her values in her cookbook. Most of her recipes came from other publications, but her choices were in some way meaningful to her. None was copied verbatim; all were altered to superimpose a personal gloss, sometimes simply, other times more radically, but clearly based on the earlier Mackenzie, Child, or other source recipe. One exception was the meat and fish section, comprising twelve entries that appear to be hers either entirely or at least partially. She states that Baked Meat accords to "my method" and Broiling Meat to "my practical rule." Her deliberate assembly of these recipes, her alterations and editorial comments, and her own writing, though limited, disclose her pleasure in cooking and tending a garden, her interest in good-quality food and attractive presentation, a sense of humour, a romantic streak, and a consciousness of safe practices. She was, as well, practical, sensible, conservative, and, of course frugal.

Our cultural background usually determines the kinds of food we cook in our own kitchen. Newer settlers from Britain in Upper Canada who harboured a sense of superiority often felt frustrated by their "Yankee" neighbours, who understood cornmeal and squash and had very particular ideas about baking. In the 1790s, Elizabeth Simcoe, wife of the lieutenant-governor, welcomed encounters with American foods in the Niagara area. She was thrilled with the breads and cakes she ate when visiting settlers born in the United States.[15] The dominant food culture of the Niagara Peninsula was North American, that is, a kind of fusion cooking of old-world recipes and methods of food preparation adapted to new, locally abundant, basic ingredients. Unfamiliar species of fish, game, fruits, and vegetables demanded fresh ideas about preservation, preparation and serving. Even the flour—such as buckwheat, corn, and rye ground at John Dennis Beamer's mill on Forty Mile Creek, which flowed through the community—was different from the old country. For example, for baking breads and cakes, new types of chemical raising agents, such as pearl ash and saleratus (forerunners of baking powders), had been invented to supplement or replace the ancient brewer's yeast that was either made at home or purchased from a local brewer. Sugar was sold in sugar loaves or cones that had to be broken apart, but in Grimsby in the 1840s expensive white sugar was less likely to be used as a sweetener than any of the grades of imported brown sugars or molasses made from sugar cane, or locally made maple molasses boiled down from maple sap.

A.B. limited herself to just seventy-two recipes (plus a few more in the gardening entries), yet she managed to cover the gamut of standard dishes familiar in Canadian farm households, particularly for cakes and puddings. From her presumably Anglo-American background came all three major types of traditional egg-enriched cakes, represented by one recipe each (Rich Plum Cake, Plain Pound Cake, Sponge Cake, plus an egg-white icing), three of the four major pastries (puff, short, sugar, but not hot suet pastry, which is seldom found in other Canadian cookbooks), two custards, several fundamental preserves (red currant, apple, peach, pear, plum, cherry, egg, onion, cucumber, beet, cabbage), and one basic recipe each for waffles, buns, and fritters. She offered much more variety in puddings, which range from fancy (Floating Island) to plain (Rennet) with fruit (three Apple), baked (Bread), boiled (Jam), stirred (Hasty), and more, demonstrating the many possibilities. However, "One [wine] sauce answers for all kinds of puddings that require sauce," she wrote, then declared a sauce of sweetened cream flavoured with cinnamon or nutmeg "old-fashioned."

The author was clearly schooled in culinary traditions from south of the border, evidenced by her familiarity with chemical leaveners, molasses, and cornmeal. For Indian Pudding, sometimes identified as the American national dish, cornmeal was substituted for wheat flour or oats, which were the principal ingredients of British puddings. Indian Pudding already had a long history in the Canadas, reaching back to encounters by the early explorers with the native people. In Upper Canada, the diet of the first settlers included the original boiled Indian pudding and the later steamed and baked styles, all three undoubtedly familiar to the Loyalists who had enjoyed this food back in pre-Revolution America. To prepare the dish, A.B. first looked at Mrs. Child's *The Frugal Housewife*, but typically she made significant changes to what she found. In one recipe a spirit of extreme frugality prevailed, for it is an egg-less version, much like the "Cheap Indian Pudding" that some cookbook authors recommended if fresh eggs were not at hand. On the one hand, Election Cake was a yeast-risen bread, characterized by its old-style cakey texture, but Americanized by its title, which was taken from Election Day, a festive holiday in the American colonies. On the other hand, Albany Cake, Cup Cake, the Gingerbreads, Fritters, and others all featured rising assistance from saleratus or pearl ash, a clear indication of new-world invention or adaptation.

She was carefully detailed in preparations for some recipes, while others were mere lists of ingredients. Election Cake, for example, reads: "Take five pounds of flour, two of sugar, three quarters of a pound of butter, five eggs, five large spoonfuls of yeast, one pint of milk, and spice as you please." Such an unadorned recipe produces panic in unconfident cooks, both then and today. As was often typical until the end of the nineteenth century, the authors of cookbooks for middle-class homes did not mollycoddle experienced housewives or servants by providing sequential step-by-step instructions, while inexperienced brides, semi-literate servants, or newly motherless young girls assuming the mantle of family housekeeper struggled without them. A.B. seems to have expected her readers to be able to apply their own knowledge, especially in cooking fish and meat. Other cookbook authors expended considerable verbiage on the niceties of roasting, broiling, baking, boiling, simmering, and grilling meat and fish, but A.B. clearly preferred to concentrate on cakes and puddings, as indeed did the readers of the three extant copies who left those pages spattered from use (see Appendix, p. 164).

Despite its silence on roasting skills and equipment, and other techniques, *The Frugal Housewife's Manual* reveals important details about the kitchen in mid-nineteenth-century Ontario farmhouses. Without suitable equipment, roasting in front of a fire was difficult; at the very least, a string was needed to dangle the meat. Mary O'Brien, a farm housewife in Vaughan Township, north of Toronto, coped as best she could in November 1830, as she recorded in her diary: "My little quarter of pork was dangling before the fire at the end

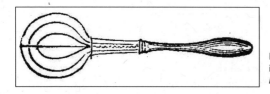

FIGURE 7.5 Flat egg-whip for beating eggs, batter, etc. *The Dominion Home Cook Book*, 1868

of a skein of worsted, for having a loaf to bake I was unable to bake it as usual in the all-accomplishing bake kettle.... [The] frying pan ... was engaged in enacting [as a] dripping pan for the pork" (Miller 1968, 141). Roasting jacks and roasting tins with a central spit were available but uncommon in Upper Canada until after the War of 1812, but by circa 1840 were in general use. A.B.'s kitchen must have been well equipped if we judge by the variety of standard cookware, utensils, and vessels itemized in her recipes and gardening instructions.

She mentions no fancy piece of equipment—no copper fish kettles or brass roasting jacks—but only common items like pickle crocks, pint measures, a pail, broad and narrow knives, wooden bowls, and fine white cloths, plus ordinary specialized tools like a nutmeg grater, an egg whip, an apple corer, a lemon squeezer, and a saw for butchering. If they are included in her chosen recipes she presumably had them in her kitchen drawers. But not specifying something did not mean she did not own it; for instance, items not mentioned by specific name but which were essential include a weigh scale, a rolling pin, a mortar and pestle, and jelly bags. Since many of her dry ingredients were measured in the old European way by pounds and ounces, obviously a weigh scale was present, whereas more "modern"—that is, North American—recipes were measured by dry volume in cups, as in Cup Cake, so named in contrast to the traditional Pound Cake, measured by weights. She did not state "use your skimmer" or "use your strainer," but merely "skim" or "strain," implying the presence of a slotted spoon for skimming and a colander for straining. But lacking either, an ordinary spoon or bowl is possible should they be all that a young housewife possesses. Similarly, A.B.'s two jelly recipes begin with the assumption that the cook already has the red currant juice ready, but to achieve that, the currant berries must have been simmered and then carefully dripped through an unmentioned conical jelly bag. Without that prior knowledge the recipe is incomprehensible. Items not required for her selection of recipes, but supportive of a well-managed kitchen like hers, such as a coffee grinder, bread pans, and a knife grinder, were standard kitchen equipment. Another piece of quotidian cookware, unrecorded by A.B., was the iron bake kettle, nicely captured in Mary O'Brien's ode: "Oh, who can number the uses and perfections of a Canadian bake kettle" (Miller 1968).

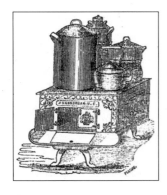

FIGURE 7.6 (above) "The kitchen." *The Canada Farmer*, 1864
FIGURE 7.7 (left) Ad for Van Norman stove, 1842, *The British American Cultivator*. Toronto Reference Library

Newspaper advertisements placed by local shopkeepers and small man-ufacturers describe the products that they made and/or sold. For example, L.D. Winchester had a small workshop at the east end of St. Catharines vil-lage where he manufactured an assortment of tin, copper, and iron wares, "among which may be found Milk Pails, Pans, Strainers of various sizes and prices, Patent Bakers, Covered Pails, Lanthorns, Pint Basins and Cups, Dip-pers, Skimmers, Funnels, Scoops, Pudding Dishes, Graters, Candlesticks, Lamp Fillers, Lard Lamps, Sheet Iron Bread Pans, &c."[16] A pudding dish was a square or round bowl, not to be confused with a pudding mould, which was a much deeper bowl with an interesting shape and was tightly covered with a cloth during cooking. A.B. also helps us to understand the local vocabulary. For example, a tin hoop in Mackenzie's original text becomes a tin dish in A.B.'s version, a dessert spoon becomes a tablespoon, and egg whites beaten until stiff become egg whites beaten until light in her Sponge Cake. She must have changed these terms, and others, in accordance with other women's use of domestic language in her Grimsby community.

The cheerful 1864 kitchen scene from *The Canada Farmer*, although dashed off as a quick sketch for an ongoing domestic column, has an inad-vertent but helpful documentary quality.[17] The housewife-cook is busily engaged in some culinary action, while her toddler and the family dog play at her feet, dangerously close to the flame, and a cat lurks by the table. Through the open door is a vista of bountiful fields, and on the shelves, man-tle, and tabletop are arrayed quite a selection of vessels and utensils. This woodcut neatly captures our sense of A.B.'s kitchen: simple, efficient, active, and not state of the art—she was a frugal housewife, after all. An air of estab-lishment and prosperity seems to exude from the image, just as it does from the cookbook, but a closer examination reveals considerable functionality. This illustration postdates A.B.'s book by over twenty years but is one of the very few Upper Canadian images of a mid-century kitchen, especially one with a hearth, which in 1864 was getting to be fairly old-fashioned, even in far distant rural areas. Her *Manual* appeared right at the point of transition from the ancient hearth to the new iron cook stove, which in 1840 had been readily available in Upper Canada for just over a decade, according to information in many newspapers and references in personal papers. It is likely that A.B., and many other housewives, still had a hearth since only two recipes for preserving peaches and boiling meats specify a cook stove.

COLONIAL CULINARY MYTHS

A few myths and fallacies about foods in our past are still trotted out by those who wish to disparage colonial foods, but such myths can be readily debunked with reference to this little cookbook. Letting A.B. speak from the pages of *The Frugal Housewife's Manual*, we immediately discover that the past was prelude to the diversity and flavourfulness of foods we are able to enjoy today.

Most egregious is the supposed bland and unseasoned food that we are accused of preferring before European and Asian newcomers to Canada awakened our taste buds to exciting unfamiliar flavours. In fact, from earliest colonial times apothecaries and grocers sold a wide range of imported spices and condiments. And recipes demanded that spices be freshly ground in a variety of combinations for curries, soups, meat dishes, and cakes. In 1840, the St. Catharines grocers Ross & M'Leod advertised Allspice, Nutmegs, Cloves, Cinnamon, and Ginger for sale.[18] A.B. uses ten different spices throughout her cookbook, ranging from nutmeg and cinnamon to "such spices as you please to add" in relatively plain cakes such as Sponge Cake, Albany Cake, and Cup Cake. In the case of fruitcakes, which were meant to last for weeks, even months—they were well fortified with brandy and wine— her recipes call for nutmeg, mace and cloves, and allspice and cinnamon. Spices were essential ingredients in puddings based on custard, rice, corn, fruit, and bread, all of which were popular year-round. Vanilla, an expensive ingredient imported from Mexico, had not yet entered the rural cook's repertoire, but A.B. flavoured her puddings with rose water and orange water, which vanilla eventually replaced.

At first glance, a rich ingredient like butter might seem excessive in the amounts found in the recipes, but let us imagine a cake that calls for one pound of fresh butter, a pound of sugar, and a dozen eggs, such as A.B.'s Rich Plum Cake or her Black Cake. Then imagine an extended family of easily ten or more around the table, plus boarders and servants—a gathering not uncommon for the time. When you study the recipe carefully and see that a pound and a half of flour are listed, plus several pounds of fruit and the all-important brandy or wine, one realizes a huge cake pan is involved. Today the end result would nicely feed the equivalent of two football teams of hungry eaters. Nineteenth-century recipes took into account large numbers of diners, not just the four servings prescribed in today's cookbooks.

We have already hinted at the role that brandy and wine played in cake baking, where alcohol ensured a moist consistency. In addition, the alcohol secured a long shelf-life for a Black (that is, Fruit) Cake, except, as A.B. warns the reader, with her usual humour, "it will keep for six months in a suitable place. You can choose the place yourself; but I would advise you to put it under lock and key." It is true that in villages and towns throughout Upper Canada, temperance societies exerted strong moral authority.[19] However, "temperance" did not mean total abstinence from alcohol. This was a time when the scourge of homemade brews left farm labourers drunk in haystacks and farmers hard-pressed to plant and harvest their crops, but it wasn't just a class problem. Ross & M'Leod of St. Catharines sold fine wines, as well as spices, advertising Cognac and Bordeaux, Brandy, Jamaica Spirits, Whisky, Holland Gin, Port Wine, and several brands of Madeira.[20] At banquets and official dinners, posh people managed to down endless glasses of claret and hock, champagne and brandy, and port and liqueurs in twenty or more toasts to the Queen, to all those present, and to everybody they could think of in between. Banquets often ended after 1 a.m., with the celebrants staggering home, usually on foot, fortunately. The misuse of alcohol led religious authorities to promote alcohol in moderation.

In many ways the eating and drinking habits of the people of Ontario took a turn for the worse after the beginning of the twentieth century. That decline can be ascribed in part to food adulteration; the loss of species of fish, game, and fruits; and the introduction of refrigerated, canned, and frozen foods, and chemical preservatives—topics for further research.

GARDENING

Precisely half of *The Frugal Housewife's Manual* is devoted to the growing and cooking of vegetables. There are few precedents in North American cookery lore for a woman writing about wielding a spade or a hoe, let alone a plough or a garden roller, as A.B. does here. Yet in British North America it was women who were in charge of the kitchen garden. A number of American food historians have observed that the early settlers in New England had neither the time nor the necessary equipment—nor, it must be said, the will—to grow vegetables other than those that could be kept over the winter in cold cellars. In Upper Canada, if the settlers had the time and the energy, they were inclined to uphold the English tradition of the kitchen garden. Joseph Pickering had reported in 1825 that "Gardens in York [now Toronto] are generally in good order, better than I have seen elsewhere in America, and the vegetables, &c. in them" (1831, 96). Six years later Isaac Fidler, an Anglican minister and gardener, was disappointed that struggling new emigrants had less time for their gardens than was usual back in England: "Gardening is, in Canada as in the States, but little cared for; and garden produce, when purchased, is very dear.... Much time cannot be devoted to horticultural pursuits, and a little time is not sufficient to keep a garden in order" (1833, 369–70).

But a lack of time was only one of several obstacles. Another was working one's way through the extravagant claims made in nurserymen's advertisements and catalogues. For the successful cultivation of vegetables and fruits, seeds with a watertight pedigree are essential. As A.B. notes in her Onion instructions, "good seed, well put in, will not fail to come up well." But in the 1840s, tracking down reliable seeds for the garden took time. Just a few years earlier, Catharine Parr Traill had complained about a "Yankee trick" of making customers pay for seeds, and then receiving the packet with nothing but "empty husks" (1836, 179).

Grimsby farmers and gardeners could purchase seeds from the store of Wm. C. Chace of neighbouring St. Catharines. Chace's advertisement for 1833 lists forty kinds of English vegetable seeds and twenty varieties of New York seeds.[21] Also, in towns all over Upper Canada one could buy seeds grown by the Shakers, who had settled near Albany in New York State. The Niagara Apothecary Store—the shop still exists as a museum in the centre of Niagara-on-the-Lake—advised newspaper readers that they had "a quantity of fresh garden seeds of all descriptions put up by the Shakers in New Lebanon, New York."[22] New (or Mount) Lebanon was just a day's cart-ride southeast of Kingston and the St. Lawrence River. As early as 1795 the Shakers had been in the business of selling reliable seeds to the public, and they were among the earliest commercial vendors to package seeds in small paper packets rather than in cloth bags or barrels.

A gardening manual published in 1835 by the Shakers of Mount Lebanon was the source of much of the gardening section in *The Frugal Housewife's Manual*. Charles F. Crosman, the Garden Deacon in the community, compiled *The Gardener's Manual*, which was then published in 1835 by the Shakers. Each spring Crosman led a parade westward with wagonloads of seeds destined for merchants along the south shore of Lake Ontario who in turn sold them to shopkeepers in Upper Canada.[23] On the back cover of his booklet are listed twenty-seven kinds of vegetable seeds, each available in a number of varieties, and inside are brief directions for planting the seeds along with a few cookery recipes. Crosman's *Manual* was sold with the seed packets in retail outlets. The seeds marketed by the Shakers intrigued the young immigrant Adam Hope. Writing in 1835 to his father back in Scotland he noted, "A great many of the Store Keepers in Hamilton keep stocks, small stocks of Garden seeds. These seeds are procured from the Society of Shakers in Columbia Co. New York State, who employ Peddlers to hawk them thro' the Canadas. They are put up in small boxes, are all neatly assorted & a Catalogue goes along with each Box, and the cost of a Box about 2 ft x 12" x 6" is $6 or $7" (Crerar 2007, 103).

The author of *The Frugal Housewife's Manual* must have had in her possession a copy of the Crosman publication. In this section A.B. took full advantage of the time-honoured tradition of "borrowing" substantially from another author's work. However, Crosman had done the same when he put together his booklet, lifting large sections out of previously published American and British gardening books such as Thomas Fessenden's *The New American Gardener*, first published in 1828. As she had done in the cookery section, A.B. made a few small changes that better adapted the Shakers' directions to local conditions. She listed twenty-six vegetables, omitting the Mustard and Saffron in Crosman's *Manual*, but adding the Bene Plant, which was the source of sesame seeds, Eggplant, and Nasturtiums, whose seed pods are pickled as a kind of caper. All of these are found in Thomas Fessenden's book. Crosman had relied on *The New American Gardener*, but Fessenden in turn cited the entire catalogue of a Boston nurseryman, John B. Russell. Like cookbook compilers, the most revered garden writers have never been too proud to adopt well-expressed sets of directions and to reproduce them as their own work! The few alterations made by A.B. reflect adaptations to local conditions. For example, she changed spellings from American to British-Canadian usages. Sometimes she makes minor additions, such as recommending a concoction of tobacco juice, soot, and ashes to discourage worms from nibbling on cabbage roots. Cooking directions often accompany the growing instructions and it is here that we find a recipe for Tomato Catchup or Catsup, "an excellent sauce or gravy for meat or fish," and an accompaniment to codfish. Properly a fruit, tomatoes can be made into pies when a little sugar is added. In 1840 tomatoes were met with widespread suspicion but A.B. assures readers that physicians recommend tomatoes as not only delicious, but harmless!

The Frugal Housewife's Manual appears to be only the second book published in all of North America that brings together sections on cookery and gardening. The first is by H.L. Barnum, an Ohio-based writer on agriculture and farming, whose *Family Receipts* (1828) was aimed at "husbandmen and housewives." Barnum cheerfully mentions that he borrowed his recipes from "the most celebrated American and European works" and then lists his sources, including *Mackenzie's 5000 Receipts*. And his gardening directions are largely taken from Thomas Fessenden's *New American Gardener*, which had inspired both Charles Crosman and A.B. It was a small world then, and it has made a full circle here.

CONCLUSION

In comparison with other cookbooks that had been imported into Canada in the nineteenth century from the United States, Great Britain, and Europe, *The Frugal Housewife's Manual* is exceedingly modest in size and production values, reflecting the likely low sales expectations of the author and publisher. In nineteenth-century Britain, cookbooks sold well—certainly better than poetry, and often better than novels—and publishers were always looking for best-sellers. Evidently housewives in Upper Canada did not embrace the *Manual*, and its influence on the foodways of its time would have been marginal, if not negligible. Reviewers in newspapers and periodicals assessed each new title as a useful contribution to the body of gastronomical literature. Regretfully, this little book did not receive that kind of attention back in 1840. Yet, at a mere 14.5 cm or 5 3/4 inches tall, its pages, as suggested here, succeed in evoking the domestic culture of rural Anglo-Canada in the mid-1800s. Until recently, cookbooks have been dismissed by academics as little more than curiosities. Today we are learning to appreciate their documentary value, their power to illuminate their times, and their archival importance as artifacts for popular culture study.

APPENDIX

Shrewsbury Cake, *The Frugal Housewife's Manual*, page 4, number 10.

Original Recipe

Mix half a pound of butter well beaten, and the same weight of flour, one egg, six ounces of sifted loaf sugar, and half an ounce of caraway seeds; form these into a paste, roll them thin, and cut them out. Bake on tin in a moderately heated oven.

Modern instructions: Interpreted by Fiona Lucas

Preheat oven to 180°C (350°F). Yield: about 30 cookies 5 cm (2") in diameter.

1 cup	250 mL	soft unsalted butter
1 cup	250 mL	white sugar
2 tsp	10 mL	whole caraway seeds
1	1	egg, beaten
2 cups	500 mL	white flour

1. Cream the butter and sugar together until very light.
2. Blend in the caraway seeds and beaten egg.
3. Blend in the flour half a cup at a time until a tender but not sticky dough forms. Divide into two sections.
4. Roll out one section on a well-floured surface to about 8 mm (¼") thin. Stamp out with a round cookie cutter. Gather up scraps and reroll.
5. Repeat with second section. Repeat with scraps.
6. Bake on an ungreased or papered sheet for 12 to 15 minutes or until very lightly golden.

Historical information

Shrewsbury Cakes were essentially caraway-flavoured shortbreads that appeared frequently in eighteenth- and nineteenth-century British, American, and Canadian cookbooks. Variations still appear in cookie collections. The text of A.B.'s recipe can be traced back through several cookbooks to at least 1769, when it appeared in *The Experienced English Housekeeper* by Elizabeth Raffald, a Manchester confectioner and baker.

NOTES

1 *The Cook Not Mad*, published in 1831 by James Macfarlane of Kingston, Ontario, is often said to be Canada's first cookbook, but in fact Macfarlane imported copies of *The Cook Not Mad*, published in Watertown, New York, in 1830, replacing the title page with his own.

2 Eleven advertisements for the cookbook appeared in the *Christian Guardian* between April 8 and November 4, 1840.

3 One copy is in the Special Collections Department (the Baldwin Room) of the Toronto Reference Library, and another is in the William Reddy Division of Archives and Research Collections, McMaster University Libraries, Hamilton, Ontario. The Toronto Reference Library copy was filmed by the Canadian Institute for Historical Microreproductions and can be viewed as microfiche number CIHM 90013 in many Canadian libraries. The text has been digitized and is accessible from Early Canadiana Online through subscribing libraries.

4 Colin Mackenzie's *Five Thousand Receipts* ... (1823) was reissued and enlarged by Hayes and Zell of Philadelphia. The American edition of this all-encompassing

compendium added a supplement by "An American Physician" in which Cookery and Confectionery were merely two sections out of fifty-four.

5   Lydia Maria Child's *The American Frugal Housewife* (1829) was originally published as *The Frugal Housewife*, but the eighth edition of 1832 included the adjective American to distinguish it from Sarah Carter's *The Frugal Housewife* published in London (1765), New York and Boston (1772), and Albany (1796), which was still circulating. There have been several reprint editions in recent years, but the 1830 edition can be viewed online at "Feeding America," the digital archive of cookbooks sponsored by the Michigan State University Library: http://digital.lib.msu.edu/projects/cookbooks/html/authors/author_child.html.

6   The 1798 edition can be viewed online at "Feeding America" (see above) at http://digital.lib.msu.edu/projects/cookbooks/html/authors/author_simmons.html.

7   See the *Christian Guardian*, Sept. 9, 1840, 183, for twenty-two lines on Mrs. Child's cookbook, the presumably male reviewer declaring, "Another shall dictate to our pen when the Housewife's duties ask attention."

8   *British Colonial Argus* (St. Catharines) on Aug. 5, 1833; *The Housekeeper's Book … with a Complete Collection of Receipts for Economical Domestic Cookery*, first published in Philadelphia in 1837, and advertised in the *St. Catharines Journal*, Aug. 20, 1840; William Kitchiner's *The Cook's Oracle*, first published in London as *Apicius Redivivus* in 1817, and advertised by Alexander Davidson in the *Niagara Reporter*, May 28, 1841; and *The Cook's Own Book* by N.K.M. Lee, first published in Boston and New York in 1833, and advertised by Alexander Davidson as above.

9   For discussion of Niagara's wine culture today, see Hugh Gayler's study in this volume.

10 Taken from the 1851 Canada West Census, Lincoln County, Grimsby Township, microfilm C-11736, 49 sheets.

11 In her article, "Female Servants in the Bush," Catharine Parr Traill, writing from near Peterborough, Ontario, observed, "Irish servants are more plentiful than English or Scotch." She goes on to describe the considerable differences between the Protestant girls and the Catholic girls. *Sharpe's Magazine* 15 (Jan.–June, 1852), 279–81.

12 Report in *The Patriot* (Toronto), Aug. 7, 1840. In the Niagara Historical Society Collection at the Archives of Ontario (F1138), there are Thomas Craig's manuscript accounts for the dinner in Niagara Town Council Papers, Scrapbooks, Misc., reel 12, 149.

13 Report in *The Niagara Chronicle*, Jan. 17, 1845.

14 *St. Catharines Journal*, Aug. 20, 1840.

15 In her diary entry for August 6, 1793, Elizabeth Simcoe wrote: "The Governor brought me some very good cakes [from St. John's Creek]. The miller's wife is from the United States, where the women excel in making cakes and breads" (1934, 183).

16 *St. Catharines Journal*, 1844.

17 *The Canada Farmer*, several issues in 1864.

18 Advertisement in *St. Catharines Journal*, Apr. 9, 1840.

19 On May 14, 1842, thirty-nine individuals attended a temperance meeting in Grimsby and signed the pledge. *Canada Temperance Advocate* 8:4 (June 15, 1842), 52. For more information on the subject of drink, see Dan Malleck's study in this volume.

20 Advertisement in *St. Catharines Journal*, Apr. 9, 1840.
21 *The Farmer's Journal* (St. Catharines), Apr. 18, 1833.
22 Advertisements placed by Starkwather and Brown for Shaker seeds offered at the Niagara Apothecary appeared in *The Colonial Advocate*, Mar. 30, 1826, and in issues up to February 1840.
23 By 1841 Crosman had left the Shaker community and with M.B. Bateman had opened the Rochester Seed Store in New York State, east of Grimsby along the south shore of Lake Ontario. As Bateman and Crosman, they advertised seeds to gardeners in the Niagara Region (*St. Catharines Journal*, Apr. 29, 1841). Peter Wetsel, a merchant in Kingston, was advertising Shaker seeds as early as 1816 (*Kingston Gazette*, Mar. 30, 1816).

WORKS CITED

A.B. of Grimsby. *The Frugal Housewife's Manual, Containing a Number of Useful Receipts, Carefully Selected, and Well Adapted to the Use of Families In General, to which Are Added Plain and Practical Directions for the Cultivation and Management of Some of the Most Useful Culinary Vegetables*. Toronto: Guardian Office, 1840.

Barnum, H.L. *Family Receipts, or, Practical Guide for the Husbandman and Housewife, Containing a Great Variety of Valuable Recipes, Relating to Agriculture, Gardening, Brewery, Cookery, Dairy, Confectionary, Diseases, Farriery, Ingrafting, and the Various Branches of Rural and Domestic Economy*. Cincinnati: A.B. Roff, 1828.

Bouchette, Joseph. *The British Dominions in North America, or, A Topographical and Statistical Description of the Provinces of Lower and Upper Canada*. London: H. Colburn and R. Bentley, 1831.

Child, Lydia Maria. *The American Frugal Housewife, Dedicated to Those Who Are Not Ashamed of Economy*. Boston: Carter, Hendee and Co., 1829.

Crerar, Adam. *Letters of Adam Hope, 1834–1845*. Toronto: Champlain Society, 2007.

Crosman, Charles F. *The Gardener's Manual Containing Some Plain and Practical Directions for the Cultivation and Management of Some of the Most Useful Culinary Vegetables: to which is Prefixed a Catalogue of the Various Kinds of Garden Seeds Raised in the United Society at New Lebanon, Pittfield and Watervliet, with a Few General Remarks on the Management of a Kitchen Garden*. Albany, NY: Haffman and White, 1835.

Fessenden, Thomas G. *The New American Gardener, Containing Practical Directions on the Culture of Fruits and Vegetables*. 8th edition. Boston: Russell, Odiorne and Co, and Carter, Hendee and Co., 1834.

Fidler, Isaac. *Observations on Professions, Literature, Manners and Emigration in the United States and Canada, Made During a Residence There in 1832*. London: Whittaker, Treacher, 1833.

Howison, John. *Sketches of Upper Canada, Domestic, Local, and Characteristic: to which are Added Practical Details for the Information of Emigrants of Every Class*. Edinburgh: Oliver and Boyd, 1821.

Jameson, Anna. *Winter Studies and Summer Rambles in Canada*. London: Saunders & Otley, 1838.

Mackenzie, Colin. *Five Thousand Receipts in All the Useful and Domestic Arts, Constituting a Complete Practical Library*. London: 1823. Reissued and enlarged by Hayes and Zell: Philadelphia, 1825.

Miller, Audrey Saunders, ed. *The Journals of Mary O'Brien, 1828–1838*. Toronto: Macmillan of Canada, 1968.

Moodie, Susanna. *Roughing It in the Bush: or, Forest Life in Canada*, v. 2. London: R. Bentley, 1852.

Pickering, Joseph. *Inquiries of an Emigrant: Being the Narrative of an English Farmer from the Year 1824 to 1830, during which Period He Traversed the United States of America, and the British Province of Canada, with a View to Settle as an Emigrant*. London: E. Wilson, 1831.

Simcoe, Elizabeth. *The Diary of Mrs. John Graves Simcoe, Wife of the First Lieutenant-Governor of the Province of Upper Canada, 1792–6*. Toronto: Ontario Publishing Co., 1934.

Simmons, Amelia. *American Cookery*. Hartford, CT: Printed by Hudson and Goodwin for the author, 1796.

Traill, Catharine Parr. *The Backwoods of Canada, Being Letters from the Wife of an Emigrant Officer, Illustrative of the Domestic Economy of British America*. London: C. Night, 1836.

Turcotte, Dorothy. *Gleanings from Grimsby*. Grimsby Historical Society, 2007.

"A LITTLE MORE THAN A DRINK"
Public Drinking and Popular Entertainment in Post-Prohibition Niagara, 1927–1944

DAN MALLECK

INTRODUCTION

Situated so close to the United States, the Niagara Region's cultural and social life is often directly affected by economic, social, and political changes "across the river." Never was this connection more clear than when looking at Prohibition-era popular culture. In 1927, the province ended its decade-long dalliance with alcohol prohibition, creating the Liquor Control Board of Ontario (LCBO), charged with enforcing the Liquor Control Act (1927) (LCA) and tightly regulating the distribution of alcoholic beverages in the province (Malleck 2003).[1] In the United States, Prohibition remained the law of the land. Indeed, unlike the provincially mandated legislation in Canada, in the United States it was a federal law with the authority of a constitutional amendment (the Eighteenth). Many thirsty Americans rushed across the border, finding that, while they could buy booze in stores, at breweries, or wineries, they were forbidden from going to a bar and consuming alcohol in public spaces. The consumption of beer in public places remained restricted to low-alcohol "light beer" (roughly 2.2 percent alcohol by volume).[2] In 1934 things changed. Partially in response to the end of American Prohibition with the passage of the Twenty-First Amendment in December 1933, the LCA was expanded to permit the tightly regulated sale of beer in hotel beverage rooms, and beer and wine in their dining rooms. As a result, the LCBO's work expanded, and a struggle began to define what was allowed and disallowed in these public drinking spaces.

While it may appear now to be an oddity, this struggle to define the parameters of public drinking had considerable social importance. Although alcohol, music, and dance may seem to accompany one another naturally in contemporary leisure space, the relative respectability of these activities did not emerge without considerable social anxiety. In *Bad Habits* John Burnham argues that various activities including drinking, smoking, swearing, sexual impropriety, and drug-taking formed what he calls a "vice constellation" in the minds of regulators and indeed many individuals from at least the late nineteenth century onward (1994). For many social reformers, to this vice constellation could be added such activities as dancing, singing, and the intermingling of the sexes (Perry 1989). Although alcohol consumption was a popular target for reformers who voiced concerns over the direction in which society was headed, those activities connected with public drinking, including dancing and popular music, also came under scrutiny, especially as they were associated with the troubles of inter-war youth culture (Comacchio 1997, 2006). Since this constellation of vices included alcohol consumption, the public drinking establishment (such as the tavern, saloon, or beverage room) was seen to be the centre of social danger. According to popular reformist thinking, to prohibit the manufacture and sale of spirituous liquors, beer, and wine was to remove a major roadblock to the development of society. Prohibition in the United States and Canada had been considered, therefore, a progressive reform of mass social improvement.

When these Prohibition regimes ended, government administrators charged with reconstructing public drinking were faced with the dilemma of reconstituting public alcohol consumption without seeming to revivify the perceived moral cesspool of the saloon. The solution in 1934 was to restrict drinking to the beverage rooms and dining rooms of properly inspected and licensed "Standard Hotels," establishments that were already being inspected and licensed by the LCBO. Since the beginning of the century, public drinking in the province was restricted to establishments that provided some form of hotel service. The LCBO in 1927 continued the work of its predecessor organization, the Prohibition-era Board of License Commissioners, and inspected and granted licences to Standard Hotels. So when the law changed in 1934, the government determined that public drinking would be permitted only in hotel beverage rooms and dining rooms—much to the chagrin of restaurant owners—with establishments deemed suitable receiving a beer or (for the dining rooms) beer and wine "authority." After a flurry of applications from well over 1,000 hotels, Ontario's new public drinking regime began in July.

FIGURE 8.1 New Statler Hotel, 70 James Street, St. Catharines, c. 1937. When it was demolished, it was known as the Harding Hotel; a Tim Hortons coffee shop now occupies the site. Archives of Ontario

With a mandate to control but permit public alcohol consumption, the LCBO had to balance the demands of social order, informed by pre-Prohibition temperance ideals about what constituted moral and immoral public behaviour, with the practicalities and business realities of operating a public drinking establishment in Ontario. These competing expectations and pressures created something of a "shake-down" period of the post-1934 LCA. The LCBO approached public drinking with specific ideas about its dangers and the best way to maintain order, but its administrators combined this concern for social order with an appreciation of the importance of beverage rooms and hotels in the social fabric. At the same time, the drinking public had its own sets of assumptions about what activities they wanted to accompany their beer, while beverage room proprietors, facing significant Depression-era financial pressures, had their ideas about how to make their businesses successful. The result is an example of the negotiation of values and rules that T.J. Jackson Lears argues characterizes the dialectical process of value creation (1985). Rather than regulatory authorities simply dictating behaviour, a rule formation process was negotiated. Kathy Peiss examines this process in her study of the development and regulation of working-class amusements in New York City (1986), and Robert Campbell describes similar negotiations in Vancouver's hotel beer parlours (2001).

This study examines how hotel proprietors in what is now the Niagara Region (Lincoln and Welland Counties, which the board referred to as the Niagara District) balanced the regulator's vision of what public drinking could look like with customers' expectations of what they should be allowed to do on an evening out. Although the LCBO inspectors and management tended to look with disfavour upon innovations that broke the rules, they also recognized the need to accommodate the demands of the public. In the process, the connection between public drinking and other popular amusements was tested. While the LCBO remained steadfast in its enforcement of rules regarding the activities permitted in beverage rooms, loopholes within the Liquor Control Act permitted hotel proprietors to tap into the demand for licensed public dancing in their dining rooms. To do otherwise would be to drive beverage-room customers back to the doors of bootleggers.

RULES OF CONDUCT

Designed consciously to reduce the temptations toward immorality, the beverage room of 1934 looked significantly different from the typical or, perhaps, stereotypical pre-Prohibition saloon, and this contrast was rooted in the LCA and the mandate of the LCBO. The board instituted a number of rules that forbade a range of social activities, part of the "vice constellation," from taking place in the beverage rooms. The stand-up bar was forbidden, and patrons were required to sit at a table and order their beer from a male waiter—a similar situation to that which existed in Vancouver's beer parlours (Campbell 2001). Gambling, singing, any performed music, either pre-recorded or live, and virtually any activity besides sitting at a table and drinking beer were forbidden. For the most part, the LCBO also forbade food in the beverage rooms, although there is some indication that they permitted small bowls of snack foods such as peanuts or pretzels. Clearly, the beverage room was intended to be a strictly controlled environment where the only activities permitted were drinking and quiet conversation. The liquor authorities frowned upon spontaneous, rowdy, boisterous behaviour, and serving a person to the point of drunkenness was illegal. To deal simultaneously with a perceived problem of prostitutes soliciting in beverage rooms and with women's demands for a space in which they could drink untroubled by drunken, lascivious single men, within a few weeks of instituting beverage room rules, the board mandated that authorized hotels needed to have separate men's and ladies-and-

FIGURE 8.2 New Statler Hotel Ladies and Escorts beverage room, c. 1937. Archives of Ontario

escorts beverage rooms. With the Beer Authority, then, came the responsibility to ensure that conduct did not get out of control.

If the beverage room rules were designed in an effort to eliminate the association between public drinking and disreputable leisure activities, the hotel dining room appears to have been designed to reinforce a specific vision of respectable drinking. All Standard Hotels were required to have dining rooms for "the traveling public," which could (and usually did) receive an Authority to serve beer and wine with meals. As with the beverage rooms, these hotel dining rooms would be strictly controlled, but the range of acceptable activities was broader than the beverage rooms; the board permitted music and later some casual dancing under clearly defined guidelines, but always with the reminder that dancing and drinking should be secondary to the sale of meals or the provision of lodgings. This permission, as I discuss later, created a loophole that Authority holders were anxious to exploit, leading to a growth in public dancing places where beer was served. With the advent of the licensed hotel beverage and dining rooms, public drinking, albeit under tight control, reappeared in Ontario.

The administration of public drinking in Ontario fit into a broad range of experiments in government control of the sale of liquor throughout the

FIGURE 8.3 New Statler Hotel dining room, c. 1937, St. Catharines. Archives of Ontario

world. Each of these liquor control regimes had different features, based on a variety of cultural and social perceptions of the problems with public drinking. In some locations, regulators considered eating, for example, to be a necessary adjunct to public drinking and required meals to be served with liquor. But in Ontario, as in British Columbia, the regulators appear to have intended to strip other forms of socialization from drinking, making alcohol a singular pursuit, and lifting it from the perceived debased centre of working-class socialization.[3] This perception of social danger in the public drinking space was the result of decades of temperance and moral reform activity, which centred on the working-class "saloon" as a hotbed of social danger (Heron 2004, Powers 1998). In the eyes of the LCBO, if people wanted to go out for a beer in Ontario, that is all they could consume in the beverage room. If they wanted to go for dinner, they could have a beer or a glass of wine.

From the LCBO records, it seems clear that many people went out for a drink with a distinct view of what should be allowed to take place. These ideas were often in marked contrast to the rules laid down by the LCBO in its near-annual *Schedule of Rules and Regulations* and dozens of "circulars" that informed the Authority holders of new rules or reiterated older ones that had been transgressed. Nevertheless, many Authority holders attempted to skirt the rules, exploit loopholes, or simply push the boundaries of what was acceptable in order to attract customers and achieve business success.

DRINKING CONDUCT IN NIAGARA

The contrast between the LCBO's expectations and public demands for activities they could undertake in public drinking establishments was especially vivid in Niagara. Sitting on the border with the United States and directly south across Lake Ontario from Toronto, and containing several vacation destinations including Crystal Beach, Niagara Falls, and Port Dalhousie, the Niagara Region was a prime location for travellers and long-term visitors, and hotel proprietors often heard persistent demands from their patrons, especially but not exclusively from travellers from the United States (Malleck 2007). Moreover, the major modifications of the 1934 LCA came just before the Depression entered its fifth year and partially as a reaction to the end of Prohibition in the United States. Since Niagara's tourist trade had benefited from a large number of thirsty American visitors and had seen a considerable boom due to Prohibition in the United States, it was vulnerable as the Depression continued and as American Prohibition ended (Dubinsky 1999, Heron 2004). A Beer, or Beer and Wine, Authority could boost a hotel's financial prospects but often came at a price: it was accompanied both by customers' expectations of what they could do in a drinking establishment, and the LCBO's expectations that the Authority holder would run a clean operation. Hotel proprietors, then, had to balance the demands and expectations of their patrons with the rules of the Liquor Control Board. Sometimes they were successful, but more often they faced the consequences.

Proprietors' attempts to massage the law into something more lucrative may be classified broadly in two categories: illegal activities and simple rule violations. Illegal activities were those that actually violated the Liquor Control Act, such as bootlegging, selling after hours, and selling to minors, and could result in a conviction. Rule violations, such as permitting singing or dancing in a beverage room, permitting immoral activities to take place in the hotel rooms (which could be illegal but often did not go to court), and allowing minors into areas where people were drinking, were incidents of breaking the LCBO's regulations but not actually violating the LCA. Such activities also would result in some sort of penalty, ranging from "a slap on the wrist" warning letter to a temporary suspension or even permanent cancellation of the premises' Authority. In examining the reshaping of the activities within the hotels, it is important to keep these differences in mind. The LCBO was attempting to create an environment where drinking was permitted but in a controlled space. To do so it needed to be permissive enough to make the legal (controlled) drinking space attractive, but restrictive enough to eliminate potentially troublesome if not outright illegal activities.

In the early years of the LCBO, hotels were often the sites of clear violations of the LCA. Prior to 1934, the LCBO employed only six inspectors for the whole province, and surveillance of the hotels was difficult. Several individuals who had been suspected or convicted of illegal activities applied for Authorities for hotels they managed. The New Statler Hotel, on James Street in downtown St. Catharines, saw a succession of managers apply for the Authority, and when they could not obtain it because of their shady past, they would move on and a new manager would be hired. In November 1927 the proprietor of the New Statler was convicted under the LCA and a new manager took his place. This manager was scrutinized and also found to be of less than ideal character. The Ontario Provincial Police (OPP) investigated his background and found that he was "quite a heavy drinker and for a time was head of the Canadian Legion Club where liquor [i.e., spirits] was dispensed very freely." They further noted that "the local police have been on the alert ... for infractions of the Liquor Control Act" since he took over the hotel (Elliot 1927). The board wrote to the manager noting that he was "a heavy drinker and have [sic] been under some suspicion in the past of irregular conduct," and that his application was not going to be approved (Dingman 1927a). The proprietors of the King George Hotel in Crystal Beach repeatedly were denied an Authority owing to the board's suspicions about the manager's character, and in 1931, the board asked the local provincial member of Parliament, W. G. Willson, to comment on this individual. Willson wrote, "being a new arrival and of the foreign race [he was Italian] he might use [the Authority] as a guise to screen the good stuff [strong beer], as the police inform me he comes from Toronto" (1931). Here xenophobia drove the concern over the manager's character and stopped him from getting an Authority; both this man's ethnic background and his big-city roots made him suspect. Crystal Beach, on the shore of Lake Erie, was an especially insular hotel community, hostile to outsiders who attempted to break into the hospitality market.

These examples of pre-emptive refusals do not mean that the LCBO was always able to screen out unscrupulous applicants. In 1927, a month after the LCA came into effect, the police raided the Alexandra Hotel in Niagara Falls and found the following beverages stored there:

8 Cartons 96 qt bottles Taylor & Bates ale in pantry off main dining room of
    hotel
36 qt bottles Taylor and Bate in ice box in bar room
3 cartons 36 quarts Taylor & Bates ale in buffette [sic] in bar-room
1 case of Canadian Club whisky in basement of hotel (Walter 1927).

The manager pleaded guilty and was fined $300 and costs. His lawyers
tried to convince the LCBO that their client should keep his Standard Hotel
Licence and Light Beer Permit, but the LCBO would have nothing of it, the
Director of Hotels explaining that "the search showed in all fourteen dozens
of beer in three places ... and one case of whiskey ... all indicative of intent
to violate the law" (Dingman 1927b). In 1930 the Foxhead Inn in Niagara
Falls was raided, and the assistant manager and head waiter, along with a
customer, were charged after the police found bottles of regular-strength
beer on tables in front of forty American guests.[4] The manager of the inn,
Howard Fox, was a respected businessman (Dubinsky 1999, 135), and in
this case he did not lose his Authority, though it may have been suspended.
The OPP reported in early 1934 (before the new LCA) that St. Catharines'
Mansion House on downtown William Street was operating as a gambling
house and bootlegging "joint" where patrons could buy regular-strength
beer. The police inspector recommended that its Standard Hotel Licence be
cancelled, since the proprietor, who also owned the hotel, would otherwise lease the place to someone who would be a "blind" for the owner's illegal operations (Shannon 1934). Some hotel proprietors saw the hotel
beverage room as tantamount to a resurrected saloon, and the board had
to correct that perception.

The sheer number of applications in 1934 meant that for much of the first
year of the new LCA's operation, the board's inspectors and the OPP spent
a lot of time retroactively evaluating and in some cases rescinding the hotel's
Authority. A key factor of this work was evaluating a proprietor's character,
scrutinizing his past, and speculating on his likelihood to cause trouble.
Reporting on the proprietor of the Lakeside Hotel in Fort Erie in 1935, Inspector Wilson Wylie observed, "[He] has some convictions against him in connection with boot legging activities and therefore suggestive that he is the
type that in all probability would court trouble" (1935e). When this proprietor went to jail one year later for non-liquor-related reasons, the new appli-
cant was considered by Wylie to be a front for the old proprietor's partner,
who would continue their "Rackets" (1936b). The proprietor of the City
Hotel in Humberstone was found to have a very spotty reputation. Combining a moral estimation of the man's character with his illegal activities, the
inspector reported that this proprietor had engaged in a love affair with a

married woman and had been convicted of bootlegging in the 1920s (Dean 1934, anon. letter to LCBO 1936). His application was denied, but a questionable background did not always condemn a proprietor to beer sale purgatory. Wylie described the proprietor of the Merritton Hotel as having "quite a record in local courts and ... the reputation of having made money from bootlegging operations," but he still received an Authority, and he appears to have built a reputable business (Wylie 1934a). Retroactive evaluations such as these enabled the board to anticipate problems before they became full-blown controversies, but it appears that they recognized the exigencies of Prohibition may have made criminals out of otherwise respectable individuals, so some forgiveness was dispensed.

PUSHING THE BOUNDARIES OF ACCEPTABILITY

This screening process was not flawless, since it permitted the board to evaluate a proprietor's or hotel's potential for rule violation only on the basis of past events. Such a system would not prevent proprietors from following in the same footsteps as the bootleggers before them. The lure of the profitability of surreptitious liquor, combined with the demands of the customers, meant that many proprietors were tempted to break the law. Newspapers and LCBO files are replete with stories of hotels being raided and the proprietors busted for violations of the LCA. Major violations included selling hard liquor, selling after hours and on Sundays, and off-site sales when people could buy beer and take it out of the hotel. Responding to a tip from the local police, Inspector Wylie visited the New Murray Hotel in St. Catharines at 1:30 a.m. and found people in the rotunda; he suspected that there had been gambling but could find no proof. Six months later he received a complaint from a resident at the hotel that they were keeping "a race tract [sic] book" and were selling liquor on Sundays, and that "loose women [were] frequenting the hotel." A few weeks later the OPP raided the place and found betting slips and suggestive evidence that a clerk had been selling liquor. Since they could not prove definitively that the proprietor was involved in the illegal activities, the board issued a stern rebuke but did not suspend the Authority (Wylie 1936a, OPP 1936). In the course of a year, the proprietor of Port Colborne's Belmont Hotel was accused of serving cocktails and allowing prostitution, gambling, and after-hours drinking in the bedrooms. After one surprise visit, when Inspector Wylie told the staff to find the manager, he was located in a local "bootlegging joint" (Wylie 1937d, Smith 1937). These activities, if not typical, were at least *stereotypical* of pre-Prohibition taverns and anathema to the LCBO's regulatory expectations.

While a notable number of hotel proprietors attempted to violate the law by engaging in these sorts of activities, the majority of hotel proprietors made a more concerted attempt to work within the law. Nevertheless, most hotel proprietors at some time faced a rebuke from the board for contravention of the rules. Many of these rule violations were for what we might call "fringe" transgressions—activities that stepped just outside the boundaries of what the board considered appropriate. Some of these activities might have stemmed from ignorance of the rules, while others were certainly intentional attempts to push the boundaries. This distinction is difficult to make, and therefore I will not attempt to analyze the veracity of reasons cited in reports or the conditions under which these violations were made, but rather consider the types of activities undertaken, and how the board responded, in order to examine the process of negotiation at the fringes of permissibility.

Since hotels were the only public establishments where drinking was permitted, and these hotels were a mixture of private rooms (bedrooms, owners' residences) and public spaces (beverage rooms, dining rooms), the nature of transgressions was complex. As noted in the case of Port Colborne's Belmont Hotel, illegal or improper activities could be confined to private guest rooms. Since the LCA permitted guests to purchase alcoholic beverages in retail stores and drink them in their rooms, the inspector had to determine the exact nature of the situation he found. Was the proprietor using the liquor-in-bedroom loophole to attract drinking clientele, or was the proprietor simply being too permissive with legitimate hotel bedroom customers? At times proprietors exploited this rule. At the Belmont Hotel, for example, where the proprietor appeared to be serving beer to customers in their rooms, the inspector found beer in the icebox. The proprietor claimed that the beer belonged to staff and was just being kept cold (Wylie 1937d). At the King Edward Hotel in Fort Erie, the proprietor asked the inspector if he could have some rooms "designated 'bedrooms, dining-rooms, or banquet rooms' as occasion requires." Inspector Wylie explained to the board that he suspected the proprietor hoped to get around rules relating to beer being served only with meals in dining rooms; the idea was that an individual could register as a guest, be assigned the big banquet room, and then be permitted to order beer for all his friends in his "bed room" (1938a). This activity persisted through the period under study here. In 1942 the Ontario Provincial Police reported to the board that, while beer was not being served after hours or on Sundays in the beverage room of Fort Erie's Niagara Hotel, "persons secure rooms and beer and probably liquor is sold in these rooms" (OPP 1942). The law permitting drinking in private hotel bedrooms proved to be a challenge to the hotel inspectors and an opportunity for proprietors to increase revenues.

Much more frequent than bedroom drinking were transgressions in the public spaces of the hotels, the beverage rooms, and dining rooms. The proprietors' ingenuity tested the limits of the board's regulations: many adopted gimmicks specifically to bring people into the establishments, some of which reflected the vice constellation, notably gambling. The manager of Fort Erie's Tourist Inn Hotel reportedly brought "ducks, geese and turkeys as prizes in gambling ventures" (Wylie 1937e). Several hotels were caught with slot machines, something prohibited by board rules and by most municipal bylaws. In 1936, the Dain City Hotel, adjacent to the city of Welland, continued to operate on standard time, thereby being open one hour after beverage rooms in Welland had to close (Wylie 1936c). St. Catharines' New Statler Hotel arranged with a local gas station to give "premiums" on the sale of gas, which "would be accepted for beer in this hotel" (Wylie 1937c). The Garden City Inn and the Ontario House, also in St. Catharines, were chastised for giving credit or cashing workers' cheques, two common activities in the pre-Prohibition saloon but against LCBO regulations, as noted in the board's Circular No. 112 (Mair 1936a, Wylie 1938c). The Bon Villa Hotel on Lundy's Lane in Niagara Falls brought in "Madame Vendus," a fortune teller, "where she may be consulted," and a week later the inspector reported the hotel held "exhibitions of Tap Dancing" (Wylie 1936d). Tactics such as these, involving a variety of popular culture forms, to bring in clients were noted and censured by the LCBO.

DRINKING AND DANCING

Although hotel proprietors might introduce a variety of strategies to draw people to their hotels, the most common approach involved music. The proprietor of Fort Erie's Maple Leaf Hotel noted in 1936, "The public seem to want to go where they can get a little more than a drink. They want to go where they can get a little enjoyment. I mean they want music" (Gizzie 1936). The desire for music was often combined with a desire for dancing, and it was these two forms of entertainment, music and dancing, that occupied much of the regulatory interventions of the board's staff throughout Ontario. Dancing was problematic for several reasons. A general concern with the moral impact of dancing on the youth of Ontario was one problem and fuelled a moral backlash against many dancing establishments (Comacchio 1997, 2006). But more than that, the board was concerned that hotel proprietors could exploit the popularity of dancing to benefit drink sales. This trend was anathema to the idea of a staid drinking space. As the board often noted, drink sales should not be the main goal of hotels, so any sort of activity that was seen as luring drinkers was discouraged. Hotel owners in Niagara, especially in Niagara Falls, a growing tourist destination, faced pressure from locals and visitors to provide that "little enjoyment." Moreover, a number of proprietors expressed concern that, were people not permitted to dance in Niagara, they would cross the river to the United States to do so (Malleck 2007). In their attempts to add music and usually dancing to their dining rooms, Niagara Falls proprietors placed themselves squarely between the Liquor Control Board's expectations of an orderly public drinking space and public expectations of an entertaining evening out.

Music in beverage rooms was strictly forbidden, yet many proprietors simply ignored these rules. Often upon entering a beverage room on his monthly rounds, the inspector would find people clustered around a piano singing popular tunes, or a Victrola or record machine providing background music while the patrons might be singing or just listening. Proprietors provided elaborate stories to hide their transgressions. When Inspector Wylie found a piano in the ladies-and-escorts beverage room of the Trennick Hotel on Bridge Street in Niagara Falls, the manager explained that the piano "was placed in this room to provide necessary music to a tap dancing class or school" (Wylie 1938a). When he entered the Grand Trunk Hotel's beverage room to find a group of people surrounding a piano, he was told that the conditions were unusual and "due to the presence of a number of Americans who had staged a party" (Wylie 1937g). An inspection of the Hotel Grimsby revealed "a three piece orchestra discoursing third rate jazz music ... in the front window of [the] Hotel.... The obvious reason for the innovation would be to direct all and sundry that there was in the village a real live tavern" (Wylie 1935i). Without exception, every time the inspector found in the beverage room a means to make music, be it a piano, a band, or a music machine, he immediately ordered it to be removed.

Group singing in the beverage room appears to reflect traditional expectations of what activities were socially acceptable in a public drinking space. As several historians have demonstrated, the interaction of public drinking and music had been a feature of the working-class tavern for generations.[5] There is little North American historical research on the activities in non-working-class drinking establishments in the early part of the twentieth century (Erenberg's work being notable exceptions), so apart from the images in popular culture and novels, we have little indication of what the so-called respectable classes were expecting in the beverage room. Yet the prohibition on anything but drinking is indicative of the driving metaphor provided by the vice constellation or, as Mariana Valverde calls it, the imaginary saloon against which regulators were fighting (1998). The board's ban on music and singing seems to be a direct reaction to the perception that singing in a drinking environment is a step on the slippery slope to debauchery. It also reflects the expectation that only drinking should take place in a beverage room. As Heron notes, there was irony in this decision, since without food or other activities, all a patron could do was sit and drink, thereby consuming more alcohol faster (2004). Yet that irony notwithstanding, the LCBO remained adamant that nothing but drinking could take place in the beverage room.

THE DINNER-DANCE LOOPHOLE

Although music in the beverage room was prohibited, the dining room was a different story. An Authority to serve beer and wine in hotel dining rooms appears to have provided the most opportunities for fringe transgressions. In dining rooms, moderate entertainment was allowed with the board's permission. The consent to offer music and dancing significantly expanded the role of the hotel dining room as a space for public entertainment. In response to their guests' requests, and probably in reaction to what was permitted at "dry" dining rooms, hotel proprietors would bring in a record player, or a record machine, perhaps a piano, or even a small band. L.W. McConkey, the proprietor of the Hotel Trennick in Niagara Falls, asked permission to have "refined music in the Dining room at meals ... such as they have at some of the Hotels in Toronto and at the Brock [Hotel in Niagara Falls]." He said that he had considered using a radio or "one of the Wurlitzer Machines," but he had received an offer "from three prominent young men in town who play piano, Bass Viol and Violen [sic] to play for Dinner hours for me in return for the priviledge [sic] of practicing their pieces in the dining room in the late evenings and afternoons" (McConkey 1938). While McConkey insisted "there would be no dancing at any time and no singing either," other hotel proprietors quickly made the leap from music to dancing. In July 1935, the board refined its rules to permit "dine and dance arrangements" under clearly delineated stipulations. Patrons had to pay at least twenty-five cents for their meal; the food check was "proof" of entitlement "to utilize the privileges of the Dining Room, and to dance"; "none other than bona-fide Dining Room patrons" was allowed dancing on the premises (Smith 1935). In short, many proprietors took advantage of these new rules and introduced some form of dancing in their dining rooms.

The dining room, then, became a central locus of the negotiation of norms around public drinking, and the dinner dance was the main focus of proprietors. By holding dances in their dining rooms, proprietors could offer that "little more than a drink." But while some proprietors might characterize their interest in providing dancing and music to customers who go out for dinner as a way of enhancing the dining experience, the syllogism more likely worked in reverse. People were going out to dance, and the appeal of drinking would entice them to dance at licensed hotel dining rooms rather than at any of the unlicensed dance halls throughout the region. Dance halls, clubs, and other organizations regularly convened some kind of dance function, but while people wanted to take liquor there, and some did, they could legally drink (only beer or wine) only in a licensed hotel, and only with dinner.[6] The combination of music, dancing, and drink remained central to the promise of economic gain for local proprietors. In post–Twenty-First Amendment United States, it was quite easy for residents to head across the Niagara River to dance halls in New York State, so keeping patrons in Ontario was an economic necessity that required many local proprietors in Niagara to push the limits of the LCBO's rules.

Permission to hold dinner dances was not automatic. Proprietors had to apply to the board and receive consent, usually after the local inspector had agreed that such an event could take place without violating the board's rules and endangering public order. Inspectors considered the size of the venue, the character of the proprietor, and the "need" of dinner dancing in the area. When Fort Erie's Mather Arms requested permission to conduct dances in early 1935, Inspector Wylie reported, "Whilst the room is of a size which would lend itself to banquets and accompanying dances, the proposal to conduct one or two dances per week as per request would undoubtedly introduce conduct which the Board would ultimately censure" (Wylie 1935a). In contrast, in 1935, when the Bon Villa Hotel in Niagara Falls sought permission to hold a small New Year's Eve party with dining and dancing to piano accompaniment, Inspector Wylie requested "sympathetic consideration of the Board to the proposal" because the place, while small, "is carefully managed and patronized by a good type of customers" (Wylie 1935g).

In these examples, the inspector considered the character of both the proprietor and the establishment, and size mattered. As one inspector noted, in small hotels it was difficult to keep the activities of a dance in the dining room separate from the theoretically much less boisterous (but stereotypically much more socially dangerous) atmosphere of the beverage room. The Western Hotel in Humberstone wanted to install a music machine in the hallway between the dining room and the ladies' beverage room, a plan the board distinctly refused, since it would permit music to be heard in the beverage room (Smith 1940). The Grand Trunk Hotel in Fort Erie faced this same problem when it attempted to hold a singalong in its dining room, resulting in a condition that "could easily deteriorate into a roadway house with its implications" (Wylie 1937f). At the Bon Villa, Wylie saw the danger of holding a tap dance show in the dining room: "patrons of the beverage room crowded to [the] dining room" (1936e). The Tourist Inn Hotel in Fort Erie was equally disadvantaged, and its aspirations to hold dances were considered suspect; Wylie reported, "My experience in this service is that [a dance] may be conducted with propriety in larger hotels where proper accommodation is provided, but in small places where dining room adjoins beverage room, the chances for violation and irregularities are multiplied. This place is small" (Wylie 1934b). The board wanted to ensure that dine and dance privileges did not create an environment throughout the hotel that would degrade the orderly social system it was trying to construct. Although dinners and dancing could take place in the same authorized premises, a night out for both activities had to be physically separate from a night out for beer.

The LCBO appears to have recognized the necessity of permitting dances, but it clearly distinguished between a dance hall where beer was sold and a licensed dining room where dancing was permitted, discouraging the former and controlling the latter. Wylie was cautiously supportive of the New Statler Hotel's request to hold dances in the dining room because the proprietor emphasized that dancing would be secondary to dining: "Assurance is given that there is no intention to run a dance hall or to conduct organized dances, the intention being to run a dining room service which will afford an opportunity to patrons between the course[s] of the meals to indulge themselves in a little tip toe" (Wylie 1935f). In contrast, when a hotel seemed to emphasize dancing instead of dining, the inspector was much more guarded. Wylie told the proprietor of the Belmont Hotel in Port Colborne that his desire to hold a "thirty-five cent dance" would probably be refused because "the charge must be more substantial than a fish-and-chip affair" (1937b). The next year, when the hotel's proprietor asked to hold a New Year's dance, Wylie was more supportive because "the dinner will be one dollar per plate.... I believe the price of the dinner will debar those who might come with the intention of having a rough time" (1936f). Yet the board's efforts to control the dine-and-dance trade were not entirely successful, because it could not oversee the activities of a hotel every minute of the evening. When Wylie visited Fort Erie's Tourist Inn in 1935 he found a piano player and a violinist providing dance music and the place so crowded that there was no place to dance and no place to seat patrons: "Beer [was] being served and in most cases no attempt made to supply food" (Wylie 1935b). As a result, the hotel was issued a one-month suspension of its Authority. When the Queen's Hotel in Port Colborne was found to be hosting purportedly spontaneous outbreaks of music and dancing in the dining room, Wylie stated, "I have no objection to a regular supper-dance, since the Hotel is well laid out for this thing" (Wylie 1937a); his concern was that permission had not been granted. It appears, then, that licensed dinner dances were to be strictly controlled; yet, often the hotel's conversion into a licensed dance hall was simply tolerated, as long as public order could be maintained.

In the Niagara Region, the pressure to hold dances in dining rooms was intensified by outsiders. Just as the lack of dancing might send locals to New York State, so too, Americans coming across the border reportedly expected something more to do than drink (Malleck 2007). In the case of the Grand Trunk Hotel in Fort Erie, many proprietors explained away transgressions to the inspector by blaming the demands of American visitors, either those on a cross-border evening out or longer-term tourists staying in resort towns like Crystal Beach on the northeastern shore of Lake Erie. Inspectors paid little heed to those explanations, demanding that impromptu dancing and singing be stopped immediately and at times arguing to the board that the proprietor should receive either a severe reprimand or even a temporary suspension of his authority, depending on the severity and frequency of such transgressions. Visiting the Mather Arms one evening in March 1935, the inspector found a beverage room "in full operation," a euphemism for disorder. He reported that he suspected these conditions were "aggraviated [sic] by a skating Carnival ... which had drawn to Fort Erie a large contingent of American citizens from across the line" (Wylie 1935c). In 1935 Wylie observed that Crystal Beach should be under the board's special scrutiny "in view of the American atmosphere that prevails ... and the possibilities of temptation to law infractions" (Wylie 1935d). The proximity to the border left some hotels tempted by the opportunities to serve a transitory but potentially lucrative drink-tourist trade.

Temptations from outsiders were not limited to the south shore of the Niagara Peninsula. Operating in the popular resort town of Port Dalhousie in the north end of St. Catharines at Lake Ontario, the proprietor of the Embassy Hotel saw the benefit of holding dances in his licensed dining room, given the many excursions arriving from Toronto and the United States. Indeed, the local council had instituted dances in Port Dalhousie, but these, held in the park, were dry (Turcotte 1986). Dances were popular social activities, and the opportunity to combine dances and drinking was tremendously lucrative, giving hotel proprietors an advantage over the "dry" competition. The Embassy Hotel was characterized by Wylie as simply "a dine and dance restaurant to which has been added some bedrooms, but the mainstay of the Hotel is the patronage by the young people of the district who come here to dance."[7]

Wylie made the manager take down the word "DANCING" (in twelve-inch-high letters) appended to the side of the hotel. When the board suggested to the proprietor that he stop pretending his establishment was a hotel and continue with the banquet and dance hall operations (a decision that meant he would have to operate as an alcohol-free establishment), the proprietor began to put more effort into the hotel operations, recognizing that the Authority to sell beer and wine in the dining room gave him a competitive edge (LCBO 1938).[8]

HOTELS IN THE COMMUNITY

The LCBO was not completely rigid in its rule enforcement regarding dancing. The dinner-dance loophole was vague enough that proprietors often begged forgiveness for transgressions, noting that they did not know they were breaking the rules. Generally, the board would not accept this excuse as valid but would issue "a stern rebuke" instead of a suspension of the authority. At times, board personnel attempted to offer clarification, especially in cases where proprietors had been considered upstanding citizens and seemed to make an honest mistake. In 1936 the assistant director of hotels, William Mair, wrote to the proprietor of the Mather Arms in Fort Erie to clarify the difference between a Banquet and a Dinner Dance:

> A Banquet is an affair sponsored by an outside Organization, to which an Hotel Proprietor may cater in his Dining Room, by way of service of food at a *substantial* charge per head, and service of Beer and Wine in accordance with the Rgulations [sic]. Music, Dancing or any other form of entertainment must be provided and paid for by the Organization sponsoring the affair....
> A Dinner Dance ... is an affair provided by an Hotel Proprietor, who has available service accommodation for such entertainment apart from his ordinary Dining Room space, and at such Dinner Dances the service of Beer and Wine may be continued only during the period allotted for the service and consumption of food by the guests and the meal price per head must be a substantial amount, and not merely a small charge for the purpose of evading the intent of the Board's desires. (1936b)

The distinction was clear. Dinner dances were to be strictly under the control of the proprietor, while community groups hosted banquets, and the proprietor had to keep an arm's-length distance from the activities the community group sponsored.

Providing space for banquets for community groups was a business strategy the LCBO embraced, and it built upon a long tradition of the role of the hotel as a community centre. Historian Julia Roberts has explored the role of the colonial tavern as an essential component of Upper Canadian communities, and although the history of hotels in communities since the 1860s is yet to be written, the hotel, especially in smaller towns, appears to have continued to provide needed public space.[9] As Arnold Smith, the deputy chief commissioner, told the manager of the Mather Arms in 1938, "The Board realize [sic] that a properly run Hotel is an asset to a community, and if the Hotel has the proper facilities the Board are [sic] Anxious [sic] to encourage the holding of social affairs in said hotels" (Smith 1938). Many hotel proprietors actively sought out and courted community groups to hold meetings or banquets in the hotel. These groups were often held up as proof of the hotels' respectability, and at times, when a hotel faced censure from the board for a transgression, hotel managers might have club presidents write to the board to advocate on the hotel's behalf. The Embassy Hotel's manager recognized this practice and wrote to the board in September 1937, listing the clubs that applied to hold banquets in his large hall: the Kiwanis Club, a local athletic association, and the manager of the F.W. Woolworth Co., Ltd. But here the lucrative nature of the banquets overtook his overtures of being a good community citizen. The athletic association's function consisted of a small dinner for six supposed members of the executive, followed by what Wylie viewed as a general public dance, contrary to the board's guidelines. The board had little patience for these sorts of transgressions, and in five years the hotel went through six managers, each leaving after his authority to sell beer was cancelled and a new person was hired by the hotel's owner to keep the place going. Using the banquet excuse as a front for a simple dinner dance was not confined to the Embassy, though that hotel's example, probably owing to the tourist culture of the community, was one of the most vivid transgressions.

Most other hotel owners were not so bold, or so sloppy, when attempting to build the clientele of local community groups. The Village Hotel in Grimsby applied to have dancing with the Lion's Club Ladies Night, meetings of the Chamber of Commerce, and an amateur moving pictures night (Anderson 1943). On a routine inspection, an OPP officer noted that the Imperial Hotel in Niagara Falls hosted "the Blacksmith's Cribbage League of Niagara Falls [who] play cribbage in the dining-room, but that no beer is served to them in this room and they go to the beverage room if they want a drink" (OPP 1943). The owner of the Fort Erie Hotel requested permission to have dances in case members of "a convention banquet or something of that kind," such as the local Lion's Club, expressed such interest; the board saw no problems with this request (Wylie 1935h). The proprietor of the Queen's Hotel in Port Colborne asked permission to hold a banquet for the local Polish

Association, and the board granted this request. However, owing to the proprietor's spotty record in following LCBO regulations, William Mair reiterated the difference between a banquet and a dance (Mair 1936c), although for each of these requests the LCBO's central administration granted permission.

The auspices of the community organization gave the event an expectation of respectability, likely because the interests of the community organization would not be motivated by profit, and therefore less likely to break the rules in order to increase revenues. The profit motive, as I have discussed elsewhere, was something about which the LCBO administration was quite suspicious (Malleck 2007). By holding community activities, the hotel managers tapped into a lucrative market and also drew on the traditional role of the hotel as a meeting place for the broader community. It therefore could take shelter in tradition and the respectability of community social groups, such as the Chamber of Commerce or the Lions Club. Whether such events boosted the hotel's credibility to the board, however, depended on how the banquets were carried out.

CONCLUSION

By introducing dancing into their dining rooms, hotel proprietors exploited a loophole in the LCBO's regulations and simultaneously appealed to traditional notions of the appropriate activities that accompany public drinking and the growing importance of dancing and live music to youth culture. A singalong around a piano might harken back to the pre-Prohibition saloon, while a "third rate" jazz band or a three-piece swing "orchestra" would draw upon the emerging youth culture's fascination with these new musical forms (Erenberg 1984, 1998). The LCBO viewed such musical activities with suspicion but, rather than clamping down, sought to regulate and moderate them. Ironically, the singalong, and its association with saloon culture, faced more scrutiny and censure than did the facilitation of couples dancing in semi-darkness—an activity, as Elisabeth Perry has shown, that was not without its perceived social dangers in spite of its bourgeois character (Perry 1989). By permitting, albeit cautiously, the introduction of dancing and music in hotel dining rooms, the Liquor Control Board of Ontario allowed hotel proprietors to take advantage of, and become involved in, developing emerging popular forms of entertainment while also regulating conduct.

The introduction of public drinking in Ontario's hotels presented a new challenge to the liquor control authorities and new opportunities for the proprietors of Niagara's hotels. Hotel proprietors attempted to push the boundaries of the liquor control regulations, and thereby participate in reshaping the drinking culture of Niagara, by introducing a variety of innovations to entice customers into their premises. Although many innovations continued to be censured, the permission to provide music and moderate dancing in the hotel dining rooms gave enterprising hotel proprietors an opportunity to tap into the public expectation of being allowed to go out to drink and dance. In effect, while the Liquor Control Board continued to regulate public drinking strictly, it permitted the development of popular music and dancing in "licensed" public spaces of Niagara. Although this situation was not unique to Niagara, the region's location on the border with New York State and its identity as a significant tourist destination for both Canadians and Americans meant that hotel proprietors faced tremendous pressure to be inventive to build and retain business. The LCBO's regulatory regime, combined with the tenacity of hotel proprietors and pressure from the public, resulted in a shift in the nature of public drinking activities in Niagara. The board's need to discourage illegality, combined with the proprietors' need to sustain their businesses, resulted in a gradual loosening of public drinking regulations and a restructured form of popular recreation less bound by conservative morality and inflexible rules.

This research was supported by an Operating Grant through a joint partnership of the Canadian Institutes of Health Research and Associated Medical Services Inc.

NOTES

1 The Liquor Control Board of Ontario establishment records are filed in the Liquor Licensing Board of Ontario fonds in the Archives of Ontario. The LLBO was created in 1946 to oversee the licensing of establishments. In 1944 the LCBO's work was divided between the LCBO (overseeing retail sales and general distribution) and Liquor Authority Control Board of Ontario (licensing establishments for public sale and on-site consumption). The LACBO was renamed the LLBO in 1946.

2 See Jaeger 2000, Heron 2004, Malleck 2007.

3 See Heron 2005, Delottinville 1981–82, Powers 1998, Rosenzweig 1983, Kingsdale 1973.

4 "$300 in Fines at the Falls," St. Catharines *Standard*, Oct. 14, 1930.

5 See Heron 2004, 2005; Kingsdale 1973; Rosenzweig 1983; Delottinville 1981–82.

6 "Was Fined $100 and Assessed Costs," St. Catharines *Standard*, Mar. 24. 1930; "Three Months in Welland County Jail," St. Catharines *Standard*, Mar. 23, 1931.

7 The LCBO set the drinking age at twenty-one. Anyone under twenty-one was not allowed to drink, nor were they allowed in the drinking establishments. There was some inconsistency in the board's policies—for example, whether people under twenty-one were allowed seating at tables in hotel dining rooms with people who were drinking.

8 See Hugh Gayler's study in this volume for the regulations governing the Niagara wine industry and the production, marketing, control, and consumption of wine.
9 See Heron 2005, 2004; Roberts 2008; Delottinville 1981–82.

WORKS CITED

Anderson, W. Letter to LCBO. Feb. 9, 1943. LLBO Establishment Files RG 36-8. Village Hotel, Grimsby file, Archives of Ontario.

Anon. Letter to LCBO, 1936.

Burnham, John. *Bad Habits*. New York City: NYU Press, 1993.

Campbell, Robert. *Sit Down and Drink Your Beer: Regulating Vancouver's Beer Parlours*. Toronto: University of Toronto Press, 2001.

Comacchio, Cynthia. "Dancing to Perdition: Adolescence and Leisure in Interwar English Canada." *Journal of Canadian Studies* (Fall 1997), 5–35.

———. *The Dominion of Youth: Adolescence and the Making of Modern Canada 1920 to 1950*. Waterloo: Wilfrid Laurier University Press, 2006.

Dean, M.G. Inspector's Report. Sept. 28, 1935. Standard Hotel files, RG 36 1-0-1511, Archives of Ontario.

DeLottinville, Peter. "Joe Beef of Montreal: Working Class Culture and the Tavern, 1869–1889." *Labour/Le Travailleur* 8/9 (1981–82), 9–40.

Dingman, W.S. Letter to [proprietor of Harding Hotel]. Dec. 27, 1927a. Standard Hotel files, RG 36 1-0-616, Archives of Ontario.

———. Letter to German and Brooks. Oct. 28, 1927b. LLBO Establishment Files, RG 36-8, Clifton Hotel file, Archives of Ontario.

Dubinsky, Karen. *The Second Greatest Disappointment: Honeymooning and Tourism at Niagara Falls*. Toronto: Between the Lines, 1999.

Elliott, WB. Memo for Dingman. ca. Nov, 1927. Standard Hotel files, RG 36 1-0-616, Archives of Ontario.

Erenberg, Lewis. *Steppin' Out: New York Nightlife and the Transformation of American Culture, 1890–1930*. Chicago: University of Chicago Press, 1984.

———. *Swingin' the Dream: Big Band Jazz and the Rebirth of American Culture*. Chicago: University of Chicago Press, 1998.

Gizzie, Mary. Letter to Smith. Oct. 16, 1936. LLBO Establishment Files. RG 36-8, Maple Leaf Hotel file, Archives of Ontario.

Heron, Craig. *Booze: A Distilled History*. Toronto: Between the Lines, 2004.

———. "The Boys and Their Booze: Masculinities and Public Drinking in Working-class Hamilton, 1890–1946." *Canadian Historical Review* 86 (2005), 411–52.

Jaeger, Sharon. *From Control to Customer Service: Government Control of Liquor in Ontario 1927–1972*. PhD Diss. University of Waterloo, 2000.

Kingsdale, Jon M. "'The 'Poor Man's Club': Social Functions of the Urban Working-Class Saloon." *American Quarterly* 25 (1973), 472–89.

Lears, T.J. Jackson. "The Concept of Cultural Hegemony: Problems and Possibilities." *The American Historical Review* 90 (1985), 567–93.

Letter to LCBO. Jan. 30, 1936. Standard Hotel files, RG 36 1-0-1511, Archives of Ontario.

LCBO. Letter to Brisson. Jan. 12, 1938. LLBO Establishment Files. RG 36-8, Embassy Hotel files, Archives of Ontario.

Mair, W.C. Letter to Cecil Day. Nov. 19, 1936a. Garden City Inn file, Archives of Ontario.

———. W.C. Letter to Robinson. Nov. 28, 1935b. LLBO Establishment Files RG 36-8, Mather Arms Hotel file, Archives of Ontario.

———. W. C. Letter to Zielski. Nov. 27, 1936c. LLBO Establishment Files RG 36-8, Ritz Hotel (Port Colborne) file, Archives of Ontario.

Malleck, Dan. "An Innovation from Across the Line: The American Drinker and Liquor Regulation in Two Ontario Border Communities, 1927–1944." *Journal of Canadian Studies* 41 (2007), 151–71.

———. "Federal Prohibition: Canada." In Jack Blocker, David Fahey, and Ian Tyrrell, eds., *Alcohol and Temperance in Modern History: An International Encyclopedia.* Santa Barbara: ABC-Clio Press, 2003: I, 229.

McConkey, L.W. Letter to Smith. Oct. 1, 1938. LLBO Establishment Files. RG 36-8, Metropole Hotel file, Archives of Ontario.

OPP (Ontario Provincial Police). Report. May 26, 1936. LLBO Establishment Files. RG 36-8, New Murray Hotel File, Archives of Ontario.

———. Report. Nov. 20, 1942. LLBO Establishment Files, RG 36-8, Niagara Hotel (Fort Erie) file, Archives of Ontario.

———. Report. Jan. 27, 1943. LLBO Establishment Files RG 36-8, Imperial Hotel file, Archives of Ontario.

Peiss, Kathy. *Working Women and Leisure in Turn-of-the-Century New York.* Philadelphia: Temple University Press, 1986.

Perry, Elisabeth. "Cleaning up the Dance Halls." *History Today* 39 (Oct. 1989), 20–26.

Powers, Madelon. *Faces Along the Bar: Lore and Order in the Workingman's Saloon, 1870–1920.* Chicago: University of Chicago Press, 1998.

Roberts, Julia. *In Mixed Company: Taverns and Public Life in Upper Canada.* Vancouver: University of British Columbia Press, 2008.

Rosensweig, Roy. *Eight Hours for What We Will: Workers and Leisure in an Industrial City, 1870–1920.* Cambridge: Cambridge University Press, 1983.

Shannon, Wm. Letter to F. E. Elliott. Feb. 7, 1934. LLBO Establishment Files RG 36-8, Mansion House file, Archives of Ontario.

Smith, Arnold. Form letter to J. G. Williams. July 11, 1935. LLBO Establishment Files. RG 36-8, St. Clair Hotel files, Archives of Ontario.

———. Letter to M. Adams. Nov. 4, 1937. LLBO Establishment Files. RG 36-8, Belmont Hotel File, Archives of Ontario.

———. Letter to Robinson. Mar. 16, 1938. LLBO Establishment Files. RG 36-8, Mather Arms Hotel file, Archives of Ontario.

———. Letter to Hudson. June 24, 1940. LLBO Standard Hotel Files, RG 36-1-0-1511, Archives of Ontario.

Turcotte, Dorothy. *Shoes and Ships and Sealing Wax: Port Dalhousie*. Erin, Ontario: Boston Mills Press, 1986.

Valverde, Mariana. *Diseases of the Will: Alcohol and the Dilemmas of Freedom*. Cambridge: Cambridge University Press, 1998.

Walter, P. Memo to District Inspector. June 30, 1927. LLBO Establishment Files. RG 36-8, Clifton Hotel file, Archives of Ontario.

Willson, W. G. Letter to LCBO. June 3, 1931. Standard Hotel files, RG 36 1-0-1496, Archives of Ontario.

Wylie, Wilson. Authority Holder's Conduct Report (Sept. 18. 1934a). LLBO Establishment Files. RG 36-8 (Merritton Hotel, Merritton), Archives of Ontario.

———. Authority Holder's Conduct Report (Dec. 8, 1934b). LLBO Establishment Files RG 36-8 (Ohio Hotel, Fort Erie), Archives of Ontario.

———. Authority Holder's Conduct Report (Jan. 9, 1935a). LLBO Establishment Files RG 36-8 (Mather Arms, Fort Erie), Archives of Ontario

———. Authority Holder's Conduct Report (Mar. 16, 1935b). LLBO Establishment Files RG 36-8 (Ohio Hotel, Fort Erie), Archives of Ontario

———. Authority Holder's Conduct Report (Mar. 16, 1935c). LLBO Establishment Files RG 36-8 (Mather Arms Hotel, Fort Erie), Archives of Ontario.

———. Authority Holder's Conduct Report (Jun. 2, 1935d). LLBO Establishment Files RG 36-8 (Palmwood Hotel, Crystal Beach), Archives of Ontario.

———. Inspector's Report (Aug. 15, 1935e). LLBO Standard Hotel Case Files, RG 36 1-0-1509, Archives of Ontario.

———. Letter to LCBO (Sept. 20, 1935f). LLBO Standard Hotel Case Files. RG 36-1-0-616, Archives of Ontario.

———. Authority Holder's Conduct Report (Dec. 4, 1935g). LLBO Establishment Files RG 36-8 (Bon Villa Hotel, Niagara Falls), Archives of Ontario.

———. Authority Holder's Conduct Report (Dec. 9, 1935h). LLBO Establishment Files RG 36-8 (Fort Erie Hotel, Fort Erie), Archives of Ontario.

———. Authority Holder's Conduct Report (Dec. 21, 1935i). LLBO Establishment Files, RG 36-8 (Hotel Grimsby, Grimsby), Archives of Ontario.

———. Authority Holder's Conduct Report (May 11, 1936a). LLBO Establishment Files, RG 36-8 (New Murray Hotel, St. Catharines), Archives of Ontario.

———. Inspector's Report (Jun. 2, 1936b). LLBO Standard Hotel Case Files, RG 36 1-0-1509, Archives of Ontario.

———. Authority Holder's Conduct Report (Jun. 13, 1936c). LLBO Establishment Files, RG 36-8, (Dain City Hotel, Welland), Archives of Ontario.

———. Authority Holder's Conduct Report (Oct. 21, 1936d). LLBO Establishment Files. RG 36-8 (Bon Villa Hotel, Niagara Falls), Archives of Ontario.

———. Authority Holder's Conduct Report (Oct. 27. 1936e). LLBO Establishment Files RG 36-8 (Bon Villa Hotel, Niagara Falls), Archives of Ontario.

———. Letter to LCBO (Dec. 15, 1936f). LLBO Establishment Files RG 36-8 (Belmont Hotel, Port Colborne), Archives of Ontario.

———. Letter to LCBO (Jan. 21, 1937a). LLBO Establishment Files RG 36-8 (Queen's Hotel, Port Colborne), Archives of Ontario.

———. Authority Holder's Conduct Report (Jan. 21, 1937b). LLBO Establishment Files RG 36-8 (Belmont Hotel, Port Colborne), Archives of Ontario.

———. Authority Holder's Conduct Report (Jun. 25, 1937c). LLBO Establishment Files, RG 36-8 (Harding Hotel, St. Catharines), Archives of Ontario.

———. Authority Holder's Conduct Report (Aug. 16, 1937d). LLBO Establishment Files, RG 36-8 (Belmont Hotel, Port Colborne), Archives of Ontario.

———. Authority Holder's Conduct Report (Oct. 14, 1937e). LLBO Establishment Fonds, 36-8 (Ohio Hotel, Fort Erie), Archives of Ontario.

———. Authority Holder's Conduct Report (Nov. 10, 1937f). LLBO Establishment Files RG 36-8 (Grand Trunk Hotel, Fort Erie), Archives of Ontario.

———. Authority Holder's Conduct Report (Nov. 19, 1937g). LLBO Establishment Fonds, RG 36-8 (Grand Trunk Hotel, Fort Erie), Archives of Ontario.

———. Letter to Arnold Smith (Apr. 12, 1938a). LLBO Establishment Files, RG 36-8 (King Edward Hotel, Fort Erie), Archives of Ontario.

———. Authority Holder's Conduct Report (Apr. 26, 1938b). LLBO Establishment Files, RG 36-8 (Metropole Hotel, Niagara Falls), Archives of Ontario.

———. Authority Holder's Conduct Report (Sept. 12, 1938c). LLBO Establishment Files. RG 36-8 (Golden Pheasant, St. Catharines), Archives of Ontario.

NIAGARA'S EMERGING WINE CULTURE
From a Countryside of Production to Consumption

HUGH GAYLER

INTRODUCTION

Niagara has played a pivotal role in the development of a wine culture in Canada. This was where it all began in the late nineteenth century, and today it is the largest grape-growing and wine-producing area in the country with over ninety estate and boutique wineries. However, talk of a wine culture is surprisingly recent and follows a century of bad Canadian wine, a Prohibition-era mentality, the heavy hand of government, which hardly promoted the industry, and a tradition that favoured beer, spirits, and imported wines over the local product. It was not until the 1970s that all this changed. The growing of different grape varieties, the development of estate and boutique wineries, a new level of entrepreneurship, and the promotion of a very different wine industry have resulted in a dramatic shift in how a growing middle class of consumers views Canadian wines.

This study examines Canada's early wine industry and why the industry in the last thirty years has seen a new, and very different, course of action for Canadian wine and a wine culture. It has led to Niagara becoming an important agritourism destination; it is associated with various middle-class lifestyle experiences here and elsewhere; and it was in part responsible for persuading the Ontario government in 2005 to legislate a greenbelt in the Greater Golden Horseshoe Area, thereby protecting Niagara's vineyards from urban development in perpetuity. However, behind the bucolic landscapes and in spite of media hype and middle-class consumerism, considerable challenges face this industry. Production is relatively small and its influence is more local than global; the heavy hand of government still casts a shadow over entrepreneurial spirit; and the big international players exert an influence that is so often resented by the little guy. Also, a certain irony remains: there is no doubt that in the hyping of the product, wine is becoming part of popular culture, but it is all too readily seen as a middle-class preoccupation and a learning experience for most Canadians.

EVOLUTION OF THE LOCAL WINE INDUSTRY

For the first hundred years of settlement in Niagara, following the American War of Independence, there was no commercial wine industry. Mixed agriculture met the needs of new immigrants. As transportation improvements took place, in particular the coming of the railway, many agricultural products could be more cheaply imported from elsewhere, and Niagara farmers had to seek different crops to give them a competitive advantage (Chapman 1994). The northern part of the Niagara Peninsula, to the north of the Niagara Escarpment, extending from the City of Hamilton to the Niagara River, constitutes one of Canada's most favourable climatic regions and has microclimate and soil conditions that are highly conducive to the growing of tender fruit and grape crops (Shaw 1994, 2005, Planscape 2003). Coined the Niagara Fruit Belt, the area's peach and cherry orchards, for example, became unparalleled in Canada, and the new and faster rail communications allowed for fresh fruit to be exported to the growing urban markets in Ontario and Quebec.

Niagara's vineyards and the resulting wine story did not exactly curry the same favour (Rannie 1978, Bramble 2009). Wine experts, or indeed any discerning consumer of wine, did not consider the various local grape varieties, collectively known as *Vitis labrusca*, to make particularly good wine. Indeed, it was far from good, with the grapes best left to the juice and jam industries and the making of fortified wines such as port and sherry. Jokes abounded about cheap and fast ways to get drunk or help strip paint. There was never any sentiment about a European-style wine culture, and parallels were not even drawn with the emerging wine cultures in places such as California, South Africa, and Australia. It was strictly an industrial product associated with wineries that were located in urban areas alongside any other factory. The name of the grape mattered little compared to the name of the company—for example, Jordan Wines, Barnes Wines, and Bright's—and it was all too often simply red wine or white wine, unromantically delivered for cheapness in metal-capped gallon jugs. For almost 100 years, it was an industry going nowhere. Canada remained firmly a beer and spirit nation, and the overwhelmingly European émigré population who wanted wine could easily obtain it from that source.[1]

The wine industry was further hampered in this period by marketing and government restrictions. In Ontario, as in other jurisdictions in Canada and the United States, the emergence of a temperance movement in the late nineteenth century, exposing the evils of "demon drink" for various religious, health, and social reasons, resulted in governments eventually prohibiting the sale of intoxicating drinks except for medicinal purposes. Although actual prohibition was short-lived, the government afterwards established the Liquor Control Board of Ontario (LCBO) to license and regulate the manufacture, distribution, advertising, and sale of all intoxicating drinks, and to be the sole retailer for local and foreign wines and spirits.[2]

The LCBO remains the Western world's largest public drinks monopoly. Any attempts to deregulate and privatize, and to open up the industry to the needs and desires of modern lifestyles, have been thwarted constantly by various vested interests, including an Ontario public who would stand to lose a billion-dollar profit being applied annually to the public purse. For much of the last seventy or more years, a Prohibition-era mentality has been promoted by the LCBO. People were now able to drink—and the private and public sector could make vast profits from manufacturing and selling drink—but they were not exactly encouraged to do so. Laughable rules were enacted concerning the purchase and consumption of intoxicating drinks. LCBO stores were (and to some extent still are) as inviting as former government-run stores in Communist Europe. Until the late 1960s, the public could not see the product they were about to buy. The "store" was in fact a line of desks where one filled out an order form for the desired product and handed it to an employee at the counter who retrieved it from the depths of a warehouse behind. So many rules were simply unenforceable. For example, one could only drink in a public place, or in public view, if the premises were licensed (as in a bar or restaurant). Drinking in a park while picnicking or on one's front porch was illegal.

By the 1920s, the economic and regulatory difficulties inflicted on wine producers in Ontario had resulted in a rationalization and reduction in the number of firms to seven for the next fifty years.[3] No new wine licences were issued during this time, and a reasonably comfortable coexistence was to be found between an unsuspecting public who drank the cheap local "plonk" and the cognoscenti who would buy the generally more expensive European product (which could be little better than foreign "plonk").[4]

EMERGENCE OF A NEW WINE INDUSTRY AFTER 1970

The post–World War II period saw tremendous change economically, socially, and politically that in turn resulted in significant changes in the wine industry and the social mores surrounding intoxicating drink. The dark chapter of bad wine and "demon drink" was about to be blown out of the water. Although a number of factors are involved, there is little doubt that the most important is the switch of grapes for winemaking from *Vitis labrusca* to *Vitis vinifera* and French hybrid varieties. Grape growers and winemakers had been experimenting for years, figuring that if these grapes could be successfully grown in similar, cool-climate regions of France and Germany, then they could be grown commercially in Niagara. However, it was not until the late 1960s that the first of these new wines was promoted (as it happens, by Bright's, one of the old wineries), and it took the public by storm. Within a decade there was a sea change in how local wines were viewed by the Canadian public.

The structure of the wine industry also changed at this time. The seven old industries rationalized until there were two. Meanwhile, in 1975, the first wine licence to be issued in half a century went to Inniskillen Winery, whose president, Don Ziraldo, became a major force in the promotion of the new industry. There are now over ninety of these small estate and boutique wineries, with a rapid growth in just the last few years. And while they still account for less than 20 percent of total wine production in Niagara, their impact has been dramatic. A wine culture was born. Winemakers won award after award in international, blind-taste competitions, with special recognition given to Niagara icewines, and a small but growing Canadian public was proud to say they drank Ontario wines. Wine was no longer thought of as a uniform industrial product, emanating from some obscure factory or bottling plant. The new wine licences went to small entrepreneurs of proven ability, who were often their own winemakers and whose skills were challenged by the vicissitudes of weather so that we could begin to think of good years and not-so-good years and the notions of vintage, rising demand, and higher prices.

The location of the estate and boutique wineries was no longer tied to industrially zoned urban areas. Indeed, planning regulations now forbade it. Wineries are an agricultural land use and have to be situated amid a certain minimum acreage of their own vineyards. The fact that they are still essentially a factory or warehouse containing crushing equipment, fermentation barrels or metal tanks, a bottling plant, and storage area is, however, offset by landscaping, hospitality facilities, a retail store, local employment growth, and often stunning architecture.

This new wine industry has been able to grow because of a wide range of institutional supports, some new, such as the Canadian Wine Institute, the Wine Council of Ontario, the Vintners Quality Alliance (VQA), and the Cool Climate Oenology and Viticulture Institute (CCOVI) at Brock University, and some of long standing, including the fifty-year-old Niagara Wine Festival. For an industry that is so small in a culture that is seemingly hostile (be it regulatory measures or a public where only a minority drinks wine), it is important that government be kept constantly onside and working for the industry. The North American Free Trade Agreement (NAFTA) after 1988, for example, had the potential of easily burying the fledgling Ontario industry with Californian imports, but the federal government was persuaded to endorse a measure of protection for the industry in return for limiting the number of non-LCBO wine outlets in Ontario. If the Niagara wine industry was to excel, there had to be an incentive for grape growers to change their ways and their crops. The joint Federal-Provincial Grape Acreage Reduction Program gave growers $50 million to tear out the *labrusca* grapes in favour of the new varieties, while legislation was passed that effectively forbade the commercial sale of wines using the *labrusca* grape.

New varieties alone do not guarantee good wine, and although physical conditions of soil and weather can play a major part and be blamed when the wine is of poor quality, so too can the education and skill of the winemaker. Academic training and research, such as Brock's CCOVI, has increasingly taken over from on-the-job, father-to-son training, and many wineries have sought winemakers with many years of experience at famous wineries in Europe and elsewhere. Government and the wine industry have introduced various incentives to help improve wine quality—for example, the VQA stamp of approval. A VQA-labelled bottle not only assures the consumer that the wine is made from 100 percent Ontario grapes, but also that it has passed a blind taste test by a panel of industry experts.

Whether or not wineries belong to the Wine Council, they all benefit from the council's considerable lobbying and marketing expertise. A wine route has been established and signposted through the Niagara Wine Region, connecting member wineries and helping to guide the approximately 8 million people, Canadian and American, who live within a two-hour drive. The council publishes and distributes widely a free annual official guide to its wineries that also includes extensive advertising by related tourist and cultural facilities (see map, p. xi, Wine Council of Ontario 2009). These ventures are undoubtedly part of a process of popularizing wine drinking.

Niagara wines have long been showcased annually by the former Niagara Grape and Wine, now Niagara Wine, Festival, held over a ten-day period at

FIGURE 9.1 Niagara Wine Route signage. Courtesy of author

harvest time in September and ending with one of North America's larger grand parades through the St. Catharines downtown. Earlier, the party spirit was, perhaps understandably, more associated with pubs and the beer tent than wine-tasting events. More recently, a tired and faltering festival has been given a shot in the arm with better promotion of the new wines, adding more events at other times of the year—for example, an icewine festival—associating wine events with a culinary experience, and changing the name of the festival, ironically by dropping the grape connection, in order to create a fresh and more up-market image.

Niagara's small estate and boutique wineries have always played a major role in the popularizing of new products (Gayler 2003). All are allowed to sell wine and associated products on-site, an important consideration when so many wineries are too small to be allowed to sell through the LCBO. Also, although regulated by the LCBO, they are able to sell directly to restaurants. Most encourage year-round wine tours and tastings, and showcasing a wider cultural experience, both on-site and in more distant urban centres, as a way of promoting a wine product to a captive audience has become *de rigueur* in the business. Choices are seemingly endless, including restaurant and banquet facilities, wine appreciation classes, conferences and seminars, concerts (jazz, classical, rock), theatre (Shakespeare in the Vineyard), antique car shows, sports competitions, and charity events. In addition, wineries get their name and products known through media advertising, from the national and local press to targeted audiences in specialist publications such as interior-design and epicurean magazines, and concert and theatre programs.

The expansion of the wine industry and the popularizing of the product among a growing middle-class audience have led to an increasing concern about the ability of the industry to sustain itself. The Niagara Wine Region sits amid a fast-growing urban area with a long history of poor planning and urban sprawl and a less than robust agricultural sector only too willing to sell out to urban interests (Gayler 2004, 2005). The fact that this area contains some of Canada's most valuable land has resulted in a fifty-year debate about the need to preserve the land for agricultural purposes, and, on paper at least, this led to some quite restrictive measures in the 1981 Regional Niagara Policy Plan (Regional Municipality of Niagara 2001). However, the uncertainties surrounding local and regional decision-making under the Ontario Planning Act, and sizeable expansions of urban boundaries into areas of valuable agricultural land, hastened the demands from 2001 to 2003 for the Ontario government to introduce more restrictive legislation. The reaction of the agricultural community was immediate and hostile and remained so through the new Liberal government in Ontario setting up a Greenbelt Task Force (2004a, 2004b) and eventually passing the Greenbelt Act (2005). However, the wine industry and the majority of the public at large could breathe a sigh of relief that finally there would be no further urban expansion into the Greenbelt (coincidentally, in Niagara, the boundaries set in the 1981 Policy Plan) and the land base would be protected in perpetuity (Gayler 2010).

A WINE INDUSTRY UNDER STRESS

There is no doubt that the Niagara wine industry has made great strides in the last thirty years, producing wines that have received global recognition and awards, if not the volumes to anywhere near meet global demands. However, at home, amid all the public support for the industry, the media hype, the agritourism, and the bucolic and cultural associations, there are signs of an industry under stress. The major actors are several with competing agendas; furthermore, there are often competing agendas within the one industry sector.

Provincial and federal governments are major actors, and, in spite of a long history of government subsidy for the agricultural sector, it is never enough and incessant demands are made on them for more. Praise for measures such as the Grape Acreage Reduction program, the Wine Content Act, protections under NAFTA, instituting the VQA, and new funding for research at the Vineland Research and Innovation Centre have been buried under the continual litany of what government has not been doing. The closing of the Cadbury-Schweppes grape juice plant in Niagara in 2007 resulted in government being criticized by grape growers that there was no replant program in place to subsidize growers to switch to wine grapes. The Ontario government is accused of not doing enough to promote local wine, remaining firmly resistant to wine (and beer) being sold in corner stores, and using NAFTA regulations to ward off the opening of VQA-only wine shops. Since the replant program is national in scope, one level of government has been quite prepared to hide behind the other.

In defending itself, the Ontario government often points to a second major actor, the LCBO, which is at arm's-length from government and which government firmly contends is in the public interest. The near monopoly of this regulatory and retail organization results in over a billion dollars in profits per annum to fuel the provincial tax coffers. There is also widespread public and labour support, and any attempts to privatize the LCBO, even by the most right wing of governments on behalf of business interests, have been studiously avoided.

Parts of the wine industry, on the other hand, have serious doubts that the LCBO is working well on their behalf. Canada is the only major wine-producing country in the world where the majority of the products consumed is not local. The LCBO stands accused of promoting this situation by giving too much publicity and visibility to foreign products in its slick in-house publications, in the positioning and shelving of products in its stores—with foreign products, and blended (foreign-local) wines closer to the doors and cash register—and excluding most of the smaller wineries from even selling their products at the LCBO. The LCBO exacts a high markup on its products, controls the prices that can be charged, and strictly limits the usual entrepreneurial practices of promotional sales and special offers. Although the major breakthrough of Sunday shopping at the LCBO promoted sales across the province, it was criticized locally for taking traffic away from the wineries' own retail outlets.

The third major player, the Wine Council of Ontario, has as its mandate the promotion of the wine industry and the lobbying of government, and there is little doubt that it does that job commendably on behalf of all Niagara wineries. However, membership is voluntary, and many of the smaller wineries do not belong; some cite the cost of membership, and the council is seen as an association of the larger wineries, promoting their interests over those of the smaller wineries.

The fourth major player includes the wineries themselves; however, the various differences between the larger and smaller wineries result in their not acting with one voice. The two largest wineries, Constellation and Andrés, produce over 80 percent of the wine bottled in Ontario and have a corporate structure and global reach that differ markedly from the estate wineries. The two have reformed from the bad old days of Ontario wine and now make quality wines and have taken over a number of the new estate wineries to improve their product line and overall corporate image. However, other wineries, the media, and the public at large criticize them because their corporate success is built in part on a deception. The smaller wineries are committed to using 100 percent local grapes to gain the VQA stamp of approval for "Made in Canada," thereby promoting Canada's wine industry. Constellation and Andrés do the same through their estate wineries. However, the major share of their business is not VQA wines but the blending of local and foreign wines, permitted under the Wine Content Act to a maximum of 70 percent foreign product. At this point comes the deception: the wineries are allowed to market this blended product as "Cellared in Canada," and an unsophisticated public will (they hope) not realize the meaning of the different nomenclature. Besides, consumers may be more attracted by the price, which is generally lower for the blended products and a reflection of economies of scale that are not possible for the estate winery. It can be argued that the blending of wine is necessary because, as yet, there are insufficient local grapes being grown. Also, there are years when Niagara grape production suffers from adverse weather conditions, making it necessary to obtain government approval for a one-off increase in foreign content above the 70 percent maximum.

The ongoing debate between the larger and smaller wineries became more rancorous late in 2009, when the Ontario government came down on the side of VQA wines (and the vast majority of Ontario wineries) by imposing a tax increase on wine sold at private wine stores in order to pay for the Wine Council of Ontario's marketing programs and the VQA subsidy program at the LCBO.[5] The 289 private wine stores in Ontario are principally owned by the two major players, Constellation and Andrés, selling mostly blended wines, while the VQA subsidy program allows the small wineries to sell for the first time at the LCBO. Changes in government policy resulted in the larger wineries withdrawing from the Wine Council of Ontario and forming a new trade organization, the Winery and Grower Alliance of Ontario; it was felt that the new group would be better able to lobby government on behalf of the larger wineries and their blended products.

The over ninety estate and boutique wineries are growing in number by the day, and when some are not members of the Wine Council of Ontario or do not subscribe to highway directional signage, it is difficult for the public to keep up with the changes. Meanwhile, rationalization and amalgamation are constantly changing the fortunes of established wineries, while famous sports and TV celebrities, including Dan Aykroyd, Wayne Gretzky, and Mike Weir, are lending their names and their money to produce wines in borrowed space ahead of building their own wineries. The nature of the estate winery can vary from the precariously financed family operation (hopefully, only to begin with) to one where the owner is looking for a second career and a place to invest capital and employ an established winemaker. It remains quite a competitive world until the Canadian product becomes more accessible to, and better accepted by, the Canadian public, let alone foreign markets.

To state the obvious, wine is possible only if there is a grape being produced beforehand.[6] Thus, the grape growers and their trade organization, the Grape Growers of Ontario, constitute a fifth major player in the wine industry. Throughout their long history, the grape growers have faced the constant vicissitudes of weather, the market needs of the wine industry, the year-by-year contractual arrangements with wineries, and the fact that a vine takes some years to bear a mature crop and respond to a market need. As a result, grape growers, along with tender-fruit farmers, have been at the forefront of lobbying government for means to obtain greater financial security and to keep open all options on what they can do with their land—their greatest asset in the future. They would argue that, with the Greenbelt legislation, better programs and greater subsidies to enable a more healthy future are wanting.

Public spats between the wineries and the grape growers, and among the grape growers themselves, often thwart the promotion of the wine industry. Wineries have been critical of the quality of the grapes being grown locally, in particular where poorer quality is considered the result of farming practices rather than weather conditions. This has encouraged wineries to extend the acreage of their own vineyards rather than rely on contracts with grape growers, as well as to justify the need for foreign imports and blended wines. Grape growers have not stood by quietly, arguing that wineries make demands on them that are often unreasonable. In part as a reaction, in 2004 a number of the larger and more successful growers formed Niagara Vintners Inc., in effect a co-operative to employ an established winemaker to produce their own wines and later opening an impressive estate winery in Niagara-on-the-Lake. Unfortunately, their efforts were short-lived, with bankruptcy following three years later.

FIGURE 9.2 Southbrook Vineyards, organic- and biodynamic-certified vineyard and winery. Courtesy of author

Although on the surface the solidarity among grape growers is legendary, the larger and more financially secure ones are not above criticizing their weaker brethren. In an industry seeking global recognition, high-quality raw material is obligatory, and as in any other private business, the weakest may well have to be sacrificed. To help prevent this from happening, attention has been focused on various measures to improve the quality of grape farming, including the recent federal-provincial initiative to improve research at the Vineland Research Station, and research and education locally at Brock University and Niagara College. Much research has been done on what might be termed sub-appellation areas within the Niagara Wine Region, recognizing that different types of grape fare better under certain microclimatic, soil, and aspect conditions in certain areas rather than somewhere else (Shaw 2006). The VQA supported these research findings, and the Ontario government passed legislation endorsing the sub-appellation areas.[7] The long-term implications behind this research are that growers may have planted a less than desirable grape variety in a particular area. This is likely to have financial implications as an industry intent on raising quality seeks optimal solutions.

The final major player in the wine industry is the consumer, and here begins a rather sorry tale. In spite of the important strides made by the wine industry, and especially the estate wineries, Canadians continue to consume more foreign wines and Canada remains a nation of beer and spirit drinkers, especially on the very doorstep of the industry in the Niagara-Hamilton areas. With so many of the small wineries excluded from LCBO stores, their entry into the major metropolitan markets in Ontario is reliant on exposure through restaurants or encouraging consumers to come to Niagara and find their way to the winery's retail outlet. It is not easy for Canadians outside the main wine-producing provinces of Ontario and British Columbia even to experience Canadian wines. It is currently illegal, under the Importation of Intoxicating Liquors Act (1928), for wineries to ship their products across provincial boundaries or for returning tourists with purchases to do likewise. Also, consumers are beholden to what government liquor stores want to stock, and no doubt the latter are influenced by history, prices, tastes, and misconceptions about the superiority of foreign wines.

The wine industry in Ontario has had only a short time to build a loyal following among consumers, and in the process it has been necessary to educate them about what they are drinking and why. This includes defeating the snob appeal of European wines, tying wine to culinary experiences,[8] and cultivating new experiences as consumers move from white to red wines or from sweet to dry wines. Building loyalty, and thus promoting sales, is not helped by a wider society that continues to be resistant to Ontario wines. In spite of much cajoling from the wine industry, Canadian airlines continue to serve foreign "plonk" (at least to their Economy passengers!), and many restaurants outside Niagara still do not offer a Canadian wine.

Building consumer loyalty through agritourism and Niagara as a wine destination is perhaps an obvious development, but it is not one without its own difficulties (Niagara Economic Development Corporation [NEDC] 2007). Niagara may attract upwards of 10 million tourists annually, but only about 5 percent ever visit a winery. Most tourists are families visiting Niagara Falls itself, and children, needless to say, are hardly welcome at a winery. Another sizeable proportion is largely local, repeat gamblers at the two Niagara Falls casinos, and for this crowd a wine experience is not a high priority. Also, Niagara's American tourist numbers have been in sharp decline since 9/11, the SARS outbreak in Canada in 2003, the declining American dollar, and the policies imposed by the Department of Homeland Security on entry and re-entry into the United States. The NEDC Report draws attention to the fact that the world-class wines from Niagara have to be matched by better ancillary experiences along the Wine Route. Beyond the wineries themselves, it concludes, there needs to be greater public and private investment in services that will round out the wine experience, including a wine museum, culinary centre, a VQA wine store, more overnight accommodations, and a re-routing of the Wine Route.

THE WINE EXPERIENCE

For the over 500,000 visitors to Niagara's wineries each year, and for the many more who purchase Niagara wines, most would be unaware of the stresses faced by the industry. The Niagara Wine Experience has been carefully nurtured by the industry, and through its media hype and on-the-ground events is seen as upbeat and rewarding. Through their investment of millions of dollars, the wineries not only have turned an old industry around but have changed Niagara's profile as a declining manufacturing employment area, put Canada on the map as a wine-producing country, and contributed to regional economic development by attracting a new tourist population and promoting various spin-off activities. The model often cited is California's Napa Valley—larger and older, but in many ways similar.

Many Ontarians can still recall the 1970s, when a wine experience, besides actually drinking wine, was the stultifying trip to an LCBO store, or rather warehouse, to be attended to possibly by an indifferent employee. For most Ontarians, the LCBO is still the principal destination. However, attempts have been made to make the stores more appealing through product display and knowledgeable employees who enjoy their work. Beyond this has come in the last thirty years the promotion of wines at the winery itself. Rather than the earlier formidable factory building that was designed to turn away the visitor, the new "factory" is an inviting edifice with staff to match. From a countryside of production, the Niagara Wine Region is now a countryside of consumption with a well-marked Wine Route directing the visitor to most wineries (Fig. 9.1). Although there is no denying that a winery is still a factory, many have tried to hide the tanks, the crushing equipment, and the bottling plant behind or inside the building in order to deflect the visitor's attention. The buildings themselves often make a stunning impression in their landscaped and vineyard settings.[9] Château des Charmes invokes comparisons with a Loire Valley château. Hillebrand could be a New England neo-Georgian house. Jackson-Triggs is an eco-friendly building reminiscent of an airport terminal. One winery, yet to be built, has commissioned a design from the internationally acclaimed architect Frank Gehry. These aesthetic evocations speak to a number of factors, including the growing capitalization of the industry, the need in a competitive age to market a brand image and destination, and a reflection of individual owners' tastes and cultural background. However, most wineries, reflecting the precariousness of a new operation, are relatively

FIGURE 9.3 Château des Charmes Winery. Courtesy of author

simple buildings, varying from a modest 1960s bungalow to a strip mall to a utilitarian warehouse. In these cases, the qualities of the wine and service are assumed to be more important than the aesthetic of the building.

This working countryside, the dispersal of wineries across a wide area, and the hundreds of thousands of visitors who are attracted annually are economic developments welcomed in Niagara. However, various concerns have been raised, indicating that perhaps the deleterious effects of these developments may turn away the very visitors the wineries want to attract. Niagara's long history of urban sprawl has resulted in residents who do not readily identify with or appreciate neighbouring agricultural operations and rural industries. Factories and warehouses masquerading as wineries, albeit architecturally appealing ones, come on the heels of a growing and visually very unappealing greenhouse industry. These are not a part of the rural idyll that so many urbanites seek, and one frequently hears the cry of why such industries cannot be contained in an urban industrial park. Moreover, wineries bring more tourist traffic to rural roads and encourage various spin-off activities that result in more development in the area. But viewing other wine regions—for example, California's Napa and Sonoma Valleys—with a much longer history and more intense development, it is clear that Niagara has a long way to go before its developments interfere with the wine experience and turn visitors away.

FIGURE 9.4 Hillebrand Estates Winery. Courtesy of author

FIGURE 9.5 Jackson-Triggs Niagara Vintners. Courtesy of author

CONCLUSIONS

Niagara's quality wines and emerging wine culture are gaining global recognition and eclipsing the more traditional roles of tourism in Niagara Falls, heavy industry, and the automotive trades, all of which are in various states of decline in the region. Niagara's wine industry is over a hundred years old, but until the 1970s it was not something with which wine experts or serious wine drinkers wished to be associated. Also, bad wine was compounded by institutional resistance and an indifferent wider public. However, changes in the grape varieties grown, the arrival in Niagara of professional and dedicated winemakers and entrepreneurs, and the growth of institutional and consumer support systems have resulted in a total turnabout. From zero to over ninety estate wineries in thirty years is a spectacular achievement, although the industry, when compared to that in other countries, remains small and more local than global.

Furthermore, it is an industry with growing pains. Niagara's wineries face various stresses exerted by the major actors in the field and their differing agendas, including government at the different levels, the LCBO, institutional supports such as the Wine Council of Ontario, the grape growers, other wineries, and last but not least, the consumer who does not come from a country with a long and good winemaking tradition and who in the main has only a sketchy knowledge of wines. However, developments in Niagara, the award-winning successes of its wineries, continuing institutional and government support, and a growing middle-class consumer base bode well for the future of the industry. There continues to be a strong social transformation in the wine industry.

NOTES

1 There is a long tradition in Niagara of immigrants from wine-producing countries in Europe, and their descendants, growing grapes on their property (even urban gardens and patios) and producing homemade wine. More recently, and for reasons related largely to cheapness, wine drinkers have been able to go to wine suppliers and bottle their own wine. In both cases, the wine must only be for home consumption and as gifts to relatives and friends and is highly unlikely to win awards in blind-taste tests.

2 For more discussion on the LCBO, see Dan Malleck's study in this volume: "'A Little More Than a Drink': Public Drinking and Popular Entertainment in Post-Prohibition Niagara, 1927–1944."

3 The old Ontario wineries were Andrés, Barnes, Bright's, Cartier, Château-Gai, Jordan, and London Wines.

4 "Plonk" is slang for "cheap" drink typically applied to inferior wine, port, and brandy. See *Partridge's Concise Dictionary of Slang and Unconventional English* (from Eric Partridge), Paul Beale, ed. (New York: Macmillan, 1989).

5 Monique Beech, "Big Wineries Split from Council," St. Catharines *Standard*, Nov. 19, 2009, A1, A7.
6 Consideration is not given here to the small production of wine from other fruits. Niagara has one commercial fruit winery, Sunnybrook Farm Estate Winery, Canada's first, established in 1993. Its wines have been awarded the Fruit Wines of Canada Quality Certified designation, the equivalent of the VQA designation for grape-based wines.
7 Sub-appellation is the formal recognition of ten unique growing areas in the Niagara Wine Region—for example, the St. David's Bench and the Beamsville Bench—and replaces the informal local terms, such as upper bench or lower bench, which had been used earlier. Details of these growing areas can be seen on the VQA website (www.vqaontario.com/theWines/appellation.htm).
8 A variety of culinary experiences pair food and wine, including that provided by Niagara College's Culinary Institute, which features, alongside its teaching program, special event and public restaurant space for food and wine, the latter coming from the college's teaching winery; a cooking school at Strewn Winery; the Good Earth cooking school, where chefs from local restaurants also promote Niagara wines; the Niagara Wine Festival's annual food and wine event set up in Montebello Park in downtown St. Catharines; and numerous charity promotions that feature food and wine.
9 Monique Beech, "The Off-the-Wall Architecture of Niagara Wineries," St. Catharines *Standard*, Dec. 31, 2007, A4.

WORKS CITED

Bramble, Linda. *Niagara's Wine Visionaries: Profiles of the Pioneering Winemakers*. Toronto: James Lorimer, 2009.
Chapman, Paul. "Agriculture in Niagara: An Overview." In Hugh J. Gayler, ed., *Niagara's Changing Landscape*. Ottawa: Carleton University Press, 1994: 279–99.
Gayler, Hugh J. "Agritourism Developments in the Rural-Urban Fringe: The Challenges of Land-Use and Policy Planning in the Niagara Region." In Kenneth Beesley, Hugh Millward, Brian Ilbery, and Lisa Harrington. eds., *The New Countryside: Geographic Perspectives on Rural Change*. Brandon and Halifax: Brandon University Rural Development Institute and St. Mary's University, 2003: 179–96.
———. "The Niagara Fruit Belt: Planning Conflicts in the Preservation of a National Resource." In Mark B. Lapping and Owen J. Furuseth. eds., *Big Places, Big Plans*. Aldershot, UK: Ashgate, 2004: 55–82.
———. "Stemming the Urban Tide: Policy and Attitudinal Changes for Saving the Canadian Countryside." In Andrew Gilg, Richard Yarwood, Stephen Essex, John Smithers, and Randall Wilson, eds., *Rural Change and Sustainability: Agriculture, the Environment and Communities*. Wallingford, UK: CABI Publishing, 2005: 151–68.
———. "Ontario's Greenbelt and Places to Grow Legislation: Impacts on the Future of the Countryside and Rural Economy." In Greg Halseth, Sean Markey,

and David Bruce, eds., *The Next Rural Economies: Constructing Rural Place in Global Economies*. Wallingford, UK: CABI Publishing, 2010: 75–88.

Greenbelt Task Force. *Towards a Golden Horseshoe Greenbelt: Discussion Paper*. Toronto: Ontario Ministry of Municipal Affairs and Housing, 2004a.

———. *Towards a Golden Horseshoe Greenbelt: Advice and Recommendations*. Toronto: Ontario Ministry of Municipal Affairs and Housing, 2004b.

Niagara Economic Development Corporation (NEDC). *Energizing Niagara's Wine Country Communities*. Thorold, ON: NEDC, 2007.

Planscape. *Regional Municipality of Niagara: Regional Agricultural Economic Impact Study*. Bracebridge, ON: Planscape, 2003.

Rannie, William F. *Wines of Ontario: An Industry Comes of Age*. Lincoln, ON: William F. Rannie, 1978.

Regional Municipality of Niagara. *Regional Niagara Policy Plan*. Office Consolidation, Publication 91, 2001.

Shaw, Anthony B. "Climate of the Niagara Region." In Hugh J. Gayler, ed., *Niagara's Changing Landscapes*. Ottawa: Carleton University Press, 1994: 111–38.

———. "The Niagara Peninsula Viticultural Area: A Climatic Analysis of Canada's Largest Wine Region." *Journal of Wine Research*, 16 (2005), 85–103.

———. *Delimiting Sub-Appellations within the Niagara Peninsula Viticultural Area*. Report prepared for Vintners Quality Alliance (VQA), Ontario, 2006.

Wine Council of Ontario. *Official Guide to the Wineries of Ontario*. St. Catharines, ON: Wine Council of Ontario, 2009.

Part IV | **LOCAL CONNECTIONS**

"KENNY-ING" | Kenny Wheeler and Local Jazz

TERRANCE COX

Kenny Wheeler is from St. Catharines, Ontario—long from, far from. A jazz virtuoso on trumpet and flugelhorn and a composer of international repute— the most important musician ever to come out of Niagara—Wheeler left here for London, England, in 1952. Since then, his distinctively accomplished musicianship has graced over 250 recordings, more than twenty as lead artist, performing his own idiosyncratic compositions, much acclaimed and emulated.[1]

Wheeler's oeuvre spans an astonishing range of idioms. Teenage beginnings in hometown swing bands led to an embrace of both small group bebop and studies in music theory while still in Niagara. From his 1960s association with the big band of John Dankworth through his engagement of free jazz (with Anthony Braxton, among others), Wheeler has never stopped exploring formats and forms. As featured sideman, he appears on various recordings of bop (with, for example, saxophonist Tubby Hayes), post-bop (with bassist Dave Holland), and on diverse U.K. non-jazz albums, includ- ing rock LPs and the original cast version of *Jesus Christ, Superstar.* Since his mid-1970s link-up with the ECM label, he has increasingly worked with European avant-garde jazzers such as Jan Garbarek, while also recording in "world music" contexts: for instance, with the Lebanese *oud* master Rabih Abou Khalil. On March 15, 2005, six decades into his extraordinary career, Wheeler was honoured by the British parliament with a House of Commons Shield, naming him jazz musician of the year.

Away from St. Catharines, Kenny Wheeler has gone long and far. And yet, for all this while on world stages, he has kept in touch with Canada and stayed especially close to the city where he came of age—and where he came to music. Wheeler has been a benign presence in St. Catharines. Often, through master classes at the Banff School of Fine Arts in Alberta and with workshops for various Canadian university and college music programs, he has memorably affected a succession of emergent musicians. As he has done for decades, Wheeler frequently still comes back to St. Catharines, welcomed each visit by jazz friends of longstanding and revered by cohorts of local players to whom he has been mentor.[2]

The trumpeter-composer Lina Allemano, an Edmonton-bred, Toronto-based recipient of his encouragement, entitles her recorded tribute to Wheeler with the coinage "kenny-ing."[3] I borrow her gerund to name the nexus of the person and the work. "Kenny-ing" involves a complex of oft-conflicting elements: the local and the global, virtuosity and effacement, prominence and anonymity, remoteness and connection, singularity and mentorship. The particulars of this definition of "kenny-ing" derive in large measure from interviews with numerous Wheeler associates, past and present, from Niagara and farther afield.

A month before his 2006 parliamentary distinction, Wheeler had been in St. Catharines, at Brock University's Sean O'Sullivan Theatre, the region's prime concert venue, where five years prior he had performed. On the second occasion, he sat anonymous among the audience for the Niagara Symphony Orchestra (NSO). Augmented by local jazz players—many of whom had been inspired by Wheeler—the NSO performed his song "Sea Lady," in an arrangement he had volunteered especially for this occasion. With a self-effacement as legendary as his musicianship, when conductor Laura Thomas announced his presence for deserved acclaim, Kenny Wheeler stayed seated, "invisible." (To receive that House of Commons Shield, he sent in his stead his son and daughter.)[4]

In Wheeler's person and career, soaring accomplishment and ceaseless self-deprecation co-exist. So, too, seemingly contrary is his need to leave St. Catharines and to stay in touch. Contradiction may be complement. The ever-changing musician who says "I don't have any solos of my own that I like completely, only those that are not as bad as others"[5] is contrastingly generous in praise of others' talents, constant as a mentor, especially supportive to youngsters from this city.

FIGURE 10.1 Wheeler with students, Laura Secord Secondary School, St. Catharines, Jan. 12, 2008. Permission of photographer Mike Balsom and music teacher David Sisler

SWING IN NIAGARA[6]

Born on January 14, 1930—in Toronto, as he pointedly asserts—Kenneth V.J. Wheeler[7] came with his family to St. Catharines in 1945. Although he got out of the city as soon as he could—and has subsequently so counselled others—it was in this small city in the Niagara Region that he became a musician.[8]

"Jitney" dances at the pavilion in nearby Port Dalhousie, on 1940s summer nights at the Lake Ontario shore, had dancers pay a nickel each to crowd the floor. To hits of the day, sweet or hot, they did the foxtrot or the jitterbug, for two choruses at best. Then came the rope. Burly fellows encircled the youthful crowd, hauling a rope of nautical thickness to clear reluctant patrons off the polished hardwood and usher them out for another nickel's worth of repeat business.

Playing for those jitney dances were local big bands with some very fine musicians. Most were to enjoy life-long careers as, quite happily, "weekend players." Newcomer Wheeler, likely the youngest on that bandstand, played in the band of tenor saxophonist Bruce Anthony. The eldest regular up there was alto saxophonist Mynie Sutton, a pioneer of Canadian popular music, who brought the spirit of jazz back home to Niagara for an extended run. Besides dancers, the Port Dalhousie pavilion attracted kids who aspired to play, who, for instance, sought out the incumbent drummer, asking for advice, offering to take over his kit during intermissions. One such, circa 1943, was Rod North. For more than thirty years, he went on to play drums, evenings and weekends, in groups led by Sutton.

Myron ("Mynie") Sutton (1903–1982) began playing jazz about the time that Louis Armstrong cut his first records. Through the late 1920s, the Niagara Falls–born Sutton gigged across the border in nearby Buffalo, New York, and toured the northern states in early big bands. Resisting invitations to go where his talents merited—to New York City and the jazz big-time—Sutton took his alto sax and road-won savvy to Montreal in the early 1930s. In the nightclubs of that "wide-open" city, on tours and at summer resorts, for almost a decade, he fronted a band called the Canadian Ambassadors, all its players from Ontario, all "coloured" (a departure from the all-white band Sutton led in Niagara). Mark Miller, in his book on Canada's "lost" jazz history, *Such Melodious Racket,* calls Sutton "the first black Canadian bandleader of any significance" in Montreal and quotes a contemporary's observation that the Canadian Ambassadors "didn't look up to the American musicians. They were better than the American musicians" (1997, 148).

Dutiful son to his widowed mother, Sutton returned to Niagara Falls in 1941. Before leaving Montreal, he recognized the extraordinary talent of a local teenage pianist, inviting Oscar Peterson to sit in on a few of the band's rehearsals. Back in Niagara Falls, he took a day job as a welder, but never stopped playing his Johnny Hodges–inspired alto sax.

Following Sutton from band to band through the 1940s gives an inkling of how vibrant and coherent the Niagara area swing scene was. The silky tone of Sutton's alto was featured in dance bands led by accordionist Peter Grecco from nearby Thorold, and then with Bob Wybrow, a pianist from Niagara Falls. Beginning in 1946, he led his own band, one that got the attention of *Down Beat,* the influential American jazz magazine, which printed a photo, perhaps drawn by the novelty of a black leader of an otherwise all-white band.

Sutton's band played those jitney dances, but only on some nights. Typically, he would alternate, turnabout through the week, with such bands as that of St. Catharines' Bruce Anthony, or of Welland's Jimmy Marando, also on alto sax. The local musical community was geographically proximate: from St. Catharines south to the Lake Erie shore resorts and Buffalo was an hour's travel; to Niagara Falls and Welland by frequent trolleys, less than half that. In this tightly interconnected and highly co-operative scene, movement from band to band was common, without rancour. Bands did not undercut each other for jobs. Even bandleaders sometimes played together. Marando so admired Sutton's playing, that, for example, he switched to tenor just to sit in the next chair and learn. Marando himself got his start auditioning successfully for Bruce Anthony in 1939. Wheeler, in recollection, describes the Anthony band as "the slightly more jazzy of the big bands."[9]

Music, family, friends, and the local—all are linked in Wheeler's beginnings. Trombonist father Wilf gave him the gift of his first cornet; Wilf Jr. also played trombone; brother Paul, clarinet and baritone sax; and sister Helen sang, also in Anthony's band. His mother's piano in the parlour of the family home on Salina Street, close to St. Catharines' downtown core, made the Wheeler home a hangout for adolescent fellow devotees of swing and then bebop. Many subsequent song titles affirm the ties of family and music: the album title *Double, Double You* puns on his father's initials; "Ma Belle Helene" plays with two sisters' names.[10]

Music also led to friendships in Wheeler's St. Catharines adolescence, ones that survive his leave-taking. Gene Lees, now a California-based jazz writer and lyricist, then living in the nearby town of Merritton, close enough to be a St. Catharines Collegiate schoolmate, writes scathingly of this "peculiarly bland" locality: "The people ... were for the most part parochial, shallow and aloof. I am told they still are. Therefore, if you found anyone who held interests in common with you, such as jazz, you clasped him or her to you, and made a friend, often for life."[11] Lees as an "oddball" teenager was not yet a jazz writer of any ilk but an intense, opinionated record collector and fan, already forming and shaping ideas that emerged in his subsequent writing. He would also—to get ahead of the story—in 1952 be instrumental in putting Wheeler on a fateful ship to London.

Wheeler, coming to St. Catharines in 1945, by serendipity found like-minded fellow musicians in his downtown neighbourhood. Taking as home turf the corner of Welland Avenue and Geneva Street (then the site of a railway terminus, a major local junction), he, with Art Talbot, Paul Lindo, and Bill Jelley, staked their nascent counter-cultural claim. There and in garages and upstairs in family homes, they shared their enthusiasm for music, including idioms beyond jazz (Stravinsky was a favourite), for latest books and ideas (Lindo was the group's intellectual), and even fashion statements (coats without lapels). One can only imagine reactions of passers-by as, circa 1946, Talbot stood out on that corner playing Charlie Parker solos on an ocarina.

BEBOP, NIAGARA-STYLE

Sometime in 1947, most likely—no one involved remembers exactly when—
jazz was presented in a concert setting for the first time in Niagara. A young
man named Gus Garriock, perhaps inspired by the American promoter Norman Granz with his "Jazz at the Philharmonic" series, rented the St. Catharines
Collegiate's auditorium and daringly presented an evening's program that featured two bands—both local, but aesthetically divergent.

Remarkable for taking the music out of its usual contexts of pavilion and
dance hall and for billing it as "jazz," this venture also echoed precisely its
moment of uneasy transition from established "swing" to upstart "bop" (also
known as "re-bop" and "be-bop": all onomatopoeic terms for the early modern jazz, originating in jam sessions by young African-American musicians
playing for themselves and for "art," featuring extended harmonies and
extensive virtuosity). First to play was a Mynie Sutton–led quintet that
included trumpeter Howard Bradley and drummer Rod North. Sutton, Niagara's premier exponent of swing, presented a set of standards and favourites
of the immediate past. Next up, however, was a quintet of young modernists:
Kenny Wheeler, trumpet; Paul Lindo, alto sax; Art Talbot, piano; Boris
Zenchuk, double bass; and Bill Jelley, drums. They played less familiar contemporary pieces such as "Robbin's Nest" and outright bebop numbers such
as Fats Navarro's "Fat Girl."

Under-attended and money-losing, not reviewed in the press, this concert, nonetheless, encapsulates the coming to Niagara of modern jazz; it
reveals, in hindsight, the cultural dynamics involved. During the late 1940s,
Niagara was prescient in its reception of musical change; it got the news
early. Conflictedly, this region was both a hotbed for major talents and a stultifying backwater that failed to foster them and led them to leave.

When a popular music dominates its era—as big-band swing did from the
mid-1930s through the war years—it pervades the culture. It plays as the
soundtrack of the times, always there, everywhere. It matters to very many,
and its manner sets the moment's style and tone, with influences beyond its
role as entertainment of common choice. From fashion in dress and dance
steps to courting rites and concepts of beauty, everything follows music's
lead. In all senses of the term, that music defines what is "in."

When, inevitably, a new idiom comes along—as bebop modern jazz did
in the late 1940s—with an explicit challenge to established musical and
social norms, it "plays out" in the culture quite differently. Most, at first or
ever, are reluctant to embrace it, but a self-selecting few do so with intensity.
By its deliberate difference and oppositional attitude, such music is fated
never to become "mass entertainment." It creates, instead, a subculture,

where its impact is profound, even life-changing. It identifies its adherents as unusual, as "into" what is "outside" the normal.

By consistent accounts of those involved, this is what happened here when modern jazz came along. The period of transition from swing to bop resonated locally much in sync and spirit with its unfolding elsewhere. As throughout the jazz world, the seemingly radical innovations heard on post-war recordings by alto saxophonist Charlie Parker and his associates startled both musicians and audiences. Bebop's often-frenzied small group performances foregrounded soloists' freedom to improvise on melodies, beat out liberated rhythms, and sound "far out" harmonies. Some listeners to these departures from practices of big-band swing—mostly youngsters—were as delighted as astonished. Others, often only slightly older, were not so sure, but a few puzzled through. Some still wish it had never happened.

Sudden conversions forged strong bonds. Afternoons in upstairs rooms, zealous converts gathered to listen to the latest records, to wonder and to argue with the cautious. Around about midnight, in solitude, one sixteen-year-old tunes in "Symphony Sid," broadcasting from New York City's Birdland, hears Charlie Parker live. He raves to another kid, who hips then a third. That reluctant fans of the "old stuff" resist the new with acrimony, that the unconvinced are suspicious, makes all the more intense its meaning and importance to modern jazz initiates. The ardour of this new music's advocates in Niagara was made more fierce by a shared perception of its being heard here in a "nowhere" place. Lees writes of late 1940s St. Catharines as "a narrow and bigoted little city." At the same time, however, the city's proximity to a porous American border allowed for a distinct musical advantage.

Enriching the 1940s Niagara swing scene were appearances by big-name American bands on tour, taking a northern turn along a circuit that might include evening stands at the Crystal Beach Amusement Park on the Lake Erie shore, at the Niagara Falls arena on Victoria Avenue, at the Brant Inn in Burlington, Ontario, and on to the Palais Royale Ballroom by the Lake Ontario shore in Toronto. Whenever this happened, union rules called for "replacement" local musicians to be hired at scale, merely to sit and enjoy. The bands of Jimmie Lunceford and Lionel Hampton came most often. That same circuit brought Benny Goodman, the Dorseys, Gene Krupa, Count Basie, and Duke Ellington. Fans could actually meet the musicians, passing a paper to the bandstand for autographs of the entire band. Bold devotees, often players themselves, might stand visiting musicians to intermission drinks. It was possible, as an awestruck Bill Jelley later did, to meet Charlie Parker in a Buffalo bar.

Together, the young bop enthusiasts valiantly attempted to introduce the modern sounds to St. Catharines audiences, with only moderate success. With tenor saxophonist Joe Calarco as bandleader, they played bebop at a "hamburger joint" on east-end Hartzel Road for a younger crowd than frequented the pavilion down at north-end Port Dalhousie. Wheeler was already arranging charts in the manner of influential innovator Claude Thornhill and growing as a musician, studying with diverse mentors: a military bandleader in Buffalo, and the Royal Conservatory in Toronto in harmony classes with John Weinzweig, a pioneer of "serial music" in Canada.[12]

This core group of modernists cut a record at a studio in Niagara Falls: the ballad "Don't Blame Me," with sister Helen on vocal, backed with "Lester Leaps In," a forward-looking improv on "rhythm" changes by Lester Young with Count Basie. They also found summer employment in the resorts of Ontario's cottage country. By most accounts, including his own, Wheeler was, as a teenage player, second best on the local scene to pianist Art Talbot. Sitting in with touring jazz stars Lionel Hampton and Al Haig, Talbot was invited by both to come along to New York, but deferred. Some time after the St. Catharines Collegiate concert, Talbot did front a trio for a while at the Club Norman in Toronto (in the upstairs lounge while Wheeler and Jelley played in the downstairs dance band). Favourable comparisons were made at the time between Talbot and the then-emerging Oscar Peterson. Accompanying vocals was his particular strength, and Jelley recalls thinking at the time that wider fame was Talbot's for the taking. For reasons unknown, he went no further; he gigged locally but with increasing reticence and has been a recluse for decades. Perhaps Talbot's fate was one Wheeler sought to avoid.

By the early 1950s, jazz no longer defined the popular music mainstream, and Niagara's two future luminaries had left the scene, off to make major contributions to jazz elsewhere. Gene Lees, in the States, would write many books about jazz, edit *Down Beat* magazine, publish his own magazine (*Jazzletter*), act as publicist for Woody Herman, and write English lyrics for songs by Antonio Carlos Jobim. Subsequently a vocalist himself, his lyrics were recorded by Tony Bennett, among others, and he collaborated with pianist Bill Evans.

In his book *Singers and the Song*, Lees argues that the big-band era came to an end partly because the trolley cars that took the audiences readily and cheaply to the continent's dance pavilions stopped running, their tracks torn up in the culture's post-war adoration of the automobile. This idea had its genesis on the trolleys that took him from Merritton to Port Dalhousie through St. Catharines' Welland Avenue–Geneva Street junction, and to performances by touring American bands at the Victoria Avenue arena in Niagara Falls.[13]

Lees suggests strongly also that, as much as Kenny Wheeler needed to leave Niagara to grow as a musician, he got essential experience and necessary camaraderie locally: enough to sustain a notoriously shy young man as he crossed an ocean to pursue his diversely prolific career. That skinny kid went from the St. Catharines Collegiate's stage to non-union gigs in Toronto (over which he got in trouble) and then to studies at McGill University in Montreal. In the autumn of 1952, Wheeler, expecting to be joined shortly by Lees, set sail for the United Kingdom.[14] To launch one writer and one musician to international prominence is no mean achievement for a short-lived, largely ignored, tightly bonded little "peninsular" late-1940s scene, when more than just the music changed.

MENTORSHIP AND MUSIC[15]

Wilf Wheeler was for years the AFM (American Federation of Musicians) local's sergeant-at-arms (son Ken still holds a St. Catharines union card). Through him, guitarist Warren Stirtzinger, near his career's start, connected to Wheeler. At a union meeting, with his brother Randy (a bassist then, nowadays playing vibes and piano as well), Stirtzinger heard the proud father who checked their cards sing his son's praises, showing off the newly released *Deer Wan*. Attracted to the LP by its featured guitarists John Abercrombie and Ralph Towner, Stirtzinger was an immediate convert to Wheeler's music and met the man shortly thereafter through Bill Jelley. Niagara's jazz community here is welcoming and crosses generations.

By the mid-1980s, Stirtzinger's relationship with Wheeler had him comfortable in requesting an arrangement for a Buffalo-based guitar ensemble he was part of. Wheeler's response nicely reiterates the links of family, friends, the local, and music: he wrote and arranged a brand-new piece called "Salina Street." In pencil on that score appears a typically dismissive "if it's any good" and then the tantalizing phrase: "could be part of the *St. Catharines Suite.*" Alas, no sign of that work, yet.

U.K. colleague Ian Carr describes Wheeler's music as having "a powerful individual atmosphere which has spawned many disciples—a kind of buoyant romantic melancholy."[16] One glance at a Wheeler chart and the complexity is readily apparent, even to one who cannot read music. "Difficult" is frequently an interviewee's first word, asked to describe Wheeler's music—and "challenging," clearly meant as a virtue, as essential to its beauty. Rick Wilkins, arranger and conductor of orchestra and strings for a 2006

CBC (Canadian Broadcasting Corporation) radio tribute concert, says: "It's beautiful, but Kenny's music is not the kinds of tunes you'd go and fake on a job. If you are going to play jazz on these tunes, you have to go to bed with them for a long time."[17]

"Distinctive," "unmistakable"—such words as these repeatedly come up in relation to Wheeler's music. Allusions get made to the greats who also put their signatures on the elements of jazz: Ellington, the arrangers Gil Evans and Claude Thornhill. Once you know Wheeler's music, the initiated insist, any newly heard work can instantly be sussed out as his. Most who so esteem his work unabashedly admit to aping it. Tyro trumpeters mimic; young composers pastiche. This is Wheeler's mentorship at its most basic and pervasive: as an exemplar of distinguished excellence.

Katie Malloch, long-time host of CBC Radio's *Jazz Beat*, casts Wheeler as "the Merlin in the Camelot of jazz … a harmonic alchemist."[18] Wheeler's musical wizardry amazes with harmonic richness. "Grown-up chords," Warren Stirtzinger calls them. Wheeler's vocabulary takes bebop's harmonic extension even further, from the root to abstruse realms. His style is described by Fred Sturm as:

> distinguished by synthetic harmonies (triads over foreign bass notes, for example), altered major-type chords (particularly major seventh with augmented 5th), extended minor chords (that frequently omit the 7th and sometimes lower the 6th degree), and dominant structures with suspended 4ths. [Wheeler] frequently structures chords in inverted forms (notably use of third inversion-placement of the chord 7th in the bass). The near absence of pure dominant chords and rare appearances of altered dominant chords are also highly significant to the sound and character of [his] works.[19]

For trumpeter-composer John MacLeod, his late-1970s discovery of Wheeler's music was "a real turnaround." Talking in his University of Toronto office, he lauded a lyricism that bridges the gap between jazz and "serious music": "His composing and his playing are so at one with each other, recognizably the same personality in both; he improvises and composes at the same level, in the same voice." MacLeod admires an unconventional approach to phrasing, to rhythm that he finds "liberating," and speculates on whether their shared Canadian-ness made this "different" music so resonant, made it immediately feel "comfortable."

In a December 2005 concert staged by JAZZ.FM91, where six Toronto trumpeters, including Lina Allemano, each paid tribute to a legend of the horn, MacLeod, described by critic Mark Miller as "wear[ing] his Wheeler on his sleeve anyway,"[20] played "Smatter" from *Gnu High* (his entry point to the canon) and a Wheeler-inspired piece of his own, "Tir na Og," paying homage to all aspects of his influence.

Guitarist Michael Occhipinti, co-leader of the Juno-winning band NOJO, calls Wheeler's melodies emotionally powerful, "operatic," with countermelodies that stand on their own, with "nothing superfluous." Occhipinti, mentored by Wheeler at the Banff School of Fine Arts in Alberta, was inspired by him to compose and to form his innovative jazz orchestra. His graduating "final exam" in composition at York University bears the title "For Kenny Wheeler."

Listening to "Aspire," from *Widow in the Window,* a piece his early writing particularly emulates, Occhipinti delights in its Wheeler-esque features: the playing that "leaps and warbles" with control, "comfortable with odd times"; the handling of format that has each part "interesting and important," that "brings out great playing." He celebrates writing that is also paradoxically unpredictable, where "the key is a moving target, but yet, once revealed, 'inevitable' in its structure."

A perceived "darkness" in Wheeler's "austere" music, consistent with its slow to mid-tempo pace, wants a second listen. Recognizing the melancholic in his melodies, Wheeler reflects: "I must be a little twisted because sad melodies make me feel very happy.... I was fifteen the first time I heard [Coleman Hawkins's recording of "Body and Soul," and] I immediately burst into tears, not so much with sadness—it just communicated to me."[21] Occhipinti hears a complementary "playfulness" in Wheeler's music. A parallel to that musical "play" manifests in the fun Wheeler has with song titles: cryptic allusions ("Unti" for untitled, the aforementioned family names), orthographic puns (*Deer Wan, Gnu High*) and palindromes ("Hotel Le Hot," "Flutter By, Butterfly," *Kayak*)—all sorts of musical wordplay everywhere ("Foxy Trot," "¾ in the Afternoon"). His "dry humour" frequently quips against himself, pervades the anecdotes musicians trade about him.

Those whom Wheeler benefits, those he has mentored, concur that his taking on the mentor role is deliberate, sustained, and extensive but that he seldom speaks about it. His involvement with young musicians means staying in touch after Banff workshops, freely distributing his scores, playing featured sideman at concerts, being a "famous" guest artist on recordings.

DUNCAN HOPKINS AND LE ROUGE[22]

One particularly enduring instance of Wheeler's mentorship is also distinctly local. Jazz bassist-composer Duncan Hopkins met his mentor fortuitously early in a career very much fostered by Wheeler. All of six months into playing jazz in the summer of 1987, Hopkins laboured through a Niagara College

FIGURE 10.2 Hopkins and Wheeler in concert at Laura Secord Secondary School, St. Catharines, Jan. 12, 2008. Permission of photographer Mike Balsom and music teacher David Sisler

Jazz Band concert in Montebello Park, downtown St. Catharines. By his own assessment not yet very good, Hopkins treasures how pianist John Sherwood and the Stirtzinger brothers overlooked his lapses, recognizing an intensity to learn and "perhaps," he says, "some potential."

Wheeler, back in town at sister Helen's, present at that concert, certainly heard something from this tall, skinny redheaded kid. Seeking Hopkins out after, he invited him to the next evening's jam session at the Ontario House in Niagara Falls, New York. Only vaguely aware of who Wheeler was, Hopkins, not knowing what he was up against, went. Assembled players from both sides of the border ventured "Everybody's Song but My Own," workshopped "Gentle Piece" (with Wheeler coaching Hopkins through tricky bass parts), and Cole Porter's "I Love You" at a blistering tempo: "I was really way over my head. Besides the fact that I was new to the instrument.... I went and found out a lot about Ken, as a person and as a player. I had a lot of fun, learned a lot.... It set me on a path of righteousness [*laughs*]."

Thereafter, the neophyte entered a deep study of Wheeler's music— music whose very existence encourages. Hopkins found in its complex of distinct virtues much to emulate. As he came to know the man, meeting regularly on Wheeler's subsequent visits, the mentorship became overt. Hopkins, in reflection, is certain that shared locality distinguished him for

FIGURE 10.3 Wheeler, long-time collaborator singer Norma Winstone, and Hopkins in concert at Laura Secord Secondary School, St. Catharines, Jan. 12, 2008. Permission of photographer Mike Balsom and music teacher David Sisler

particular attention. Here's Hopkins on Wheeler as teacher: "If you like this sound [Wheeler says], I'll tell you how I get to this point and I'll encourage you to find your point of happiness, your zenith. This is what I did and maybe you can find a way through my path." Graduating from Brock University in St. Catharines with a "day-job" degree in economics, Hopkins paralleled Wheeler's move to Montreal, studying at McGill University for a while with bassist Michel Donato. "Fired up," he soon found school a hindrance and gigged in Montreal and studied with Donato privately.

Wheeler's mentorship became formal at the Banff School of Fine Arts in the summer of 1991. Successfully auditioning before iconoclastic composer-saxophonist Steve Coleman, Hopkins came to Banff an "agile player" and left a nascent writer of jazz. Instead of trumpeter to bassist, the link becomes composer to composer. At Banff, Wheeler's master-class expositions on his own works gave Hopkins inspiring insights into the process. Using the example of "Heyoke," from *Gnu High*, Wheeler illustrated his rich harmonic, counter-melodic, interval-leaping, key-shifting system: "First I compose," says Wheeler, "then I decompose." This method, he puns, makes him a "composter" of music. On another occasion, Wheeler describes his method of composing as "sitting at the piano for hours, getting rid of ideas."[23]

From that Banff summer to the present, Wheeler has boosted Hopkins the composer. Offering critiques in person, in voluminous correspondence and in terse phone messages ("Tell the bass player I like his music. That is all"), Wheeler soon insisted Hopkins record, raising the ante by offering to play on what in early 1993 became the bass player's debut disc, *Le Rouge*: "It was all Kenny's doing, not only through inspiration but through his actual encouragement. In fact, more than encouragement, he sort of told me to do it. More than encouragement, it was direction." Many aspects of Wheeler's mentorship converge in this recording. Here is his extended hand, extensively. Recorded at the home studio of John MacLeod (also a "flawless" engineer), *Le Rouge* includes tracks where Wheeler plays songs conceived by Hopkins in Wheeler mode, meant for his playing, including "Mr. Banff" (its title inspired by a Wheeler rebuff of an insistently unknowing New York student's "Who are you?"—with Wheeler claiming to be the Alberta school's namesake).

Prior to the one day-long session with Wheeler, the band (Lorne Lofsky, guitar; Kevin Dempsey, drums; John Hassleback Jr., trombone; John Sherwood, piano; Hopkins, bass) in rehearsals had producer Bill Melymuka, on trumpet and flugelhorn, playing the Wheeler parts ("with difficulty, poorly," he says).[24] As a young Niagara Falls high-schooled player, Melymuka eased into local jazz just prior to the bassist. They grew as musicians together, with Hopkins introducing his peer to Wheeler's music. By the early 1990s, graduated in music production from London, Ontario's Fanshawe College, Melymuka was another local devotee of Wheeler, thrilled to be in the same room as his exemplar. On a recording done directly to two-track stereo, no overdubs or remix possible, Melymuka's chief task was the proper balancing of studio and instruments by miking and physical arrangement.

Prior to the recording session, Wheeler, sensing Hopkins's anxiety, began to joke about as an antidote for nerves, claiming, for instance, to have forgotten his horn but offering to "sing a few songs, if you like." Melymuka recalls him poring over charts as if for the first time, but playing them cold, executing each with due diligence to the needs of the piece. Looking at the Art Blakey-like score for "Freneticism," asked to take first solo, Wheeler opines, "This is the kind of song people ask me not to play on." Holding firm to his own aesthetics, however, Wheeler balks at a passage in "Mr. Banff": "How do you want me to play this bit here, because I refuse to play it as written." Hours on, Hopkins was about to call the session, but Wheeler insisted they do more, knowing, Hopkins thinks, that they were "in the moment."

CONCERTS IN ST. CATHARINES

As a tribute, Hopkins had long wanted to produce a St. Catharines concert, featuring Wheeler and whoever he wanted to play with. Adamantly, Wheeler said "Nothing doing!" and, indeed, offered to record what became *Le Rouge* instead. Eventually, such a concert did happen, as music, family, friends, and locality again conjoined.

Deb Slade, director of Brock University's Centre for the Arts, received a phone call from Helen Hill (née Wheeler) in late spring 2000, saying her brother, coming home that September, was interested in playing at Brock. His never having played a concert in St. Catharines since his departure was, she said, a "travesty." Although the centre's season was already booked, Slade readily agreed to a special added event. Wheeler had indicated a preference to play with local pianist John Sherwood, who, when contacted by Slade, agreed as well to produce the concert.[25] But even as plans for the concert were being set by trans-Atlantic telephone, Wheeler expressed his doubts to Sherwood about a Kenny Wheeler concert in St. Catharines: "Will anyone come?" he asked.

Yes they did, in the hundreds, to an unusual Sunday night engagement, on September 17, 2000. An all-but-full house included a reunion gathering of the Wheeler clan, to hear a select quartet of Wheeler, long-time associate Don Thompson on vibes, producer John Sherwood on piano, and Duncan Hopkins on bass. At this juncture, Hopkins, touring down east with his quintet (featuring John MacLeod on trumpet), was about to fly to London, joining Wheeler's young U.K. associates in a first-time British tour. Set to depart from Halifax, Nova Scotia, he eagerly came back home, now an established jazz musician and composer, to play with his mentor. That night, the quartet played each other's works and a few standards and had an obviously good time before an appreciative audience—many of whom were aware of being witness to artistic justice.

Over the years, Helen Hill also had spoken with principal percussionist and associate conductor Laura Thomas about the Niagara Symphony Orchestra performing Wheeler's music.[26] When the NSO determined in its Pops series to celebrate Niagara music, Thomas, charged with programming, led off with local jazz, her "first love." (For many years, she directed and drummed with the Niagara College Jazz Band that included Sherwood, the Stirtzingers, and young Hopkins.) A year before the jazz-themed concert, Thomas phoned Wheeler in the United Kingdom, seeking permission to orchestrate a work of his. Making more or less a "cold call," she alluded to the Stirtzingers link and noted a distinct warming in his reception. As discussion of the concert ensued, piqued by its focus on jazz's local roots and continuing presence,

Wheeler asked about pieces already selected, the tempos, the sequencing of the concert, the better to choose his own work for inclusion. He suggested "Sea Lady," then unknown to Thomas.

In follow-up calls, it dawned on Thomas that Wheeler was not only onside with permission, he was offering to orchestrate. This was more than she had ever wished for. They set a schedule for the task, working backwards from the February 2005 concert date. The scores arrived well on time and Thomas is still not sure if it was deliberate or happenstance, but for the concert itself, so did Wheeler. Afterwards he was very positive, very happy with the jazz-enhanced NSO's playing of his music, and signed Thomas's now-treasured copy of the score.

Thomas recalls first listening to "Sea Lady." She was so taken by its "so strong, so lyrical" melody, she, a percussionist, did not notice its "odd" 5/4 meter. She exulted in how Wheeler the composer voices chord extensions so that the piece can be heard as polytonal or as having a second basic triad in its further reaches, creating "a richness not heard in regular tertial harmonies." An accomplished arranger for the orchestra herself, she praises his skill at orchestration, especially loving "the way he used the winds."

At that concert, Beth Bartley sang "Sea Lady," with its lyrics by long-time Wheeler collaborator, vocalist Norma Winstone. A violinist as well as vocalist, Bartley and her musical and domestic partner, the guitarist Mark Clifford, perform locally and internationally and record as the duo Vox Violins. She is also a composer, with a musical education that includes conservatory and university studies, and as she speaks with punctuations of awe at Wheeler's achievement, she peruses the score for "Sea Lady." She notes the "cleverness" of the music, how, in the key of C with gentle modulations, it evokes its liquid subject: "Melodically, he uses every semi-tone—and so wonderfully!—it creates a line like a mermaid floating in the sea. And then harmonically, it's the same thing! How can he use every lush chord possible …? He's taken all this and he's made this gorgeous sea of music."[27] Shaking her head in admiration, she launches into an *a cappella, sotto voce*, in-the-kitchen rendering of "Sea Lady," for the sheer pleasure of it.[28]

CODA

The relationship between Wheeler and St. Catharines is curiously conflicted. Wheeler has spoken often with Hopkins about their city in common. As noted, it was a shared locality that spurred the early mentoring, but Wheeler, also early on, told Hopkins he had to leave St. Catharines: "Canada, if you can, St. Catharines, for sure." Yet, having left (with stints of study in New York

FIGURE 10.4 Wheeler (far right) onstage with local musicians, Cat's Caboose, St. Catharines, 2007. Courtesy of Bill Melymuka

City with Dave Holland and in Denmark with Niels-Henning Orsted Peder-sen, and now resident outside Toronto), Hopkins sees the many virtues of the St. Catharines jazz scene, including precisely the fostering and self-effacement so characteristic of Wheeler: "I don't know if it's in the water or what...." Of Wheeler's particular reticence about St. Catharines, Hopkins concludes:

> He's sort of famous now, but St. Catharines had nothing to do with it.... He had to leave, but he's the same guy, whether here or in London, but London recognized it and St. Catharines didn't. Maybe there's a bit of antagonism about that, I'm not sure.... There's an underlying sense that he wants to have a belonging here, but he never really belonged. He had to leave to find him-self and his music.

In the late spring of 2007, Wheeler, back again in town, gave advance notice of his willingness to sit in at the Randy Stirtzinger-led gig at Cat's Caboose, a south-end St. Catharines bar that features jazz on Saturday after-noons. All of the regulars—both full-time and "weekend" players—were keen to share the bandstand with him and gathered mid-week for an unusual rehearsal, working up the Wheeler book. On the day, with the city's jazz fans alerted and present, Wheeler disappointed the players by calling for standards, beginning with "Green Dolphin Street" and ending with his perennial favourite, "Body and Soul." (Frankly, I think he just wanted to play some standards, for once.) Only as an encore did he accede to one of his own, a work with the aptly ironic title "Everybody's Song But My Own." Both his play-ing and its final gesture were superb and self-effacing—quintessentially Kenny Wheeler.

APPENDIX: KENNY WHEELER: A SELECTED DISCOGRAPHY

Thanks to graduate research assistant Laura Wiebe Taylor for her work on this discography.

1964

Cleo Laine and John Dankworth. *Shakespeare and All That Jazz*. AFF 196

1967

Spontaneous Music Ensemble. *Withdrawal*. Emanem 4020

Kenny Wheeler. *Windmill Tilter*. Fontana STL-5494 (also listed as Kenny Wheeler and the John Dankworth Orchestra), 1969, Fontana STL 5494

1969

Clarke-Boland Big Band. *At Her Majesty's Pleasure*. Black Lion BLP 30109

1973

Kenny Wheeler. *Song for Someone*. Incus 10

1975

Kenny Wheeler. *Gnu High*. ECM 1069

1977

John Taylor, Norma Winstone, Kenny Wheeler. *Azimuth*. ECM 1099

Kenny Wheeler. *Deer Wan*. ECM 1102

1979

Azimuth with Ralph Towner. *Depart*. ECM 1163

1983

Kenny Wheeler. *Double, Double You*. ECM 1262

1987

Tim Brady/Kenny Wheeler. *Visions*. Justin Time JTR 8413-2 (listed by some sources as 1985)

Kenny Wheeler Quintet. *Flutter By, Butterfly*. Soul Note 121 146-2

1990

Kenny Wheeler. *Music for Large and Small Ensembles*. ECM 1415/16

Kenny Wheeler. *The Widow in the Window*. ECM 1417

1992

Kenny Wheeler. *Kayak*. Ah Um 012

1995

The Upper Austrian Jazzorchestra. *The Upper Austrian Jazzorchestra Plays the Music of Kenny Wheeler*. West Wind WW 2097

1996

Kenny Wheeler. *Angel Song*. ECM 1607

Kenny Wheeler/Norma Winstone/John Taylor with The Maritime Jazz Orchestra. *Siren's Song*. Justin Time JTR 8465

1997
The Kenny Wheeler and Sonny Greenwich Quintet. *Kenny and Sonny Live at the Montreal Bistro*. Justin Time Just 114
Kenny Wheeler and Paul Bley. *Touché*. Justin Time JIT 97

1998
Kenny Wheeler-Brian Dickinson. *Still Waters*. Hornblower HR 99105 (listed as 1999 or 2000 by some sources)
Kenny Wheeler. *A Long Time Ago*. ECM 1691

2000
UMO Jazz Orchestra with Kenny Wheeler and Norma Winstone. *One More Time*. AL 73202

2003
Kenny Wheeler. *Dream Sequence*. PSI 0304

2005
Kenny Wheeler. *Where Do We Go From Here?* CAM 5004
Kenny Wheeler. *What Now?* Sunny Side 285005

A Small Sample of the Diverse Recordings with Wheeler as a Sideman
Ronnie Scott. *Live at Ronnie Scott's*. CBS REALM JAZZ 52661, 1968
Anthony Braxton. *New York, 1974*. Arista AL 4032, 1974
Globe Unity. *Improvisations*. Japo 60021, 1977
The United Jazz+Rock Ensemble. *Live in Berlin*. Mood 28 628, 1981
Bill Frisell. *Rambler*. ECM 1287, 1984
Dave Holland Quintet. *Seeds of Time*. ECM 1292, 1984
Claudio Fasoli. *Welcome*. Soul Note SN 1171, 1986
Steve Coleman. *Rhythm in Mind*. Novus 63125-2, 1991
Duncan Hopkins. *Le Rouge*. Counterpoint CPR 002, 1993
Rabih Abou-Khalil. *The Sultan's Picnic*. Enja ENJ-8078 2, 1994
Jacek Kochan. *Alberta*. Gowi CDG 47, 1995
Jane Ira Bloom. *The Nearness*. Arabesque Recordings AJ0120, 1995
Stefan Bauer. *Coast To Coast*. IGMOD IG-49702-2, 1996
The Stan Sulzmann Big Band. *Birthdays, Birthdays*. Village Life 99108VL, 1999

NOTES
1 See Appendix for a selected discography of Kenny Wheeler's works.
2 On a recent January afternoon radio broadcast from JAZZ.FM91in Toronto, host Larry Green noted it was Kenny Wheeler's birthday and saluted him as "the pride of St. Catharines." Unfortunately, this is not so. Beyond intersecting circles of friends and jazz fans, to most St. Catharines residents, Wheeler is, proverbially, without honour, an unknown.
3 Tribute to Wheeler available on William Carn and Lina Allemano, *Old Souls* (CAP 101, 1998).

4   Matthew Van Dongen, "Britain Honours Legendary Trumpeter," *St. Catharines Standard*, Mar. 17, 2005, B2. Wheeler did, however, attend the ceremony at the Canadian High Commission in London on May 3, 2007, inducting him into the Order of Canada as an Officer. His citation reads: "A trumpeter, composer and arranger, Kenny Wheeler is considered a giant of jazz who has helped put Canadians on the map internationally. Admired by musicians and fans alike as an innovator whose work serves as a cornerstone, he has recorded more than 20 albums and played with the biggest names in the business. He has created new directions in both composition and arrangement, and his works are studied in music courses around the world. Humble yet generous, he is a beloved teacher and guide to younger musicians, who cite him as an example and inspiration."

5   Ian Carr, "Kenny Wheeler," *Jazz: The Essential Companion* (London: Grafton Books, 1987), 538.

6   The facts, opinions, and direct quotations in this section and the next, involving the Niagara jazz scene in the 1940s and '50s, are taken from the following lengthy interviews: with Rod North, St. Catharines, July 20 and July 30, 1999; with Bill Jelley, St. Catharines, July 24, 1999, and Feb. 3, 2006; with Jimmy Marando, in nearby Welland, Aug. 11, 1999. My thanks to them and to all the other interviewees cited below.

7   "Kenny" is how Wheeler is known to most, so named on all his works. But many friends call him "Ken," which is how, for instance, he also signs his Christmas cards.

8   In 1945, the population of St. Catharines was 35,210, about one-quarter of the present population.

9   Gene Lees, "Come Back Last Summer, Part One," *Jazzletter* 12:3 (March 1993), 5. Lees devotes two issues of his *Jazzletter* (P.O. Box 240, Ojai, CA 93024-0240) to reminiscences of these times and of his links to Kenny Wheeler. "Part Two" is 12:4 (April 1993). Augmenting my interviews with its participants, Lees's memoirist essays are a major source for this conjuring of Niagara's jazz scene of the 1940s into the 1950s.

10 "When you write a tune for one member of the family, you must then write a song for all the others. So, I thought I'd kill two birds with one stone. So, for my sisters Mabel and Helen: 'Ma Belle Helene.'" Kenny Wheeler, quoted by Katie Malloch, introducing the song "Phoebe," named for "one of his mischievous granddaughters," on the broadcast of *A Long Time Ago* (see note 15, below). Among the myriad of family tribute titled songs, he honours his wife with "Three for D'reen."

11 Lees, *Jazzletter* 12:3 (March 1993), 2. First noticing Wheeler in the school band at assemblies, Lees imagined how much his friend suffered in its out-of-tune confines. St. Catharines Collegiate yearbook pictures of the era document Wheeler's school band membership.

12 Serial music, also known as twelve-tone music, refers to the compositional methods initiated by Arnold Schoenberg in 1923 ("composing with twelve tones which are related only with one another") and subsequently taken up by Anton von Webern, Alban Berg, Igor Stravinsky, Pierre Boulez, and others. From Alex Ross, *The Rest Is Noise: Listening to the Twentieth Century* (New York: Farrar, Straus, Giroux, 2007): "Twelve is the number of steps it takes to go from middle C on a

piano to the next C above or below. Twelve consecutive notes make up what is called the chromatic scale, so named because it suggests all the colours of a spectrum. A particular arrangement of twelve notes is called a series or row. The idea is not to consider the row a theme in itself but to employ it as a kind of fund of notes, or intervals. The composer can run the row in retrograde (go backward from the last note). Or he can use an inversion (turn it upside down).... The retrograde inversion goes back to front and upside down. The composer can also transpose the row by moving it up or down the scale" (194–95).

13 I ventured this point in a magazine article, which Rod North sent to his friend Gene Lees. In a subsequent e-mail (Jan. 5, 2000) Lees wrote: "Your surmise that my ideas about the interurban trolleys underlay the piece I wrote on the decline of the bands is correct. That old trolley line ran from Port [Dalhousie] to St. Catharines to Thorold, where it split into lines going to Niagara Falls and Welland."

14 An obvious question is why his destination was the United Kingdom instead of the more usual, and readily accessible, United States, jazz's homeland. Bill Jelley offers the possibility that Wheeler wished to avoid Jelley's fate: off to the States to play, the drummer was drafted into the Korean War. Lees cites Ian Carr's answer that Wheeler sought a "non-competitive" alternative to the "gladiatorial" jazz world of the States. Alternatively, Lees explains the going to England as "almost by accident," spurred by Lees's casual remarks in a late-night Montreal café that Canadians did not need a work visa there. *Jazzletter*, 12:3 (March 1993), 6–7, and 12:4 (April 1993), 8.

15 This section draws on interviews with the following: Warren Stirtzinger, in nearby Beamsville, Feb. 10, 2006; John MacLeod, Toronto, Feb. 15, 2006; and Michael Occhipinti, Toronto, Feb. 16, 2006.

16 Ian Carr, p. 537, as quoted in Gene Lees, *Jazzletter*, April 1993.

17 Wilkins and Malloch are quoted from the broadcast of CBC Radio Two's *On Stage* from the Glenn Gould Studio in Toronto, Apr. 23, 2006. The concert *A Long Time Ago* featured Wheeler's music exclusively, as performed by Wheeler on trumpet and flugelhorn; Phil Dwyer, saxophones; Don Thompson, piano; Jim Vivian, bass; Terry Clarke, drums; plus Rick Wilkins conducting a large orchestral ensemble, with arrangements by Wilkins, Thompson, and Dwyer.

18 From introductory remarks, *A Long Time Ago*.

19 Fred Sturm, *Kenny Wheeler: Collected Works on ECM*. UE 70007, 1997, not paginated.

20 Miller, now retired as jazz critic for *The Globe and Mail*, reviewed this concert. See Mark Miller, "Players Trumpet Masters' Influence," *The Globe and Mail*, Dec. 8, 2005, R5.

21 Sturm, not paginated.

22 Matter in this section derives from an extensive interview with Duncan Hopkins, after a gig in an east-end Toronto pub, Feb. 15–16, 2006.

23 Quoted in an an e-mail from pianist John Sherwood, Nov. 8, 2007.

24 Insights into the recording of *Le Rouge* are courtesy of an interview with Bill Melymuka, St. Catharines, May 6, 2006.

25 Interview with Deb Slade, Centre for the Arts, Brock University, Nov. 29, 2007.

26 Interview with Laura Thomas, by e-mail and telephone, Nov. 27–29, 2007.

27 Beth Bartley, interviewed in St. Catharines, Nov. 4, 2007.

28 Ms. Bartley, backed by local Wheeler-influenced jazz players, also sang "Sea Lady" in a concert celebrating Niagara music and musicians that was part of the Popular Culture Niagara conference, "Popular Culture and the Local," held at Brock University, May 13, 2006.

WORKS CITED

Lees, Gene. *Singers and The Song*. New York: Oxford University Press, 1987.

Miller, Mark. *Such Melodious Racket: The Lost History of Jazz in Canada*. Toronto: Mercury Press, 1997.

Sturm, Fred. *Kenny Wheeler: Collected Works on ECM*. UE 70007, 1997.

THE MUSIC STORE AS A COMMUNITY RESOURCE

NICK BAXTER-MOORE

INTRODUCTION

The Niagara Region has a rich and varied musical history. In part because of its location on the border between Canada and the United States, between southern Ontario and western New York, close to major centres such as Toronto and Buffalo and on tour routes between the two, the region has hosted performances by major artists and been subject to the latest musical trends. It has produced or become home to musical notables: jazz greats such as musician-writer Gene Lees and trumpeter-flugelhorn player Kenny Wheeler (see Terrance Cox in this volume); Canada's polka king and multiple-Grammy-winner Walter Ostanek; Neil Peart, drummer and principal lyricist of Rush; 1980s "hair" bands Honeymoon Suite and Brighton Rock; jazz pianist John Sherwood; and James Bryan (McCollum), jazz guitarist, former member of the Philosopher Kings and one-half of Prozzak. More recent rising stars from the region include jazz bassist Duncan Hopkins, multiple Aboriginal Music Award winners, The Pappy Johns Band, singer-songwriter Ron Sexsmith, "screamo" band Alexisonfire and Dallas Green's side project City and Colour, Welland's Attack In Black, and transplanted Nova Scotians The Trews. And there are vibrant local music scenes in most of the towns and cities that make up the Niagara Region.

As the growing literature on the spatial dimensions of popular music demonstrates, the development of local sounds, scenes, and musical communities depends on the support of local infrastructure, institutions, and community resources. Inventories of such resources typically include live performance venues, supportive radio stations and community newspapers, recording studios, record labels, and record stores. A notable omission from this list is the local music store. By "music store" in this context, I mean not a record store, which sells CDs, possibly vinyl, increasingly DVDs and other entertainment-related paraphernalia. Rather, "music store" here denotes a *musical instrument store*, an emporium that specializes in the sale of musical instruments and accessories but also offers a variety of other music-related products and services to local musicians and would-be musicians.

In this study, I report some of my findings on local music stores, so defined, in Niagara. I argue that the music store is an institution worthy of study because it performs multiple functions in support of local musicians and their music-making, which often go beyond purely commercial transactions to make the store a community resource, not only for professional musicians but also for amateurs, hobbyists, and the young musicians from whose numbers may emerge the next generation of stars, or, at least, the next generation of local bands.

MUSIC STORES IN NIAGARA

I conducted my research in a number of music stores in Niagara, with particular emphasis on four stores located in St. Catharines and Thorold, neighbouring cities that, with a combined population of around 150,000, constitute the largest conurbation in the region. The research strategy was largely qualitative and ethnographic in nature. I engaged in overt, semi-participant observation[1] of the physical layout and use of space, and the activities and social interactions in the music stores, during regular visits to each of the principal sites ("Old" Thorold Music, Thorold Music, Mike's Music, and Ostanek's Music Centre), at least once a month, and often two or three times a week. I conducted on-site interviews with music store owners, managers, and employees, and with selected musicians and other customers in the Niagara Region. The primary fieldwork, especially the interviewing, was conducted in the period between October 2004 and March 2006; less formal observation has continued in most of the stores, and any significant changes that may have occurred in their operations after the primary fieldwork are reported below. Other sources of evidence for the study include music store websites, local music store advertising, references to stores in the local press, name checks, and acknowledgments in the liner notes of CDs by local bands, and—to establish broader context—observation of and interviews with owners and staff of music stores outside the Niagara Region.

"Old" Thorold Music

The original Thorold Music store, now known as John's Thorold Music, was established in 1964 by Elio (Al) Moretti and still occupies the same stone building on Front Street in downtown Thorold, which Moretti bought from the Salvation Army in the mid- to late 1960s ("around 1968," he recalls). He ran it as a family business until the late 1970s, when heart problems forced him to retire for a while. His sons managed the store briefly in its current location and then moved the business to larger premises on Glendale Avenue in St. Catharines (see Thorold Music, below). Moretti leased out the building before re-opening his music store in 1997. To distinguish it from the store operated by his sons, it became popularly known as "Old" Thorold Music.

The store is jammed with instruments, on floor (mostly guitars and amplifiers) and walls (more guitars, violins, mandolins, handmade mountain dulcimers, and other less standard fare), as well as drums and boxed merchandise in the crowded basement. There are usually between eighty and one hundred guitars on stands on the main floor, so many and so crowded that one can't reach some without endangering others. They are mostly seconds or low-end "knock-offs," the kind parents buy for their kids just beginning lessons on guitar or bass or drums. The price range is appropriate for Thorold, largely a working-class community. "Old" Thorold Music may not make a lot of money in sales—for Moretti, "it's not a business, it's a hobby"—but it performs other functions for the local community, musical and otherwise. In 2006, Al Moretti retired again and renamed his store John's Thorold Music in honour of his youngest son.

("New") Thorold Music

The store now officially known as Thorold Music (sometimes "New" Thorold Music) is located on Glendale Avenue in south suburban St. Catharines, about a mile from the "Old" Thorold Music and close to both the 406 Highway, a major traffic route across the peninsula, and the Pen Centre, the largest mall in the Niagara Region.[2] Thorold Music was founded in 1980 by Dan and Leo Moretti, sons of Elio (Al) Moretti; a third brother, Bob, later joined the firm, and in 2004 Bob and Leo were running the store. Bob Moretti died of a heart attack in April 2006, after which Leo became the sole active proprietor.

In February 2008, the Thorold Music store was gutted by a fire that destroyed most of its inventory and severely damaged the building. When the store re-opened in December 2008, it was somewhat smaller than its former self, but there is both room and ambition to expand. The following description is based on the store's appearance when the main body of this research was conducted. It was then the largest music store in the region, with a total floor area of 7,000 square feet. It also carried the widest range of instruments, including pianos and keyboards (one of the few stores still to do so), mandolins, banjos and ukuleles, strings (mostly violins and cellos), and some brass and winds, in addition to the guitars, basses, percussion, amplifiers, and accessories (the staples for other stores). Most were priced in the mid- to mid-high range, with a few low-end models for family or first-time purchasers. According to Bob Moretti, Thorold Music catered to a diverse clientele.

Mike's Music

Brock University geography graduate Mike Palermo established Mike's Music in 1998; it is the newest of the four stores described here. Housed in a single unit of the Pine Centre Plaza, a large strip mall—Thorold's main off-street shopping venue—it's about four blocks from the "Old" Thorold Music store and about a kilometre from the "new" one. Aware that he was entering a fairly competitive market, and operating in a small space, Palermo decided to specialize: he concentrates on guitars, basses, and drums, along with amplifiers and accessories, and is the only local dealer carrying certain brands.

FIGURE 11.1 Mike's Music, Pine Centre Plaza, Thorold. Courtesy of author

As a result of his niche-market strategy, a small but significant proportion of Mike's Music Store customers are from outside the Niagara Region, coming particularly from south-central Ontario (Hamilton, Kitchener/Waterloo) and western New York State. At the same time, local customers are offered accessories, equipment service and rentals, music lessons (guitar, bass, and drums only), and the convenience of location in a multi-outlet mall that provides, if not one-stop shopping, at least one-parking-space shopping. Mike's also attracts a younger clientele, on average, than the other stores.

Ostanek's Music Centre

Situated on Geneva Street in downtown St. Catharines, Ostanek's Music Centre is named for its founder, Walter Ostanek, accordion player, Canada's king of Slovenian/Cleveland-style polka, multiple Grammy Award nominee and three-time winner, inductee into numerous musical halls of fame, and Member of the Order of Canada. In the 1950s, while pursuing a music career, Ostanek sold guitars from the basement of a Thorold dry goods store and briefly co-owned a music store in Niagara Falls before opening up on St. Paul Street in downtown St. Catharines in 1964, moving to the current location on Geneva Street around 1980. Given Walter's age and continuing musical commitments, son Rick now runs the store.

In 2004, the front half of the 2,000-square-foot store was filled with drum kits, percussion, and accessories, the back half with over 200 guitars (about 100 acoustic, 70 to 80 electric, 30 to 40 basses), most hung up around the walls, while amplifiers, equipment, and more guitars on stands crowded the floors. In early 2005, Ostanek's expanded by acquiring the adjacent store, which became the drum room, allowing the guitar stock and space to expand. Due to its downtown location, Ostanek's draws a diverse crowd: practising musicians, hobbyists, parents with kids in tow, high school students, punks, goths and "emos,"[3] all jockeying for space and for the attention, if needed, of the sales staff.

The Competition

Given their relative proximity within the major population centre of the Niagara Region, these four businesses are direct competitors with each other in certain respects, but they also compete with a number of other music stores in St. Catharines and Thorold, elsewhere in Niagara, and outside the region. In St. Catharines, both Niko Music Gallery, in Ridley Square Plaza in the rapidly expanding suburban west end, and Ryson's United Studios of Music, the oldest surviving music store in the city (in business since 1938) on Court Street in the city's downtown, sell musical instruments and sheet music.

They offer other music-related services, but their principal business is the provision of music lessons, largely but not exclusively classical and conservatory-based. These longer-established competitors were recently joined by Music City, an independent store that opened in May 2007 in Lake Square Plaza in the north end of St. Catharines, where owners Sean and Miranda Oakes hope to build a local clientele.

In other cities in the Niagara Region, both Central Music in Welland and Murphy's Music in Niagara Falls attract customers from St. Catharines and Thorold looking for specific brands or services, since, as noted, most stores in the region tend to specialize in particular makes of guitar, drums, amplifiers, and other equipment. J&B Music in Fort Erie and The Music Depot in Port Colborne cater almost exclusively to local clienteles, offering a wide range of services to musicians, other performers, and community groups. Moreover, as in most urban centres, musical instruments, amplifiers, and other accessories may also be purchased in Niagara at other kinds of stores, especially big-box stores and pawn shops, hock shops, and other businesses selling euphemistically labelled "pre-owned" goods. Local music stores have traditionally also faced competition from larger enterprises in the nearby cities of Buffalo, Hamilton, and Metropolitan Toronto;[4] paradoxically, as this challenge has receded to some extent, a new one has surfaced in the form of the Internet as a source of both material goods and information.

THE NEGLECTED MUSIC STORE

Since the early 1990s, one of the principal areas of research and publication in popular music studies has focused on local "sounds" and "scenes." Particular attention was paid to cities in the United States or Britain where currently popular sub-genres of rock and pop—often loosely categorized as "alternative" or "indie" rock—had taken root. These included the "Madchester" scene in Manchester and the "indie" rock scene of Liverpool in England; the "grunge" sound emanating from Aberdeen, Olympia, and, later, Seattle, all in Washington State; the alternative rock scene of Athens, Georgia; and the highly politicized "indie" rock scene in Washington, D.C., among many others.

Although attempts have been made to generalize the concept of "scene" to include "translocal" and even "virtual" sites of music production and consumption, the term has most frequently been applied to musical practices in a particular locality, "where performers, support facilities and fans come together to collectively create music for their own enjoyment" (Bennett and Peterson 2004, 3). The importance of "support facilities," otherwise called "institutions" or "infrastructure," is emphasized by a number of writers.

According to John Connell and Chris Gibson in *Sound Tracks*, their comprehensive overview of the cultural geography of popular music, sounds and scenes typically develop where there is

> both a "critical mass" of active musicians or fans, and a set of physical infrastructures of recording, performance and listening: studios, venues (with sympathetic booking agents)—spaces that allow new musical practices—and even record companies (or alternative labels) and distribution outlets.... The most famous scenes (those responsible for distinct "sounds") have all built upon local popular support (or at least cult status), and featured particularly vibrant combinations of venues, local production and methods of local information flow and exchange (such as radio and street press). (101–102)

Recording studios, venues, record labels, sympathetic booking agents, supportive mass media—these are all cited by Connell and Gibson as institutions that facilitate the development of local sounds and scenes. Others also note record stores—indeed, the index to *Sound Tracks* contains four mentions of "music stores," all of which refer to record retailing—but the musical instrument store is conspicuous by its absence.

Similarly, in an edited volume on key concepts in popular music and culture, Sara Cohen illustrates a discussion of the formation of local music "scenes" with examples drawn from her research on "indie" rock culture in Liverpool. While institutions, or what Charles Landry (2000) terms the "hard infrastructure," play a facilitating role in Cohen's formulation, people serve as the basic building blocks of the scene, which is really constituted by the "soft infrastructure," the networks and regularized patterns of interaction that occur among the scene's members. "Such relationships," she writes, "involve a regular circulation and exchange of: information, advice and gossip; instruments, technical support, and additional services; music recordings, journals, and other products" (Cohen 1999, 240–41).

Cohen also writes of "the day-to-day struggle to raise funds in order to rent or purchase instruments" (1999, 240) and credits a number of businesses and organizations—record shops, rehearsal spaces, recording studios, live performance venues—that help to support local scenes. However, she does not mention among these institutions the local music store, even though this is where funds, once raised, will be spent "to rent or purchase instruments," where many musicians will turn "for technical support and additional services," and which is often a source of the "information, advice and gossip" that also contribute to the scene's formation. In fairness, it should be noted that, in Cohen's book-length study of Liverpool's rock music culture, she *does* mention music stores, albeit briefly in the introduction, noting that she rarely had problems contacting musicians in her research, in part because clothing and music stores displayed notice boards "crowded with advertisements placed by bands searching for new members or by individuals looking for bands"(1991, 1). Later in the same volume, she notes that the "three best-known shops selling rock music equipment … and other music shops acted as grapevine centres for musicians" (51). Thus, though Cohen acknowledges the role of the music store as a site of communication and recruitment for bands and musicians, she neglects its many other crucial functions.

In part, this neglect is due to the emphasis placed by popular music scholars on local means of mass production and dissemination of local *sounds*, which tend, by the dictates of popular music as a business, to be transitory (see, for example, Burnett 1993, Stahl 2004) and on local variations in audience tastes and consumption patterns, otherwise generally known as *scenes*, which often transcend a particular place (Straw 1991, Peterson and Bennett 2004) and are also relatively ephemeral. Such research tends to privilege those institutions and infrastructural elements that directly assist the creative process (for example, recording studios, record labels), and the dissemination and consumption of particular styles of popular music, as in the emphasis on radio stations, supportive DJs and reporters, record stores, and, especially, performance venues.

Music stores are institutions that do not readily fit into these categories. They are not transitory; successful ones, at least, tend to outlive particular sounds or scenes. Also, while local sounds or scenes tend to be tied to particular musical styles, music stores, especially in smaller markets—indeed, in all but the largest cities—cannot usually afford to cater only to musicians in a particular genre or sub-genre. Hence, their longevity and breadth of clientele may result in music stores being viewed as constants, part of the background, and therefore of little use in accounting for short-term changes in musical sound or audience tastes.

THE MUSIC STORE ON THE SCENE

As both Will Straw and Holly Kruse have observed, popular music communities tend to be both more stable and more lasting than ephemeral sounds and scenes (Straw 1991, 373–74; Kruse 1993, 37–39). Hence, it is largely in ethnographic studies of local music communities, which focus on the musicians rather than their musical styles or their audiences, that music stores warrant some discussion, even in passing. For example, in his analysis of the development of underground musical careers in Honolulu, Fumiko Tagasuki observes that music stores often provide employment to musicians, either as sales staff or as teachers for musical instrument instruction, in addition to their more obvious function as a source of instruments and accessories (2003, 82, 84–85, 86).

While Tagasuki identifies ways in which music stores support local musicians, Mavis Bayton argues in her book *Frock Rock* (1998) that the hyper-masculine atmosphere of music stores is an obstacle to young women interested in becoming rock musicians.[5] According to Bayton, the music store is one among a number of forms of "public space" from which young women generally feel excluded:

> The fact that both customers and assistants are overwhelmingly male means that music shops are their preserve, and, therefore, boys are more at home than girls.... Young women ... typically find trying out equipment a severe trial. Because they are scared of showing themselves up and being patronised or put down by the assistants, they are inhibited in what they perceive to be a male arena. (30–31)

However, having briefly established early in her study that music stores may be among the constraints that discourage girls and young women from becoming rock musicians, Bayton pays little to no attention to them in subsequent chapters. For example, while she delineates a number of routes by which women *do* become actively engaged in rock, she fails to report how the women musicians she studied either avoided or negotiated their way around the constraint of the male-dominated music store or, in her chapter "Joining a Band," where they obtained their instruments and equipment.

The most notable exception to the general neglect of the music store in popular music studies is Ruth Finnegan's book *The Hidden Musicians*, an ethnographic analysis of music-making at the local level that focuses on "networks" (Finnegan's preferred term) of amateur musicians—representing all types, forms, and genres of music—in the English city of Milton Keynes in the early 1980s. Even for amateur musicians to practise their art, Finnegan suggests, "there has to be some system for the supply of the necessary equipment and for the material and non-material support that musical performance demands" (1989, 273). First among the institutional supports that Finnegan identifies are music stores. She discusses numerous ways in which the music stores of Milton Keynes and nearby towns served as important resources for local musicians, including the supply of instruments, equipment, and sheet music, offering music lessons and employment opportunities, and serving as "a source of expert advice and communication" (274). Finnegan concludes that the stores played "a significant role in local music ... which went beyond just the sale of musical materials, *important though that itself was.* They were also both formally and informally involved in the musical life of the area, providing skills and services as well as equipment, and they and their staff were part of local musical networks" (277, emphasis mine).

In the following pages, I build on existing observations of the functions of the music store made by Finnegan, Tagasuki, and others to develop a more formal typology of music store activities. Eight sets of activities may be identified on the basis of their relative importance to the business of different stores and for their respective contributions to the maintenance of a local community of popular musicians. They are listed here roughly in the order in which they would appear on a continuum ranging from the "most commercial" to "least commercial" (or "most community-oriented") activities: sales of musical instruments and equipment; sales of sheet music and music books; music instruction; equipment rentals; repairs, service, and fine-tuning of instruments and equipment; source of employment; communication and recruitment; and meeting place and community centre. In most towns and cities, there are other commercial establishments that provide some, but not all, of these services—usually the sale of musical instruments, equipment, music books, or provision of music lessons. Such establishments are significant to this analysis in that they often compete with music stores and threaten their economic viability without necessarily fulfilling the social or networking functions essential to sustaining a musical community, but only music stores, as defined in this study, perform all of these functions to varying degrees.

PRINCIPAL FUNCTIONS OF MUSIC STORES

Instrument and Equipment Sales

Sales of instruments and equipment may be divided into two groups: primary and secondary sales. *Primary sales* involve the purchase of instruments and the basic tools required to play (for singers, this would also include microphones); *secondary sales* encompass all other items the musician or prospective musician might acquire to enhance the playing of the instrument: strings, reeds, picks, bows, drumsticks, replacement cymbals, amplifiers, and additional electronics—perhaps later, PA systems and other stage equipment.

By definition, all music stores sell (or offer for sale) musical instruments, although the number and range of instruments, and their prices, differ substantially from one store to another, as does the relative significance of sales among the various sources of business income. In most stores, much of the visible space, whether on the ground, walls, or ceiling of the main floor, is

FIGURE 11.2 Ostanek's, Geneva Street, St. Catharines. Courtesy of author

devoted to guitars acoustic and electric; six-string, twelve-string, and bass; and their accessories, including capos and cases, picks and pick-ups, straps, strings, and tuners. Ostanek's, Central Music, and Thorold Music have separate climate-controlled rooms for their most expensive acoustic guitars. Drums, drum kits, and accessories are common fare, and all sell harmonicas, usually blues harps rather than the more complex multi-octave chromatic instruments ("mouth organs") played by virtuosos such as Larry Adler. In larger stores, drums are usually in the basement or in a separate room clearly distinguished from the main sales area.

Most stores specialize in particular brands, although these change over time, partly in response to consumer taste and fashion, and partly in response to the competition. For example, in 2006 Mike Palermo, owner of Mike's Music, started carrying Ovation guitars because Thorold Music was moving away from this brand. Many stores also stock a few examples of other popular-music stringed instruments, usually banjos and mandolins; as befitting the musical accomplishments of its founder, Ostanek's also has a range of accordions. Apart from Thorold Music, most stores specializing in popular-music instruments are moving away from pianos and keyboards, which some view as increasingly unprofitable. As Rick Ostanek explained, keyboards are less popular in part because fewer bands now feature them. Moreover, because digital technology is changing so rapidly, they date very quickly, and a store has to turn over its inventory fast to make any money on them.

In some smaller centres, instrument sales are largely seasonal (especially around Christmas) and constitute a relatively small proportion of business. In late January 2006, for example, The Music Depot in Port Colborne had fewer than twenty guitars, including basses, on display and there were empty hangers on the wall. In the larger Thorold Music, guitars are the principal stock-in-trade and, with keyboards, the biggest source of sales revenue. Ostanek's has approximately 200 guitars on display at any time, Thorold Music around 150. Spend more than fifteen minutes in any of these stores, large or small, on any afternoon, and at any time on a weekend, and one will hear guitars being played—sometimes by prospective purchasers, sometimes by "tire-kickers,"[6] sometimes by sales staff demonstrating the instrument for a customer or whiling away the time on a slow business day.

Several store owners and managers observed that selling a musical instrument is a long-term process. Bob Moretti of Thorold Music called it a process of "helping customers achieve their aspirations," whether to learn to play an instrument; to play one better; or to find the perfect guitar, keyboard, or saxophone that fits hands, personality, preferred musical style, or desired sound. Almost never does a customer buy the first guitar that he or she picks up, strums, plugs in, plays again, or prices. According to Moretti, the principal sales strategy is to make sure that "customers keep coming back until they buy whatever it is they've decided they want in *our* store." For this reason, there is usually little pressure to buy a particular brand or model, and sales staff in all local music stores are paid hourly wages and not on a commission basis.

An important *secondary* source of revenue in most stores is the sale of electronic sound equipment, ranging from small practice amplifiers to PA systems complete with microphones, mixing boards, sound monitors, and speakers, and from simple one-way volume switches and Crybaby wah-wah pedals to complex digital-effects producers and home recording equipment. This part of the business is, to a major extent, an offshoot of instrument sales. For example, a father having purchased an electric guitar for his child or for himself also needs an amp and later, perhaps, decides it would be fun to use a fuzz box or wah-wah pedal so he can pretend to be Jimi Hendrix playing the riff from "Purple Haze."

For other secondary sales, inexperienced buyers and new musicians tend to return to the store where they bought their first instruments. For more experienced musicians/buyers, price and brand availability are influential for more expensive items, while location is often a determining factor if the item is cheap or required urgently—for example, replacement strings or a new pair of drumsticks. Sean Oakes, co-owner of the new Music City store, admits that the future of his business relies in part on persuading prospective customers in north St. Catharines that, to purchase secondary items at least, they don't need to travel downtown to Ostanek's or across the city to Thorold Music.

Sales of Sheet Music and Music Books

All music stores in Niagara sell music books, ranging from basic primers ("Learn to play guitar") to books covering specific styles (blues harp, ragtime piano), lyrics, chords and tabs for guitar and piano for the Country Hits of 2005, Classic Rock Hits of the 1970s, or the songs of individual bands and artists from ABBA to ZZ Top. Even in the Internet age, when music books can be easily purchased online and sheet music is downloaded at home, music books remain steady sellers. Instructional books are consistently in demand, but songbooks for particular artists also continue to find a market, especially bands such as The Beatles, AC/DC, Pink Floyd, and Led Zeppelin. Lyrics, chords, and tabs may be common Internet fare on a variety of websites, but these are often unreliable and infested with annoying pop-ups. As Bob Moretti of Thorold Music observed, downloading song lyrics or tabs from the Internet may be cheaper, but "it takes time to find the right version of a song and even then you don't know if it's in the right key or even if the lyrics are correct."

Few stores now sell individual pieces of sheet music. Generally, individual song sheets are too expensive at $6 or $7 each, whereas music books, containing all the songs from an album or a collection of songs from a particular artist, retail at around $25 or $30. Although some stores will order individual items, Rick Ostanek explained, "you just don't make money from sheet music in a town this size. It's too easy to end up with a lot of dead stock." Moreover, sheet music and music books are often used as a free service or resource. Rather than buying the music, store patrons will subvert the commercial process by consulting these resources to check their own arrangements of a particular song, sometimes openly, sometimes surreptitiously, jotting down chords on a scrap of paper before returning the sheet or book to the sales rack.

Music Instruction

Most music stores in Niagara offer, or used to offer, music lessons. For a number of local businesses—Ryson's or Niko's in St. Catharines, or the wonderfully named Fun School of Music in the west Niagara town of Grimsby—music lessons are the primary function. For music stores in smaller centres, such as J&B Music in Fort Erie, music instruction is an important part of the business and a steady source of income. According to Sean Oakes of Music City in north St. Catharines, income from music lessons was the principal reason his new business survived its first summer in 2007, disproving the nay-sayers who suggested he was "nuts" opening his store in May, since the summer months are acknowledged by most owners to be the slowest time of the year.

Al Moretti offered lessons at the original Thorold Music before his first, enforced, retirement. His sons continued that tradition at the new Thorold Music, at least for a while. According to Bob Moretti, music lessons are potentially a good moneymaker, but "must be taken seriously" to turn a profit. His store allowed the musician-instructors to run the operation, which proved to be a mistake; teaching was suspended in the late 1990s, in part because it wasn't profitable and some instructors proved unreliable, and partly because better use could be made of the space formerly devoted to instruction.

Mike's Music and Ostanek's still offer in-store music lessons for guitar, bass, and drums. In 2004, Ostanek's refurbished and expanded its instructional space to five rooms, only to find that this part of the business, although lucrative, was growing too large to manage. Since December 2005, Ostanek's has contracted out its music lessons, providing the space in return for rent. During store hours, students may enter and leave the instructional space through the shop, although there is a separate entrance for after-hours customers.

Instruction in many other instruments is offered in the Niagara Region's school system, beginning in Grade 4 with string orchestra, Grade 5 for brass and winds, and percussion in Grade 6. There are also school board–based jazz bands, which are really big bands or show bands, in which brass and winds greatly outnumber the players in the rhythm section (keyboards, guitar, bass, drums). Music conservatories and other institutions, including Niko's and Ryson's in St. Catharines and music stores in smaller towns, offer training in piano and other instruments primarily associated with orchestral or classical music.[7] Those who are plugged into the local music community might know if a particular instructor at one of the music schools is inclined toward rock or jazz; otherwise, to learn blues or folk guitar, jazz bass, or rock drumming, the principal choices are either private tutors or the local music store.

Equipment Rentals

Bands that want to go beyond simply rehearsing in someone's garage or basement need equipment—not just guitars, drums, and personal amplifiers, but microphones, a mixing board, speakers, and sound monitors, all of which are part and parcel of any gig, no matter how small the space. When starting out, both solo artists and groups often lack the money to buy these items or don't know what they need, so they borrow stage equipment from other bands or rent it from music stores.

In major centres where several stores are easily accessible, equipment rentals have traditionally been a highly competitive business, whether the customer is a band needing (extra) equipment for a gig, a theatre or dance group requiring sound, or a venue in need of a PA system for one night only. Although some bands remain loyal to a particular music store, especially if a band member can get an employee discount, most shop around for the best deal or for equipment compatible with their own. Managers of venues almost always shop around, although cost considerations may sometimes be tempered by a calculus involving sound quality, service, pick-up versus delivery and, where necessary, willingness or ability to explain effectively how to use the technology. In smaller cities, such as Fort Erie or Port Colborne, the music store is often part of a broader enterprise providing stage lighting and sound equipment for local theatre companies, high schools, and hotel-based conferences, as well as musicians.

In recent years, for many stores, technological advances and changes in business opportunities have affected the relative importance of equipment rentals for local musicians. At Ostanek's, for example, PA systems are still an important part of the sales side of the business, but rentals are less lucrative than they used to be. According to Rick Ostanek, since there are now relatively few large venues featuring live music in Niagara and because equipment costs have fallen, most bands and soloists can afford to buy what they need to play an average bar, club, or restaurant gig.

Repairs and Service

All music stores offer instrument and equipment repairs. Services offered in larger stores extend from simple wiring repairs to substantial modification of guitars and basses to improve the playing action, including changing the profile of bridges, nuts, and frets, or sanding the neck better to fit the hand. Music stores face competition in some of these areas from luthiers, who specialize in servicing and customizing instruments and equipment, as well as building them to order. A number of Niagara musicians, for example, told me to take a guitar that needed "fine-tuning" to Freddy Gabrsek, who builds, customizes, and repairs guitars, trading under the name of Freddy's Frets in Welland, a few miles south of St. Catharines and Thorold. Gabrsek has restored guitars for, among others, Rush lead guitarist Alex Lifeson and Leroy Emmanuel, former Motown session player and now leader of the local band LMT Connection. He also builds guitars to order, although with prices for acoustics starting around $3,500, he's not in direct competition with most of the music stores in this respect. The skills and reputations of local luthiers[8] mean that some repair jobs taken to the principal music stores are so routine as to be boring; an employee at Ostanek's complained that a lot of kids bringing their guitars in for service really just want a change of strings, a task they haven't yet figured out how to do for themselves.

However, the service function frequently involves more than a simple commercial transaction. Rather than bringing an instrument in for modification—important though this may be—customers often come to the service desk simply to seek advice on how to get the best performance out of an instrument, or how to combine analog and digital equipment to create a specific sound. In other words, the service function is often as much a community-related activity as a commercial one.

Career Opportunities

As a partial corollary of other roles (especially music instruction, repairs, and service), music stores perform the important task of employing musicians. Thus far, the discussion of the functions of music stores has concentrated mostly on commercial transactions that result in revenue for the store "at the expense of" customers, whether they are musicians, would-be musicians, or parents of would-be musicians. But, by employing musicians as sales personnel, as service and repair technicians, and as teachers providing instrument and general music lessons to customers, stores help to support musical careers and, indirectly, to subsidize performance venues. To the extent that the majority of venue managers in the Niagara Region are, according to both musicians and music store proprietors, notoriously cheap, it follows that most would-be professional musicians in the region need a day job—and where better than working in a music store?

Stores that offer music lessons employ musicians and pay them at a rate that may not be union scale but which is, at least, above minimum wage in Ontario. Moreover, the vast majority, if not all, of the sales and service personnel in music stores, at least in St. Catharines and Thorold, are or have been practising musicians. In Thorold Music, all eleven full- and part-time employees in 2004–05 played regularly as solo performers or in local bands. Musicianship is not the sole criterion for employment in a music store—Mike Palermo acknowledged that "talent doesn't necessarily translate into a good employee"—but is a very important factor in the hiring process.

The music stores' employment of musicians has important sociological consequences: staff members are accomplished in their musical ability and their command of the technical specifications and jargon, which a minority of customers demands. Also, and not coincidentally, they are predominantly male.

Together, these traits foster a certain atmosphere in music stores to such a degree that they appear to be intimidating spaces for potential customers, particularly for women and others who lack musical or technical skills and the vocabulary to feel comfortable in a hyper-masculine and somewhat technologically and musically elitist environment.

When asked why all the sales staff in his store were male, one owner responded that he'd never received job applications from women and he claimed never to have thought about the extent to which music stores are (almost) exclusively male environments. Another owner acknowledged, "We have had two or three applications from women to work here. I would be hesitant to employ one because all the guys would be chasing her around morning, noon, and night instead of doing their jobs." This owner also commented that the number of women purchasing musical instruments for their own use is increasing, although they rarely came into the store alone: "Mostly they come with a friend, usually a male friend, or boyfriend, husband, or whatever," he observed, while not appearing to make connections to possible causes. In a third store, the attitude of the staff might best be described as "laddism," a brand of adolescent sexism that mixes elements of patriarchy and misogyny, desire, and exclusion, applied indiscriminately to all women customers.

An exception is the Fun School of Music, co-owned by Brock music graduates Denise Blaney and Jennifer McKillop, with their respective partners. The Fun School opened in Grimsby in August 2006; Blaney and McKillop had previously run the school in nearby Beamsville, about a twenty-minute drive from St. Catharines. They carry a small range of instruments for sale or rent, but the principal function of the Fun School is music instruction—particularly for children. Half the instructors are female, a conscious decision according to Blaney, who contends that the atmosphere in other music stores in the region is intimidating for girls and women.[9]

Such observations are congruent with the findings of other researchers. According to one of Mavis Bayton's informants, Fran of the band Sub Rosa: "You go in and all the blokes are sitting in one corner talking about some riff that they came up with last night, totally ignoring you. They are very patronising. They see that you're a woman and they think, 'How did you dare come in our music shop?'" (Bayton 1998, 31; Bayton 1997, 41–43; Leonard 2007, 49–50). Like Bayton's respondents, women musicians interviewed for this study observed that they are routinely ignored by sales and service staff in music stores, especially when stores are crowded with other (male) customers. As one woman noted of her experience of taking her guitar in for service, "The guys totally ignored me, but immediately descended on [her spouse].

I pretty much had to reach over the counter and grab the guy by the throat to get his attention."

However, Bayton and others who seek to account for the structural or systemic biases against women's participation in rock bands overlook another advantage to working in a music store if one is a musician, other than the pay and, perhaps, employee discounts on purchases and rentals. There is also the possibility that, on a Friday or Saturday afternoon, a regular customer in the store or on the phone will say to one of the employees, "I need a guitarist [or a drummer or a keyboard player] tonight—any of you guys free?" To the extent that there is gender imbalance among music store employees, there is likely to be a similar bias in the structure of opportunities that such employment provides for career advancement.

Communication and Recruitment

The music store is an advertising and communications centre and a broker between bands looking for players and individuals looking for bands. Every music store has a bulletin board where bands and musicians—and those offering other services, whether they are music instruction or recording studios, CD manufacturing or tattoos—advertise their desires, needs, and opportunities. The size and placement of the bulletin board vary from store to store and may signify the extent to which owners or managers view their store as serving a community function rather than, or in addition to, a purely commercial one. Ostanek's, for example, provides three boards, each about three feet by two feet, located close to the main entrance from the parking lot and immediately visible to customers. In Central Music in Welland or Thorold Music (before the fire), a single board is buried at the back of the store, hidden by a door leading to the basement, and difficult to find without assistance from staff.

Despite its unpromising location, the bulletin board at Thorold Music was well used. Most visits to the store found messages overflowing the board onto surrounding wall space; at any one time, on average, there were over twenty ads from musicians seeking bands or bands looking for musicians, and another dozen or so advertising other services or events: tattoo parlours, recording facilities, music lessons, CD releases, music appreciation nights at a local church, and so on. Some of the ads are replicated in other stores; some are unique to individual stores. Usually, genre and the advertiser's perception of the store's clientele, rather than its location, are the principal determinants of ad placements. The casual observer might wonder why some ads are still there, as in "Bass player needed immediately" and "Bass player looking for band"—until one looks at the fine print of each ad, especially

FIGURE 11.3 Bulletin board, the music store's communications centre. Courtesy of author

the connotations of specific musical influences: "Korn, System Of A Down, Red Hot Chili Peppers" in one ad, and "Eagles, Crosby Stills and Nash, Poco" in the other.

Bulletin boards, store windows, and other store surfaces also offer opportunities for bands and venues to announce upcoming gigs. In addition, all the local music stores provide space, usually in prominent locations by the door or the cash desk, for music-related publications, most notably the leading local weekly independent cultural paper, *Pulse Niagara*, as well as alternative music "freebies" such as *Exclaim!* and *Gasoline Magazine*, and the Canada-wide but largely Ontario-centric *Musician's Newspaper*, the principal function of which is to offer non-commercial advertising space to aspiring musicians seeking bands and to aspiring bands seeking musicians.

Community Centre

The music store also serves as a meeting place for local musicians. On almost any Saturday morning, a visitor to what is now called John's Thorold Music on Front Street in downtown Thorold will find a "session" taking place, with up to a dozen mostly "senior" or retired musicians playing a mix of Anglo-Celtic folk, blues, standards, and especially, traditional (1950s to '60s)

FIGURE 11.4 Saturday morning session, John's Thorold Music. Courtesy of author

country, sometimes remembering what it was like to play this music in front of an audience, but mostly participating for the pure enjoyment and companionship in playing the music, any music. As one regular customer described the store, "This place is a drop-in centre for lonely musicians." So important are these jam sessions to the community surrounding the old Thorold Music store that a visit in February 2006 found John and his manager, Ray, cleaning out the basement so that drum kits could be moved downstairs from the main floor to make room for the session players, even though Ray complained that the store made no money from the sessions: "Those guys come in here to spend time, not money."

While John's Thorold Music may be an atypical example, given its confessed "hobby" status, other music stores also serve, to a greater or lesser extent, as drop-in or community centres for local musicians. The music store is a place to connect, to find out what's going on, to learn which venues are hiring and which band has a new gig, to check out new instruments or new equipment, to meet up with friends (some of whom may work there, as salesmen or instructors; others may be regular customers), or just because that's what one does on a Saturday. A visit to the music store is often part of a ritualized routine associated with being part of a local musical community or scene.

The relationship between music store and musical community is changing, however. According to Rick Ostanek, twenty years ago, practising musicians constituted about three-quarters of his store's regular customers; now they amount to about one-quarter of the regular clientele, the remainder being hobbyists and families. This shift partly reflects a reduction in opportunities for full-time musicians. Most local musicians now have a day job outside of, or only tangentially related to, music. This, in turn, is principally due to a decline in the number of local venues, especially larger, well-paying ones that feature live music. A handful of musicians in the region subsist just by playing; several more make a living through playing and teaching—in music stores, as private tutors, or through the school system—or by working in music stores or in other music-related jobs (record stores, recording studios, DJs, or engineers for radio stations). Others work in a wide variety of occupations by day and play at night and on weekends. Few have time to hang out in the music store on weekdays, which is why the social function of the stores picks up on Saturdays, or around 5 p.m. on weekday afternoons as musicians and hobbyists leave work.

THE FUTURE OF LOCAL MUSIC STORES

Music stores do not simply sell musical instruments and equipment. As described in this study, they are multifunctional institutions that provide numerous services to local musicians of varying degrees of expertise and ambition. At the same time, the relative importance of the activities delineated here varies from store to store and, in most cities, towns, and even smaller communities, the music store is not the only institution performing many of these functions. "Big-box" stores sell musical instruments, at least for beginners; private tutors and school boards may provide music lessons; luthiers may service both instruments and equipment; schools, community centres, and local bookstores may offer some of the communications and networking opportunities. But none of these other institutions or actors fulfils the same combination of activities or functions that music stores typically provide in a specific locale.

Today, however, the local music store is under threat. In southern Ontario, but not yet in Niagara, a number of formerly independent music stores have been taken over by larger chains such as Long and McQuaid. The Internet has made inroads into certain music store activities, especially sales of equipment and sheet music and music books, and, to a lesser extent, some of its communications functions. A further challenge to the economic survival of the local store is posed by the emergence of new rivals in the "first guitar" market. In the 1960s, for example, Sears, K-Mart, Woolco, and other department stores rivalled music stores as the place to buy "entry-level" guitars. In the last two decades of the twentieth century, such alternatives to music stores became less influential in the beginner market. Now, however, suburban "big-box" stores such as Best Buy, Walmart, and Future Shop are offering "starter" packages—guitar, amplifier, and instructional booklet, plus accessories—at prices with which few specialist music stores can compete, irrespective of the quality of the instruments on offer.

At the same time, there is a danger of placing too much importance on what I have called "primary sales"—that is, largely, instrument sales—among the activities of music stores, both for their economic viability and role in sustaining local musical communities. Although primary sales are the largest source of income for some of the bigger stores, the business model of many of the smaller stores relies more on income from other activities, particularly music lessons and rentals of musical and related equipment, as well as "secondary sales" of smaller ancillary items. Moreover, except as objects to be discussed and occasionally coveted, new guitars and equipment are not usually the principal reason that more experienced musicians visit their local music store. Most practising musicians have been using their favourite instruments and equipment for a number of years. Only what some music store employees call, slightly disparagingly, the "gear freaks" (who tend to be hobbyists rather than professional musicians) continue to look for and sometimes buy additional guitars, other instruments, more equipment, in search of a better sound, something easier to play, more special effects, or simply the cachet of being able to choose between a vintage Fender Strat, a '52 Gibson Les Paul Goldtop, or a Martin D-45 acoustic the next time they jam with their friends.

As this study of Niagara music stores demonstrates, for many members of a local music scene or community, it is not necessarily the range of instruments or amplifiers or other expensive products on sale that attracts them to a local music store, but rather the opportunity to socialize or network, to seek out gigs, find out who is playing where and when, or simply to gossip with others. Hence, while music stores are defined in part by the sale of musical instruments and equipment, it is their multifunctional nature that makes them an important community resource. However, music stores are businesses and, for many, sales of musical instruments and accessories are the most important source of revenue without which they may not survive to provide their more community-oriented activities and services.

Thanks to Andy Bennett, Tom Kitts, Barry Shank, and, especially, the editors of this volume for comments on earlier versions and drafts of this chapter. Thanks also to the owners and staff of music stores in Niagara and elsewhere who, mostly cheerfully, put up with me hanging around and asking questions.

NOTES

1 Observational activities were overt to the extent that they were carried out in public view and because music store owners and staff knew that I was conducting research in the store. For most customers, however, I was just another patron chatting to the staff, trying out a guitar, asking questions about the local music scene, or simply "hanging out." Some local musicians who were patrons of the stores under study were aware of my research but did not (despite occasional threats to the contrary) blow my cover.

2 Note that "Pen" in the Niagara Region is an abbreviation of "peninsula," not "penitentiary."

3 "Emo," short for "emotional," describes a youth subculture, a music sub-genre and a fashion style linked most recently to pop-punk bands such as Good Charlotte or Sum 41. The lyrics often focus on teen anxiety and vulnerability, sometimes mutating into "screamo," a more aggressive and emotional musical form, exemplified by the St. Catharines–based band Alexisonfire. Niagara was home to a sizable "emo" subculture when this research was being conducted, and many "emos" hung out at both Ostanek's and Mike's Music after school and on Saturdays.

4 At one time, local *professional* musicians would go to Toronto or Buffalo for most of their instrument and equipment needs. As local music stores have grown and increased the range of merchandise and the number of brands they carry, most musicians can find much of what they need locally. As one salesman said, "If you want to play five or six Martin guitars in the $2,000 to $3,000 range before making up your mind, you might have to go to Toronto or some other major city. But if you want to try out a couple, you can do that at Thorold Music. If you know which Martin model you want, you can order that at two or three local stores, or directly from the manufacturer via the Internet. Toronto is not the draw it used to be, not for most players."

5 Sara Cohen elsewhere makes a similar argument in accounting for the "maleness" of the "indie" rock scene in Liverpool, arguing that gender relations are shaped by "the scene's own music institutions where a male culture and atmosphere usually predominate. This includes ... music instrument and record shops which are largely staffed and frequented by men" (1997, 23).

6 "Tire-kickers" are, according to staff in some stores, those customers who are perceived to play around with the merchandise with no intent to purchase but, rather, to kill time. They may inquire about prices or specifications but are interested only if the merchandise is on sale and prices are deeply discounted. One branch of The Hock Shop in St. Catharines (now closed) used to display a large sign proclaiming "No Tire Kickers" in front of its musical instruments, which were, in any case, separated from potential customers by a waist-high, locked gate. Experienced

music store staff are pretty good at distinguishing between tire-kickers and genuine (potential) customers.

7 Music camps, including those sponsored by the Niagara Symphony, also provide instruction for young musicians.

8 Paul Saunders, in Wainfleet, in the southwest of Niagara, is another luthier who was recommended for specialized repairs or modifications by both musicians and even some music store employees.

9 Other studies in this volume also point to the gendered nature of social practices and local institutions. See, in particular, "'Hollywoodization,' Gender, and the Local Press in the 1920s: The Case of Niagara Falls, Ontario;" "Frolics with Food: *The Frugal Housewife's Manual* by 'A.B.' of Grimsby;" and "Electricity from Niagara Falls: Popularization of Modern Technology for Domestic Use."

WORKS CITED

Bayton, Mavis. *Frock Rock: Women Performing Popular Music.* Oxford and New York: Oxford University Press, 1998.

———. "Women and the Electric Guitar." In Sheila Whiteley, ed., *Sexing the Groove: Popular Music and Gender.* London and New York: Routledge, 1997: 37–49.

Bennett, Andy, and Richard A. Peterson, eds. *Music Scenes: Local, Translocal, and Virtual.* Nashville: Vanderbilt University Press, 2004.

Burnett, Robert. "The Popular Music Industry in Transition." *Popular Music and Society* 17:1 (1993), 87–114.

Cohen, Sara. "Scenes." In Bruce Horner and Thomas Swiss, eds., *Key Terms in Popular Music and Culture.* Oxford: Blackwell, 1999: 239–50.

———. "Men Making a Scene: Rock Music and the Production of Gender." In Sheila Whiteley, ed., *Sexing the Groove: Popular Music and Gender.* London and New York: Routledge, 1997: 17–36.

———. *Rock Culture in Liverpool: Popular Music in the Making.* Oxford: Clarendon Press, 1991.

Connell, John, and Chris Gibson. *Sound Tracks: Popular Music, Identity and Space.* London and New York: Routledge, 2003.

Finnegan, Ruth. *The Hidden Musicians: Music-making in an English Town.* Cambridge: Cambridge University Press, 1989.

Kruse, Holly. "Subcultural Identity in Alternative Music Culture." *Popular Music* 12:1 (1993), 33–41.

Landry, Charles. *The Creative City: A Toolkit for Urban Innovators.* London: Earthscan, 2000.

Leonard, Marion. *Gender in the Music Industry: Rock, Discourse and Girl Power.* Aldershot: Ashgate, 2007.

Peterson, Richard A., and Andy Bennett. "Introducing Music Scenes." In Andy Bennett and Richard A. Peterson, eds., *Music Scenes: Local, Translocal, and Virtual.* Nashville: Vanderbilt University Press, 2004: 1–15.

Stahl, Geoff. "'It's Like Canada Reduced': Setting the Scene in Montreal." In Andy Bennett and Keith Kahn Harris, eds., *After Subculture: Critical Studies in Contemporary Youth Culture*. London: Palgrave/Macmillan, 2004: 51–64.

Straw, Will. "Systems of Articulation, Logics of Change: Communities and Scenes in Popular Music." *Cultural Studies* 5:1 (1991), 368–88.

Takasugi, Fumiko. "The Development of Underground Musicians in a Honolulu Scene, 1995-1997." *Popular Music and Society* 26:1 (2003), 73–94.

BACK TO OUR ROOTS | How Niagara Artists Centre Became Popular Again

ROSLYN COSTANZO

INTRODUCTION

Saturday, September 13, 2003, was a defining day for the Niagara Artists Centre (NAC).[1] That evening, *Lilli-Putting*, a site-specific miniature golf installation, opened at the converted warehouse in downtown St. Catharines to a crowd of over 250 local residents, artists, and members. The show combined work by twenty new, long-standing, and founding members and reconciled NAC's present with its past. NAC's member artists were invigorated and the public excited by the return to this type of witty and collectively driven contemporary art programming, which had defined the artist-run group (the Niagara Artists' Co-op), since its inception in the '70s.[2] The space was filled with artists, art lovers, and mini-golf enthusiasts. From a vantage point outside the building, revellers spilled onto the fire escape and street, sharing their experiences of the unconventional par 711 course. In a review in *Pulse Magazine*, G. Pardie enthused, "I was amazed by the turnout, not only the sheer [number] of people putting, but the diversity of people, everyone from old fogies and little kids, to artists and lawyers…." (2003). *Lilli-Putting* made contemporary visual art fun and unpretentious, dissolving social barriers between art and the general local public in the process. Since the '70s, few NAC exhibitions could boast such popularity.

The local relevance of many of the "art objects" in the exhibition solicited the community's attention. Founding NAC president John Boyle constructed a hole resembling a ship passing through the Welland Canal, a prominent feature of the St. Catharines landscape and a symbol of industry, local history,

263

FIGURE 12.1 *Lilli-Putting* group installation, 2003. Niagara Artists Centre Archive

and the working class. Don Dormady, NAC board member at the time of this writing, fashioned his hole after a map of the downtown core, allowing locals to putt through their own streets. *Lilli-Putting*, which was originally proposed by NAC members Sandy Fairbairn and Dennis Tourbin in the mid-'70s, evoked those early projects by the co-op members who went to great lengths to involve the local community, earning them "an enviable reputation for craziness and positive innovation" (Barber 1974). As such, *Lilli-Putting* signified the start of a new era at NAC, one built on this artist-run group's long effort to put community at the centre of its contemporary visual art projects.

    In 2001, concurrent with the appointment of Stephen Remus as director, NAC underwent a community-focused renaissance. A keystone of NAC's current programming is the rediscovery of art happenings carried out by the founding members of the civic-minded collective in the early '70s. This populist and entertaining approach is unique among the more than 100 artist-run centres across Canada and renews the spirit of a mission statement issued by the Niagara Artists' Co-op in 1974: "NAC's new and intensified interaction with a much more representative public than before seems to be having a positive influence on the art being produced. If this is the case, and if it continues to be a natural and honest process, then it is a welcome development that will surely contribute to a strong and distinctive Canadian culture" (press release). NAC's recent resurgence has resulted in an increase in membership of more than 300 percent as well as some of the highest exhibition attendance records since the '70s. Exploration of NAC's history brings into relief the organization's uncommon and as yet unpublished contributions to the development of artist-run culture in Canada. Artist-run history exists on the margins of Canadian cultural research and, as a regional movement, has generated only a small body of writing. This case study takes a revisionist retrospective approach to the activities of NAC as a regional centre bound to the specifics of its environment and indicative of Canada's national identity as a culmination of disparate geographic and cultural perspectives. Regionalism as practised by NAC's first wave of artists leveraged local identities as a means of realizing a shared national experience. Today, as Canadian art institutions embark on the task of rethinking Canadian art in an era of globally linked media technologies and the predictable internationalist preoccupations that ensue, it is critical that regional artist-run centres continue to assert themselves by revisiting their cultural history from the perspective of the nation's "front lines"—that is, local communities. If regional artist-run centres focus intently on what is culturally unique in their communities—in the manner of the Niagara Artists Centre—they can continue to participate meaningfully in the diversity of Canadian culture.

SIGNIFICANCE OF NAC'S HISTORY

In its first decade, the Niagara Artists' Co-op developed a reputation for collectivist programming activity that was innovative, irreverent, and sensitive to its public. It was built on a socio-centric brand of contemporary art activity that began in the late '60s. Considered a regional artist-run centre due to its location outside of major cities, NAC played an integral role in creating a pluralistic vision of Canadian culture. The challenge for centres such as NAC has always been to assert their relevance in a contemporary visual arts culture dominated by trends in art-making emanating from national and international urban centres. Today, large Canadian public museums and galleries grapple with a new public reality that includes a rich cultural diversity and the demands of citizens who insist on responsive, community-minded institutions. Regional artist-run centres have historically demonstrated strong ties to their communities owing to the necessarily modest, targeted scale of their activities and their direct involvement with the public in the communities where they are situated.

In many ways NAC was a pioneering organization of the artist-run movement, adopting Canadian regionalism as a philosophy for art-making that validated an artist's connection to the community in which he or she lived. Regionalism, for many of its early practitioners, evolved from an assertion of Canadian "nationalism" that privileged the local. The rigorous nationalistic tendencies associated with the naissance of artist-run activity in the late '60s and early '70s were a response to the perceived lack of Canadian identity owing to the cultural domination of Canada by the United States. The situation was further exacerbated for liberally minded artists by the controversial involvement of the United States in the Vietnam War. John Boyle, painter and founding president of the Niagara Artists' Co-op, illuminates his nationalist inclinations in a passage from "Working Together":

> More than 50% of the few available teaching and administrative positions in the colleges and universities are filled by non-Canadians, primarily Americans, closing that avenue effectively to artists in the regions, while at the same time imposing American standards at the highest levels, heightening the alienation of these artists, frequently less inclined than their big city colleagues to so called "international" trends. (1974)

The artist-run movement was also largely driven by the emergence of a liberal working class with a heightened social consciousness. Their advocacy for artist rights, for instance, led to the founding of Canadian Artists Representation (CAR), an organization whose goal remains the promotion of a socio-economic climate conducive to the production of visual arts. Writer and curator Barbara Fischer contends:

> Artist-run spaces owe their existence to the rebellious energy of youth culture in the 1960s and early '70s, its search for "alternative" values (opposed to the existing parental and sociopolitical order), and the resulting proliferation of alternative social organizations. Predominantly psychosocial rather than political in nature ... these "counter institutions" sought to emphasize community and an intimacy of social relations, to counter the individualizing, fragmenting, and repressive aspects of social organization. (1992)

Many original and early NAC members, including Boyle, Fairbairn, and Tourbin, were key figures in the work to establish artist rights organizations and the payment of standardized artist exhibition fees. NAC and the handful of other artist-run centres founded in the late '60s and early '70s blazed a trail for the collective emergence of artist-run culture in Ontario that followed.[3]

"Amid Ontario Vineyards," a 1970 article in the *Toronto Star*, drew attention to the burgeoning artist-run movement in Ontario and cited as a catalyst the notion of regionalism propagated by the late artist Greg Curnoe and others in London, Ontario: "'Regionalism' in recent years has consisted primarily in the belief that it's possible—perhaps even necessary—to create significant art in various regions independent of the so-called 'International style' emanating from New York" (no byline, Apr. 11). For these artists, regionalism focused on celebrating what was uniquely Canadian and on the lateral dispersion of culture from the major city centres to local communities. Boyle and like-minded artists believed that "the 'interrogation' of their own habitat is as valid as that of anyone else." In an issue of *Open Letter* entitled "We Are Not Greg Curnoe," Ontario-based artist and writer Richard Hill describes Curnoe's regionalism as an initiative "to engage local values, issues, and history in a variety of contexts, from the local to the international" (2002).[4] Gail Dexter Lord elaborates on the implication of the local community in regionalism: "Greg lived in a marginal country, which had become so marginalized relative to the influence of the United States—that we did not have an acceptable word for being part of your own community, for home, for nation, for active citizenship. So 'regionalism' became that word" (2002). Curnoe's commitment to his community is reinforced in a letter to the Canada Council requesting a grant for Region Gallery, a co-op gallery he founded in London, Ontario, in 1962 to showcase the work of local artists: "We are not using regionalism as a gimmick but rather as a collective noun to cover what so many painters, writers, and photographers have used—their own immediate environment—something we don't do in Canada very much." Regionalism facilitated social interaction between an art community and its public, which took precedence over the traditional exhibition and reception of art objects. *Lilli-Putting* is one example of NAC's resurrection of the group-show format and socially focused programming.

In the beginning, NAC had close ties to the regionalist movement from London, about 150 kilometres west of St. Catharines, through the relationship between Boyle, a London native, and Curnoe. Although Boyle left London for a teaching job in St. Catharines in 1962, he maintained an active friendship and working relationship with Curnoe, strengthened by their mutual involvement with the Nihilist Spasm Band, a "kazoo-free-music group."[5] In *The History of Painting in Canada*, Barry Lord positions Boyle as the community-minded mentor to the other members of the Niagara Artists' Co-op, in line with both Curnoe's and the late Jack Chambers's roles in the London scene:

> Like both Curnoe and Chambers, Boyle has also helped to build the organizations needed for the independence and collective self-reliance of Canadian artists. Just as Curnoe had encouraged Boyle and many others in London, so Boyle in turn inspired younger artists and writers in the Niagara area to depict the people and places they know. (1974, 239)

NAC's director, Stephen Remus, notes that a regionalist approach worked in the past and continues to work at the centre: "It allows us to esteem our collective work without trying to unify our expression as artists. What's most important is who we are, where we are, and what we're doing." In short, NAC's current renaissance is indebted to the regionalist agenda of the early members led by Boyle, who linked the centre so fundamentally to its community in the first place.

FOSTERING AN IDENTITY

Since the '70s, there have been ebbs and flows in the level of community involvement with NAC, corresponding to the appointment of various board presidents and directors and accompanying cultural agendas. Tobey C. Anderson, artistic and administrative director at NAC from 1990 to 1998, and a proponent of the regionalist ideals of the founders, cites Remus's current tenure as director as beneficial to the organization based on his interest in the premise of the collective: "I'm very happy with NAC ... right now. We're seeing the ideal model happening" (interview 2005). Anderson would know: He was hired as director of NAC in 1990 after being asked to apply for the position by John Moffat and other founding members of the Niagara Artists' Co-op with whom he had forged friendships during their mutual involvement with CAR in the '70s. When Anderson took over, however, he faced a similar predicament to the one Remus would find himself having to navigate some ten years later. The founders, who maintained an interest in the operations of the centre, had sought out Anderson for a reason. The board of directors was governing the institution independent of the policies and the artist rights delineated within, which had defined the socially and politically conscious collective at its formation and which Anderson, along with the founders of NAC, had advocated for so strongly in establishing CAR.[6] Most significantly, Anderson was faced with the task of refocusing the organization after the speedy proliferation of artist-run centres across Canada in the '80s, and the subsequent shift in the way artist-run initiatives operated: the very fabric of the movement had changed.[7] The shift that occurred was one whereby many of the vibrant and active project-based collectives like NAC evolved into artist-run centres and were crippled under the bureaucratic weight of their permanent gallery facilities. This, along with a steadily increasing number of artist-run initiatives exploring their candidacy for government funding from the Canada Council, completely changed the dynamics of the organizations. Anderson explains the process at NAC:

> NAC moved into its first permanent gallery facility in 1980 and had to start operating more like an institution than a collective. They applied for operational funding as opposed to the project funding they customarily received,

and got it, hired Pete Wing as the first NAC director and established a more formal board. They went from a project-driven collective to a small institution concerned with writing grants that satisfied increasingly strict funding guidelines determined by the Canada Council and the Ontario Arts Council, leaving less time and energy to focus on the socio-centric brand of artistic programming the collective was founded on. (interview 2009)

In 1990, Anderson faced the very situation that A.A. Bronson had criticized in 1987:

Suddenly there were galleries (and other hybrids) by artists popping up all over the country: Open Space in Victoria, Video Inn and the Western Front in Vancouver, the Parachute Centre for Cultural Affairs in Calgary, Plug-in in Winnipeg, Artspace in Peterborough, the Music Gallery, Fifteen Dance lab and Art Metropole in Toronto, Véhicule in Montreal, Powerhouse in Montreal, the Centre for Arts Tapes in Halifax and many more. We called upon our Canadian tendencies, the bureaucratic tendency and the protestant work ethic, and soon there were little artists' bureaucracies having exhibitions and promotions and educational programmes and video workshops and concert series and anything else you might care to think of in this parody of that museum world we all supposedly were trying to escape. (167)

The pattern of government-funded dependency established by this paradigm shift in artist-run culture has persisted since then. For example, Clive Robertson, cultural critic and co-founder of the Parachute Centre for Cultural Affairs in Calgary, states, "The processes of professionalization we have embraced in turn have reformed our own organizations, erasing certain functional and ethical distinctions" (2004).

During the '80s, the community involvement that NAC was born of necessarily took a back seat to the bureaucratic concerns of keeping the facility running. Anderson, however, took simple measures to successfully realign the centre with the ideals of the founders. He instituted a policy that outlined a commitment on behalf of the centre to "maintain artist fees and project related expenses above minimum CARFAC [Canadian Artists' Representation/Le Front des Artistes Canadiens] rates," an operating guideline that NAC observes to this day. Significantly, Anderson also set to work organizing a variety of events and exhibitions for NAC's twenty-second anniversary (nothing had been done on behalf of NAC's leadership to commemorate the organization's twentieth in 1989), which, along with policy changes that recognized the artists and their locality, reinstated a close connection to the local arts community as the *raison d'être* of the centre. Anderson explains, "We re-cultivated the local group shows the original collective was founded on and organized two exhibitions of work by artists from across the Niagara Region—

Watershed and *Whirlpool*. There was an incredible turnout to both exhibitions" (2009).

When Anderson stepped down as director in 1998, the membership was over 300 strong and the organization was operating with a budget surplus. Anderson's legacy demonstrates, through practice, the importance of upholding the regionalist roots of the centre in supporting those artists and stakeholders in NAC's immediate community. Significantly, Remus began his involvement with the organization as a volunteer during Anderson's tenure as director. Remus makes Anderson's influence along with that of the founding members of NAC apparent:

> In the number of years I worked as a volunteer at NAC I met many of the old guard of regionalist artists including Tobey C. Anderson, John Moffat, Alice Crawley, John B. Boyle, Sandy Fairbairn and the late Dennis Tourbin. They all instilled in me the belief that the best artists made work that was connected to where they were—the community they were living in. Coming from small-town Ontario, I gravitated to the regionalist sensibility of the art world right away, it just made sense.

Like Anderson, Remus is empathetic to the "old guard" of regionalists and rigorously promotes NAC's relationship to the community. He identifies as his main goal making NAC an organization "that supports local artists first and foremost.... I am following the original model put in place by John Boyle and others." Remus's push to increase the organization's profile in the community is also a strategic move in an attempt to grow the centre and re-establish it among those organizations recognized for their unique contributions to a national cultural identity, as was the case in the '70s.

The need to recultivate the regional Niagara community can be found in the programming prior to Remus's tenure, which focused on the international art scene and alienated NAC from its immediate location in St. Catharines. Exhibits of work by internationally respected Canadian artists such as the Toronto-based sculptor Tom Dean in 2001 and the exhibition *Light Ship*, which occasioned the collaboration of Netherlands-based artists Hanna Boon and Petra Halkes, did little to spark community interest in NAC. These exhibitions obscured the importance of local cultural producers in favour of an artistic hierarchy upheld by the larger Canadian public art institutions that funnel the works of recognized artists through their doors. Without engaging the local community, this type of programming contradicts the reasons for establishing regional artist-run centres in the first place.

The original co-op was founded by a growing population of artists living in the region to address their situation as artists residing and working in a small community that offered very few opportunities for the exhibition of contemporary art. They also wanted to acknowledge their desire to stay in the community rather than relocate to a large urban centre, thus fostering a sense of local importance. John Moffat, founding secretary of NAC, recalls, "[We] started talking to each other about how to improve our lot, living in a small community and being able, in some ways, to control our own destiny. There was only one [commercial] gallery in town—very little other opportunity if you wanted to stay here" (lecture, 1992). The outcome of the collective's desire to "control their own destiny," as Moffatt professed, is attested to by reporter John Barber in the early '70s: NAC "has proven itself to be a model for Canadian artists mired in the incompetence of patronizing systems and the exploitations of dealers, collectors and administrators who control their livelihoods without contributing to the production of fine arts" (1974). NAC effectively eliminated the conventional role of the institutional curator/critic as "gatekeeper" (Robertson 2004), and the members began working together on projects in 1969. Eventually they rented the small coach house at Rodman Hall Arts Centre and used it collectively, before the term "artist-run centre" was coined.[8] The minutes from a Niagara Artists' Co-op meeting in 1971 describe their plans: "The Co-op members inspected the new NAC building and the following possible uses of the building were discussed: regular meeting place, social gatherings, small in-depth exhibitions, work shop concept, office space, storage space, library facilities, lectures" (Dec. 17, 1971). The members initially operated on a project-by-project basis, joining together to work collectively on a happening, exhibition, or event and then disbanding to continue individual art pursuits. They used the coach house to stage lectures and small exhibitions and rented other facilities in St. Catharines to accommodate larger projects and aid in public dissemination. At times, the backdrop for the artists' work was the city of St. Catharines itself, implicated as it was in many of the co-op's public projects.

The degree to which the co-op engaged the local community is the most outstanding aspect of the early NAC projects, and through the overt adaptation of these projects by Remus, NAC has been able to survive and excite a new generation of artists and art enthusiasts. Notably, Remus, who was not a pioneer of the original movement, has revitalized NAC's regionalist roots, visibility, and permanence in the downtown core. Remus was born in 1969—the year the original Niagara Artists' Co-op formed—and his spirited guidance has educated a new generation, including me and fellow NAC board members, about regionalism and the important role it still plays in the cultural fabric of my community.

COMMUNITY-BASED PROGRAMMING

Linkage between the contemporary NAC and the original co-op was articulated visually in the *Niagara Ego Exposition* in 2004. The exhibition was a spin-off of the *Johnny Canuck Canadian Ego Exposition* of 1974 and celebrated the latter's thirtieth anniversary. It was also the third in a series of hugely successful annual community group shows after *Lilli-Putting* (2003) and *Spring Run* (2002). These annual shows were implemented to recapture the community-based dynamism of the seventies. In its combination of new miniature works by both founding and current NAC members, the *Niagara Ego Exposition* poetically imparted the revitalization of a social agenda that reconciled past and present. The show included a miniature chesterfield, a miniature model of a faceless block of suburban housing, and a miniature Tom Thomson-esque landscape with a silhouetted Jack pine in the foreground.

The *Johnny Canuck Canadian Ego Exposition* of 1974 took the task of local dissemination to new heights, often engaging other small Ontario communities. The original *Johnny Canuck* show is a portable Plexiglas display case measuring 38 inches high, 10 inches deep, and 25 inches wide, divided into 68 compartments measuring 3.5 inches square. Each cube features artwork by one of sixteen NAC artists. The exposition opened in St. Catharines, then toured to towns in Ontario that share place names with more famous world cities. A couple of NAC members would roll into town with the *Johnny Canuck* show in the trunk and quickly set it up in offbeat, public locations in Ontario: the *Paris Star News*, a meat market in Dublin, an abandoned mill in Brussels, the Damascus General Store, and the Vienna Barber Shop and Billiards Hall. Touted in the press as "Canada's Smallest Touring Art Exhibition," the show was self-effacing and modest and poked fun at the instant validity afforded an international art exhibit. (In a prophetic twist *Johnny Canuck* was eventually sponsored by the Centre culturel canadien on a tour of locations in Europe including Paris, Brussels, Belgium, and London.) The portability of the exhibition enabled the dissemination of NAC's art to the public in a convenient way. The choice of venues for the tour reflected the co-op's desire to extend its work to people living in small towns outside of the Canadian city centres. In an article detailing NAC's collective exhibition history, John Barber writes, "Most of these luckily-named Ontario hamlets had never had an art exhibition before, and the *Ego Exposition* ... worked well in enacting the Company's belief in Art for the People" (1974). The tour of the *Johnny Canuck Canadian Ego Exposition* contributed to the collective's reputation for wry humour and its established knack for cultural subversion as a means of commenting on Canadian cultural and economic subordination to Europe and the United States. In comparison to their grand

FIGURE 12.2 *Niagara Ego Exposition* miniature group show, 2004. Niagara Artists Centre Archive

European art-capital namesakes, the Ontario towns on the tour route typically were relegated to a glaringly obvious second class—befitting the show's purposeful irony.

Two additional art happenings are emblematic of NAC's early social agenda—and commitment: *Niagara Now '72* art and billboard exhibition, and the *Storefront Art Blitz* and its affiliated banner, print, and bus projects of 1973. By placing social interaction above the cultural and static art object, these projects, along with the *Johnny Canuck Canadian Ego Exposition*, collapsed aesthetic, geographic, and social barriers that traditionally render the fine arts insular and elitist. The *Niagara Now '72* art and billboard exhibition comprised colour reproductions of work by fourteen of the co-op artists, displayed on billboards throughout St. Catharines. NAC offered bus tours of the billboard route that commenced at the gallery. Maps of the route were also available to those who preferred to follow the tour on their own. The billboards allowed the members of the co-op to disseminate their work to a larger and more varied local audience and to weave their work into the very fabric of the community. Subsumed into the vernacular of advertising, the billboard exhibition engaged a broader audience and precluded the need to function as an institutionalized mediator between art object and audience. In a contemporaneous issue of *artscanada*, Robert Johns credits NAC's billboard exhibition as a successful effort to subvert institutional authority: "Normally the public goes to an art gallery in order to find its artists. The billboard show dramatically demonstrated that the artist need not go there to find his public. In that sense, such a show bypasses 'The Gallery' and suggests that although the audience of art lovers is largely a

FIGURE 12.3 *Storefront Art Blitz* in downtown St. Catharines, 1973. Niagara Artists Centre Archive

creature (i.e., a creation) of the galleries, art itself need not be" (1972). Johns further emphasizes the impact of the co-op's mission to preserve and improve the local community, and to popularize the arts in the region: "[The exhibition] underlined the role of the city as something to be played in and looked at quite apart from its all too common function as a barracks for workers in the industrial cattleyards."

The following year in 1973, the city, and more specifically, the downtown core, was played as the stage for the *Storefront Art Blitz*, and the accompanying banner show, print project, and bus project. NAC members launched a month-long interdisciplinary art, lecture, and workshop series in the old L. Hattey Company Store, a department store on St. Paul Street, the main thoroughfare in downtown St. Catharines. The work of NAC members, and a group from London, Ontario, was exhibited in the storefront space. A slide show of work by guest artists from Czechoslovakia was also shown. On-site lectures and workshops were offered by visiting artists, including Curnoe, who gave a slide show on Canadian folk art; Michael Snow, who installed a permanent mural at Brock University and showed slides and films; and Dennis

FIGURE 12.4 Banner show in downtown St. Catharines, part of *Storefront Art Blitz*, 1973. Niagara Artists Centre Archive

Tourbin, who entertained the audience by reading his humorous and unorthodox poetry to the sound of a household vacuum cleaner. In conjunction with the storefront activities, fifteen silk-screened banners by members of the co-op were hung on the lampposts on St. Paul Street. The interdisciplinarity of the event engaged a wide audience. Equally popular was the headquarters for these events, a converted storefront on downtown St. Paul Street. Writer and curator Donna Wawzonek alludes to the implication of location on the audience and the social perception of art: "With a street level picture window and a front entrance, the space is more accessible, visible and safe for the uninitiated to explore" (2000).

The exhibition and sale of prints at the local K-Mart store widened the co-op's aim to appeal to the "working man" demographic. In the proposal for the print project, print master Craig Oliver articulated the co-op's aim to disseminate its art to a larger local audience and, in turn, make art accessible to everyone: "Although the prices will compete with those of commercial products, our concern involves placing CANADIAN ART PRINTS into the Community as opposed to making large profits. If any profits are realized they may be put into another Co-op project" (1972). To these ends, an edition of seventy-five unsigned prints of each of the twelve original designs by the co-op members were sold for about five dollars each, and a limited edition of twenty-five signed prints sold for between $40 and $85 each, or $450 for a set of twelve. When the *Storefront Art Blitz* ended, the co-op rented a converted school bus, which they decorated with the banners formerly hung on St. Paul Street, and filled with the series of prints and other small works by co-op members. The bus rented for $1,300, including a fee to be paid to a co-op artist to act as a docent to inform the public about the co-op and its projects. The purpose of the bus component of the *Blitz* was to bring Niagara art to those who might not otherwise get a chance to see it. The bus travelled to London, Burlington, and Niagara Falls, making stops at public spaces, including the Pen Centre shopping mall in St. Catharines. More than 650 people attended the opening day and about 4,000 people moved through the exhibition over the course of the month (Minutes, 1993). These impressive figures proved that the co-op's initiative to place the community at the centre of its artistic activities was working.

In 2002 NAC attempted a community outreach project that borrowed from the success of the *Storefront Art Blitz* of 1973. The 2002 *Spring Run* exhibition was produced in collaboration with the City of St. Catharines and the Downtown Association. Selected NAC member artists were given one of twelve identical fiberglass castings of rainbow trout to paint or augment as they saw fit. Local businesses in the downtown merchant district chose a "fish" to hang in their store for one month, and members of the community were encouraged to visit the businesses and collect stamps of the fish. A collection of all twelve fish stamps entitled the bearer to enter a draw for a variety of prizes. This initial venture extended NAC's reach into the community by combining the visual arts with the interests of small enterprise and the civic-guided aims for the city's downtown revitalization. At the conclusion of *Spring Run*, the entire "school of fish" was installed in the foyer of the main branch of the St. Catharines Public Library for a year, making NAC's populist place highly visible in the community.

CONCLUSIONS ABOUT NAC TODAY

NAC is acutely aware of the importance of socio-centric programming. More than ever before, programming is designed to explore the community, its strengths and shortcomings, in witty and satirical ways, to engage the people of Niagara in local art as part of the larger milieu of contemporary Canadian visual art. In his essay on Greg Curnoe, Oliver Girling argues, "Without

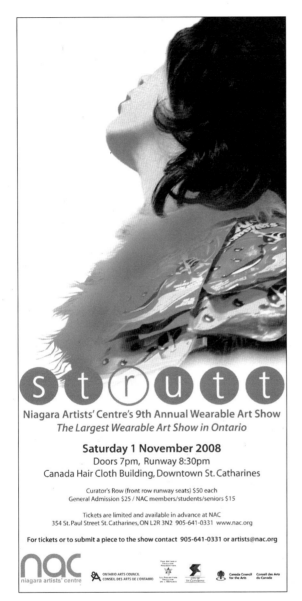

FIGURE 12.5 *Strutt* 2008,
NAC's major annual
fundraiser. NAC Archive

a place to stand, there's no point of view, no loyalty, none of the meaning that grows out of connectedness" (2002). Girling's claim that one's physical and ideological bond with a community and a locale is a precondition to understanding larger issues within culture is an ideology long favoured by NAC. By looking to its co-op origins and resurrecting programming strategies developed by its first wave of members, NAC has found a continuing vital place for itself in the popular consciousness of Niagara.

Hot Shots, a fundraising exhibition and event that took place in September 2007, also demonstrated NAC's renewed tendency to deepen cultural connections within the local community. Over 100 disposable cameras were distributed to St. Catharines radio and television personalities, performers, musicians, athletes, writers, politicians, and business and civic leaders, with instructions to capture on film visions of their "Garden City" (as St. Catharines identifies itself). One photo from each roll of film was selected for exhibition at a gala event and auction. *Hot Shots* was a hot ticket in a busy September in St. Catharines, typically dominated by the beginning of Brock University's academic year and Niagara Wine Festival events. NAC was filled to capacity, and representatives from each tier of government attended and spoke at the event. The following excerpt from a letter written by St. Catharines resident and NAC member Norm Bradshaw attests to the success of this outreach effort:

> Thank you to [Steve], the board and all the volunteers for a fantastic show! It was a packed event and the enthusiasm for the exhibit, NAC and Art was such a great thing to see, hear and feel. You created a brilliant event which engaged the community, further developed relations with our politicos, made headlines around town and really advanced NAC's presence and prestige.

While labouring to forge strong bonds in its immediate community, NAC also is working diligently to assert itself nationally. But it will do so on its own regionalist terms. In addition to developing a concerted capital campaign effort, one of the first of its kind among Canadian artist-run centres, NAC is also developing a plan to screen contemporary video work onto the mist and cataract of Niagara Falls, making this "wonder of the world" the largest "silver" screen on earth. How this on-site event alters the tourist gaze along with local perceptions of the Falls remains to be seen, but such an event, if it does come to fruition, promises to expand upon NAC's original goal by addressing the global through the local in a new way.

Since 2001, NAC has undergone significant change. Remembering lessons of projects from the past, such as the *Storefront Art Blitz* of 1973, NAC sought a permanent home with public visibility and a welcoming design in the downtown core and in 2006 bought a large two-storey storefront building (354 St. Paul Street) that accommodates two exhibition spaces. The building purchase was made possible by the benevolence of NAC board member Don Dormady and makes NAC one of only a half-dozen artist-run centres in Canada to own its facility.

The catalyst for NAC's current popularity and organizational growth was a return to the programming models from an early and energetic phase of its history as a co-op with a vision. The revived annual member group shows served to affirm the value of work by local artists and found a social place for NAC activities in the consciousness of the community. As well, the member group shows are team exercises that build the collective muscle needed to buy and renovate buildings and stage successful fundraisers and capital campaigns.[9] Through a distinct regionalist art practice—one that is not too taken with its own self-importance and that cares as much about the person on the street as the newspaper critic with a column—NAC is providing an effective popular response to the new public realities facing Canadian cultural organizations.

Thanks to Tobey Anderson, Clive Robertson, and John Boyle for participating in my research. I am especially grateful to Stephen Remus for his assistance and insight and, most of all, for his spirited leadership of the Niagara Artists Centre.

NOTES

1 Originally called the Niagara Artists' Co-op, NAC modified its name to the Niagara Artists' Company during its warehouse era on Bond Street (1996–2005). In 2006, NAC moved to its current location at 354 St. Paul Street under the name Niagara Artists' Centre. (More recently, the apostrophe was dropped from the name.)

2 NAC is an artist-run centre that has served the Niagara Region since its formation in 1969, making it one of the oldest organizations of its kind in Canada. The term "artist-run centre" (ARC) describes those galleries and art spaces that emerged in Canada in the late '60s and early '70s. Also called parallel galleries, these venues developed in response to the lack of appropriate exhibition spaces for artists whose priorities were non-commercial and whose early careers were not recognized with exhibitions in institutional or public galleries. Those ARCs that receive government funding have status as non-profit and, often, charitable organizations. Typically, one or more staff manages them, and a board of directors, mainly comprising practising artists, guides them. The underlying premise of ARCs gives artists creative control over their work, against the constraints and demands of the market.

3 Other early artist-run initiatives included Region Gallery and Forest City Gallery in London, Ontario, as well as Intermedia in Vancouver and A Space in Toronto.

4 *We Are Not Greg Curnoe* is an issue of *Open Letter* that chronicles the proceedings of a symposium of the same name sponsored by the Art Gallery of Ontario and the Ontario College of Art and Design, in Toronto, on the occasion of the exhibition *Greg Curnoe: Life and Stuff* in 2001.

5 Donald Alexander's documentary *Why Are They Making All That Noise?* (2001) features the Nihilist Spasm Band in performance and conversation. The film shared

the Best Documentary Award at NIFF (Niagara Indie Film Fest) in 2001. For further information on the Nihilist Spasm Band, see http://www3.sympatico.ca/
pratten/NSB/.

6   The founders of NAC had incorporated the mandatory payment of exhibition fees
and the payment of artists' travel costs according to the CAR minimum fee schedule into the policy and procedures manual. However, when Anderson took over
in 1990, the board was not governing according to this policy.

7   In *From Sea to Shining Sea*, the catalogue for an eponymous exhibition in 1987
at the Power Plant in Toronto chronicling the history of artist-directed activity in
Canada from the post-war period to the present, a diagram illustrating the number of artist-run centres funded by the Visual Arts Section of the Canada Council
(which doesn't even include the many centres funded by the Media Arts Section
of the Council at that time), shows 11 centres at the end of 1975 compared to 46
centres just over ten years later (Bronson 1987, 162).

8   Rodman Hall is a historic mansion situated in St. Catharines, built by Thomas
Rodman Merritt in the mid- to late 1860s. Rodman Hall remained a private residence for generations of the Merritt family until it was sold to the St. Catharines
Art Council in 1960 and subsequently named Rodman Hall Arts Centre. Rodman Hall boasts a permanent collection of over 850 contemporary and historic
paintings, drawings, prints, sculptures, and outdoor installations. In 2003 Rodman Hall was purchased by Brock University and its legacy as a public art gallery
lives on.

9   NAC's major annual fundraiser, *Strutt*, is a juried wearable art show that draws
large crowds and is supported by arts funding agencies and community and corporate sponsors.

WORKS CITED

Anderson, Tobey C. Personal interviews conducted Feb. 27, 2005, and Aug. 10,
    2009.

Barber, John. Untitled article. *Arthur* 10:12 (Jan. 1974).

Boyle, John. "Working Together." *Twelve Mile Creek* 1 (1974): no pagination.

———. "We Are Neither Regionalism Nor Internationalism." *Open Letter [We Are
    not Greg Curnoe]* 11:5 (Summer 2002), 98–99.

Bradshaw, Norm. "A Job Well Done." E-mail to Stephen Remus, Sept. 16, 2007.

Bronson, A.A. "The Humiliation of the Bureaucrat: Artist-run Spaces as Museums
    by Artists." In *From Sea to Shining Sea* (1987). Reprinted from *Museums by
    Artists*. Peggy Gale and A.A. Bronson, eds. Toronto: Art Metropole, 1983:
    164–69.

———, and Power Plant. "Notes." In *From Sea to Shining Sea*. Toronto: Power-
    Plant, 1987.

Fischer, Barbara. "YYZ—an Anniversary." *Decalog: YYZ 1979–1989*. Scott Mitchell,
    ed. Toronto: YYZ Books, 1992: 5–31.

Girling, Oliver. "That Was a Suit!" *Open Letter [We Are not Greg Curnoe]* 11:5
    (Summer 2002), 39–42.

Hill, Richard. "Introducing: A Tale of Two Regionalisms (and Two Internation-alisms)." *Open Letter [We Are not Greg Curnoe]* 11:5 (Summer 2002), 88–90.

Johns, Robert. "The St. Catharines Billboard Show." *artscanada* 29:4 (Oct./Nov. 1972), 53.

Lord, Barry. *The History of Painting in Canada* Toronto: NC Press, 1974.

Lord, Gail Dexter. "Citizen Artist." *Open Letter [We Are not Greg Curnoe]* 11:5 (Summer 2002), 91–93.

Moffat, John. "NAC Anniversary Lecture." Niagara Artists Centre, St. Catharines. Apr. 10, 1992.

NAC Archive. Niagara Artists Centre, St. Catharines.

———. "Amid Ontario Vineyards." *Toronto Star* (Apr. 11 1970). 1970/1971 file.

———. Evaluation of the completed *Storefront Art Blitz*. Minutes of NAC General Meeting (Apr. 19, 1973). Board Minutes 1971–1990 file.

———. Untitled press release (undated). 1975 file.

———. Niagara Artists' Co-Op minutes (Dec. 16, 1971). Minutes 1971–1990 file.

Oliver, Craig. Proposal for the Co-Op Print Marketing Program, Nov. 2, 1972. Board Minutes 1971–1990 file. NAC Archive, St. Catharines.

Pardie, G. "G. Stands for Green." *Pulse Magazine* (date unknown). 2003/2004 file. NAC Archive, St. Catharines.

Remus, Stephen. Personal interviews conducted Dec. 8, 2004; Aug. 12, 2005; Oct. 25, 2007.

Robertson, Clive. "Looking Back While Moving Forward—A Response to Infest: Artist Run Culture and the Formation of a New National Association of Artist-Run Centres." *Fuse Magazine* 27:2 (2004), 26–36.

Wawzonek, Donna, and Andrew Hunter. *Shifting Territory: Artist-Run Centres and Exhibition Practice*. Ottawa: Gallery 101, 2000.

Part V | **BORDERLINE MATTERS**

ENTERTAINING NIAGARA FALLS, ONTARIO | Minstrel Shows, Theatres, and Popular Pleasures

JOAN NICKS
JEANNETTE SLONIOWSKI

INTRODUCTION

In most studies, the minstrel show, with its complex historical roots, is identified as a quintessentially American popular form. However, in a review-essay of three studies on minstrelsy, Philip Gura observes that historians "have not taken the time to consider fully the ways in which this popular entertainment spoke to its audiences ... [and] how deeply one of its main characteristics, the blackface convention, was embedded in European and American culture generally." Gura points to the proliferation of minstrelsy *outside* the United States, and suggests, "We must try to account more thoroughly for minstrelsy's immense popularity in other countries.... Equally obscure is the subject of the phenomenon's continuing popularity into later decades and even into our own century" (1999, 614).

Gura's observations raise obvious questions from a Canadian perspective: what *of* blackface minstrelsy in Canada, and why did it continue here deep into the twentieth century—specifically in Niagara Falls, Ontario, known globally as a popular tourist destination and hardly at all as a community (incorporated as a city in 1904)? Geographically located at the Ontario/New York state border, and not far from Toronto, Niagara Falls was a strategic site for touring blackface comics, part of what Gerald Lenton describes as "small-time" vaudeville that endured into the early twentieth century (1983, 147). In this cross-border community, the ubiquitous stereotypes and practices of blackface minstrelsy persisted in local amateur shows.

We approach this study on local amateur minstrel shows in the spirit of W.T. Lhamon Jr., for whom the "job of criticism" is "not to scorn or judge" minstrelsy's codes and gestures, "but to find some way ... to grasp at their implication" (1998, 226). Our study inflects Mel Watkins's notion of tracing "performance genealogies" (1996, x): for our purposes here, to understand the periods, practices, and places of minstrelsy in the local community. Michel de Certeau's notions of "use" also echo throughout this study (1988, 35)—"use" meaning common community practice where "everyday life invents itself by poaching in countless ways on the property of others" (xii). Blackface minstrelsy by white performers thrived on racial poaching in the United States in the nineteenth century and in the early twentieth century gained popularity as a local practice in Niagara Falls and nearby communities.

We argue that, by the 1920s, blackface amateur shows were nurtured in Niagara Falls, Ontario, as if a home-grown form and that the shows functioned as a carnivalesque outlet for the expression of local ambivalence about racial and class issues in an era of increased immigration and economic stress in the community. Local newspaper discourse is key here, promoting public acceptance of blackface in an era when Frank H. Leslie (1876–1969), the entrepreneurial owner-publisher of the *Niagara Falls Evening Review*—the "dean of this city's business life" (Feb. 4, 1960)—shaped his paper, and thus readers, with his conservative social views.[1] The *Review*'s coverage played up the civic value and moral rationale of the amateur shows, for a common good as in, for example, the promotion of the Rotary Club's annual charity minstrel show that urged "citizens ... [to] join in the Christian experience" (Nov. 28, 1927, 7). Thus, the newspaper socially "approved" the racial slurs of blackface, leaving audiences to enjoy the carnivalesque disruptions and the musical numbers without being troubled by minstrelsy's racist codes.

ENTERTAINING NIAGARA FALLS

The citizens of Niagara Falls enjoyed a variety of entertainment in the early 1900s.[2] Baseball, basketball, and hockey competed with live theatre, vaudeville, early films, and concerts for people's leisure, along with chautauquas and wild west and medicine shows that drew large crowds. Amid such activities, the blackface minstrel show grew to be one of the most common and enduring forms of live entertainment in Niagara Falls and the greater Niagara area. Minstrel shows were performed in any venue that could accommodate performance, whether in vaudeville and movie houses or school gyms, church auditoriums, or community halls. These shows were surprisingly long-lived, lasting until the early 1960s when, according to

Niagara Falls performer-producer Bob Lamb, members from the NAACP (National Association for the Advancement of Colored People) in Niagara Falls, New York, visited his group at Christ Anglican Church and asked that their annual minstrel shows—now widely considered to be racist and offensive—be discontinued.

The amateur minstrel show flourished in Niagara Falls long after local people enjoyed vaudeville and short-reel films at the Princess Theatre (1908–14), located near the Whirlpool Rapids Bridge in an extant building at 4238 Bridge Street, which in recent years has served as a tavern and strip joint or stood vacant. Like many early small store-front playhouses, the vaudeville bills at the Princess featured singers, musicians, animal acts, acrobats, and blackface comedians.[3] Early newspapers from the nearby city of Welland printed stories and commentary on the numerous amateur and professional touring blackface shows playing there in the late 1800s. Niagara Falls, New York, more than double the size of its Canadian counterpart, had several live theatres in the early 1900s that featured blackface performers and short-reel film programs. Since frequent border-crossing was cheap, easy, and commonplace during this period, Canadians enjoyed and also participated enthusiastically in minstrel shows and other entertainments on both sides of the border—a decided perk and a defining aspect of everyday life for people who lived close to Niagara's Canada–United States border (even in the post-9/11 era, local residents with proper identification [lately, passports] are largely inconvenienced only by traffic delays, and those with Nexus passes pass quickly through designated gates).

Touring professional minstrels made their most frequent appearances in Niagara Falls in movie theatres in the early 1900s, mostly disappearing when professional vaudeville faded from the movie houses in the early 1930s. Although not local in origin, amateur blackface endured as a popular form of community entertainment enjoyed by large audiences on both sides of the border and throughout the Niagara Region. Local movie theatres were important civic institutions and did far more than merely screen films; they were centres for ethnic performances, talent shows, beautiful baby contests, and religious lectures; they ran movie clubs for children, reported election results, and hosted drama, opera, and minstrel shows. Many of the minstrel shows were presented in the Web Theatre on Main Street, often produced by service clubs as charity events.[4] In the 1950s and early 1960s, the Niagara Falls Collegiate auditorium was filled to capacity for amateur minstrel shows produced and performed by local church groups.

MINSTRELSY'S PORTABLE CODES AND CONVENTIONS

Minstrelsy goes back to the nineteenth century antebellum era, and numerous writers have studied its historical movement within the United States from a folk form into a highly commodified popular entertainment across North America and Europe.[5] Eric Lott emphasizes that blackface minstrelsy was "always implicitly structured by an economics of slavery" in its "northern interracial contexts…. Minstrel-show versions of the South made black culture available to whites in a way that permitted its insertion into a burgeoning leisure industry" (1993, 41). Handbills from 1820 and 1848 reproduced in Lott's study show a black farm labourer dancing on a wood shingle, creating a crude stage that delineates his performance space (23, 26–27); formally suited white bystanders help to make theatre of the performance, but also appear to be edging close to the action as if overtaking it. Lhamon argues that "young blacks … were dancing a free identity in a place that valued it, against a backdrop of enslavement" (1998, 16). Kevin Phinney writes of the later commercial form of blackface performed by black people, who "made a success of blackface and their purgatory in it by sheer force of will" (2005, 56).

In the development of commercial minstrelsy in the nineteenth century, *white* blackface performers adopted and dominated the minstrel form of stock figures, caricatures, and stage conventions. Performers "corked up" in concoctions of soot or burnt cork and water or grease, a mask that amused and evoked racial, social, and class characterizations. Two nineteenth-century classic figures were the highly coded Zip Coon and Jim Crow. Phinney describes Zip Coon as "the original black dandy … given to flamboyant dress and equally florid speeches … often rife with grammatical errors" (38). More modern traces of Zip Coon's strutting urban type can be found in the cool "hood" operators in "blaxploitation" movies of the 1970s and in hip-hop performers parading their "bling." Jim Crow, as described by Phinney, is "Zip Coon's poor southern relative," a shuffling, stoop-shouldered figure in "tattered coattails" (41). His creation is attributed to Thomas D. Rice, a white performer who became famous in the late 1820s for his blackface song and dance in imitation of an arthritic old black man (Lenton 1983, 21). In nineteenth-century minstrelsy, the term "jumping Jim Crow" meant staged performance of this iconic character (Phinney 20), and the discriminatory term "Jim Crow" later became shorthand code for laws and social practices associated with the oppression of Southern blacks (41). Taking a rich historical and aesthetic perspective on Rice's Jim Crow, W.T. Lhamon argues, "Elites first repudiated Jim Crow not because he was racist, but because he was not racist enough…. The phenomenon of Jim Crow spread beyond its home….

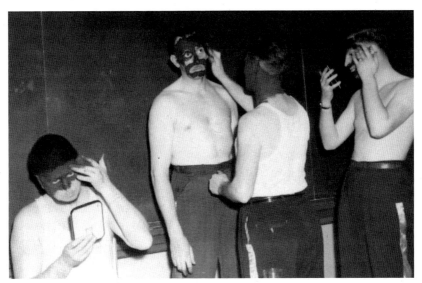

FIGURE 13.1 Corking up, Chi-Rho "Merry Minstrels," 1951, Christ Anglican Church. Courtesy of Bob and Shirley Lamb

This public applauding Jim Crow was living in much more racially mingled neighbourhoods ... already living belly to belly, white on black, black on white.... It was people in power who most needed that social division.... More important, they could propagate and codify their beliefs" (2003, 11).

The generic minstrel show consisted of three parts: prologue, olio (middle part), and afterpiece. Comedy, music, and specialty numbers made up the contents, and local amateur groups adapted the tropes of the minstrel show to their own needs using scripts readily available from sources such as Samuel French, a New York distributor of countless blackface materials and song sheets.

The prologue typically consisted of a chorus that opened the show with sentimental songs. Stephen Foster's "Oh! Susanna" was a favourite. Phinney calls Foster "a songwriter for hire" who wrote "blackface dialect" songs made famous on the American minstrel circuit in the nineteenth century (50). In his analysis of Foster's compositions, Charles Hamm notes that Foster's minstrel songs of the mid-1850s "are a far cry from the 'nigger songs' of the early minstrel show" in that black dialect was all but gone from the composer's lyrics (1979, 213–14). Still, the use of dialect persisted in minstrel practice. Sentimentality was common to many popular songs in blackface repertoire, such as "My Mammy" with its evocation of a mythic old South. In the Niagara Falls minstrel shows, performers for whom "south" mostly involved crossing the border to New York State sang such songs. The early newspaper convention of publishing sheet music of popular songs for readers to play in their parlours encouraged the use of minstrel repertoire ("Kiss Your Minstrel Boy Good-Bye," *Record*, Sept. 21, 1911). Perhaps the sentimental songs softened the racist dialect of the "coon" songs for producers and audiences.

In its coverage of the 1923 Merudelion Lady Minstrel Show at the Web Theatre on Main Street, the *Review* reports—without editorial comment and oblivious to the slur—that the chorus sang the tune "Cooning 'neath the cotton pickin' moon" (Apr. 25, 1923, 4). For Niagara Falls audiences, the racial slurs of blackface minstrelsy had been cast early by touring comics. The newspaper repeated the racist rhetoric, for example, in a Princess Theatre ad promoting "Edith Barton, Refined Coon and Character Singing Comedian [sic] (*Record*, 1910, Aug. 15) and in another Princess ad for the farce comedy "The Hottest Coon in Dixie" (June 2, 1911). Phinney notes that "a craze for so-called 'Coon songs' kept bigotry alive" in the United States in the early1900s (70). By the time the craze spread to Niagara, it had been well honed and was welcome—thus went without editorial comment by the *Record* and the *Review*. Though the *Review* took high-minded editorial positions in the 1920s against the folly of Hollywood life (see our "Hollywoodization" study in this volume), the newspaper never questioned the slurs of blackface minstrelsy.

The middle part of the conventional blackface show, known as the olio, was a carnivalesque interplay of stage business, soloists, tap dancers, skits, and in some cases drag numbers performed by the front-row cast and guests. The End Men were pivotal front-row figures, typically in the Niagara Falls shows seated three to a side. "Corked-up" blackface caricatures, they wore satin suits, oversized ties, and curly wigs and engaged in jokes and quips with the smartly attired white Interlocutor, who commanded centre stage. Jules Zanger calls blackface minstrelsy a "theater of misrule" and refers to the olio section as "being at the heart of the ritual of the minstrel show":

> They, the End Men, are unqualifiedly Black; they speak in dense 'Minstrel dialect,' and move, dance, clown, and sing in terms of the elaborate caricature the Minstrel show devised. He, the Interlocutor, seated at the center of the stage, dresses with great resplendence, speaks in high-flown, multi-syllabic, 'learned' speech, is intensely dignified, and is always White. Much of the humor of the Minstrel Show results from the dialogue and patter flowing between the Interlocutor and the End Men, and from the contrasts in the two modes of speech that are used.... The resultant laughter of the white audience is directed primarily at the discomfiture of the Interlocutor and only secondarily at the foolishness of the End Men who, in this regard, are acting as instruments of the white audience's will. (1974, 33)

FIGURE 13.2 Ad for "Alabama Jubilee," Knights of Columbus, 1952. Courtesy of Rev. Msgr. Ferrando

In 1953, the St. Ann's–St. Patrick's Knights of Columbus minstrel group performed a show called "Killarney Bound," directed by St. Ann's parish priest, Vincent Ferrando. It was an Irish take on an earlier blackface show, "Alabamy Bound" (1951). A skit in the olio section of the "Killarney Bound" script references the group's minstrel show history. The local audience, made up of family, friends, and supportive church-goers, would have understood the ploy of injecting an aimless "black man" who appears on stage briefly as a lost but known minstrel type from prior shows. The Irish Pat and Mike characters are ethnic clichés but speak in the lingo of black-face, with no substantive changes made in the "Killarney Bound" script. Ignorance remains a central trope in the locution of all the characters, except for the white, elegantly suited Interlocutor at centre stage. As dead-pan questioner, he controls stage business, pace, and order—in the script and on stage:

Enter blackface stranger [stage direction]

Stranger: "Hey, they'ah, boy; who's the boss man roun' heah?"

Interlocutor: "What can I do for you?"

Stranger: "Well, I heah you fellas was scoutin' for some talent for a minstrel show and I think I'm yo' man (starts to sing "Way Down Upon the Swanee River").

Mike: "Well, me buck, you're barkin' up the wrong tree this year because this is an Irish Minstrel Show"

Stranger: "Awrish Show eh—Northern or Southern?"

The "black" stranger's joke served several purposes, first as obvious reference to the American cultural divide of North and South. For audience members from St. Patrick's church (commonly called St. Pat's), north and south would have suggested a long divided Irish culture; for members from St. Ann's church (located in the centre of the Italian settlement in Niagara Falls), north and south would have kindled memories of the part of Italy from which their immigrant parents came.[6] Not only does minstrelsy's black dialect persist in local amateur shows, the conventions and local inflections were maintained by the assumed "contract" between stage and audience—as Susan Smuylan argues in her study on 1950s backface shows: "The audience agreed to the ideas being promulgated in the shows and found further ease in the racial masking during which white middle-class people constructed, expressed, and reinforced their racialized class positions while not taking responsibility for their actions" (2007, 17).

FIGURE 13.3 Chi-Rho "Merry Minstrels," Christ Church Hall, 1949. Courtesy of Bob and Shirley Lamb

Typically the afterpiece (third part) of the generic minstrel show is a big musical finish employing the entire chorus and cast, featuring such songs as "Missouri Waltz" and "Sleep Kentucky Babe" (Chi-Rho "Merry Minstrels" program, 1949) and up-lift repertoire such as "I Had a Little Talk with the Lord" ("Merry Minstrels" program, 1951). The minstrel show format was simple and flexible, and its carnivalesque character potentially, but rarely, unsettling for cast and audience familiar with each other but not with black people in a largely white community. The trick of these amateur minstrel shows was to play them for laughs and sentimentality—with competent production values and skilled actors and singers—making local references and craftily satirizing citizens and city officials but without serious insult.

SERVICE AND PLEASURE

With casts that could run from thirty to fifty players, theatres and auditoriums in Niagara Falls would be filled with friends, relatives, and supporters of the benefit performance for some worthy cause—as in the case of the Rotarians' long-running annual minstrel shows in aid of the city's crippled children. In the 1920s, civic-minded boosterism was vital to the city's development, and accounts in the *Review* promoted the minstrel shows as special local events and significant entertainment featuring talented local performers.[7] Ads, front-page write-ups, and promotional inserts ensured that venues were packed. A letter to the Rotary Club president from Mayor Stephens, published on the newspaper's front page, signalled official endorsement of the service club's annual benefit show (Nov. 9, 1927). An insert announcing the show, signed by Wm. Musgrove, chair of the Board of Education, served the same purpose (Nov. 3, 1927, 4). In short, minstrel shows meant good citizenship.

The *Review* embellished its own promotional role in its front-page coverage of the 1927 Rotary Club minstrel show, under the running headline "ROTARIANS IN A FINE SHOW/Local Club put on Excellent Entertainment. Enjoyed from the Beginning to the End/Program was Full of Good Things/Is repeated again tonight":

> The Rotary Minstrel Show ... at the Web Theatre last night more than fulfilled expectations *aroused by the advance notices* [emphasis ours], and the audience, which packed the theatre, enjoyed to the full, the amusing repartee on the part of the end men and their dusky 'complected' companions who were effectively arranged on the stage in a double semi-circle around Interlocutor Dr. A.B. Whytock.... The minstrels, wearing shiny black faces, and wigs which were in many cases a trifle askew, looked resplendent, in coats featuring pink lapels and blue waistcoats, while their huge, white collars, above the blue bow

ties, would be an inspiration for a Dutch maid's best cap.... The monotony of intermission was relieved with negro songs and other selections contributed by the Power City trio. (Feb. 24, 1927)

Interviews with producers, directors, and performers involved in local minstrel shows in the 1940s and 1950s all emphasized the pleasure of doing the shows, though Shirley Lamb, who was the youngest member of the Chi-Rho group at Christ Anglican, explained the domestic challenge for women:

> A lot of husbands could give you a hard time for even being in these shows. It was a concentrated effort for five weeks, and he [Shirley's husband Bob] knows I enjoyed it. And he just never started giving me a hard time. He made it easier for me and ... just sort of stepped in where I couldn't, and they [their children] always had one or the other of us with them, not even babysitters, unless it was a grandparent when we would go out for our anniversary. (interview May 18, 2005)

Putting on amateur minstrel shows was social glue for local groups—service clubs, youth and church groups, Protestant and Catholic. Retired high school principal Jim Smith recalls carrying props uphill from the Web Theatre to Lundy's Lane Methodist Church (now L.L. United) for minstrel shows produced by the church's young men's club. The St. Ann's–St. Patrick's Knights of Columbus shows were collaborations under the skilled direction of Monsignor Vincent Ferrando, a clergyman new to Niagara Falls in the 1950s. As a young priest in Toronto in the 1940s, Ferrando became an experienced and popular director of minstrel shows. Kitty Decicco commented that her protective Italian father agreed to her involvement in minstrel shows only because it was under St. Ann's Church auspices; the upshot is that she met cast member Carl, the man she would marry (interview June 29, 2005). Monsignor Ferrando, like Bob and Shirley Lamb of the Chi-Rho group at Christ Anglican, saw similar purposes (beyond charity) in the pleasure of producing and performing in these amateur theatricals: keeping religious youth and couples socializing within the church.

RACISM OF BLACKFACE PRACTICE

White performers dominated minstrelsy, but historically blackface was also an opportunity for blacks performing in blackface to make a living in entertainment. At worst, their performances manifested racial self-effacement, as depicted in Spike Lee's scathing satire *Bamboozled* (2000). Kevin Phinney describes the "core" of minstrelsy practice, "a paradox that has played out in American society ever since its introduction":

To many a white mind, there remains something mystical and primal about the black experience. So to imitate blacks—in essence, to slough off the 'white man's burden' of reserve and decorum—blackface entertainers were able to tap into a wider or at least a different vocabulary of behaviors. At the time, white people would never have given themselves over to the wild physical gyrations of a Jim Crow ... or the transcendental state blacks could reach through song. By creating the shell of a Negro with the application of burned cork, though, whites opened a portal to their own hidden creative impulses. (2005, 42)

William J. Mahar also discusses the slippery effect of blackface: "[B]urnt cork was a *masking device* allowing professional and amateur entertainers to shield themselves from any direct personal and psychological identification with the material they were performing" (1999, 1). He concludes: "At their best, minstrel comedians were social satirists; at their worst in regional amateur productions—the comics joined their neighbors in denigrating members of other ethnic groups in their own communities. Minstrel performers, even the rank amateurs, assumed, if only for an evening, that all races, classes, professions, and genders were fit subjects for comedy" (6).

In his study of blackface in the Hollywood musical, Arthur Knight discusses how blackface song and dance numbers were integrated into movie plots as late as the mid-1950s (2002, 30). With the inception of sound film and the popularity of movie-going, many Hollywood musical films played on both sides of the Niagara border. In 1928, the *Review* featured wire stories on *The Jazz Singer* (d. Crosland 1927), the first sound feature, starring vaudevillian Al Jolson, and celebrated the sound conversion of the Capitol Theatre (formerly the Queen, built in 1913) where the film played.[8] Hollywood musicals with stars Judy Garland, Mickey Rooney, Eddie Cantor, Bing Crosby, and Fred Astaire performing in blackface legitimized the production of minstrel shows, and it is no surprise that staged minstrel shows thrived locally as late as the early 1960s. For more than half a century many Niagara Falls shows were presented, in the recreation centres of major industries (Cyanamid, Nabisco), the Y.M.C.A., and the auditorium in the first city hall on downtown Queen Street. Some shows were sufficiently popular and polished to tour the region and beyond. A minstrel show put on by Houck Brothers Garage was "Headed by a big Chevrolet carrying a calathumpian [*sic*] band. The cars drove through the city announcing the show" (*Review*, Jan. 24, 1929, 4).[9] In 1929, the Home and School club at Stamford High School sponsored a show titled "What Makes a Nigger Prowl" (Feb. 16, 4; Feb. 19, 7). A local truckers' group put on at least one minstrel show. The numerous bands, orchestras, and weekly

FIGURE 13.4 Chi-Rho Minstrels, Niagara Falls Collegiate, 1955. Courtesy of Bob and Shirley Lamb

dances meant that local talent and recreational musicians were ready-made for the blackface minstrel shows and the occasional street parades to advertise them.

PLEASURE AND LICENCE

Apart from the obvious attractions of minstrel shows—music and comedy, skillful professional performers, enthusiastic and socially prominent amateurs, and pleasure for both audience and entertainer—why was the amateur minstrel show so popular and long-lived in Niagara? Niagara Falls is hardly the seething, sometimes violent, multicultural mix of the large American urban centres where minstrelsy came into its own commercially as white, working-class entertainment. One historical answer to this question is both simple and complex: entertainment, licence, and popular resistance, in the carnivalesque sense developed by Eric Lott in his Bakhtinian/carnivalesque inspired study: "Theatrical displays of 'blackness' seemingly guaranteed the atmosphere of license so central to working-class entertainment in [the 1830s]. And blackface provided a convenient mask through which to voice class resentments of all kinds—resentments directed as readily at black people as toward upper-class enemies" (68). Lott argues that the minstrel is a "Janus-faced figure" (30), one side of which was clearly and unapologetically racist, the other "linked to social and political conflicts that issue from the weak, the uncanny and the outside" (29) as it became "an oppositional, almost underground cultural form" in the 1830s (63).

The attitude of the 1830s described by Lott plays out early in the Niagara Region newspapers. A clear example is this 1869 account in the St. Catharines *Evening Journal*, headed "Dars Music in De Sole":

> On Saturday evening Deacon Aminadab Dorsey, one of the bright refulgent luminaries of Coon town, and the organizer of the colored brass band, made himself the observer of all observers. He visited the music store of Mr. Soper, and there obtained a big drum. Brudder Dorsey thereupon saddled himself with this monster tom-tom.... In his right and left "muffin hooks" he held a pair of mammoth drum sticks, and the manner in which he belabored the parchment with them should put to shame the sons of William who operated so emphatically on the 12th of July. A crowd of admiring juveniles followed Mr. Dorsey to Coontown, where he gave a free exhibition of his musical skill. 'Dar,' said he, concluding, 'dat's suffin' like drum playing I tell ye, chillen. I'se a hoss an' two mules on dis business, an' more too.' (Aug. 2, 1869)

The writer seems to favour "Coon town" over the WASP "sons of William."[10] However, the assumed dialect and physical description mimic the caricature of blackface comedy for the amusement of readers who also knew the conventions and would get the joke, thus subscribing to the writer's clever sense of superiority.

A 1907 example from the Welland *Telegraph* is written under the guise of a letter to the editor, with apology for replacing the paper's regular reviewer with someone identified as an "amateur dramatic critic." Written in the black dialect of minstrel shows, the long-winded piece begins with the illiterate salutation, "Dere Editor." With tongue planted firmly in racist cheek throughout, the writer titillates readers, boosts interest in a local minstrel show, alludes to stage business, and evokes Jim Crow: "Into their voice and axshuns ... the most hart rendering bathos and trajedi. One sez, I hev an allful secret, never again will I be able to look my wife and children in the face. Wot hev you did aste the other one. Then the fers one sez I voted for jony crow ... where at the audience had a harty laff" (Jan. 17, 1907, 1).

Adopting the lingo of blackface, these regional Niagara examples of newspaper discourse have the effect of approving racist posturing for the white community, though, as Lhamon explains, the term racism "was not widely used" until after World War II: "The figure Jim Crow emerged, therefore, about a century before people began systematically conceiving racial issues the way people overwhelmingly do now" (2003, 10). Canadian historian Barrington Walker has remarked that racial discrimination in Canada was "*de facto*," not "embedded" in law, and that blacks did not fit into the "grand

narrative" of Canadian culture.[11] Since bylines weren't yet a press convention locally, the convenient use of racist speech in early newspapers could
"pass," perpetuate racial stereotyping, and skirt accountability. As entrepreneurial practice, the newspapers courted readers and businesses, and the
sometimes racist prose taken from minstrelsy suggests such use was acceptable, as no complaints were printed. We cannot dismiss this disposition as
small-town thinking alone, for it replicates wide social contradictions attached
to blackface practice.

The following accounts in the Welland *Telegraph* (Welland is the county
seat, a short distance from Niagara Falls) show how prolific regional minstrel
activity was at the turn of the twentieth century, including women's performance groups:

> The minstrel show put on the boards at the town hall on Wednesday and
> Thursday evening by the 44th Regiment minstrels was a great success. The
> crowd was large at both performances, and the entertainment was of the
> best. Those able critics, the lady minstrels, were out in force, but they had
> to admit that it would keep them busy to keep ahead of the new burnt cork
> aggregation (*Telegraph*'s Niagara Falls column, Apr 22, 1902).
>
> An old time minstrel show will be given in the [Niagara Falls] City Hall ...
> for the benefit of the Church of Our Lady of the [*sic*] Peace, Falls View (June 7,
> 1906, 8).
>
> A large audience packed the Township Hall on Ferry Street ... to the limit
> of its capacity, when the Old Time Minstrels gave an entertainment ... ren-
> dered by the company of black and white-faced artists ... six end-men in
> burnt cork. (Nov. 29, 1906, 10).
>
> The Booster Club Minstrel show on the evening of St. Patrick's Day was
> an artistic and financial success. The audience was so large as to completely
> fill the hall, and, indeed, many had to stand throughout the performance.
> (Mar. 20, 1908, 1)

Local newspaper accounts and promotions typically reported that the
entertainment offered in Niagara Falls was "the best" and that venues were
"packed"—"to the doors" (*Record*, Feb. 20, 1909). Promotion for the Bohemia
Comedy Company at the Princess theatre promised "a high class Minstrel
show, full of good songs, good singers and bright music" (Feb. 20, 1911). In
1908 in the *Record*'s City and Vicinity section, this write-up appears under the
header "SPECIAL PROGRAMME AT THE PRINCESS":

> Manager Taylor has arranged for a particularly strong bill on Christmas
> Day at his pretty little theatre, headed by Rieff and Clayton, said to be one
> of the strongest teams in vaudeville. They do [a] singing and dancing act.
> This is followed by one of the funniest black-faced comedians ever seen in

this district. A new line of moving pictures and a new illustrated song complete what will undoubtedly be the best yet at the Princess (Dec. 24).

Amateur nights at the Princess and at theatres on the American side in the early 1910s were a popular forum for local people to display their talent (*Record*, Sept. 20, 1910), in a community where singalongs were homely pastimes and the two music stores on downtown Queen Street sold pianos and music books and offered lessons. One contest at the Princess promised the winner stage time in Buffalo, New York, in professional minstrel shows, though typically the porous international border crossing at Niagara Falls facilitated the flow of American entertainment forms to the Canadian side. When console radios were mass-marketed, they could be purchased in stores on both sides of the Niagara border, and listening to Buffalo radio stations became common. The latest Capitol recordings were sold at Thorburn's Drugstores. With three stores in Niagara Falls, Ontario, by 1912, Thorburn's was a familiar source of popular culture, regularly advertising the sale of theatre tickets and new releases of music records. A 1923 article in the *Review* boosted a highly advertised American attraction, the revival of big-time minstrelsy on tour: "the unusual spectacle of two great minstrel shows in one ... at the Web theatre.... That minstrelsy is about to come into its own again is evidenced by the big advance sale which has marked the announcement of the Gus Hill and Honey Boy Evans Minstrels" (Nov. 27, 1923, 3). The local taste for amateur blackface and the city's border location were factors in this revival of big-time minstrelsy coming to Niagara Falls.

READING RACE AND RACISM IN NIAGARA FALLS NEWSPAPERS

A concern that naturally arose in pursuing the cultural context of local minstrel shows was the racial atmosphere in Niagara Falls, a small city with a very small black population, which was experiencing an influx of new immigrants into what had been a largely Anglo-Saxon area. Most immigrants were of European origin, primarily from Italy and Eastern Europe. There was a small but culturally significant population of the descendants of slaves who had fled the United States through the Underground Railroad, as well as the descendants of former Canadian slaves, and a much larger African-American population in Niagara Falls, New York, many of whom had journeyed north looking for industrial jobs in the more prosperous industrial part of the United States.[12]

This view of race has been largely taken from the newspapers, which were, given the era, strongly ambivalent about racial issues. For Pierre

Machery, every text consists of "a confrontation between several discourses: explicit, implicit, silent and absent" (1978, 82–89). The explicit discourse on race, found mostly in the editorial section of the Niagara Falls newspapers, is of course, the official Canadian, highly laudatory view of immigrants, mostly humanistic in its stance against bigotry and even gender discrimination. But the newspapers on the whole, both inside and outside of the editorial section, have a sense of themselves as representing the view of a general "*we,*" an indigenous and successful group, loyal to the British Empire. Outside of the editorial section, they speak with a more ambivalent voice on matters of race and gender—in Machery's terms, implicitly *for* the community. Readings from the *Daily Record* and the *Review* between 1908 until the early 1930s demonstrate that the *we*, although loyal to their white ethnic and cultural pasts, have also developed a sense of themselves as Canadian, as separate from Britain, with certain disagreements with British policy and annoyed with a perceived preference given to recent English immigrants with respect to their easy acquisition of managerial and higher paying jobs. A letter to the editor in Sept. 22, 1931, expresses this concern: "Is it not time that the born Canadian be given a chance?" (*Review*, 4). The writer complains that the Canadian born do not have equal access to government jobs and that English and "Scotch" immigrants are given priority over native Canadians. During the Depression years, this is a particularly heated debate. There is also ambivalence toward the Canadian government, which from time to time was thought to interfere unjustly with local matters of the border and its lucrative commercial and cultural traffic.

At the same time, the newspaper's editorial view of new immigrants, in general, echoes the official welcome to much needed new workers to Canada, but also firmly maintains the idea that while the newcomers come from good European stock, "*we*" will, and indeed must, make them accept "*our*" culture and values. What is often cheerfully implicit here is the easy dismissal of the value of other cultures—*they* will be acceptable when *they* become like *us*. A 1929 editorial in the *Review* proposes that rather than forcing the "foreign born," in this case Ukrainians and Finns, into segregation, "the first step toward making them good Canadians is to befriend them. Then they will be inclined to listen sympathetically to our advocacy of British and Canadian ideas" (Aug. 10, 1931, 2). This is a clear example of what Robert Budde refers to as "Canadian Anglocentric and Assimilationist Cultural Rhetoric," which posited the cultural superiority of the *we* and proposed the assimilation of the others into the seemingly better values and practices of the Anglo majority (2004).[13]

Frequently, demonstrations of racial ambivalence can be found in the *Review*. A "humanist" editorial claims, "The Heart of Humanity Beats Alike Regardless of Hue"—"Humanity is essentially the same the world over, whether the skin be yellow, or brown or white" (Feb. 12, 1931, 2). Yet, in the same year the *Review* prints "fearful" headlines like "BROWN MEN TO RULE THE WORLD, CLAIM OF FILIPINO LEADER" (Jan. 24, 1931, 1). The newspaper carefully couched the story of an attempt by the African Brotherhood of America to buy land in Ancaster, Ontario (near Niagara), for the purpose of building a hospital, orphanage, and old age home. No editorial comment is made about the burning cross found on the property, nor any remark when "Col. E.W. Clifford, one of the Ancaster commissioners, says the authorities were doing their best to stop the proposal, and planned sending a delegation to Toronto to wait on the Provincial Secretary, Hon. Leonard Macaulay to see what can be done about the matter" (May 6, 1931, 3). By May 12 the *Review* reports that Ancaster managed to prevent the building project by quickly rezoning the land to prevent the erection of hospitals within the village boundaries.

For Ella Shohat and Robert Stam, "Eurocentrism," the myth of the west, conceives of itself as "a single 'universal' regime of truth and power" in which "colonialist institutions attempted to denude peoples of the richly textured cultural attributes that shaped communal identity and belonging, leaving a legacy of both trauma and resistance" (1994, 16–17). They argue that Eurocentrism is both "a discourse and a praxis" (19)—both of which come through in the newspapers of the time. For example, in the City News section of the *Review* non-Anglo-Saxons were routinely identified by ethnic background when arrested for crimes ranging from public drunkenness to assault or gambling, while Anglo-Saxons were not.[14] Not once is any Anglo-Saxon identified as such, appearing instead as a name without a race or the race that has no race. It also was not uncommon for the *Review* to print a laudatory story about a black lawyer, teacher, or athlete on the front page and a racist cartoon a few pages later (Mar. 25, 1929).

The *Record* often indulged in sensational "fear headlines" concerning race. Chinese immigrants are suspect in numerous articles, Eastern Europeans particularly after the Communist Revolution, and Italians are associated with various crimes including bootlegging, violence, and a rash of bombings (exploding stills) that arose from time to time in Niagara Falls. Chinese immigrants—a small population in Niagara Falls, about whom little has been written—are frequently suspected of engaging in the white slave trade while sensational headlines discuss the peril of Europeans and white missionaries during the Boxer Rebellion (1900) in China. Orientalism was at

MYSTERIOUS BILLY SMITH
GoT WALCOTT'S GOAT BY
NIBBLING AT THE TOP
OF HIS HEAD..

FIGURE 13.5 White on Black
boxing match. *Niagara Falls
Evening Review*, Mar. 25, 1929

its height in this period with, among other things, the great popularity of
Sax Rohmer's Dr. Fu Manchu novels (1913). One story in the *Review*, with
a boxed headline highlighted in large, bold font, exclaims that Niagara is
home to a "White Slave Plot: fourteen girls missing in district" (Nov. 2,
1927). A number of these girls were subsequently found dining in a Chinese
restaurant and the Chinese owners were arrested; later it was determined
that the young women were merely having dinner and the Chinese proprietors were set free, but the story by that time had been relegated to the
back pages of the paper, and no headlines announced the innocence of those
arrested.

Frequently in this era, the newspapers perpetuate the myth that the
United States exclusively is home not only to the Ku Klux Klan but other anti-
black racism and violence, while Canada would seem to have a more exem-
plary record on this score. This has been a persistent Canadian myth perhaps
beginning with Upper Canada's abolition of slavery between 1793 and 1819

and support of the Underground Railroad. The newspapers often cite examples of racial violence and lynching in American cities, decrying any attempt by the Klan to infiltrate Canada. At the same time, the *Record* expresses disapproval of a group of former slaves from Oklahoma wanting to escape racism in the United States and relocate in Manitoba on the grounds that black farmers could never survive the freezing temperatures of that province, and also because white farmers were upset about this migration (Apr. 27, 1911, 1). The paper reports, "Churches are opposed to the movement and the Dominion Government similarly regards it. It is recognized that the climate of Western Canada is unsuitable for negroes, and every effort will be made by organizations interested in keeping them in the South to show the folly of their attempting to make a livelihood in this country" (May 30, 1911, 1). In the end, the Canadian government prevented most of them from coming.[15]

Small as it was, Niagara Falls had its share of racial difficulties with a prosperous, well-placed, and largely Anglo-Saxon establishment seeing itself as the mainstream, with their views expressed as the implicit *we* of the newspaper. But newspapers are made up of a complex of discourses and social forces, driven not only by the voice of a cultural elite with its suppressions and absences, but by numerous voices seeking to be heard, as well as the need to court readers and sell papers. No clear voice spoke for the "others" in the period up to the 1930s, and few letters to the editor were published. Others are largely absent in the pages of the Niagara Falls, Ontario, papers, except when breaking the law or being colonized; however, others do appear in the advertisements for increasingly successful Italian and Jewish businesses and for movies at the local theatres, especially the Tivoli (1927–31), known pejoratively as "the Garlic," located in the Ferry Street area where early Italian, Jewish, and Black families settled. Social columns in the newspaper occasionally noted a meeting of an ethnic organization, although this in itself indicates a kind of separation. Male ethnic names and sometimes photographs did appear in the Sports Section, particularly spectacular successes like black heavyweight boxing champion Jack Johnson, popularly referred to as "Big Smoke Jack Johnson," who defeated, among others, Canadian Tommy Burns (Dec. 26, 1908). However, there was considerable controversy, both in Canada and the United States, over whether the movies of Johnson's very popular fights should be shown, since the sight of a black boxer beating a white opponent was considered distasteful, and perhaps dangerous.[16]

DRAWING CONCLUSIONS

Given this state of affairs, the popularity of the minstrel show in Niagara Falls becomes clearer. As Lott and others argue, the minstrel show was one of the first indigenous forms of American popular entertainment—not Canadian in origin at all, but popular nonetheless in its local manifestations. Shohat and Stam, as well as Lott, while pointing to the Americanness of this form, also note that all Eurocentric societies have tended to portray others, particularly black people, as licentious, sexual, and rebellious, safely transferring their own illicit desires upon the other. All cite the symbolism of the popular practice of "blackening up" the face before committing acts of riot and rebellion "directed both against authority and, sometimes, against Blacks" (Shohat and Stam 20, Lott 89–107). Lott notes that white performers and audiences took a "ludic, transgressive glee" in minstrel performances (77). In a small city such as Niagara Falls, clearly accommodating, but not always happily, influxes of new immigrants with new ideas and different cultures, the minstrel show not only provided a socially approved form of community activity and an accepted way to express racism and fear outside of official discourses, but also expressed covert sexual desire and poked fun at authority.

In the course of this research, we interviewed several people who produced, directed, and performed in minstrel shows. We have been surprised by what has been said, and not said, in the interviews. The interviewees have all been elderly, and all but one white. No one, save for the one African-Canadian interviewee, Wilma Morrison, long-time volunteer at the Norval Johnson Heritage Library in Niagara Falls, expressed any discomfort with the shows.[17] On the contrary, all remember the shows with great fondness and recalled the performances as innocent fun for charitable purposes and the delight of local audiences. No one expressed a racist view; in fact, the issue of race was hardly mentioned. This absence or denial is not specific to Niagara Falls alone, but it is Eurocentric, and unthinkingly so.[18] However, odd moments emerged: Monsignor Ferrando, long retired from his duty as St. Ann's parish priest and an experienced producer of minstrel shows, began his interview by saying, "Oh yes, we did many minstrel shows but it was all very clean"—we had not asked anything about the content of the shows at this point. One woman (preferring anonymity for this anecdote) told us of an act gone wrong where she was supposed to begin a mock striptease in a minstrel show. A missed cue by another performer left her with little to do but begin to disrobe, clearly enjoying both the moment and the retelling of it. Bob Lamb told us of a show where the performers aimed jokes at the pillars of the church; he enjoyed this ribbing (a convention of blackface scripts) although the butts of the jokes apparently did not and the practice was "discontinued" in later shows.

These stories all point to what else goes on under the guise of an evening of fun and song. Blackening the face seemingly freed the performer to say and do things that would not be acceptable otherwise. In fact, audiences returned year after year to savour the skewering and merriment of these shows through conventions familiar to them. Blackface as a form was a means to express racist views "all in fun" and to escape a racist past by absenting the idea of racial discrimination and slavery, depicting black characters as happy and content in stereotypical roles. The explicit issue of race seems to be "disappeared" from the minstrel shows in Niagara Falls by local newspapers and by our interviewees, although it is clearly present but suppressed or shaped into different forms. The reaction to an influx of racial "others" in the community, and some general discontent and resistance, are an important part of this phenomenon.

Cross-border vaudeville tours brought blackface to Niagara Falls and spurred the appetite for amateur minstrel shows on the Canadian side. In specific instances, there were cross-border collaborations with American groups. The 1934 *Phunny Phollies and Minstrels,* presented in Niagara Falls, New York, at the Gorge Terminal Auditorium, was a showcase of blackface know-how produced under the auspices of Niagara's leading industries and performed by their employees.[19] As a young man newly hired by the Canadian Niagara Power Company, Leonard Heximer was invited to perform in this well-executed extravaganza with full orchestra. Lacking a black demographic of any size, Niagara Falls, Ontario's predominantly WASP population served charity, community pleasure, and popular culture through amateur minstrel shows of more modest scale than the *Phunny Phollies and Minstrels* spectacle. The local newspapers, producers, performers, and audiences all appear to have been blind to the racism in the entertaining minstrel shows. Questioning the racist representation of blackface was primarily a post-1950s wake-up call. With black activism taking hold in the United States, minstrel shows were perceived as anachronisms of a racist past and changing present, as Bob Lamb told us: "By that time it had become very much out of fashion so we just did it as a variety show, basically the same type of thing but only with everybody with a white face … it was just sort of a reminiscence type of thing and that was the end of it. We never did any after that" (interview May 18, 2005).

In *Black Like You* (2006), John Strausbaugh rails at the spectre of a politically correct American culture that has buried discussion of blackface. He blames "extremist multiculturalism" ("racist to the core"), identity politics, and "idealized groupthink" in right-thinking American culture (30). He claims that the very term blackface has become "the *ne plus ultra* of hate speech, and therefore taboo" (14), but establishes ample evidence of the continuation of blackface in current American popular culture, particularly in fringe, carnivalesque stand-up comedy. We would add to such a list the sexist, good ol' boy stunt comedy, *The Dukes of Hazzard* (d. Chandrasekhar, 2005), where a laboratory gag misfires, leaving the white male protagonists covered in soot and playing dumb about their "blackface" appearance until confronted by a group of threatening black men. Playing dumb or claiming licence is common cover for doing blackface. In 2007, Wilfrid Laurier University's Winter Carnival made national news when, as reported in *The Globe and Mail*, a group of white students in blackface parodied Jamaicans (Feb. 24, 2007, M-1). The editor of the student newspaper is quoted as saying, "There's a culture right now that says it's okay to fool around. That's what the Waterbuffaloes were doing … dressed up like Jamaicans" (M-4). This incident was reported widely by the media and posted on YouTube as both entertainment *and* exposé—at once a mixed public response of ignorance and outcry on the subject of blackface today in a cultural moment when ambivalence toward Caribbean-Canadians and other ethnic groups is increasingly present in the popular media. This is the very trajectory that Smulyan perceives in arguing that amateur minstrel shows were a bridge to "popular, participatory entertainment" in the "formation of a consuming middle-class" (2007, 40).

Until our study, Niagara's minstrel show history has not been researched or documented from *any* perspective, except anecdotally in one paragraph in a nostalgic, undated document by a Rotary Club member.[20] In this context, redressing a common public misperception that blackface minstrelsy was incidental or absent in Canada's past became a necessity,[21] to bring into public view how Niagara Falls entertained itself in a period when newspaper discourse and boosterism influenced the public mood and the taste for blackface minstrelsy—apparently without any inkling of the racial degradation.

Thanks to the many people who took time to share stories and memorabilia of their involvement in minstrel shows, to the ever resourceful Andrew Porteus and helpful staff at the Niagara Falls Public Library, as well as Lynne Prunskus and Edie Williams, Brock University Special Collections, to Wilma Morrison of the Norval Johnson Heritage Library, and to graduate student research assistants Dilek Mutlu, Olga Klimova, and Joanna Robinson.

NOTES

1 For over sixty years F.H. Leslie was a highly respected publisher, citizen, and promoter of Niagara Falls. In 1914, he started the city's second daily paper, then in 1918 purchased *The Daily Record* (the "opposition" daily "in a one-paper field") and merged the two into the *Niagara Falls Evening Review*. In 1960 Leslie recollected, "For many years I wrote all the editorials, did reporting, was advertising manager at times, also circulation manager." A long-time Rotarian, Leslie was appointed chair of the Rotary International Advisory Board in 1940, "with jurisdiction over the whole dominion" (*Review*, 1960, Feb. 4). Following three generations of family ownership, in 1973 the paper was sold to the Thomson chain—a corporate pattern subsuming many small newspapers. For subsequent owners, see endnote 9 in "'Hollywoodization,' Gender, and the Local Press in the 1920s: The Case of Niagara Falls, Ontario," in this volume.

2 Our sources have been the local newspapers: *The Daily Record*, *Niagara Falls Evening Review*, Welland *Telegraph*, Welland *Tribune*, and St. Catharines *Standard*—and archival documents, interviews, memorabilia, and fieldwork.

3 See Paul Moore's study in this volume, "Early Movie-Going in Niagara: From Itinerant Shows to Local Institutions, 1897–1910," for an account of the very first film screenings in the Niagara Region in the late 1800s.

4 The Web Theatre, built on the site of Kick's Hotel (at 1956 Main Street in the south end of Niagara Falls), was fitted with sound technology by the Biamonte family and reopened as the Hollywood Theatre in 1931. Under the Canadian Theatres Group (Zahorchak family), it was renovated and re-opened in 1957 as the Princess Theatre. The theatre's closing coincided with the opening of the Niagara Square Cinemas in 1977. Today the little-used building is known as the Serbian Cultural Centre.

5 See Bean, et al. (1996), Knight (2002), Lhamon Jr. (1998), Lott (1993), Mahar (1999), Phinney (2005), Toll (1978), Zanger (1974).

6 A darker interpretation is that the "black" stranger's displacement within an Irish minstrel show embodies the ethnic slurs endured by Catholics and Italians in Niagara Falls. For discussion of the "black Irish" myth, see www.darkfiber.com/blackirish. For a gloss on slurs against Italians, see "The Racial Slur Database—Italian" at www.rsdb.org//search?q=italian&sprt=reasons, accessed Sept. 30, 2009.

7 See "Hollywoodization," in this volume, for discussion of boosterism.

8 The Capitol Theatre was demolished in 1964 to make way for the Lincoln Trust Company head office. Today, a Toronto-Dominion/Canada Trust bank occupies the site at 4463 Queen Street, Niagara Falls, Ontario.

9 Callithumpian means "a noisy boisterous band or parade" (*Merriam-Webster Online Dictionary*, Oct. 21, 2008). Callithumpian bands paraded through the streets to promote touring, and sometimes local, minstrel shows.

10 The annual July 12 Orange Day parades in Ontario celebrated Protestant King William of Orange's defeat of Catholic forces in the Battle of the Boyne in Ireland (1690). Today such parades have all but disappeared except in a few small communities in Ontario.

11 Barrington Walker is professor of history at Queen's University, Kingston. He delivered the paper "Jim Crow in Canada" at the Two Days of Canada conference on the theme Race and Identity in Canada, Brock University, Nov. 2–3, 2005.

12   Historically, in this period the border between Niagara Falls, Ontario, and Niagara Falls, New York, was extremely open. Both cities recognized, politically, culturally, and socially, that they were often substantially closer to each other than to other cities in their own countries.

13   On April 12, 1911, a bold headline appears on the front page of the *Record*: "NEW IMMIGRATION METHODS: Canadian Replicas of English Towns, Families Re-united." The article praises the government of Manitoba, which was trying to attract English immigrants because it is "in the interest of each town and of the Dominion that as many persons of British nationality as possible should be attracted to Canada to prevent the English race being swamped by foreigners who are daily pouring into this country." The encouragement of the families of British immigrants is seen as the best way of ensuring that new Canadian cities and towns will develop along the model of the mother country. Although the *Record*'s "official" statements on immigration seem to imply that all are welcome, some were more welcome than others.

14   This practice makes it appear that to be an Anglo-Saxon in this period is "normal," and that Anglo-Saxons do not have an ethnicity.

15   The Saturday May 6, 2006, *Globe and Mail* reported the third in a series of violent racist incidents in Halifax, Nova Scotia, that week. Arsonists burned a valuable black archive and community centre. One of the officials of the archive commented, "When I saw it burning it looked like something from Alabama"—here again, comparing Canadian racism with the American experience.

16   These articles about Johnson appear throughout the *Daily Record* in 1910 and 1911.

17   The Norval Johnson Heritage Library is located next door to the R. Nathanial Dett British Methodist Episcopal Church (a designated historical site) on Peer Street in Niagara Falls. Despite numerous attempts by Morrison, and by us, we were unsuccessful in getting interviews with the few remaining elderly black members of the community. Morrison informally speculated that they likely did not wish to talk about the past, and especially about minstrel shows (which they would not have attended).

18   In an informal conversation about local minstrel shows, a woman from nearby St. Catharines, the largest city in the Niagara Region, remarked, "Oh, I remember as a child that we [white people] couldn't go to those picnics at Port Dalhousie." In this completely unprompted and telling response, she took it for granted that we knew the picnics in question—namely, the annual Emancipation Day celebrations that drew large crowds of black people to Port Dalhousie from Buffalo and Toronto and beyond. From her perspective, it was white people who were discriminated against in this instance.

19   The employee-performers represented the following companies from the American and Canadian sides of the border: Niagara Falls Power Company, Niagara Gorge Railroad Company, Niagara Electric Service Corporation, Niagara Junction Railway Company, Canadian Niagara Power Company, and Niagara Gray Bus Line.

20   The Niagara Falls Rotary Club produced annual minstrel shows from the 1910s through the 1930s at least. In an undated document, *Rotary—An Appraisal,* club historian E.H. Brown writes: "In other years, we have put on minstrel shows,

each playing two nights to S.R.O. houses. Never has there been a finer brand of camaraderie than was experienced at the minstrel practices. Past District Governor Willox directed the shows until other Rotary duties prevented, and the more recent shows were directed by Past President J. Reg Matthews. Each did a fine job" (7).

21 A prime example is the Burnt Cork: Traditions and Legacies of Minstrelsy International Symposium held at the University of Toronto, March 28–29, 2008, featuring diverse presentations and performance, displaying the range and richness of blackface study as local and transnational topic.

WORKS CITED

Bean, Annemarie, James V. Hatch, and Brooks McNamara, eds. *Inside the Minstrel Mask: Readings in Nineteenth-Century Blackface Minstrelsy.* Hanover, NH, and London: Wesleyan University Press/University Press of New England, 1996.

Budde, Robert. "Codes of Canadian Racism: Anglocentric and Assimilationist Cultural Rhetoric." In Cynthia Sugars, ed., *Home-Work: Postcolonialism, Pedagogy, and Canadian Literature.* Ottawa: University of Ottawa Press, 2004: 245–56.

de Certeau, Michel. *The Practice of Everyday Life*, trans. Steven Rendall. Berkeley: University of California Press, 1988.

Gura, Philip F. "America's Minstrel Gaze." *The New England Quarterly* 72:4 (Dec. 1999), 602–16.

Knight, Arthur. *Disintegrating the Musical: Black Performance and American Musical Film.* Durham and London: Duke University Press, 2002.

Ferrando, Reverend Monsignor Vincent J. "Killarney Bound" script. Niagara Falls, ON: Knights of Columbus (April 23, 1953).

Hamm, Charles. *Yesterdays: Popular Song in America.* New York: Norton, 1979.

Lenton, Gerald Bartley. *The Development and Nature of Vaudeville in Toronto from 1899–1915.* University of Toronto (unpublished dissertation), 1983.

Lhamon, Jr., W.T. *Jump Jim Crow: Lost Plays, Lyrics, and Street Prose of the First Atlantic Popular Culture.* Cambridge, MA: Harvard University Press, 2003.

———. *Raising Cain: Blackface Performance from Jim Crow to Hip Hop.* Cambridge, MA: Harvard University Press, 1998.

Lott, Eric. *Love and Theft: Blackface Minstrelsy and the American Working Class.* New York: Oxford University Press, 1993.

Macherey, Pierre. *Theory of Literary Production.* London and Boston: Routledge and Kegan Paul, 1978.

Mahar, William J. *Behind the Burnt Cork Mask: Early Blackface Minstrelsy and Antebellum American Popular Culture.* Urbana and Chicago: University of Illinois Press, 1999.

Phinney, Kevin. *Souled America: How Black Music Transformed White Culture.* New York: Billboard Books, 2005.

Shohat, Ella, and Robert Stam. *Unthinking Eurocentrism: Multiculturalism and the Media.* New York and London: Routledge, 1994.

Smulyan, Susan. *Popular Ideologies: Mass Culture at Mid-Century*. Philadelphia: University of Pennsylvania Press, 2007.

Strausbaugh, John. *Black Like You: Blackface, Whiteface, Insult and Imitation in American Popular Culture*. New York: Penguin Group (USA), 2006.

Toll, Robert C. "Behind the Blackface: Minstrel Men and Minstrel Myths." *American Heritage* 29:3 (1978), 93–105.

Watkins, Mel. "Foreword." In Annemarie Bean, James V. Hatch, and Brooks McNamara, eds., *Inside The Minstrel Mask: Readings in Nineteenth-Century Blackface Minstrelsy*. Hanover, NH, and London: Wesleyan University Press/ University Press of New England, 1996.

Zanger, Jules. "The Minstrel Show as Theater of Misrule." *Quarterly Journal of Speech* 60:1 (1974), 33–38.

ELECTRICITY FROM NIAGARA FALLS
Popularization of Modern Technology for Domestic Use

NORMAN R. BALL

INTRODUCTION

In the early decades of the twentieth century, readily available electricity generated by the waters of the Niagara River didn't just sell itself.[1] Various groups had to be sold on the use of electricity. People had to learn why they might want electricity and what they could do with it. In this study I begin by establishing why electricity at Niagara Falls was so controversial and provide some necessary background to attitudes toward electricity in the Niagara Frontier,[2] then examine how it entered mainstream life, particularly the lives of women in the home. My interests here should lend a deeper understanding of the history of one of the world's great tourist destinations.

The Canadian Niagara Power Company pioneered large-scale hydroelectric generation at Niagara Falls, Ontario, and in 1905 the Rankine Generating Station started producing electric power for regional customers.[3] At that time Canadian Niagara had the world's largest generators, turbines, and electrical production capacity, and pioneering companies had to do everything possible to stimulate demand for electricity in order to recoup their heavy capital investments. As part of this process, Canadian Niagara launched a clearly defined strategy aimed at promoting greater use of electricity in the home. They succeeded in popularizing electricity for home use—in the kitchen and wherever one ate electrically prepared meals. Canadian Niagara's efforts to win women over to electricity began with advertising, special offers, and electric cooking demonstrations, and culminated in the showroom and cooking school that opened in the new company headquarters in Fort Erie, Ontario, in 1928.

Technological change occurs within a context, and earlier events had helped create an atmosphere of controversy and mistrust of electricity generated at Niagara Falls. By the 1890s, when technology emerged that would invite investment in large-scale hydroelectric power generation at Niagara Falls, the Falls had suffered through decades of rancorous debate over the future of North America's most heavily visited natural site. Should the Falls be primarily a scenic wonder and site for spiritual rejuvenation? Or should it be a centre for massive industrial development along with tawdry, carnival-like tourism? In the 1880s, after enduring years of organized pressure, the State of New York and the Province of Ontario succumbed and each established a park, at Niagara Falls, Ontario, and Niagara Falls, New York. However, neither park answered the basic question that bedevilled Niagara: Could beauty, some semblance of nature, and enjoyable mass-tourist experiences coexist with industrial development at the Falls?[4] The Ontario park did not receive any government funding and desperately needed to sell hydroelectric power generating rights to finance a free park for tourists. But the prospect of large generating stations, reduced water flow over the Falls, and images of overhead power lines reignited smouldering resentments over the future of Niagara Falls, Ontario. There was more. In the early 1890s, technology was changing so quickly that disagreement continued over the type of technology to use. The financial stakes were very high and a brutal public scare campaign, launched by Thomas Edison, which included electrocuting live animals, raised public fears. In short, Niagara Falls, Ontario, was already a very controversial place by the mid- to late nineteenth century. The prospect of electricity generated from the waters of Niagara was misunderstood and feared, circumstances that made the potential use of electricity in the home a daunting promotional task.

In choosing to explore the culture of domestic electricity through the Canadian Niagara Power Company and its customers in places such as Niagara Falls, Bridgeburg, Fort Erie, Ridgeway, and Crystal Beach, I am expressing a strong belief in the value of cultural studies based on regional experiences with technology. Such studies yield a more nuanced understanding of social and technological change than do the macroscopic studies of provincial or national trends. Regional studies remind us that in a societal context, technology is less about devices themselves and more about what happens when technology becomes part of a community and daily life.

THE ROCKY ROAD TO POWER FROM THE FALLS

When Father Hennepin first encountered the Falls in 1678, they were so huge, so loud, so mist-shrouded, and so dissimilar to anything he had experienced, that exaggeration was the only tool to capture what he had seen and experienced. He wasn't, as some would have it, the first of many Niagara liars, but the first of many robbed of their rational faculties by the power of Niagara. Although the Falls were impressive to look at, they were an economically disastrous impediment to navigation. If only there were waterwheels equal to Niagara, the water could be turned into money. Even smaller wheels turned by tiny fractions of Niagara's flow promoted industrial growth, particularly on the American side. With more industry and more tourism, complaints intensified by the 1830s and continued to grow. Some complained about the bad roads to get to the Falls and trees that obscured the view.

American river and Falls frontage property had been auctioned off to promote development and it certainly succeeded. Americans were criticized for the mills, factories, and assorted shoddy workshops that littered the landscape and whose outfalls dribbled down the walls of the Niagara Gorge in full sight of tourists in Canada. Niagara Falls, New York, specialized in industrial ugliness, with a dash of tawdry tourism.

In Canada, things were different. A strip of Falls and river frontage the width of one surveyor's chain (66 feet) was reserved to the Crown and, with a few exceptions, was supposedly unavailable for legal occupancy or business development—though the niceties of land ownership or legal leases did little to interfere with business. While it had some industry, the Ontario side of Niagara specialized in hassling, and sometimes abusing, tourists. It was not factories that made people angry—it was the touts and shysters who focused single-mindedly on fleecing tourists, even beating up visitors who did not pay sufficient money in fares, entrance fees, tips, or, most outrageously, exit fees to leave supposedly free attractions. A royal commission looked into the abuse of tourists at Niagara Falls in 1873.[5] The evidence was damning and the recommendations were sound. Curiously, the document was never published and little changed.[6]

For most of the nineteenth century, visitors who came to see one of the wonders of the world found instead unsightly industry on the American side and were harassed by dishonest drivers, guides, and businessmen with their hired thugs on the Canadian side.[7]

Spurred by intense and protracted public pressure from both sides of the Atlantic, matters came to a head in the 1880s, with the creation of public parks on either side of the Niagara River. In the United States, where the river frontage had long since been auctioned off, the state repurchased

FIGURE 14.1 Scenic river view with polluting factory outfalls in background. c. late 1800s. Courtesy of author

appropriate property for what would become the New York State Reservation at Niagara Falls and provided it with an annual budget.[8] In Ontario, Premier Oliver Mowat was adamantly opposed to spending public funds on a park but was forced to take action. Rather than putting the new park under the jurisdiction of a government department, he created a commission to oversee the park's operation. It was a cynical yet brilliant move: Mowat had another place for patronage appointments. Better still, even though the provincial government guaranteed debts incurred by the commission, they did not appear in financial statements as government debt. Whereas the New York State Reservation on the American side was adequately funded and provided with land by the state, its Ontario counterpart, the Queen Victoria Niagara Falls Park (QVNFP) Commission, had no government budget and had to find the money to buy up land and existing businesses.[9]

It wasn't easy. The park commission borrowed over half a million dollars before the park officially opened on May 24, 1888, and soon discovered that its revenue projections were hopelessly optimistic. The commissioners desperately needed money; large-scale hydroelectric power generation right inside the park offered a way out of their dilemma.

During the Queen Victoria Niagara Falls Park Commission's first decades, electrical technology was changing at a dizzying pace, comparable to changes in the computer industry during the 1990s. By the 1890s, large-scale plants big enough to do justice to the potential at Niagara Falls seemed feasible. And any company wanting to generate power on the Canadian side of the river would have to deal with the QVNFP Commission, which controlled the land along the river and could lease rights to divert water for power generation.

Electricity also offered a way to solve, or at least manage, another problem. The commission had cleaned up the tourist business inside the park, but outside the park it lacked control over the hackmen who picked up tourists from the wharves or the train station, charged them exorbitant rates, were often rude and uncooperative, did not pay attention to where tourists asked to go, and often delivered them to the worst tourist traps that paid the hackmen for bringing in business. If power could be generated at the Falls, an electric railway from Queenston to Chippawa could bypass the hackmen.

The commission could not find one group to do both things, but eventually found two separate groups of investors, one to build a railway with its own generating station, another to create a large-scale hydroelectric plant to sell power to customers outside the park.[10] With initial annual payments of $10,000 from the Niagara Falls Park and River Railway and $25,000 from the Canadian Niagara Power Company, the QVNFP commissioners faced a brighter future, and the prospect of generating hydroelectric power at Niagara Falls, Ontario, seemed imminent. The electric railway, with its own generating station in the park, moved ahead quickly, but the Canadian Niagara Power Company fell years behind schedule.[11] Nevertheless, both companies faithfully paid their annual rents to the park commission.

Opponents of generating power within the park claimed that the reduced volume of water tumbling over the precipice would make the Falls appear less majestic and that buildings would be a blight on the landscape. Inventor Thomas Alva Edison made the situation even worse in what is known as the War of the Currents. The profitability of Niagara's electric power depended on a large market, and the power-starved industries of Buffalo represented a potential market. That prospect propelled Edison into the most unsavoury crusade of his life. Edison and others had grown rich from his DC (direct current) system. However, because DC power must be generated, transmitted, and used at the same voltage, it would be too inefficient to transmit as far away as Buffalo. The newer AC (alternating current) technology, developed by Nikola Tesla and supported by George Westinghouse, was the answer. It could be generated at one voltage, increased to a higher voltage for efficient, cost-effective transmission and then, many miles away, stepped down to a lower voltage for safe use by customers.[12]

The War of the Currents was a dirty war, with Edison arguing that AC was more dangerous than DC. His supporters went so far as to stage public electrocutions of animals by AC and prevailed upon prison authorities at Sing Sing Prison to execute condemned criminals with high-voltage AC power. When Tesla and Westinghouse won the contract for lighting the 1893 Columbian Exposition in Chicago, Edison tried to block them by claiming patent infringement on a light socket design. Tesla and Westinghouse found another design. In the end, the dazzling lighting of the Great White Way at the exposition showed the world that AC had won the day. The battle eventually ended when Edison quietly adopted AC.

The early power companies in Niagara Falls, Ontario, built attractive buildings, and people realized that hydroelectric power was here to stay. Although the Columbian Exposition in Chicago in 1893 enhanced the public image of electricity, the 1901 Pan American Exposition in Buffalo was just as dazzling and had even greater local relevance. The big question was no longer choosing between a scenic waterfall and generating electricity; rather, it was about deciding how much water went to each activity. Public interest in electricity was high, and when the Canadian Niagara Power Company's generating station (now Rankine Station) opened in 1905, complete with the world's largest turbines and purpose-built viewing area, visitors flocked to see where electricity came from, even writing ahead for assurances they would be admitted and gladly paying the admission charge (which was donated to a local hospital). Visiting dignitaries invariably found the generating station on their itinerary. Technical societies held annual meetings there so members could view the hydroelectric generating facilities as well as visit the usual attractions of the falls. Hydroelectric power at Niagara Falls was certainly part of popular tourist interest.

FROM EXCITING NEW TECHNOLOGY TO WORKADAY ESSENTIAL

What did electricity mean for the people of Niagara Falls and the nearby communities? For a few local residents, electricity meant jobs working for electric companies. For a far greater number, electricity meant the gradual transformation of work and home life that came with the wider use of electricity.

Within the electric industry, the effort to increase power consumption is called "load building." Large-scale electric generating facilities—whether thermal or hydroelectric—required heavy initial investment before any power could be generated, transmitted, and sold. To recover their initial investment, generating companies needed to find new customers and new uses of electric power for existing customers. By late 1906, a high-voltage line ran from Niagara Falls, Ontario, to Fort Erie and over the Niagara River to Buffalo. With the lucrative Buffalo market secured, Canadian Niagara could pay more attention to the Canadian market.

In most towns, electricity first showed up in street lighting. On November 14, 1907, the "electric fluid" lit up Fort Erie's arc lamps and the light banished "shadows from the village streets" that were "as brilliantly illuminated as in the full glare of the noon-day sun." The race was on. In 1910, the neighbouring village of Bridgeburg hired Canadian Niagara and surpassed rival Fort Erie, by having more electric lights; all 50 of them were 32-candle-power incandescent lights. Three years later, Fort Erie responded by ordering 25 new 200-candlepower incandescent lamps that outshone Bridgeburg's 32-candlepower lights. Nearby Erie Beach, Ridgeway, and Crystal Beach followed in short order.[13]

Streetlights were only a start. Businesses turned to electricity to modernize and attract more customers. In Bridgeburg, electricity dramatically transformed the newspaper and printing company that started in 1895 as the *Canadian Free Press*. It soon changed its name to the *Bridgeburg Review* and added a sub-edition, the *Fort Erie Times*, for its smaller neighbour. Even before the arrival of electricity the company bought a gasoline-powered drum cylinder press, to replace a hand press and a foot-treadle-powered press. When electricity arrived, the company bought a new press said to be "among the largest of its type built" and one of only two of that size in Canada at the time. This high-capacity press opened the way to new work with time-sensitive jobs, such as printing daily programs for the Fort Erie racetrack. It was a demanding job with only a few hours between receiving the list of horses, jockeys, and other information, and delivering the program to the track.[14]

Individual households presented another load-building front. By 1920, about one in three Canadian homes had been wired, and nearly all urban centres of more than 5,000 residents had power, mainly used for electric lighting. Appliances that we now take for granted were rare—the electric iron was the only appliance that was well established at that time. Bigger and more appliances were clearly the key to greater electric power use in the home.

When the Canadian Electrical Association (CEA) held its two-day summer meeting at Alexandria Bay, New York, in 1919, A. Monro Grier of Canadian Niagara presided over the Commercial Light and Power Sales Committee deliberations, which concentrated on encouraging greater electric power consumption in the home. Delegates agreed that selling major appliances to the well-to-do was not difficult, but building a mass market meant selling to households in all income ranges. Here there were parallels to the early automobile industry: cars were for the affluent until Henry Ford introduced the first affordable automobile. Now the electrical industry was waiting for the "Ford of the Electric Range Business" that could be readily "sold to people of very moderate means, such as mechanics, factory workers, etc." for about sixty dollars.[15]

One of the CEA members from Trois-Rivières, Quebec, explained that his company extended credit to purchase stoves over a period of time and attracted some customers, but the most important development was rethinking the question of how to attract new buyers. The marketing department stopped trying to sell expensive ranges to new buyers and concentrated on selling "a two-plate cooker, which is a rather cheap proposition, with a little portable oven to be used on top, as an entering wedge. When once these are installed and used, the lady of the house will not go back to any other method of cooking, and she will, some way, persuade her husband to put in a larger range when she has demonstrated to him that she cannot do the necessary cooking on the small two-plate burner."[16]

The industry had hit on something important: "It is electric *cooking* rather than the electric *stove* itself that we are selling these days."[17] Sell electric cooking and then let rising expectations lead to sales for more expensive ranges. Electric stoves offered obvious advantages: electromechanical thermostats ensured better heat control, and better-insulated ovens produced less heat in an already hot kitchen. Electric stoves were easy to keep clean, did not emit smoke, and did not need coal or wood hauled into the kitchen and stored.

Decisions to adopt technology are heavily driven by perceived advantages and comfort. In this case, one CEA delegate suggested the electric industry follow the gas industry, which had set up programs aimed at "educating their customers how to use gas stoves." The same delegate had learned "from agents who sell electric stoves that the great fault with all the people who use them is that they have been accustomed to using gas stoves, and they start to use electric stoves the same way."[18] Shortly after this conference, the Canadian Niagara Power Company under the leadership of A. Monro Grier entered a new line of business: selling domestic appliances and educating their customers on how to use them.

The electric bill delivered in late November 1922 to Canadian Niagara customers included an invitation "to attend a special demonstration of electric cooking during the week beginning Monday, Nov. 27th." Separate demonstrations in Fort Erie, Bridgeburg, and nearby Ridgeway ensured that every customer could attend without travelling far. Each location offered customers the same chance to "spend a pleasant hour learning about clean heat." Electric stoves were still so rare that the company stressed the importance of experience: "You must see an electric range actually cooking to appreciate its value." Seeing was part of the experience of electricity; helping women feel comfortable was another part of the experience. Although anyone could attend, it was a women's event, "conducted by courteous women who will cheerfully explain how electric cooking conserves food, lightens labor and economizes both time and money." There would be no

FIGURE 14.2 Ad in the *Fort Erie Times*, Apr. 27, 1928. Fort Erie Historical Museum

fast-talking, intimidating hucksters. The purpose was to encourage long-term change based on understanding how to "enjoy the comfort and economy of clean electric cooking," and thinking about other ways electricity would improve home life.

Of course, money had to be considered, and Canadian Niagara announced that all customers would receive a 25 percent reduction in the cost of electric current in the home. There was more. Anyone who acted quickly and ordered a new Westinghouse Electric Range before December 15, 1922, received free installation and connection to existing house wiring. What about range buyers in an unwired house? These customers could buy the range on a time-payment plan and Canadian Niagara would "pay your contractor for wiring your house, and bill you for the amount in twelve monthly payments." To those who wanted to enter the electrical world with lighting but not yet buy a range, Canadian Niagara offered a time payment plan for the cost of wiring alone. At the time, deferred payments or time payment plans were new in retail sales. (Historically, this form of payment—along with new paint technology that gave customers a colour choice other than black, and the design genius of Harley Earl—allowed General Motors to jump ahead of Ford in sales.)

Canadian Niagara emphasized comfort and trust as factors in adopting electric appliances. In one early mailing campaign, the company sent postcards that could be returned for more information on electric range and house wiring offers. Part of the message read, "If you are acquainted with one of our employees and prefer to talk with him, put his name below." The name might be someone from a local church or service club, a neighbour or the meter reader if a customer already had basic service. A company in a small market could offer this kind of personal service.

In October 1923 the company emphasized the experience of electric cooking in this ad:

Come and See Electric Cooking!
Taste the products of an Electric Range—or bring your
Roast, bread or pie and have it roasted in a
Westinghouse Electric Range
The Clean, Cool, Carefree Way to Perfect Results! (*Fort Erie Times*)[19]

Now customers could take something home that had been cooked electrically, a way of convincing people to adopt electricity. To help make 1923 the year of the electric Christmas, another Canadian Niagara ad suggested choosing from one or more of four modest gift suggestions: an electric iron; a two-slice, one-side-at-a-time electric toaster; an elaborate coffee maker; or a single-element hot plate.[20]

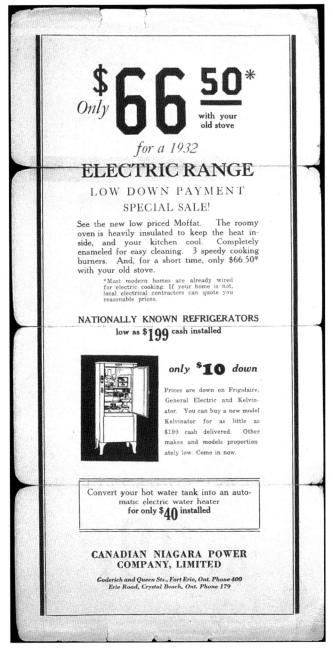

FIGURE 14.3 Likely a handbill delivered to local customers in 1932. John Burtniak collection

Five years later, on April 2, 1928, Canadian Niagara opened its new electric service centre and headquarters at the corner of Queen and Goderich streets in Fort Erie. It joined the previous year's opening of the Peace Bridge (connecting Fort Erie and Buffalo) as another symbol of Fort Erie's modernity. An understandably proud reporter for the *Fort Erie Times* proclaimed it "one of the most beautiful electric service buildings on the continent" and declared, "Its graceful tower fittingly serves as a symbol of our future."[21]

Some older Fort Erie residents remember that children would run into the building on a hot afternoon, gulp down ice-cold water from the refrigerated drinking fountain, and race out just as quickly. Others recalled the wonderful Christmas lighting and special displays in the plate-glass windows that always seemed better than anything anywhere else, even in Toronto. Others remember the beautiful marble floor, the fine woodwork, and the brass tellers' cages. Some of the most cherished memories are about the showroom, the demonstration kitchen, and the food, evoking Canadian Niagara's campaign to win more hearts and homes over to living electrically.

When the new Canadian Niagara Service Centre opened in 1928, a newspaper announcement made it seem like a dream world:

> a complete model kitchen ... including every helpful aid from electric dishwasher to cake mixer and ironer. A domestic science expert will be in charge ready to show you their wonderful convenience—and how they relieve you of household drudgery.... In the main foyer with its graceful domed ceiling are displayed charming bridge and table lamps just as you might arrange them in your own home. There too you will find all the newest electric servants designed to do your sweeping and cleaning, washing and ironing, cooking and refrigerating.[22]

But there is a gap between merely viewing a new technology in a showroom, and being ready to buy and use it. The Canadian Niagara Power Company bridged that gap with education, carried out by women trained in branches of domestic science. One such expert was Audrey Troup, who had studied at MacDonald College in Guelph before joining Canadian Niagara as a dietitian in the late 1930s. At a time when few women drove, the dietitians shared a company station wagon. On a home visit to help a customer cook with her new electric stove, Troup might also provide advice on the placement of electric lamps and other domestic uses of electricity. In addition to providing advice and information over the telephone and creating recipes, she conducted surveys of customers' needs and preferences. Dietitians also visited local schools to teach girls about using electricity in the kitchen to make

FIGURE 14.4 Queen Street Service Centre/showroom, Fort Erie, c. 1928. FortisOntario

better and more convenient meals. During World War II, Troup and the other dietitians contributed to the conservation of food by teaching people proper canning techniques.

Audrey Troup helped make the demonstration kitchen a crucial instrument in the campaign to increase domestic use of electricity. The demonstration kitchen was separate from the showroom and displays. Set on a platform two steps above the seating area, it was dominated by two stoves, a sink, and a refrigerator. Sometimes other appliances, such as electric mixers, counter-top ovens, hot plates, and coffee-makers were part of the demonstrations.

Doris Dunn was probably the best-known member of the demonstration kitchen. Known as Aunt Dorrie, she was a commanding, no-nonsense, chain smoker who spent her entire working life with the company. She created memorable feasts for the board of directors that are the stuff of company legend. The cooking classes ceased around 1950, and I have been unable to locate anyone still living who attended them, though Shirley Athoe (retired from Canadian Niagara) remembers that her mother was one of the Fort Erie area women who took classes. Her happy mother would "come home and try the things she had learned."

Women brought recipe cards home after each lesson. The cards were the most important link between Canadian Niagara's cooking school and the prospect of increased electricity sales to homes and thus dependence on electric stoves, refrigerators, mixers, and a growing list of electric appliances. Fortunately, a number of these recipe cards have survived, and they tell a story about applying a new technology to the needs of women in the 1930s and 1940s: preparing weekday family meals, creating Sunday dinners, contributing to church suppers and picnics, or impressing visitors on special occasions. Electricity was built into every recipe, a constant reminder that success as wife, mother, daughter-in-law, homemaker, or hostess depended on electricity.

One didn't just freeze ingredients, one did so "according to directions of electric refrigerator." Ingredients that otherwise might have been beaten by hand were to be stirred "with electric beater." There was even a right way to boil water: "using HIGH heat on surface unit on electric range." Similarly what might have once read as "simmer rhubarb with water until tender," now instructed "using LOW heat of surface unit on electric range." When baking, "bake in electric oven."[23]

THE WORLD IN A BOX OF RECIPE CARDS

About twenty linear inches of surviving recipe cards fit into an original wooden file box from the 1920s or 1930s and a small cardboard box.[24] All the cards are in subject groupings separated by labelled file dividers, largely organized alphabetically. With the exception of one file divider for "Buying Foods, etc." all of the cards in the cardboard box are for meals: Broiler Meals, Cooker Meals, Oven Meals, One Dish Meals, Roaster Meals. The wooden box is organized by the type of dish or where it fit into the overall meal plan: Desserts—Frozen, Desserts—Puddings, Desserts: Miscellaneous, Drinks, Egg Dishes, Entrees (Croquettes, Fritters, Patties, Ramekins, Timbales), Frostings, Fillings, Glazes, Appetizers (Canapés, Cocktails, etc.), Beverages, Breads—Baking Powder, Bread—Yeast, Cakes, Candies, Cereal Dishes, Cheese Dishes, Cookies, Fish, Fruits, Meats, Poultry and Game, Preserving—Canning, Preserving—Jellies, Jams, Marmalades, Preserves, Preserving—Pickles, Relishes, Spices, Salads, Salad Dressings, Sandwiches, Sauces, Seafood, Soups, Soup Accompaniments, Stuffings, Vegetables.

The recipes are an informative mix of the familiar and the unfamiliar. Icebox cookies (so called because the dough has to be cooled for several hours before it can be sliced and baked) are often linked with the introduction of electric refrigerators in the 1930s,[25] but Canadian Niagara never called them by that name. The Canadian Niagara Cooking School had recipes for Butterscotch Refrigerator Cookies (1930–1931), Refrigerator Neapolitan Cookies (1937–1938), and Fig Refrigerator Cookies (undated). The name "refrigerator cookies" helped people aspire to an electric future.

The cookie recipe reproduced here is a representative example of the recipes used to help women convert to electricity.

Butterscotch Refrigerator Cookies

½ cup shortening
1 cup light brown sugar
1 egg slightly beaten
½ teaspoon vanilla extract
2 cups sifted all-purpose flower
½ teaspoon cream of tartar
½ teaspoon soda
½ cup finely chopped nut meats

Cream shortening, using high speed of electric mixer. Add sugar and beat until creamy, then egg and flavoring. Reduce to low speed; add mixed and sifted dry ingredients; then chopped nut meats. Pack into small bread pan lined with wax paper; chill in electric refrigerator for several hours or over night. Cut into two or three strips, and slice thinly. Place one inch apart on greased baking sheet. Bake in preheated electric oven. Temperature: 400 degrees (F.) Time: 8–10 minutes

Yield: 5 to 8 dozen cookies.

Specifying the speed of the electric mixer for different operations implied that one needed this appliance to ensure that the cookies turned out properly. Cooks soon discovered that one electric appliance led to another. This recipe specified both temperature and baking time. The Date-Nut Pudding (1935–1936) gives the temperature as 325–400° (F.) and the time as 1 to 2 hours, along with the note that "the variance of temperature and time is noted to show that this recipe may be used with various types of oven meals."

THE APPEAL OF ELECTRICITY IN THE KITCHEN

A close examination of the surviving recipes and other information suggests that there were at least four factors that the company considered important in persuading women to make greater use of electrical appliances in the kitchen. Electricity in the kitchen had to be perceived as economical, convenient, a support to women's roles, and a measure of the smart and up-to-date woman, in the best sense of the words.

Electricity = Economy

Low down payments and low monthly payments provided the illusion of economy. The real test was the cost of electricity. As more people signed up in the 1920s and 1930s, Canadian Niagara reduced the cost per kilowatt-hour. In addition, many cooking school recipes were designed to reduce power consumption. For example, the Strawberry Tartlets recipe called for "low heat of small surface unit of electric range."

The Depression-era recipe for Steamed Green Asparagus with Eggs saved electricity by using the small heating unit and cooking the eggs and asparagus together in the same "deep utensil."[26] Most important, one was to "Cook until steaming, using HIGH heat of small surface unit on electric range; turn switch to LOW until last 10 minutes of cooking; then to OFF and finish with heat stored in unit."[27] Other recipes, such as Steamed Celery Cabbage, used the same electricity-saving technique of doing the final cooking with residual heat stored in the unit."[28] An undated recipe for Butter Steamed Green Beans instructed the cook to cover the beans "with lettuce or moistened cabbage leaves. Place on small surface unit of electric range, using HIGH heat for 8 minutes, turn unit OFF for 20 minutes." The stove was off two and a half times longer than on because, in addition to retaining steam inside the pot, the lettuce or cabbage leaves served as insulation to conserve more residual heat for cooking.[29]

Some recipes even called for a particular type of stove designed to keep heat in, that is, one with a well cooker. In a Mince Meat recipe we find: "place in WELL cooker. Cover cooker. Turn switch to HIGH until steaming vigorously. Turn to LOW and continue cooking for 1 hour. Place in sterilized jars while hot. Seal" (Desserts 1936–37). I remember the well cooker in my mother's first electric stove in Hamilton in the 1950s. It was a top-of-the-line four-burner white porcelain stove with side oven and warming oven, storage drawers, clock, and timer. The front left burner looked just like the other elements, but it could drop down into the stove about ten or twelve inches. This was the "well." The circumference of the top of the special aluminum pot had a flat lip that protruded about three-quarters of an inch and rested on the stovetop. What we called "the pot in the hole" was particularly useful for recipes such as soups, stews, large quantities of potatoes destined for potato salad for church or family picnics, spaghetti or macaroni—nobody used the word pasta in those days—and Christmas puddings. My five-foot-tall mother liked the sunken pot because she could see into it easily and felt it was much safer: kids couldn't knock it over and it stayed still when she was stirring or dishing up from it. In hot weather, it did not heat up the kitchen nearly as much as the other stove elements. The stove was very well insulated, and my father would point out that this arrangement saved electricity.

Being economical meant more than not wasting electricity. By the 1930s growing industrialized food processing had introduced a confusing array of products and advertisements. Behind the divider marked "Buying Foods etc.," the Canadian Niagara Power Company Recipe Card Collection has seventeen instructional cards dedicated to buying food wisely, providing an astounding amount of advice that covers topics such as evaluating advertisements and buying according to nutrition, health, and economy, rather than by habit and custom. The instructional cards included "newer knowledge of nutrition" and food purchasing by category and meals. Food tables conveyed extensive easy-to-follow information on caloric content, organized on the basis of how much of a given item provided 100 calories.

Careful reading of these instructional cards reveals an educational philosophy similar to the recipes: increased knowledge led to greater confidence and a feeling of freedom or independence to make decisions. It was best "to judge quality for yourself" rather than just buying "by grade." And the consumer, not magazines and the advertising industry, could "decide whether you will buy in the sanitary, and more expensive package form, or in bulk and provide your own containers." The "Buying Foods etc." section is another example of the message that it takes more than the purchase of equipment to benefit from electricity in the home. How to adapt to a culture of economy in the broader context of food and electricity was vital.

Electricity = Convenience

New technology tends to be associated with *promises* of convenience while delivering more work and greater inconvenience.[30] The recipe cards collection actually includes ways to reduce women's work. About 40 percent of the cards are for full meals arranged under the following categories: Broiler Meals, Cooker Meals, Oven Meals, One Dish Meals, and Roaster Meals. Although these recipes involved a range of ingredients and almost invariably had more than one course, very few required precooking individual ingredients, and the food cooked on its own for an hour or so. Cooking in only one part of the stove used less electricity than multiple units and threw less heat into the room. The combination of appetizing meals and the relative economy of electricity might help sell an unwilling husband on the need for an electric range.

Women using ranges were among the best advocates for electric cooking. A visit to the home of friends for a delicious meal—including dessert—cooked completely in the oven while people socialized might have led to persuasive discussions on the need for an electric range. Perhaps they ate this oven meal: Canadian Bacon Roast with Pineapple, Smothered Potatoes, Squash Squares au Gratin, and Stewed Fruit. Each uncooked dish could be prepared in advance. Then "Arrange complete meal in cold oven of electric range. Allow space on all sides of utensils for even circulation of heat. Turn oven bottom switch to HIGH heat or BAKE. Temperature: 325 degrees (F.) Time: 1 ½ to 2 hours." Once everything is in the oven, there is nothing further to do except add some final ingredients twenty minutes before mealtime.

Some of the well-cooker meals were ingenious. One involved "Fricassee chicken, 6 onions, peeled, 6 prunes, 6 sweet potatoes, pared, Chocolate Pudding." One would "arrange potatoes on top of chicken in well-cooker, alternately with onions. Add prunes to use as a garnish. Place pudding on top and cover. Turn Switch to High heat until steaming vigorously, then turn to Low. Time 45–60 minutes."[31] It was a remarkably easy one-pot meal, even though the chicken had to be prepared in a skillet first and the chocolate pudding made and poured into a greased mould and covered in wax paper before it went into the well-cooker. Numerous other recipes followed a similar pattern.

Electricity Supports Women's Roles

The adage "a woman's work is never done" expresses the idea that women perform many domestic tasks again and again. Preparing meals, cleaning up, washing, ironing, and mending clothes were part of an endless cycle.[32] Electric irons often represented electricity's first entry into women's work, but cooking electrically brought far more dramatic changes.

In the home, the woman was wife and mother in the nuclear family. Frequently, she was hostess to two extended families—one by birth and one by marriage—as well as friends. Women also took part in large-scale cooking for church socials, picnics, family reunions, weddings, funerals, and other gatherings. Many of the cards from the Canadian Niagara cooking school went beyond recipes to full meal or menu suggestions and instructions that recognized women's varied roles. "School Luncheon Suggestions," for example, offered three separate menus, each of which has additional sandwich options.

A card on "The Filling" for sandwiches began with the observation, "This depends entirely upon your imagination ... start your imagination roving," and listed items such as "highly seasoned ground meat, chicken, ham, onion juice, mayonnaise" or "lobster, crab meat, tuna fish, mayonnaise, plus a bit of lemon juice." Permission to be imaginative was an important part of forward thinking and freedom associated with being a modern electric cook. Sometimes the imagination needed help. Something "Special for the Younger Generation" suggested, "4-H Club Members: Spread circle of bread with cream cheese. Decorate with green ring of green pepper with 4 knobs. Cut out small straight pieces to make the 4-H insignias." Children too young for 4-H might like "animal crackers paired and put together with cream cheese to which a small amount of grated orange rind and cream has been added."

Many recipes for individual dishes make six to eight servings, reflecting the fact that families were bigger than they are today. The numerous dessert and pie recipes prove the prominence of dessert as part of an evening meal, but also imply its competitive importance—particularly true for pies—at extended family gatherings and church suppers. Many women never wavered from "a particular recipe." If someone wanted to try something new, Canadian Niagara offered numerous suggestions. A single recipe card titled "variations of standard cream pie" opened the door to several different pies with a common starting point: butterscotch, chocolate, banana, coconut, pineapple, chocolate chip, and date.

Fillings were important, but reputations rose and fell on pie crusts. Many admired pie-crust makers were rather vague on how they made theirs, and some people—particularly husbands or fathers—found it wise to be equally vague on who made the best crust. For those new to pie-making, the Canadian Niagara cooking school stepped in with advice: "ideas as to what comprises an excellent pie vary with individuals: crust must be light and tender, but may be flaky or crumbly, according to the method employed."[33] The school recognized that "baking methods vary," outlining variables along with the reassuring words, "equally good results may be obtained by any of these methods, when using a reliable, heat-controlled electric oven." Different pastry recipes were supplied,[34] along with advice on the use of lard, butter, and hydrogenated fats as shortening, depending on whether one wanted "flaky tender" or "crumbly tender crust."[35]

The school's instruction went beyond teaching women how to cook. In helping them understand cooking and how to achieve different results, it gave women confidence to try something new. It guided women on the mammoth tasks associated with cooking for large gatherings, with recipes designed to feed fifty people: Cabbage *Maitre d'Hotel*, Potato Salad, Mashed Potatoes, Chicken Salad, Veal Salad, and Health Salad. Quantity recipes for more unusual dishes such as "Raisin Sweet Potato Patties"—to "serve hot as accompaniment to meat"—lent sophistication to a woman's own recipe files.

Electricity = Smart and Up-to-Date

Being smart or up-to-date meant getting beyond the ordinary without being eccentric. Consider the "Waffle Pastry," which the cook was to "bake in preheated electric waffle baker," with the suggestion to "serve as canapés with spreads, or as a short cake with fruit." A note on "richer pastry" might set one apart and perhaps lead a guest to ask for the recipe.

Before the introduction of home refrigerators with freezer compartments, homemade ice cream required hard physical work: cranking the ice cream maker, ice chips, and rock salt that froze the mixture was messy—usually a job for men and any available children. Moreover, ice cream was reserved for special occasions, family picnics, or church socials. The freezer compartment in electric refrigerators made it much easier to prepare ice cream and other frozen desserts such as sherbets and mallobets (sherbets made with marshmallows). A woman who made her own frozen desserts might go one step further with a recipe that put ice cream in the electric oven. The "Pineapple Mint-Ice Cream Pie" called for canned crushed pineapple and sugar to be cooked over "low heat on surface unit of electric range" until syrupy, flavoured to taste with peppermint, coloured green, and poured into a baked pie shell, covered with ice cream, topped with meringue, and "placed in preheated electric oven until brown."

Presentation is important to the culinary arts. In addition to basic instructions for making frozen desserts, the Canadian Niagara Cooking School provided tasteful suggestions for unusual presentations: for sherbets or ices served in "a small orange half-shell ... [c]ut orange in half crosswise; remove all pulp and inner white rind. Chill shells thoroughly in electric refrigerator before filling" (1939–40). To make the meal even smarter, it might have started with "Marinated Mushrooms" served as "Hors d'Oeuvres with salad" (1935–6).

Making ice cream without making a mess, boldly serving frozen desserts in an orange half-shell instead of one's best china, marinating mushrooms for hors d'oeuvres, and attempting dishes your guests had never eaten, these were the kinds of things that modern women did in movies.

CONCLUSION

Once electricity had cleared a number of hurdles, such as opposition to industry at Niagara Falls, the Canadian Niagara Power Company worked to increase home consumption of electricity. Through its cooking school and head office showroom in Fort Erie, the company concentrated on helping local women accept and become skilful in using electricity in the home. Did these efforts actually contribute to greater use of electricity and to electricity becoming an important part of local culture? Or would it have happened anyway? The popular media—magazines, newspapers, film, and radio—equated modernity and electricity so effectively that historian of technology Jane Busch has concluded, "the single most prominent appeal in all the range advertising was to modernity, a subjective quality that sold ranges by connoting fashion and status."[36] In the case of Niagara, with its immense production of electricity, the domestic appeal of electric appliances was highly cultivated in, and for, local communities.

There was something special about Canadian Niagara customers. A 1929 article in the *Niagara Power Service* magazine titled "Canadian Villages Reach High Kilowatt-Hour Average" reveals that one in four domestic customers in Bridgeburg had an electric range, one in five in Fort Erie. The "exceedingly high" average of 1,464 kilowatt-hours of power use per year for Fort Erie households and 1,922 for Bridgeburg was "exceptional, especially in towns of the size of these Canadian villages." The article suggests, "The Slogan 'The Town of Electric Homes' may well be applied to these sister towns located across the river from Buffalo on the Canadian shore."[37] Yet the article fails to mention something that made these figures even more astounding: unlike many other electricity markets, cheap natural gas was readily available in this part of the Niagara area. Indeed, since 1901 Bertie Township had been sending its surplus natural gas to Buffalo by pipeline.

Electric utilities were quick to point out the disadvantages of using coal- or wood-fired kitchen stoves. Because wood and coal had to be carried into the house, and the ashes carried out, the electricity industry painted them as cumbersome and dirty ways to cook. Electric stoves heated up more quickly than coal- or wood-fired stoves, but gas stoves heated up more quickly than coal, wood, or electric. This feature made gas stoves the biggest competitor to electric stoves, particularly if gas was as cheap and plentiful as it was in Bertie township.[38]

Property owners, usually farmers, who let the gas company drill on their land got $50 a year, plus an unlimited gas supply if the company struck gas. Late in life, Mr. Sumner Beam, born in 1898, recalled that when he was a child his family "never had electricity, no electricity at all." Gas had been discovered on a nearby farm. "Why, of course we had gas then in the house. Gas for heating and everything. There was no limit on the amount of gas you could use, and of course a lot of it was wasted … there was no end of it."[39]

Ruth Carver, born in 1903, grew up with coal oil lamps. She and her husband didn't have electricity in the 1920s, but they tried to use technology to reduce her workload. She got a hand-powered washing machine just before the birth of her fifth and sixth children (twins) and "that took a lot of strength. Sometimes I thought I would rather do it by hand, but you'd get along faster, and then I had the hand wringer, too, so I could wring them out. I didn't have to wring by hand." The Depression brought two more children, sixteen months apart, and a gasoline-powered washing machine. The next step up was electric. "When we got the electric in I sure was happy over that! No more having to crank that [gasoline engine] over." Electricity made a great difference in her life: "Sure was a happy day when it came! I think I appreciated the electric motor more than anything."[40] For Ruth Carver and her husband, like so many others, electricity represented a big step in the reduction of a woman's workload.

In 1936 Canadian Niagara electrical janitor Leonard Heximer married Margaret Fretz, a young woman from Ridgeway. They started married life with a stove that Leonard's brother bought for them from Fort Erie's Queen Street Service Centre. When Leonard died, this attractive four-element Moffat with a stovetop oven and timer was still working after over seventy years of use. His estate donated the stove to the Lundy's Lane Historical Museum in Niagara Falls. Shortly before he died, Leonard told me that his brother bought the wedding-gift stove from Canadian Niagara because the company only sold good products and stood behind them with their own repair department and a solid reputation. The stove was a testimony to the belief in the wisdom of buying locally from a company you trusted, and Canadian Niagara was considered trustworthy.

During the research for writing *The Canadian Niagara Power Company Story* (2005), many of the people I interviewed—customers, employees, retirees—stressed the importance of trust and communications in business and daily life. Canadian Niagara's ads and actions reveal much more than the idea of modernity. The company had a particular view of how to reach and shape communities: help people feel comfortable and confident, and let people see for themselves how electricity would affect them. Canadian Niagara's approach to cooking was based on fitting into and meeting community and individual needs rather than fitting people to the technology. In small communities where people knew each other well, word of mouth, trust, and personal contact were more important than in larger communities.

Canadian Niagara did not offer a travelling kitchen road show that came into town to dazzle the locals and then leave. Rather, its kitchen showroom was a permanent local fixture, there year after year. A trusted company and local employer with a reputation for honesty and good service, Canadian Niagara sold good-quality products and stood behind them with their own repair department. There was no need to worry about what would happen if something broke. The company and, with it, electricity and its many domestic uses were part of local culture.

Thanks to friend and colleague John Burtniak for his continuing interest, knowledge, and polite comments. And to my wife, Philippa Campsie, my thanks for her continuing patience and sound editorial advice; and to the Canadian Niagara Power Company whose generous support and access to documents was matched only by its unwavering commitment to telling it like it is. My thanks also to Sandra and Frank Flake for giving me access to the Canadian Niagara recipe cards and to the Canadian Niagara employees and retirees who took me into their confidence and sometimes asked me to turn off my tape recorder.

NOTES

1 The waters of Niagara might refer to all of the water flowing through the Niagara River, which is also an international boundary. Or it might refer to all of the water flowing over the spectacular precipice where two cities called Niagara Falls have grown up, one in New York State and one in the province of Ontario, across the Niagara River.

   The advent of the era of generating power from the waters of Niagara added another meaning or necessary distinction. To produce power, water was taken from the Niagara River upstream of the Falls, directed to penstocks and the turbines that drove electric generators, and then returned to the Niagara River downstream of the Falls. Water diverted for power development reduced the volume of water that could flow over the waterfall. This meant that the waters of Niagara took on two distinct meanings: that which flows over the Falls, or the precipice; and that which is temporarily diverted from the river and does not go over the Falls. This reduction in volume of water going over the Falls, and with it, potential loss of scenic beauty, accounted for much of the opposition to using the waters of Niagara for power development.

   Some call this entire geological feature Niagara Falls. However, Niagara Falls is generally subdivided into the Canadian, or Horseshoe Falls, and the American Falls, which is sometimes seen as two rather than one waterfall. Niagara Falls is often referred to as the Falls, the implication being that it has no equal. Niagara Falls is also the name of the two cities located on either side of the Canada–U.S. border and often is used to refer to the two public parks—one American and one Canadian—at the Falls.

2 Just as the people of the United States of America have co-opted the term America to refer to one of many countries in the Americas, they have also interpreted the term Niagara Frontier to mean only the American side of the Niagara River. A definitive book on both sides of the river clearly sees two frontiers. See John N. Jackson, John Burtniak, and Gregory P. Stein, *The Mighty Niagara: One River, Two Frontiers* (Amherst, NY: Prometheus Books, 2003), 21–25, for a historical introduction to the idea of the Niagara Frontiers. The Niagara Peninsula, which extends as far from Niagara Falls as Hamilton, Ontario, is too large to suggest the area discussed in this study, and, with the advent of regional government, Niagara Region has a geopolitical meaning.

3 This study draws in part on my research of the Canadian Niagara Power Company papers (Archives Canada), for Norman R. Ball, *The Canadian Niagara Power Company Story* (Erin Mills, ON: Boston Mills Press, 2005).

4   The drive that ultimately led to the creation of the New York State Reservation at Niagara Falls, New York, and the Queen Victoria Niagara Falls Park, on the Ontario side, is often referred to as the Save Niagara Movement, though that term was not used until 1905 and refers to the campaign to oppose further reductions in the volume of water diverted from the Falls for production of power. For an introduction to late nineteenth-century dissatisfaction with the state of affairs at Niagara Falls and the creation of public parks, see William Irwin, *The New Niagara: Tourism, Technology, and the Landscape of Niagara Falls 1776–1917* (University Park, PA: Pennsylvania State University Press, 1996). Irwin deals almost exclusively with the United States. See also George Seibel, *Ontario's Niagara Parks 100 Years: A History* (Niagara Falls, ON: Niagara Parks Commission, 1985); Ronald L. Way, *Ontario's Niagara Parks: A History* (Niagara Falls, ON: Niagara Parks Commission, 1946); and Charles M. Dow, *The State Reservation at Niagara: A History* (Albany, NY: J.B. Lyon Co., 1914), which deals with both Canada and the United States. For an excellent compilation and analysis of writing from 1832 to 1914 on preservation of the Falls, see Charles Mason Dow, *Anthology and Bibliography of Niagara Falls* (Albany, NY: J.B. Lyon, 1921), Vol. 2, Chapter XI, "Preservation of the Falls," 1059–74.

5   The events at the Falls itself and those in the town of Clifton, which in 1881 became the town of Niagara Falls, Ontario, were inseparable.

6   Dawna Petsche-Wark and Catherine Johnson, *Royal Commissions and Commissions of Inquiry for the Provinces of Upper Canada, Canada and Ontario 1792 to 1991: A Checklist of Reports* (Toronto: Ontario Legislative Library, 1992) refer to the "Ontario Royal Commission to Inquire Into Alleged Abuses Occurring in the Vicinity of Niagara Falls." The commission was established June 24, 1873. The sole commissioner, Hon. E.B. Wood, submitted his report the same year. It was never published but a handwritten copy survives in the Archives of Ontario, Ontario Government Record Series RG 18-14, Records of the Royal Commission to Inquire Into Alleged Abuses Occurring in the Vicinity of Niagara Falls. Petsche-Wark and Johnson (106–107) also mention a 1960 Royal Commission related to Niagara Falls, which was never published and for which there is no known copy: *Royal Commission re Purchase of Parts of Lot 23 in the Township of Niagara by the Niagara Parks Commission and the Subsequent Resale to Mr. A.A. Schmon and Purchase by Mr. Charles Daley.*

7   This state of affairs on the Canadian side is best described in the report itself and by the evidence and exhibits gathered by Hon. E.B. Wood, sole commissioner for the 1873 *Royal Commission to Inquire Into Alleged Abuses Occurring in the Vicinity of Niagara Falls.*

8   There are many variants of the name, and even documents published by the commissioners were inconsistent. The official name appears to be the New York State Reservation at Niagara Falls; however it is frequently referred to as the New York State Reservation, the State Reservation at Niagara, or the State Reservation at Niagara Falls.

9   There is a prevailing belief that the Queen Victoria Niagara Falls Park Commission, now the Niagara Parks Commission (NPC), is required by the Act establishing it to be financially self-sufficient. There is no such legal requirement; rather the practice was forced upon the NPC by government expectations and tradition.

There is also a prevailing belief that no other parks in Ontario were established using the commission model until the establishment of the St. Lawrence Parks Commission in the 1950s. In fact, Premier Whitney created Burlington Beach Park using the self-funding commission model in 1910, and in 1921 Premier Drury used the same model for the Long Point Park. See Ball, *A Niagara Parks Commission Anniversary History*, forthcoming.

10 For additional detail on various failed attempts to find investors and the eventual arrangements, see Ball, *The Canadian Niagara Power Company Story* (2005), 23–27.

11 Ibid., 23–40. The delay was partially intentional. The American parent company, the Niagara Falls Power Company, had already started generating power in Niagara Falls, New York, and wanted to delay development in Canada until it had solved certain technical problems and to take advantage of the most recent technology at a time of rapid technological change.

12 There were other proposals for transmitting power. One would have used the energy from the falling waters of Niagara Falls to run a compressor to produce compressed air. The compressed air would be sent to Buffalo in hitherto untested high-pressure pipelines, where it would turn the generators in neighbourhood DC power plants.

13 Ball 2005, 93–95.

14 Ibid., 95. In 1932 the *Fort Erie Times*, the *Bridgeburg Review*, and the *Bertie Township Herald* merged to form the *Times-Review*.

15 Canadian Electrical Association, *Proceedings of the Annual Convention*, 1919, 100–101, as quoted in Ball, *The Canadian Niagara Power Company Story* (2005), 112.

16 Canadian Electrical Association, *Proceedings of the Annual Convention*, 1919, 111, as quoted in Ball, *The Canadian Niagara Power Company Story* (2005), 112–13.

17 Ibid., 113.

18 Ibid., 114.

19 Ibid., 115.

20 See Ball, *The Canadian Niagara Power Company Story* (2005), 115–16, for the full *Fort Erie Times* ad of October 19, 1923. The original is in the collection of the Fort Erie Historical Museum, Ridgeway, Ontario.

21 Westinghouse/Canadian Niagara Power Company advertisement, *Fort Erie Times*, Vol. 29, no. 6 (Dec. 7, 1923), 5, as quoted in Ball, *The Canadian Niagara Power Company Story* (2005), 116.

22 Unidentified newspaper clipping titled "New Service Building," Louis McDermott Reference Collection, Fort Erie Historical Museum, Ridgeway, Ontario, as quoted in Ball, *The Canadian Niagara Power Company Story* (2005), 125.

23 These are simply given as representative instructions. Individual recipes and their significance are discussed in the section that follows.

24 Frank and Sandra Flake own the Canadian Niagara Power Company Recipe Card Collection.

25 See Lucy Waverman, "Timeless Treats from the Past," *The Globe and Mail* (Sat. May 31, 2008), in which she writes, "Icebox cookies became popular with the introduction of electric refrigerators in the 1930s."

26 The term *utensil* appears to be used in the recipes to refer to any kind of cooking vessel, in this case, what we would call an asparagus cooker or pot. Sometimes

utensil refers to a steaming rack that one put inside a saucepan to keep the ingredients above the steaming water.

27 Vegetables, Steamed Green Asparagus With Eggs, 1936–1937.

28 Vegetables 1937–1938.

29 Vegetables, Butter Steamed Green Beans, n.d. Another undated recipe, Steamed Lima Beans, is less specific on times but cycles through HIGH to bring to steaming, LOW for an unspecified time, and then "Last 10 minutes of cooking OFF position."

30 Part of the reason is that new technology opens more options and with it greater expectations. Meeting these expectations, rather than holding to old standards and expectations while using the new technology, increases work load and negates potential time- and work-saving from new technology—the essential message in historian Ruth Schwartz Cowan's *More Work for Mother: The Ironies of Household Technology from the Open Hearth to the Microwave* (New York: Basic Books, 1983).

31 This recipe appeared under the title Well-Cooker Meal in the Boiler Meals section where it and a number of other cooker meals had been misfiled. Actually it is the divider that appears misfiled.

32 Comedian Joan Rivers parodied this aspect of housework. "I hate housework. You make the beds, you wash the dishes and six months later you have to start all over again."

33 Pastry and Pies 1938–1939.

34 See for example, "Pastry" undated, "Plain Pastry" 1938–1939 (which included the Standard Method and the Never Fail Method), "Plain Pastry" 1930–1931, "Hot Water Pastry" 1930–1931, "Mexican Pastry" 1935–1936, and "Pastry" 1935–1936. There also are recipes for crusts such as "Cheese Roll Crust" for casserole topping or "Gingersnap Crust" to use with the filling from the Pumpkin Chiffon Pie recipe.

35 Shortening 1938–1939.

36 Jane Busch, "Cooking Competition: Technology on the Domestic Market in the 1930s," *Technology and Culture*, Vol. 24 (Jan. 1983), 240.

37 "Canadian Village Reaches High Kilowatt-Hour Average," p. 8 of two unidentified pages titled *Niagara Power Service*, no publication data other than Oct. 9, 1929, for B. N. & E. [Buffalo, Niagara & Eastern Power Corporation] stock quotations. This was found in the Canadian Niagara Power Company papers Box 22, File 4, prior to their reorganization by Archives Canada.

38 For further discussion of the relative advantages of gas and electric stoves, see Ball, *The Canadian Niagara Power Company Story* (2005), 116–19.

39 Fort Erie Public Library, transcripts of interviews with senior citizens, Mr. Sumner Beam, #072, 1–2, 6, 33.

40 Ibid. Mrs. Ruth Carver, #011, 12, 15, 19.

WEAVING LOCAL IDENTITY
The Niagara Region Tartan
and the Invention of Tradition

GREG GILLESPIE

INTRODUCTION

In the spring of 2007 the Niagara Regional Police Pipe Band (NRPPB) created a new tartan to mark its thirtieth anniversary. The band unveiled the tartan at an annual tug-of-war competition between local Canadian and
American police services held on the Rainbow Bridge in Niagara Falls. Surrounded by the community, tourists, and members of local organizations,
the band led its team to the centre of the international bridge while proudly
displaying the new tartan. Although the Niagara Regional Police (NRP) lost
the match to their American counterparts, the community responded
favourably to the new "Niagara Region" tartan. Newspaper reports recorded
the event, retold the creation of the plaid, and set the tartan within the
approval of local government and community organizations.[1] Newspapers
expressed the band's desire to create a new tartan that reflected the community of Niagara—they wanted "something that's ours."[2] Despite the newness
of the Niagara Region tartan, the unveiling of the plaid marked the expression of regional history, identity, and the invention of a local tradition.

I analyze the local meanings woven into the Niagara Region tartan by situating the plaid as an invented tradition, as a recently constructed artifact
of material culture, and explain the role that local and international organizations played in the authentication, codification, and institutionalization of
the tartan. In accomplishing these tasks, I also provide additional historical
and cultural context on tartan generally, such as addressing the origin of
tartan and the proliferation of tartans drawn from popular culture. I close

by considering the Niagara Region tartan as a commodified expression of Highlandism, a historically marginalized Scottish identity traditionally associated with the tourist industry in Scotland and abroad.

Over the last two decades, the notion of tradition invention forwarded by Eric Hobsbawm and Terence Ranger has received much scholarly attention, including critique of the concept's heavy ideological assumptions. Tradition invention studies focus on the deconstruction of tradition and seek to "expose" the historical "realities" behind traditions and myths. Also called "bubble-bursting" studies, research like this suggests that invented traditions are laughable, fake, or invalid as cultural forms. Even the etymology of the term contributes to confusion about what tradition inventions means. In common usage, invention typically suggests newness and tradition implies something old (Tuleja 1997, 3–4). However, tradition need not imply an ancient lineage, and invention simply refers to discovering something. Moreover, Hobsbawm and Ranger failed to define the concept specifically and, as a result, scholars have loosely used the idea across numerous academic literatures (1992, 1–14). The concept of tradition invention includes a number of implicit assumptions. Hobsbawm and Ranger seem to suggest that tradition is static and reactionary rather than being constantly adaptive and creative.[3] This contributed to the false notion that tradition and modernity stand in juxtaposition. The notion of tradition invention carries the suggestion of manipulation or imposition and implies that some traditions are more genuine and authentic than others. Hobsbawm and Ranger failed to distinguish between the traditions they viewed as invented and other forms of tradition.[4] They also failed to explicate how traditions require continual reinvention and interpretation. Traditions are temporal and a reflection of the social, cultural, and historical contexts of their renewal. Perhaps most importantly, invented traditions and practices and artifacts of material culture, such as the Niagara Region tartan, carry meaning. These symbolize local community and represent a people's connection with a shared past. In my view, proving or disproving the authenticity of the tartan as an invented tradition is a fruitless exercise (Basu 2007, 123). Authenticity is a cultural construct and as such classifications of authenticity are relative and dependant on the determiner (Tuleja 1997, 3–4). Whether or not we view an invented tradition as authentic misses the point. People take meaning from activities and artifacts of material culture regardless of their age. Even a new cultural activity can be perceived as highly rule-bound and ritualized. Traditions glossed with the veneer of authenticity typically support some sort of underlying social, cultural, or economic agenda. Of greater interest here are the processes through which invented traditions are draped with notions of authenticity to construct them as official or traditional. Put differently, I am interested in the processes through which the tartan became acknowledged as an institutional and community symbol, to better appreciate the role local organizations and government play in the creation of these symbols, the ways in which they invest them with meaning(s), and how they are integrated into local popular culture.

LOCALITY AND THE ORIGIN OF TARTAN

The origin of tartan rests with locality. Many believe in the mythology of tartan—that the fabric represents an ancient familial association. However, the cultural history of tartan in Scotland suggests that the fabric was first linked with geography. The colours selected for tartans were subject to the dyes available from local vegetation. The skill of the weaver determined the complexity of a given pattern or sett. With everyone in a given locality subject to the same weaver, tartans became linked with specific regions. In this way, tartans were loosely associated with particular groups of families who lived in a feudal association with each other. The point is that cultural identity provided through tartan was one of locality as much as family (Ray 2001). Despite the mythology of tartan suggesting a connection between Highland clans and their ancient plaids, tartan was codified and invented in its modern form during the first half of the nineteenth century. Two brothers, claiming (falsely) to be descendants of Charles Edward Stuart, published the *Vestiarium Scoticum* in 1842 (Wilton 2007, 6–7).[5] The first book to illustrate and codify tartans effectively, *Vestiarium* was received eagerly by the weaving industry and came under sustained criticism only in the twentieth century.[6] Despite the relatively recent invention of the ancient clans and their tartans, the myth still serves to support the tartan, weaving, and Scottish tourist industries. The mythology of tartan has proved an effective merchandizing strategy for almost 200 years. A recent 2007 estimate of the tartan industry suggests it contributes over £350 million to the Scottish economy each year.[7]

The origin of the kilt was one of necessity and, like tartan, reflected the geography of Scotland. Wearing trousers that would stay wet in the Highlands simply was not practical. A knee-length garment with long woollen hose dried faster and provided a more practical alternative for the demands of the Highland environment. Called a *feileadh-mhor* or great plaid, the original version of the kilt included one long piece of tartan material that wrapped around the waist and was secured to the shoulder with a brooch. If needed, the *feileadh-mhor* provided a travelling sleeping bag. The Highlander simply removed the shoulder brooch and wrapped the material around his upper body. Despite the claims of historian Hugh Trevor-Roper in the 1980s, the kilt is not an invented tradition (Trevor-Roper 1992, 15–42; Hobsbawm 1992, 1–14). Although some might quibble or outright disagree with the details of his account (and scholars have), he is correct that the *feileadh-mhor* was adapted over time to the *feileadh-beag*—the small plaid—the modern version of the garment we are familiar with today. He is also correct that many invented traditions accompany the creation of the modern kilt. The kilt's national significance to Scotland, for example, is an invented tradition of Highlandism from the early to mid-nineteenth century.

WEAVING THE COLOUR AND CODE OF THE NIAGARA REGION TARTAN

Intended as a grassroots community organization, the Niagara Regional Police Pipe Band participated primarily in parades and charitable events within the Niagara Region since its inception in 1977. In the last few years the band developed a competitive focus and divided into two bands: the grade four level band serving as a "youth band" to teach and cultivate young players, and their grade two level band serving as the primary competitive group. The grade two band travels to Glasgow, Scotland, each year in August to attend the World Pipe Band Championships and recently finished twelfth in their grade of competition. The band receives no financial support from the police department.

As the band approached its thirtieth anniversary in 2007, Detective Sergeant Dave Hunter, the band's president and drum major, and piper Mike MacNeil developed an idea for a new tartan. The idea emerged, at least in part, out of simple necessity. With the advent of the grade four level group, the band faced a uniform shortage and required new uniforms to replace worn kilts. Most importantly, the band wanted to mark the thirtieth anniversary in style and decided to create a new tartan, something more reflective of the community and locality. The band situated the new tartan carefully. A news article on the band's website noted that despite the creation of the new tartan, it remains "true to Niagara." The new tartan strengthens its "roots in the region" and fosters "growth in the region's youth" through its new grade four band. With these objectives in mind, the article stated, band members "set out on a journey to identify their true colours and the connection to Niagara." The band made clear its purpose: "to create a new tartan to reflect the uniqueness and specific colours that accurately identify the Niagara Region," and "a long lasting legacy for Niagara."[8]

The story behind the creation of the tartan, on web pages for both the Niagara Police Pipe Band and the Regional Municipality of Niagara, emphasizes the importance of the symbolism woven into the colours and design of the tartan:

> Dark blue represents the vast waters of the two Great Lakes, Erie and Ontario. Light blue signifies the Niagara River and the Welland Canal, traversing the region adjoining the Great Lakes, [and] prompting international commerce and allowing a myriad of activities for residents and visitors. White is representative of the mighty Niagara Falls [and] its voluminous rising mists and raging white water rapids. Green symbolizes the fertile, rich and vibrant agriculture of our region [as well as] the world-renown[ed] parks and recreational areas. Red is significant of our rich military history. It is a tribute to our predecessors who by their valiant endeavours have preserved our way of life and our great country.[9]

Intended to serve as a "representation of the Regional Municipality of Niagara," the emphasis on the colours of the tartan—representing, symbolizing, and signifying—encourages a particular reading of the cultural landscape of Niagara that focuses on tourism and history. The colours are intended to symbolize the primary landmarks of the region. Many of these, including the Great Lakes, the Niagara River, the Welland Canal, and Niagara Falls, as well as the "myriad of activities for residents and visitors," highlight the region's primary tourist attractions. Noting the military history of Niagara, specifically the War of 1812, links past and present in a discourse that emphasizes Niagara's British Loyalist tradition.

INSTITUTIONALIZING TARTAN, ENCODING LOCALITY

Local government, namely the Regional Municipality of Niagara, played an important role in the creation and institutionalization of the tartan. Both the Cultural Committee and Regional Council approved the tartan and lent their institutional authority to the project.[10] These committees, and their elected representatives, added the approval of the communities of Niagara. Although the colours of the Niagara Region tartan highlight the region's cultural landscape, they were also chosen to reflect the colours and meanings of the Coat of Arms of the Regional Municipality of Niagara. Encoding the tartan with its own meanings, and yet also deriving symbolic meanings from the Regional Coat of Arms, ensured the reading of the tartan as an authoritative and authentic symbol of the Niagara Region. The shield is the centrepiece of the Regional Coat of Arms and integrates Niagara's present and Loyalist past. The green background represents the rich agricultural land and abundant parks

FIGURE 15.1 "Colour Coat" for the Regional Municipality of Niagara. Permission of the Office of the Regional Chairman of the Regional Municipality of Niagara

of the region, and the blue and white band symbolizes Niagara Falls and the Niagara Escarpment. The twelve blue chevrons represent the locks of the Welland Canal and also Niagara's twelve municipalities that bind the region together.[11] The gold lines symbolize the natural wealth that flows from Niagara. The Royal Crown, set in gold, recognizes Niagara's strong Loyalist tradition and symbolizes the site of Upper Canada's first parliament in Newark (Niagara-on-the-Lake). Queen Elizabeth II personally approved the inclusion of the Royal Crown. These symbols are also invoked in the official blazon and stylized logo of the Regional Municipality of Niagara.[12] Leaning on the authority of the Region's Coat of Arms, approved by both the Queen and the Chief Herald of Canada, the band used Niagara's cultural and tourist landscapes to encode the tartan and naturalize the design as an "official" symbol. The approval set the tartan alongside the official symbols of the region: the Regional Coat of Arms, Niagara Police Crest, Regional Logo, and the Chain of Office. The tartan, now an official symbol of the Regional Municipality, draws on the governmental and institutional authority of all these symbols. The tartan, like the coat of arms, and the regional logo exist as symbols representative of the locality of Niagara.

In addition to the institutionalization by local government, the Niagara Region tartan leaned on the authority of the Niagara Regional Police Service.[13] Immediately following the Regional Municipality's approval of its Coat of Arms in 1995, the NRP recreated their logo, adopting the shield and the regional motto, "Unity, Responsibility, Loyalty." The NRP website states that it now has "a symbol created specifically for the Niagara Regional Police, one that represents our community, our peoples and our heritage."[14] The Niagara tartan, drawing on the Coat of Arms shared by both the Regional Municipality and the Regional Police Service, binds the three symbols together.[15] The Chief of Police, Wendy Southall, gave her enthusiastic support to the project.[16] Although the band is primarily made up of civilian community members, the tartan carries the institutional authority of the Niagara Regional Police both figuratively and symbolically. Even the insignia of the pipe band worn on their Glengarry bonnets employs the police crest backgrounded by the saltire.

THE RULES OF AUTHENTICATION

The Scottish Tartans Authority (STA) played an important international role in the authentication of the Niagara Region tartan. Leading weavers and tartan retailers formed the Scottish Tartans Authority in 1996. The STA Board of Governors is drawn from both the public and commercial sectors in addition to members of the International Association of Tartan Studies (IATA) and the Tartan Education and Cultural Association (TECA). The purpose of the STA is to promote knowledge of Scottish tartans, their origins, manufacture, use, history, and development and to study, record, and stimulate research on the subject. The STA is a registered charity, and companies within the Scottish tartan industry provide operating funds.

In addition to providing an institutional acknowledgement, the authentication of the STA includes the codification and regulation of new tartans. The Niagara Regional Police Pipe Band submitted its application, and the tartan is now registered as number 7110 "Niagara Region." As one of its primary objectives, the STA compiles and maintains the International Tartan Index (ITI) to record and document all known tartans, historical and contemporary. This resource, available free to the general public, provides a dependable and accountable information resource. Although "unofficial," the Scottish tartan industry acknowledges the ITI as the current standard. As of this writing, the STA, in conjunction with the Scottish National party, just created an official Scottish Tartans Registry and pushed forward with plans to establish a worldwide heritage visitor centre and interpretative museum.[17]

The process of authentication, codification, and regulation of new tartans into the ITI includes several stages. The process begins with the designation of a new tartan into one of seven categories: Clan/Family refers to tartans designed for a clan or family and for use by anyone of that name and its variants. District, into which the Niagara tartan was registered, refers to tartans associated with a particular geographical area or district. Corporate identifies tartans designed for the sole use of a particular business or corporation. Commemorative refers to tartans that memorialize an event or individual. Personal refers to tartans designed and produced for individuals or individual families and usually not available for wider use, and Fashion designates tartans designed for the fashion trade. Military refers to tartans used by military organizations.[18] The STA charges a fee for tartan designing and recording services depending on the category of the tartan. There is no legal requirement to register a new tartan.

As the acknowledged worldwide authority on tartan, the institutional approval offered by the STA carries weight. The approval of the STA means more than a simple institutional authentication; it provides a *Scottish* institutional authentication. This is particularly important in diasporic countries like Canada, the United States, New Zealand, and Australia. The STA encourages the registration of new tartans with the ITI to ensure that the new tartans are globally recognized. This also avoids the duplication of tartans in name or appearance and the replication of unauthorized tartans. The process begins with a Tartan Recording application. The STA researches the proposed tartan against all others in the ITI. If none exists, the new tartan is provisionally recorded. After the new tartan has received provisional acceptance, the tartan is weaved and the STA provides a signed Tartan Recording Certificate. The STA requires special permissions for Family/Clan and District tartans. If, in the case of Family/Clan tartans, the new tartan is intended for use by everyone with that name or all those with recognized surname variants, the application must be submitted and supported by the clan chief or clan society. Supporting documentation must accompany the application. Tartans named after countries, states, provinces, districts, towns, cities, and companies, or that reference central or local government must also be accompanied by a letter of authorization.[19] The application for the Niagara Region tartan included the institutional approval of the Regional Municipality of Niagara, its Cultural Committee, and the Niagara Regional Police Service.

LOCALITY IN TARTAN DESIGNS IN CANADA AND ONTARIO

The invention of the Nova Scotia tartan offers an instructive case study in relation to the development of the Niagara Region tartan. Created in 1953 and officially adopted by the province of Nova Scotia in 1955, the Nova Scotia tartan was the first provincial tartan in Canada. The tartan emerged as part of the government's efforts to create an authentic folk handicraft revival in the early 1950s (McKay 1994, 207).[20] The tartan first appeared in a larger wool mural depicting life in Nova Scotia. Part of the mural included a shepherd wearing the tartan and a lone shieling in the background.

According to historian Ian McKay, the tartan rested at the centre of a process of "Tartanism." Tartanism was a particular way of reading Nova Scotia, for both tourists and Nova Scotians, as the "Scot-land" in Canada (McKay 2007, 206). The designer conceived of the tartan as a "direct imprint of the Terence Bay landscape," which contributed to its approval and commercial success. The tartan emphasized the dark blue of the water and the light blue of the sky, and the dark and light green of the evergreens and deciduous trees characteristic of the province. The designer used white from the saltire and gold from the lion rampant of the Nova Scotian provincial flag. The gold also represented Nova Scotia's royal character (Major 1972, 191–214).

Through encoding the cultural landscape into the design, the tartan became a naturalized symbol of all of Nova Scotia (McKay 2007, 209).

Application was made to the Lord Lyon in Scotland to register the Nova Scotia tartan officially. The Lord Lyon considered the application highly irregular as the tartan represented a region rather than a people, and a political unit rather than a familial clan. The application was approved but with the proviso that the Nova Scotia tartan could not be used in place of traditional clan tartans. As McKay states, "The tartan was duly registered. A symbol supposedly confined to pre-industrial clans had now been appropriated by a modern state. Over the next forty years, provinces, cities and even Queen's University would be clamouring for the honour of their own recently invented tartans" (McKay 2007, 210). Through this development, along with others related to tourism in Nova Scotia, the success of the tartan as a commercial tourism product was assured. In the context of local and regional tourism, "tartan had cash value" (McKay 2007, 211).

The clamouring for tartans in the wake of the creation of the Nova Scotia tartan led to the development of numerous tartan precedents in the province of Ontario. The province has a number of tartans, including the Ontario Centennial, the Ensign of Ontario (the unofficial provincial tartan for decades prior to 2000), and the Official Ontario tartan. The Province of Ontario adopted the Official Ontario tartan in 2000. Loosely based on the tartan of Sir John Sandfield MacDonald (the first premier of Ontario in 1867), Bruce County MPP Bruce Murdoch initiated a private members bill to create the Ontario tartan. Designed in conjunction with the Department of Scottish Studies at the University of Guelph, the tartan emphasized the following colours: green for the forests and the fields, red for the Aboriginal people, blue for the waters of Ontario, white for the sky above the province.[21] District tartans in Ontario exist for the Highlands of Haliburton, Durham, Lanark, Muskoka, and Northern Ontario. A number of district tartans exist for cities and local governments within the province, including Barrie, Kincardine, Guelph, Ottawa, and Thunder Bay. A tartan exists for the townships of Inverary, Englehart, and Porcupine.

The regional governments of Bruce County and Essex County are the only two counties in Ontario with registered tartans. These two specific examples provide points of comparison and context as they relate to local identity and tartan. Bruce County is located in western Ontario around the Bruce Peninsula, and the county tartan reflects a specific emphasis on the Bruce Clan tartan and immortalized the clan's legacy and history in Ontario. The Bruce County tartan is derived from a combination of the Bruce Clan tartan and the family colours of James Bruce, the Earl of Elgin and Governor General of

FIGURE 15.2 Niagara Regional Police Pipe Band in a Legion Parade, Niagara Falls, Ontario. Permission of Chief Wendy Southall, NRPS

Canada when Bruce County incorporated in 1867. The creation of the tartan marked the centennial of Bruce County in 1967. The primary colours of red, yellow, and green specifically reflected those of the Bruce Clan tartan. To these white and blue were added to represent the 367 miles of shoreline bordering Lake Huron and Georgian Bay.[22] The Bruce County tartan was registered in Scotland and patented in Canada. In 1973 the Women's Institutes of Bruce County assumed responsibility for all tartan promotions and sales. All proceeds are used for projects beneficial to the residents of Bruce County.

The Essex County tartan, unlike the Bruce County example, attempted to naturalize the tartan by invoking specific images of the cultural landscape of Essex located in southwestern Ontario. Edythe Bakes of Leamington designed the Essex County Tartan in 1981, and the Essex County Council officially adopted the tartan in 1983. Bakes employed specific colours to signify the beauty and wealth of the region. Golden yellow represented the sunshine and the harvest of local grains, corn, soybeans, barley, oats, and wheat. Green symbolized the spring fields and red signified Leamington, known as the "Tomato Capital of the World." Blue represented the skies and waterways, white for the salt mines and fish, and black for the automotive industry.[23] In these ways the Essex county tartan, following the Nova Scotian model, appears as an extension of the cultural landscape. Bakes registered the tartan both in Scotland and Canada. She wished to donate the proceeds from the tartan to local charities and in 1985 the Women's Institute in Leamington took responsibility for marketing the tartan. The Women's Institute annually makes donations to the Leamington District Memorial Hospital, the Salvation Army of Leamington, and the Essex Food Bank.

TARTANS AND POPULAR CULTURE

The proliferation of district tartans since the development of the Nova Scotia tartan in the 1950s parallels the proliferation of tartans generally. The STA authorizes tartans across numerous categories each year and include Commemorative, Corporate, Fashion, Education, Military, Personal, and Sports. A small sampling of these are tartans created specifically for films—*Braveheart* (d. Gibson, 1995) and *Rob Roy* (d. Caton-Jones, 1995)—and those that support film tourism in Scotland. Others one might not expect include the Roslin tartan in reference to the Rosslyn Chapel from the movie *The Da Vinci Code* (d. Howard, 2006) and the tartan for the green ogre from *Shrek the Third* (d. Miller/Hui, 2007). Tartans exist for sporting figures and teams such as the Formula One driver Jackie Stewart, golfer Colin Montgomerie, wrestler Rowdy Roddy Piper, the Toronto Blue Jays, and the racing horse Red Rum. Tartans also exist for Dr. Who's trusty companion K9 from the late 1970s, Scrooge MacDuck, *The Wombles* children's television show in the United Kingdom, and for online communities like www.xmarksthescot.com. There are tartans for energy drinks like Red Bull, Iron Bru, fashion designer Tommy Hilfiger, musical groups like The Dropkick Murphys, and educational institutions like the University of Calgary, Laurentian University, and Queen's University.

There are two perspectives on the proliferation of tartans. The more traditional perspective suggests that tartans are static and unchanging. That is, tartans should represent only clan and family affiliation, and the unique timelessness of tartan rests in its unchanging character and tradition. This perspective may stem from those involved with clan societies and organizations. The other perspective is more post-modern and emphasizes fluidity and plurality of interpretation. This view suggests that tartan has been and remains an evolving art form. This vantage point positions tartan as temporal and reflective of the social, cultural, and historical context around its creation. This perspective, readily adopted by the tartan industry, serves to support growth and profit by emphasizing the new in tartan design and culture. Although both perspectives have merit within tartan culture, a third point of view might integrate both perspectives. Paradoxically, I would suggest that the plurality of tartan rests within its seeming rigidity—the fixed lines and setts of a tartan belie its adaptability as a form of expression.

TARTAN, HIGHLANDISM, AND MARGINALITY

Academics and some members of the Scottish community feel that Highlandism represents a discourse of oppression. The argument suggests that the romantic ideology of Highlandism, represented through an emphasis on key symbols such as tartan, kilts, and bagpipes, perpetuates a derogatory ethnic stereotype.[24] Highlandism finds its origins at least as early as the eighteenth and early nineteenth centuries and has had an enduring legacy in how Scots at home and abroad understand and celebrate Scottish identity. During these two centuries, specific images of the Highlands and Highlanders solidified in Western culture. The 1715 and 1745–46 Rebellions, the Prohibition of Highland Costume, the success of Highland regiments in the British Army, the creation of the Highland Society of London, the Highland Clearances, the works of Sir Walter Scott, the establishment of Highland Tourism, and the Romantic Movement, all contributed to the reconsideration of the Highlander from uncouth, uneducated Jacobite rebel, to that of gallant, loyal, kilted soldier—and the transformation of the Highlands from a barren desolate waste to a sublime, mist-swept landscape (Clyde 1995). The construction of Scottishness-as-Highlandism served two interrelated functions. The regional identity and symbols of the Highlanders—emphasizing tartan and kilt—became the identity and symbols of Scotland nationally.[25] This ensured a token cultural distinctiveness from England. However, Highlandism also drew Scotland further into the grips of political, economic, and cultural union with England after 1707.

Highlandism continues to marginalize Scottish culture today. The pervasive expression of Highlandism across contemporary literature, television, and film, as well as Highland Games and Burns Suppers, simplifies the Scottish language to a set of token words and phrases and reduces Scottish identity to a set of superficial consumables like tartan knick-knacks, scarves, and tea towels. Highlandism is a marginalizing discourse that situates Scotland as primitive, backward, and descendant in its relationship with England and the rest of the world. Highlandism trivializes the Scottish people and situates Scottish culture as laughable. The Niagara Region tartan presents an opportunity to discuss the expression of local identity but *cannot* be separated from the cultural history of tartan as it relates to the historical marginalization and commodification of Scottishness and Highland Scottish identity in particular. Although not the perspective of the majority within the broad Scottish community, the creation of tartans alongside the commercial tourist industry encourages the Highlandist discourse and reminds us of the extent to which expressions of Scottish cultural identity remain colonized.

CONCLUSION

The Niagara Region tartan provides a case study of the way in which an invented tradition emerged as a naturalized symbol constructed with the patina of authenticity. The constructed authenticity of the tartan suggests continuity with Niagara's past. This connection confers a sense of cultural legitimacy on the plaid. Local organizations, such as the Regional Municipality of Niagara and the Niagara Regional Police Service, as well as international organizations like the Scottish Tartans Authority, played important roles in the codification, institutionalization, and authentication of the Niagara Region tartan. These leading institutions in policing, government, and Scottish culture contributed their approval, and thus their institutional authority, to the tartan as a symbol of the Niagara Region. The tartan emerged, not as the expression of a singular community pipe band, but as an established, and commodified, official symbol of the Niagara Region, following a long list of registered, official Ontario and Canadian tartans. Many of these draw on the example provided by the provincial tartan of Nova Scotia and interweave the local cultural landscape with notions of the local and the regional. Like the Nova Scotia tartan, the Niagara Region tartan accomplishes more than this. Alongside the local, the tartan—based in commodified products constructed to generate revenue from the local tourist industry—also celebrates the marginalizing discourse of Highlandism; that the Niagara Region tartan is the only commodified official symbol of the Regional Municipality of Niagara speaks to this point. The newness of the tartan precludes a full understanding of its integration into the local tourist market. However, the international tourist destinations in Niagara, specifically Niagara Falls and Niagara-on-the-Lake, will no doubt provide the band with unique commercial opportunities in the future.

NOTES

1 St. Catharines *Standard*, May 14, 2007, A5; Niagara Falls *Review*, May 14, 2007, A2.
2 *Review*, May 14, 2007, A2.
3 For an excellent critique of the invention of tradition, see Mark Salber Phillips, "What Is Tradition When It Is Not Invented?: A Historiographical Introduction," in Mark Salber Phillips and Gordon Schochet, eds., *Questions of Tradition* (Toronto: University of Toronto Press, 2004), 3–32.
4 However, the academic literature on invented traditions remains robust. A small select sampling of recent interdisciplinary research includes Sulayman Khalaf, "Poetics and Politics of Newly Invented Traditions in the Gulf: Camel Racing in the United Arab Emirates," *Ethnology* 39:3 (2000), 243–61; Chris Watkins, "Inventing International Citizenship," *History of Education* 36:3 (2007), 315–38; David Schweingruber, Alicia Cast, and Sine Anahita, "A Story and a Ring: Audience

Judgements About Engagement Proposals," *Sex Roles* 58:3–4 (2008), 165–78; Stephen Hutchings, "Saint Petersburg 300: Television and the Invention of a Russian (Media) Tradition," *Television and New Media* 9:1 (2008), 3–23; Robert Trumpbour, "Rituals, Invented Traditions, and Shifting Power: The Role of Communication in the History of Stadium Construction," *Journal of Communication Inquiry* 31:4 (2007), 310–30; Anne Eriksen, "Our Lady of Perpetual Help: Invented Tradition and Devotional Success," *Journal of Folklore Research* 42, 3 (2005), 295–321.

5   Wilton is the Director of the Scottish Tartans Authority.

6   See D.C. Stewart and J.C. Thompson, *Scotland's Forged Tartans* (Edinburgh: Paul Harris Publishing, 1980).

7   Neil McInnes, "Tartan Boosts Scottish Economy by 350 Million." Scottish Enterprise Official Website, July 9, 2007. Available at www.scottish-enterprise.com/ sedotcom_home/news-se/news-fullarticle.htm?articleid=211436, accessed Aug. 10, 2007.

8   Available at www.nrppb.org, accessed Apr. 10, 2008.

9   Available at www.regional.niagara.on.ca/living/region/tartan.aspx, accessed Apr. 10, 2008; and also www.nrppb.org, accessed Apr. 10, 2008.

10 Regional Municipality of Niagara, Minutes of the Culture Committee, Oct. 23, 2006, and Apr. 2, 2007; Regional Municipality of Niagara, Minutes of the Police Services Board, Apr. 26, 2007, and May 24, 2007.

11 The twelve municipalities are Fort Erie, Grimsby, Lincoln, Niagara Falls, Niagara-on-the-lake, Pelham, Port Colborne, St. Catharines, Thorold, Wainfleet, Welland, West Lincoln. The Regional Municipality of Niagara adopted its coat of arms in 1995 on its twenty-fifth anniversary.

12 Available at www.regional.niagara.on.ca/living/region/coa.aspx, accessed Apr. 10, 2008; and also www.regional.niagara.on.ca/living/region/logo.aspx, accessed Apr. 10, 2008.

13 In 1971, following the formation of the Niagara regional government, local police forces were incorporated into the Niagara Regional Police Force, later renamed the Niagara Regional Police Service—one of Ontario's largest police services. www.nrps.com/nrp/history.asp, accessed Aug. 25, 2009.

14 Available at www.nrps.com/nrp/crest.asp, accessed Apr. 10, 2008.

15 Available at www.regional.niagara.on.ca/living/region/tartan.aspx, accessed Apr. 10, 2008.

16 Ibid.

17 Available at www.tartansauthority.com/Web/Site/ScottishTartansAuthority/ introduction.asp, accessed Apr.10, 2008.

18 Available at www.tartansauthority.com/Web/Site/Tartan_Recording/Tartan Recording.asp, accessed Apr. 10, 2008.

19 See the tartan recording application available at www.tartansauthority.com/ Web/Site/Tartan_Recording/tartan_recording.asp, accessed Apr. 10, 2008.

20 Also see Ian McKay, "Tartanism Triumphant: The Construction of Scottishness in Nova Scotia, 1933–1954," *Acadiensis* XXI (1992), 5–47.

21 The debate over the Tartan Act in 1997 is available at www.ontla.on.ca/committee -proceedings/transcripts/files_html/1997-08-20_m036.htm.

22 Information for this paragraph on the Bruce County tartan available at www.bruce museum.ca/bchist_tartan.php, accessed Apr. 10, 2008.

23 Information for this paragraph on the Essex County tartan available at www.countyofessex.on.ca/countyhistory/coetartan_home.asp, accessed Apr. 10, 2008.
24 See Chapter 6 entitled "The Making of Highlandism, 1746–1822," in T.M. Devine, *Clanship to Crofters' War: The Social Transformation of the Scottish Highlands* (Manchester: Manchester University Press, 1994), 84–99; and Chapter 1 entitled "Highlandism and Scottish Identity: The Origins of Contemporary Ethnic Expression," in Ray, *Highland Heritage*, 17–44.
25 Devine, *Clanship*, 84–99.

WORKS CITED

Basu, Paul. *Highland Homecomings: Genealogy and Heritage Tourism in the Scottish Diaspora*. London: Routledge, 2007.

Clyde, Robert. *From Rebel to Hero: The Image of the Highlander, 1745–1830*. East Lothian: Tuckwell Press, 1995.

Hobsbawm, Eric. "Introduction: Inventing Traditions." In Eric Hobsbawm and Terence Ranger, eds., *The Invention of Tradition*. Cambridge: Cambridge University Press, 1992.

Major, Marjorie. "History of the Nova Scotia Tartan." *Nova Scotia Historical Quarterly* 2 (1972), 191–214.

McKay, Ian. *The Quest of the Folk: Antimodernism and Cultural Selection in Twentieth-Century Nova Scotia*. Montreal: McGill-Queen's University Press, 1994.

Ray, Celeste. *Highland Heritage: Scottish Americans in the American South*. Chapel Hill: University of North Carolina Press, 2001.

Trevor-Roper, Hugh. "The Invention of Tradition: The Highland Tradition of Scotland." In Eric Hobsbawm and Terence Ranger, eds., *The Invention of Tradition*. Cambridge: Cambridge University Press, 1992.

Tuleja, Tad, ed. *Usable Pasts: Traditions and Group Expressions in North America*. Logan, UT: University of Utah Press, 1997.

Wilton, Brian. *Tartans*. London: Aurum Press, 2007.

CONTRIBUTORS

NORMAN R. BALL is a historian of technology and Director of the Centre for Society, Technology and Values, Faculty of Engineering, University of Waterloo. He is author of *The Canadian Niagara Power Company Story* (2005) and is writing a history of the Niagara Parks Commission, to mark the occasion of its 125th anniversary in 2010. His wide work experience includes archivist, museum curator, and engineering magazine columnist.

NICK BAXTER-MOORE is Associate Professor in the Department of Communication, Popular Culture and Film at Brock University. His current research interests include the touring strategies of the Trans Siberian Orchestra, the concert-going habits of Bruce Springsteen fans, and the history of Crystal Beach amusement park.

MARIAN BREDIN is Associate Professor in the Department of Communication, Popular Culture and Film at Brock University. Her research interests include Aboriginal and indigenous media, communications policy and cultural politics, and Canadian television. She is co-editor of two forthcoming collections: *Indigenous Screen Cultures* and *Canadian Television: Text and Context*.

ROSLYN COSTANZO resides in Toronto and is active in the contemporary art scene and the Niagara Artists Centre (NAC), located in downtown St. Catharines. Her research interests are contemporary art and the emergence of artist-run culture in Canada between 1970 and 1980.

TERRANCE COX is a writer of poems and non-fiction and a "general practitioner" in the Humanities at Brock University. His published collections include a "spoken word with music" CD, *Local Scores* (2000), the prize-winning book *Radio & Other Miracles* (2001), and a second CD, *Simultaneous Translation* (2005).

HUGH GAYLER is Professor of Geography at Brock University. He specializes in urban geography and has published on various aspects of suburbanization and urban expansion into areas of high resource value.

GREG GILLESPIE is Assistant Professor in the Department of Communication, Popular Culture and Film at Brock University. His research focuses on Scottish studies, sport studies, and game studies, and he is author of *Hunting for Empire: Narratives of Sport in Rupert's Land, 1840–1870* (2008). He is from the town of Grimsby in the Niagara Region.

BARRY KEITH GRANT is Professor in the Department of Communication, Popular Culture and Film at Brock University and co-editor of this volume. The author or editor of over a dozen books, his work has been widely published in journals and anthologies. He is the editor of film books for Wayne State University Press and Blackwell Publishing.

RUSSELL JOHNSTON is Associate Professor in the Department of Communication, Popular Culture and Film at Brock University. His research on Canadian media history includes *Selling Themselves: The Emergence of Canadian Advertising* (2001), as well as articles in magazines, journals, and edited collections.

FIONA LUCAS, whose interest in Canadian culinary history began in 1987, is co-founder of the Culinary Historians of Ontario. Her first book, *Hearth and Home: Women and the Art of Open Hearth Cooking,* won silver in the 2007 Canadian Culinary Book Awards.

PHILLIP GORDON MACKINTOSH is Associate Professor of Geography at Brock University. His SSHRC-funded research of historical-cultural and social geographies of class, gender, and race includes bourgeois, masculine performativity in nineteenth-century Masonic lodges, the domestic embourgeoisment of public space, and racialized park planning in Edwardian Toronto.

DAN MALLECK is Associate Professor in Community Health Sciences at Brock University and editor-in-chief of *Social History of Alcohol and Drugs: An Interdisciplinary Journal*. His research focus is the history of the regulation of alcohol and drugs, currently liquor regulation in public places in Ontario from 1927 to 1944.

PAUL S. MOORE is Associate Professor of Sociology, and in the Graduate Program in Communication and Culture at Ryerson University. He is the author of *Now Playing: Early Moviegoing and the Regulation of Fun* (2008) and several articles on the history of movie exhibition and promotion in Canada. With Sandra Gabriele, he is currently researching a history of the weekend newspaper in North America.

JOAN NICKS is Adjunct Professor in the Department of Communication, Popular Culture and Film at Brock University and is co-editor of this volume. Her writing on film and media has appeared in various edited anthologies and journals. She and colleague Jeannette Sloniowski have been long-time research collaborators and are co-editors of *Slippery Pastimes: Reading the Popular in Canadian Culture* (2002).

GEOFF PEVERE is a long-time broadcaster and film critic. He is co-author, with Greig Dymond, of *Mondo Canuck: A Canadian Pop Culture Odyssey* (1996).

MICHAEL RIPMEESTER is a cultural/historical geographer at Brock University. He has published in the areas of historical geographies of eighteenth- and nineteenth-century Ontario, the ideological foundations of the lawn, and landscapes of public memory. His teaching focuses on power and resistance in the context of everyday landscapes.

JEANNETTE SLONIOWSKI is Associate Professor in the Department of Communication, Popular Culture and Film at Brock University. She is co-editor of the TV Milestones series (Wayne State UP) and is completing a monograph on Jack Webb's *Dragnet*. Her work on film, television, and popular culture has appeared in various journals and edited books.

LAURA WIEBE TAYLOR is a Ph.D. Candidate in the Department of English and Cultural Studies at McMaster University, investigating intersections of popular culture, mass media, and interdisciplinary theory. She has published on film, popular music, and speculative fiction and spent twelve years in campus radio as a volunteer programmer.

MARY F. WILLIAMSON is a culinary historian whose publications focus primarily on foods and cookery of the nineteenth century. She contributes regularly to *Culinary Chronicles* (Culinary Historians of Ontario). Before retiring as Fine Arts Bibliographer at York University, she authored studies of Canadian art publications and book and periodical illustration.

INDEX

musicals, 295
Musician's Newspaper, 255
musicians: employment, 245–46,
    252–54, 257; recruitment of,
    254–55
Muskoka, 4, 8
"My Mammy" (song), 289

NAACP, 287
Nabisco Ltd., 295
NAC. *See* Niagara Artists Centre
NAFTA. *See* North American Free Trade
    Agreement
Nathaniel Dett Memorial Chapel,
    308n17
National Association for the Advance-
    ment of Colored People, 287
Native Friendship Centre. *See* Fort Erie
    Native Friendship Centre
Native peoples, 45–65; 57; employ-
    ment, 56–59; heritage, 52–54, 57,
    59–60, 62; Iroquoian tradition, 54;
    land claims, 27, 28, 29, 30; rela-
    tionship with government, 53,
    61–62, 64n2
Native rights, 50
natural gas, 331
natural gas appliances, 318
natural landscape, 50–51, 63
New American Gardener, 163, 164
New Murray Hotel, 178
New Statler Hotel, 171, 173, 174, 176,
    180, 184
New Thorold Music. *See* Thorold
    Music
New York City, 218
New York State Reservation, 313–14,
    334n4, 334n8
Newman, Mayor Charles R., 110
newspapers, xxix, 3, 72, 93–95,
    99–101, 112–13; editorials
    107–10; racism in, 299–303
newsreels, 76, 101
Newstalk 610. *See* CKTB
Niagara Apothecary Store, 162
Niagara Artists Centre, xxviii, 263–81

Niagara Artists' Co-op, 263–81
Niagara at Noon (radio show), 127,
    133
Niagara College, xxii, xxv, 205, 211n6
Niagara College Jazz Band, 225–26,
    229
Niagara District Broadcasting Com-
    pany, 123
Niagara Ego Exhibition (art exhibition),
    272, *273*
Niagara Electric Service Company,
    308n19
Niagara Falls (N.Y.), xxiii, 98, 109,
    113–14
Niagara Falls (Ont.), City of, xxii, xxiii,
    45, 93–117, 175, 180, 181, 187,
    218, 312; entertainment, 285–310;
    population, 299; social conditions,
    102–3, 112
Niagara Falls (waterfalls), xxvi, 54, 97,
    97, 278; cultural and spiritual
    aspects, 56, 312; diversion of
    water, 316, 333n1; hydroelectric-
    ity, 312, 313–16, 333n1; in
    movies, 70–72, 88; industrial
    development, 313
Niagara Falls arena, 221
Niagara Falls Collegiate, 287, *296*
Niagara Falls *Daily Record*, 69, 72, 88,
    93, 97, 98, 100, 103, 109,
    300–303, 307n1
Niagara Falls (N.Y.) *Gazette*, 98
Niagara Falls Park and River Railway,
    315
Niagara Falls Power Company, 308n19
Niagara Falls Power Company, 335n11
Niagara Falls *Review*, xxixn3, 56, 72,
    93, 94, 95, 96, 98–100, 101, 102,
    103, 106–7, 109–10, 112–13,
    115n8, 286, 290, 293–94,
    300–303, 307n1
Niagara Falls South, 78, 79
Niagara Fire Brigade, 17
Niagara Fruit Belt, 196
Niagara Gorge Railroad Company,
    308n19

Books in the Cultural Studies Series
Published by Wilfrid Laurier University Press

Slippery Pastimes: Reading the Popular in Canadian Culture edited by
Joan Nicks and Jeannette Sloniowski
2002 / viii + 347 pp. / ISBN 0-88920-388-1

The Politics of Enchantment: Romanticism, Media and Cultural Studies
by J. David Black
2002 / x + 200 pp. / ISBN 0-88920-400-4

Dancing Fear and Desire: Race, Sexuality, and Imperial Politics in Middle
Eastern Dance by Stavros Stavrou Karayanni
2004 / xv + 244 pp. / ISBN 0-88920-454-3

Auto/Biography in Canada: Critical Directions edited by Julie Rak
2005 / viii + 280 pp. / ISBN 0-88920-478-0

Canadian Cultural Poesis: Essays on Canadian Culture edited by Garry
Sherbert, Annie Gérin, and Sheila Petty
2006 / xvi + 530 pp. / ISBN 0-88920-486-1

Killing Women: The Visual Culture of Gender and Violence edited by
Annette Burfoot and Susan Lord
2006 / xxii + 332 pp. / ISBN-13: 978-0-88920-497-3 / ISBN-10: 0-88920-497-7

Animal Subjects: An Ethical Reader in a Posthuman World edited by
Jodey Castricano
2008 / x + 314 pp. / ISBN 978-0-88920-512-3

Covering Niagara: Studies in Local Popular Culture edited by Joan Nicks and
Barry Keith Grant
2010 / xxx + 378 pp. / ISBN 978-1-55458-221-1